Health Sector Reforms in Orissa

Health Sector Reforms in Orissa: Lessons for Developing Countries

By

Subrata Kundu

CAMBRIDGE SCHOLARS PUBLISHING

Health Sector Reforms in Orissa: Lessons for Developing Countries,
By Subrata Kundu

This book first published 2010

Cambridge Scholars Publishing

12 Back Chapman Street, Newcastle upon Tyne, NE6 2XX, UK

British Library Cataloguing in Publication Data
A catalogue record for this book is available from the British Library

ISBN (10): 1-4438-2343-0, ISBN (13): 978-1-4438-2343-2

Dedicated to my Parents

TABLE OF CONTENTS

ABBREVIATIONS USED

ADMO	Additional District Medical Officer
AHO	Assistant Health Officer
AIDS	Acquired Immune Deficiency Syndrome
ANMs	Auxiliary Nurse/Midwives
AP	Andhra Pradesh
ASCI	Administrative Staff College of India
BEE	Block Extension Educator
CBHI	Central Bureau of Health Intelligence
CBHI	Central Bureau of Health Intelligence
CBR	Crude Birth Rate
CDMO	Chief District Medical Officer
CDR	Crude Death Rate
CEHAT	Center for Equity into Health and Allied Themes
CHC	Community Health Centre
CMIE	Centre for Monitoring Indian Economy
CPR	Couple Protection Rate
CSO	Central Statistical Organization
CT	Computerized Tomography
DANIDA	Danish International Development Agency
DEO	District Education Officer
DFID	Department for International Development
DFW	Director Family Welfare
DHH	District Headquarter Hospital
DHS	Demographic and Health Survey
DHS	Director Health Services
DIO	District Information Officer
DLO	District Leprosy Officer
DMET	Director Medical Education and Training
DMO	District Malaria Officer
DTO	District Tuberculosis Officer
ECG	Electrocardiogram
ECTA	European Commission Technical Assistance
EEC	European Economic Community
EIF	Equipments Instruments and Furniture
ESI	Employees State Insurance
EU	European Union
GDP	Gross Domestic Product
GNP	Gross National Product
GOI	Government of India

GSDP	Gross State Domestic Product
HDI	Human Development Index
HIV	Human Immunodeficiency Virus
HMIS	Health Management Information Systems
HSR	Health Sector Reforms
IAS	Indian Administrative Service
ICDS	Integrated Child Development Scheme
ICRIER	Indian Council for Research in International Economic Relations
IEC	Information Education and Communication
IMF	International Monetary Fund
IMR	Infant Mortality Rate
IPD	Integrated Population and Development
ISM and H	Indian System of Medicine and Homeopathy
ISPs	Indigenous Service Providers
LHV	Lady Health Visitor
MAC	Medical Aid Centre
MBBS	Bachelor of Medicine/Bachelor of Surgery
MCH	Maternal and Child Health
MCI	Medical Council of India
MDGs	Millennium Development Goals
MHU	Mobile Health Unit
MLA	Member of Legislative Assembly
MMR	Maternal Mortality Rate
MO	Medical Officer
MOHFW	Ministry of Health and Family Welfare
MP	Madhya Pradesh
MPFPs	Mid-Term Plans for Financing
MPHS (F)	Multipurpose Health Supervisor Female
MPHS (M)	Multi Purpose Health Supervisor Male
MPHW (F)	Multi Purpose Health Worker Female
MPHW (M)	Multi Purpose Health Worker Male
MRI	Magnetic Resonance Imagery
NACO	National AIDS Control Organization
NCDs	Non Communicable Diseases
NFHS	National Family Health Survey
NGOs	Non Governmental Organizations
NHP	National Health Policy
NPA	Non Practicing Allowance
NRI	Non Resident Indian
NSS	National Sample Survey
NSSO	National Sample Survey Organization
O&G	Orthopedics and Gynecologist
ODA	Overseas Development Assistance
OECD	Organization of Economic Cooperation and Development
OHSDP	Orissa Health Systems Development Project
PARIKAS	Parivar Kalyan Salahkar Samities

PF	Plasmodium Falciparum
PHC	Primary Health Centre
PHC (N)	Primary Health Centre (New)
PIP	Project Implementation Plan
PMC	Project Management Cell
PRIs	Panchayati Raj Institutions
PSPU	Policy Planning and Strategic Unit
RBI	Reserve Bank of India
RCH	Reproductive and Child Health
RGH	Rourkela Government Hospital
RGI	Registrar General of India
RNTCP	Revised National Tuberculosis Control Program
SAP	Structural Adjustment Programme
SBHI	State Bureau of Health Intelligence
SC	Sub Centre
SCs	Scheduled Castes
SDH	Sub Divisional Hospital
SDMO	Sub Divisional Medical Officer
SDMU	State Drugs Management Unit
SH&FWSRC	State Health & Family Welfare Sector Reform Cell
SHC	Subsidiary Health Centre
SHS	State Health Systems
SHSDPs	State Health Systems Development Projects
SIDA	Swedish International Development Cooperation Agency
SIHFW	State Institute of Health and Family Welfare
SPR	Slide Positive Rate
SRC	Sector Reform Cell
SRS	Sample Registration Survey
STs	Scheduled Tribes
TA	Traveling Allowance
TB	Tuberculosis
TCS	Tata Consultancy Services
TFR	Total Fertility Rate
TN	Tamilnadu
TOT	Training of Trainers
TT	Tetanus Toxoied
U5MR	Under- Five Mortality Rate
UGPHC	Upgraded Primary Health Centre
UK	United Kingdom
UN	United Nations
UNDP	United Nations Development Program
UNFPA	United Nations Population Fund
UNICEF	United Nations Children's Fund
UP	Uttar Pradesh
USA	United States of America
UT	Union Territory

WB	West Bengal
WB	World Bank
WHO	World Health Organization
WTO	World Trade Organization
ZSS	Zilla Swasthya Samiti

LIST OF TABLES

LIST OF FIGURES

LIST OF APPENDICES

ACKNOWLEDGEMENTS

The idea of this book occurred to me when I was doing my Post Doctoral Fellowship at IIM Bangalore, India. While most part of this book is based on my PhD work, there has been lot of reorientation to make this study relevant for developing countries. The book will also be very useful for developed countries, given the rise in health care costs and the increasing number of uninsured.

In the process of writing this book, there were many individuals who played a significant role.

First of all, I am very thankful to my PhD supervisor Dr. Rama V Baru for her continuous help and providing me the space to do my work in my own way, with minimum intervention, during the process of writing my thesis. This helped me to provide a shape to my work, the way I wanted it to be and retain my own style.

Secondly, I am very thankful to all my senior interviewees from donor agencies, from government of India and from government of Orissa, for their exceptional cooperation in spite of having their busy schedules. In this regard my special thanks to former health secretary government of Orissa, Ms Meena Gupta. I am also very thankful to my respondents at the districts of Sundergarh and Khurda for their valuable cooperation.

I am very thankful to Shri B K Jena, the then additional secretary, Ministry of Health and Family Welfare, Government of Orissa, for his constant help during my stay at Bhubaneswar. I am also very thankful to my friends Ellora, Subhajit and Manas, who provided timely logistic support for my fieldwork at Bhubaneswar. I am also very thankful to CASA, Bhubaneswar for their logistic support for my fieldwork at Khurda district.

For my research I had to visit various libraries in Delhi. In this regard I am very thankful to the Jawaharlal Nehru University library, documentation unit of CSMCH centre, JNU; Ratan Tata Library, Delhi University; World Bank documentation unit, New Delhi; DFID documentation unit, New Delhi; European Commission documentation unit, New Delhi. I am also very thankful to the staffs at Directorate of Health Bhubaneswar, CDMO office Sundergarh and CDMO office Khurda, for their help in providing relevant data.

Finally, I am solely responsible for any lacunae in this book.

Subrata Kundu

INTRODUCTION

Definition and classification of reforms

The Oxford dictionary defines the word 'reform' as to 'make changes in something so as to improve it' and as 'form again'. And it defines a reformist as a person who supports gradual political and social reform. That means reform is basically gradual in nature and tries to bring changes in the system or structure to improve its functioning. It is not a radical change. Cassels defines Health Sector Reforms as *changing health policies* according to priorities and along with this bringing reform in the institutions to implement these policies.[1] Whereas World Health Organization defines health sector reforms as a continuous process which brings some fundamental changes in the policy and institutional arrangements, which is carried out by the government.[2] Thus the WHO definition says that reform has to be a *continuous process* and it involves *some fundamental changes in policy, which is supported by corresponding institutional arrangements* to implement it. Significantly it says that it has to be implemented by the government of a country. Analysis of other definitions of health sector reforms suggest that *any fundamental changes in health policies according to the changing priorities and a corresponding institutional changes to implement it has been termed as health sector reforms.* The institutional change can be in terms of structures of financing and provisioning. In structures of provisioning and financing, a wider role for the private sector could be seen. Also the decentralization measures in these two aspects could be thought out in a federal kind of polity like India or Canada. However the interpretation of these changes could be termed at best as systemic changes. Systemic changes are those in which any system tries to adapt itself according to the changing circumstances. Therefore it has more interest in maintaining the status quo.

If we bring the elements of *health sector reforms* from the wider understandings of *response of the system to new challenges* than we would

---

[1] Cassels , 1995.
[2] WHO, 1997.

have to include different initiatives by any government to face the new health challenges at any point of time in the history of healthcare. For example there has been a shift in population policy in India since it was conceptualized in the early 1950s. This could be a reform element according to the current understanding. Even the Alma Ata declaration of late 1970s, which emphasized on primary healthcare or for that matter the 1994 Cairo conference in Egypt, which emphasized on a holistic approach to population could be termed as a reform initiative. There was another important issue related to our understanding of health sector reforms. The reforms in health sector are basically seen as a phenomenon of the 1980s and 1990s. Therefore, if we include elements according to our above understanding than we would have to *decontextualise* the phenomenon of 'heath sector reforms'; for than the reforms have existed in health sector since the provision of healthcare services was taken up by any nation state in the history of the world.

Role of a theory[3]

Therefore there is need for a definition which would not only contextualize the phenomenon, but it would also bring out the dominant trends in the field of healthcare. Before giving a definition of reform, it is necessary to discuss about the role of a theory in explaining a social phenomenon. It has to be understood that, a theory or a paradigm does not try to explain everything about the social reality. In his classic *Structure of Scientific Revolution,* Thomas Kuhn wrote, "To be accepted as a paradigm, a theory must seem better than its competitors, but it need not, and in fact never does, explain all the facts with which it can be

---

[3]According to Goode and Hatt, "Without no system, some ordering principles, in short, without theory science could yield no predictions. Without prediction there would be no control over the material world.... It can therefore be said that the facts of science are the product of observations that are not random but meaningful, that is theoretically relevant. The development of science can be considered as a constant interplay between theory and fact." P- 9. See *Methods in Social Research by William J. Goode and Paul K. Hatt, MacGraw-Hill Company, 1981.*

In a subject dealing with health sector reforms why the necessity of defining the role of theory or even quoting Kuhn from his famous *Scientific Revolution?* There are several reasons, one of them is that the way *public health* has been taught in various universities in the world, the way text books on *public health* has been written and the manner in which the issue of *public health* is being dealt with in terms of various preventive measures suggest that the term *public health* has been accepted as a *truth statement*, as a given category having universal meaning. However just like any other scientific discipline public health also is a *constructed category* and hence the challenge also lies here to understand the mechanisms through which knowledge is generated in this field. This would place the discipline in its proper context. For example this would help us to see that at present there is not a single definition of public health, which is accepted universally. There are many definitions of the term and there are very few books, which have tried to address this epistemologically significant question. Similarly over the later half of the twentieth century quantitative methods has been equated with proper way of doing research or to generate scientific data. This can be observed from the syllabus of public health departments of various universities all over the world as well as from the national and international public health journals. The quantitative method has been given the status of *the scientific method.* This argument has been extended in the later part of this chapter where it has been argued that quantitative method is only a tool of research as qualitative method is. The real question is about how a phenomenon is problematised and accordingly a quantitative or qualitative method can be used and therefore the nature of a problem defines whether a quantitative method would help to address it better than qualitative method or vice versa.

confronted."[4] It can only claim to be explaining certain trends or dominant aspects of a phenomenon in the social world. It can never explain all the facts. For if a theory tries to explain everything it would try to become a truth statement, which is fallacious[5].

If we look at most of the definitions of health sector reforms[6], they have tried to include almost every big or little change in the health sector as an element of reform. For example the change in the approach from Maternal and Child Health or MCH in the early nineties to Reproductive and Child Health or RCH in the late nineties has been termed as a reform element. If this is the case than we could also include the change in approach towards the population policy in India from the early fifties onwards as a reform element! And for that matter any other initiative taken in the field of health services sector after independence, which tries to bring a change in approach, could be termed as a reform measure. For example, the adoption

---

[4] Kuhn S. Thomas, *The Structure of Scientific Revolutions*, Chicago University Press, 1962, pp- 17-18.

[5] "Each science and each specialization within a broader field abstracts from reality, keeping its attention upon a few facts of a given phenomenon rather than upon all aspects". P- 9. See *Methods in Social Research by William J. Goode and Paul K. Hatt, MacGraw-Hill Company, 1981.*

[6] *Definitions of Health Sector Reforms:*

1- "Health Sector Reforms involves a significant, purposive effort to improve the performance of healthcare systems."- WHO Website visited on 18th October 2005.

2- "It is a fundamental rather than an incremental change, which is sustained rather than one-off and purposive in nature." – Cassels, 1997. Further elaborating on this Cassels says, " Health Sector Reforms include:

- Improving the performance of civil service.
- Decentralization of power and resources.
- Improving function of national health ministries.
- Broadening health financing mechanisms.
- Introducing managed competition."

3- Health Sector Reforms as a "Group of projects that include communicable diseases, Reproductive and Child Health Programme and Health System." – Interview with a senior World Bank Official, The World Bank Delhi Office, March 2002 by Rama V. Baru.

4- Heath Sector Reform is a "Mixed bag of donors, projects and the government of India. Overall there is singular lack of vision among all these actors when it comes to Health Sector Reform."- Ibid.

5- It is a "Sustained, purposeful change to improve the efficiency, equity and effectiveness of the health sector."- Berman, 1995.

of Primary Healthcare Approach after the Alma Ata declaration could be termed as a reform measure. Even the Vitamin 'A' campaign in the state of Orissa has been termed as a reform initiative! Therefore the context of the 1980s and 1990s of twentieth century as the beginning of Health Sector Reforms has to be recognized.

It is being argued here that initiatives by the state or central governments might be taken to improve the quality of healthcare services but these are smaller measures within the dominant trends of giving a *greater role to the private sector* in the domain of healthcare. In this frame health or good health is seen as the responsibility of an individual, rather than of the community or of a state[7].

There are some authors like Peter Berman who have defined reforms in technical terms.[8] By giving or trying to interpret in technical terms, an effort seems to have been made to give it the power of a natural science, which can not be questioned.[9] Defining in technical terms also takes away the chance to look at the historical context for the emergence of a phenomenon.

Defining health sector reforms

Let us first have a look at the elements of reform. It has to be remembered that there are different definitions about reform. Here we would be using the definition of reform as *any initiative by the state since the later part of twentieth century, which tries to reduce the role of government in health sector while creating a space for a larger role for the private sector.* Therefore this definition has three important characteristics; one is that it has located health sector reforms in the context of 1980s[10]. This distinction is very important as many of the definitions on health sector reforms have tried to overlook it. It is also important to mention here that while the beginning of health sector reforms has been contextualized in 1980s, this definition does not try to exclude initiatives by different states in twenty

---

[7] This also suggests selective role for state -- preventive services are state responsibility while curative is individual responsibility.

[8] It suggests about the liberal capitalist model of economic growth giving primacy to the market.

[9] See how Foucault has discussed about *method* in his book "History of Sexuality".

[10] The period, which saw the beginning of the ascendance of neo liberal policies in various countries across the world, which got further accelerated after the collapse of former Soviet Union and the formation of World Trade Organisation in 1995.

first century as reform elements. Because the basic idea is that the state trying to create a larger space for the private sector since 1980s. Another important distinction is that while the role of government gets reduced, that space is occupied by the private sector due to the deliberate policy of the state. The third distinctive aspect is inherent in the definition although it is not explicit and it is that the reforms in the health sector needs to be located within broader economic liberalization or economic integration of various countries with the world economy i.e. health sector reforms carry an ideological content.

However it is important to make it clear that the above definition is a conceptual category and it does not claim to explain all the changes happening in the healthcare sector in recent times, nor does it try to explain all the policy initiatives taken by the different governments around the world with regard to the health sector. On the other hand this definition captures the dominant trends being introduced in the health sector in India and abroad, beginning with the decade of 1980s, which has the potential of affecting the totality of the health sector in the long run.

Traditionally health has been seen as a domain of the government even in countries, which followed a liberal capitalist model of development. However with the oil shock of the 1970s many of the governments in the world faced fiscal crisis, along with this the collapse of the former Soviet Union in 1990 created an atmosphere where liberal capitalist model was seen as the only model of economic development.[11] In this model the private sector and the market forces play a dominant role with the state playing as a facilitator. The assumption is that *market has its own rationality* and in the long run would benefit all even though at the initial stage there would be 'hardships'.[12]

This argument has also been extended to the health sector. Now health is seen as an *individual responsibility*. After the 1990s it has been observed that the governments around the world were increasing the scope for private participation in the health sector. The scope of private participation may vary from one country to another. This private participation may be

---

[11] Baru R. V, "Private Health Care in India: Social Characteristics and Trends", Sage Publications, New Delhi, 1998.

[12] See for example Amartya Sen's understanding of the notion of Development from his different writings. Although he talks about inclusion of the poor in the overall development framework, he places his faith in the market forces in the long run.

on a small or large scale but it is redefining the concept of 'health for all'. With this the issues of universality and equity are also involved. Because this private participation is happening in an era when the market plays a dominant role in the process of world economic growth. Any kind of control by the state is seen or perceived negatively.

What is not reform?

For defining the concept of Health Sector Reforms it is equally important to identify what it is not[13]. Health Sector Reforms is different from *systemic changes*. Systemic changes are any initiative by the state to maintain the 'efficiency'[14] of the system so that it could produce optimum output[15]. Therefore systemic changes are not specific to a particular time period as compared to health sector reforms and hence we could say that systemic changes are an integral part of any health system. Systemic changes exclude any initiative by the state for increasing private participation or for decreasing the role of state from the health sector[16].

In this introductory section we have given a new definition of health sector reforms keeping in view different country experiences. Apart from defining what is reform we have also explained about those aspects, which could not be termed as reforms. Before giving a definition of health sector reforms we have tried to explain the role of a theory in explaining the social phenomenon. This was because the field of Public Health has been accepted as a given category and as a result the phenomenon of health sector reforms has been assumed as being out there in the field. Therefore we have argued that health sector reforms were a constructed category and

---

[13] In a lecture on "Class and Power" given at Jawaharlal Nehru University, New Delhi on 18th October, 2005, Professor Andhre Betteille, mentioned that the Marxist definition of 'class' was an important way of defining a concept, for apart from mentioning about 'what is class' it also says 'what is not class'.

[14] We can mention 'efficiency' as 'the best way/means to achieve certain targets/objectives'.

[15] Here it needs to be mentioned that the term 'efficiency' has been associated with health sector reforms by various definitions as if the health systems in different countries before 1980s were never interested to make themselves efficient to achieve their objectives!

[16] This distinction has been made for our clarification for even the health sector reforms could be mentioned as systemic changes! Therefore this distinction has been made to prevent a teleological argument.

hence they required a definition, which would help to classify them into a group of phenomenon, which could be studied scientifically.

Using our new definition of health sector reforms, in first chapter we have discussed about review of literature, which has looked at the process and experience of health sector reforms in various countries of the world.

CHAPTER ONE

REVIEW OF LITERATURE

The decade of nineties

In the nineties Human Development Index or HDI was used for the first time by UNDP[1] and it identified three measures like longevity, education and per capita income to measure a countries HDI. With the adoption of this index by the United Nations the whole notion of *development* was reduced to some measurable index. This also caught the imagination of various world leaders and finally in the year 2000 Millennium Development Goals[2] were adopted for which targets were set to be achieved by the year 2015.

The adoption of HDI index by various countries also brought into front the idea that the sectors like education and health requires the role of state not only for regulation but also for financing and provisioning. Thus the agencies like World Bank, which had been in the forefront of giving the argument that the state had a very little role in social sectors, started to argue for a larger role for the state in these areas,[3] in the later part of the nineties. However a close look shows that these arguments have remained only at the realm of ideas and has not been implemented at the ground level.

There was another event that shows a different direction of movement in the nineties and it was the 1994 Cairo Conference on Population, which emphasized a change in approach to population policies. It suggested about integrating population control with maternal and child health. It

---

[1] UNDP suggests United Nations Development Program.

[2] It is interesting to note that at present the donor agencies like World Bank and European Commission or DFID have set their developmental funding in accordance with the targets of Millennium Development Goals.

[3] This could be observed from the annual documents of the World Bank.

talked about interlinking the issue of population growth with larger aspects of development. These were lofty ideals as it presented a case for respecting human life particularly for women and to give people more power to control their lives. However the agreements at Cairo could not bring any substantial changes in various countries population policies[4]. One of the major reasons was that the dominance of liberal model of economic growth around the world nullified any movement toward these goals.

Another significant event in the 1990s was the formation of World Trade Organization or WTO in 1995 with 144 member countries agreeing for free trade among them. The formation of WTO legitimized the opening off of various economies of the world and those that were out of this group were in the danger of facing the blocked of these 144 countries. The importance of WTO could be observed from the fact that China, which was not a member of the WTO, tried to give many concessions[5] to USA to become a member. WTO was being seen as one of the few democratic institutions at the international forum where its rulings have been followed by every member country[6]. The arrival of WTO has further legitimized a liberal model of economic growth and the democratically elected leaders at the national level have left with few choices for taking economic decisions, which could address the immediate needs of the poorer sections of their population.

HSR: A review of International experience

The adoption of a liberal capitalist model of economic development[7] by different countries around the world not only created an atmosphere for greater role for the market in larger economy, it also legitimized the *rationality*[8] *of market forces* in the social sectors like health and education. With the collapse of communism in former USSR and its disintegration led to the adoption of market economy by the newly created countries out

[4] This has been observed by various authors.
[5] In terms of access to its market.
[6] For example see the speech by Indian Prime Minister Dr. Manmohan Singh published in Indian Express, 22 October 2005.
[7] After the collapse of communism in the former USSR.
[8] The *rationality of the market forces* means the inherent assumption that if market is left on its own without any state intervention than it can produce best results for every body in the long run. However this is an unquestioned assumption or an assumption, which is not based on verifiable research.

of it and also by the East European countries which were earlier following a socialist model of growth. Similarly communist China had liberalised its economy in the late seventies of the twentieth century.

Thus major powers in the world and most of the countries except perhaps Cuba have accepted the liberal capitalist model of economic development where the private sector and the market forces are playing the dominant role and the state is trying to facilitate this process through favorable legislation and playing the role of a regulator to promote fair competition among the various private players. Along with economic liberalization many developed and developing countries have allowed the increasing role of private sector in the healthcare. This was the trend in UK, USA, China, Canada, Australia and many of the countries of Europe where the private sector was playing a dominant role in different aspects of healthcare.

Now let us have a look at the process and experience of reforms in health sector in various countries.

United Kingdom[9]

Over the years the healthcare system in UK had been based on National Health Service or NHS, funded from central taxation. The NHS created in 1948 had the universal coverage and was based on the principles of equity. However in the 1990s the market elements were introduced to make the system *efficient, effective, and responsive to the needs of the patient* and adoption of management practices of the private sector. While in the 1980s the NHS was being under funded, the reforms in the early 1990s focused on *structure and management* of NHS. The effort was to utilize the existing resources 'efficiently' to improve performance. To generate additional resources private finance was encouraged. The reforms in NHS were closely linked with the reforms in education and civil service and with the then government's approach to public sector reforms.

One of the major assumptions of reform initiatives taken was that the competition between NHS healthcare institutions would produce greater

[9] For reviewing the experiences of UK we have referred to Hunter, 2002; Allen, 1997; Collins, Green and Hunter, 1999; Coote and Hunter, 1996; Dobson, 1999; Ethoven, 1985, 2000; European Health Management Association, 2000; Ferlie, Ashburner and Fitzgerald, 1996; Ham, Hunter and Robinson, 1995; Hazell and Jervis, 1998; Hunter, 1992, 1996, 1998; James and Manning, 1996; Klein, 1998; Le Grand, 1999; Maynard and Bloor, 1996; Pollock, 1995; WHO, 2000.

efficiency and responsiveness to the users. However there were no independent studies to assess the impact of reforms introduced between 1991 and 1997 in NHS. Beginning with early 1970s a series of organizational and managerial changes were introduced to improve the efficiency and the effectiveness of healthcare provisioning through NHS. However these initiatives were taken to improve the functioning of National Health Services. At that time the element of large scale privatisation of public sector had not emerged in the public domain.

In the 1980s there were allegations of under funding of NHS, however the reforms focused on utilising the existing resources judiciously, rather than increase in funding. In this context a review of the entire NHS was done by the prime minister's office rather than the department of health in 1988. The NHS review suggested introduction of new management practices, introducing competition among the institutions of NHS and creating more user choices. The basic idea was to generate greater efficiency among the NHS healthcare institutions and responsiveness to the users of healthcare.

As part of reform initiative within the NHS, a patient's charter was created which mentioned about patients rights with regard to issues like, right to information about services available in a particular institution, waiting times, guaranteed admission date in a hospital etc. However these were not legal rights and critics were of the view that this had raised expectations among the public which the NHS was not in a position to provide with its then existing resources.

Therefore the reforms introduced in the NHS were not based on pure scientific evidence and had more to do with the ideology of privatisation. Thus while the Conservative government led by Thatcher tried to give role to the private sector in healthcare provisioning within the publicly funded NHS, the Labour government elected in 1997 continued with this practice of mixed provisioning of healthcare.

Sweden[10]

The healthcare system in Sweden was based on central planning and the wider philosophy of welfare state from 1950s to 1989. By 1990 the debates shifted toward *competition, markets and privatisation.* The reform initiatives like Health and Sickness Care Law in 1982, *decentralized all responsibility for medical care to the counties, including decisions on allocation of resources.* The right to set standards for training and ensuring quality remained with the central government. The new law encouraged the private sector and as there was no regulation of private practitioners, the healthcare expenditure increased rapidly at the primary level care.

Similarly the Adel Reform in 1991 shifted the responsibility of primary care of the aged from counties to the municipalities. This has been termed as a successful reform initiative as it reduced the number of days spent for in-patient care by the elderly. The care guarantee reform 1992, made it mandatory that the patients could seek treatment in any county if their own county did not treat them within three months. As it was observed that the clinic chiefs used to keep long waiting lists because it provided justification for budget increases. As a result of this new initiative, the queues for elective surgeries had shortened significantly.

Another significant reform initiative was the Huslakare reform in 1993, which made it mandatory that every resident of Sweden to register with a primary care physician. The bill encouraged the private physicians who could set up practice without restriction and could compete for contracts as primary care providers. This new initiative not only increased the number of private physicians but it also increased the cost of primary level care. At the county levels experiments were made where by the provision of services was left for the private players, which would be reimbursed by the public authorities. The idea was that the private players would be efficient and would reduce the cost of care.

Thus the reforms in Sweden in 1980s and in 1990s were not due to the inefficiencies or ineffectiveness or inequity in the medical care system, rather it was mostly ideologically driven.

---

[10] For reviewing the experiences of Sweden we have referred to Twaddle, 2002, 1999, 1997,1994; Bergstorm, 1992; Esping-Anderson, 1990; Hadenius, 1988; Korpi, 1978; Landstingsforbundet, 1990,1991.

Canada[11]

The healthcare system in Canada popularly known as 'medicare' by the Canadians consisted of ten provincial and three territorial health insurance plans. Over the years although health was seen as a provincial responsibility, the federal government had played important role in funding and setting national standards for the provincial health insurance programs. Prior to World War II, when the modern Canadian healthcare system was adopted, the costs of hospital and medical care were primarily paid by individuals as out-of-pocket expenditures.

However due to slow economic growth and increasing deficit and debt load, the share of federal government's expenditure for provincial healthcare declined from 38 percent in 1988 to 33 percent in 1994. The decline continued till the year 1999. This increased the healthcare costs of provincial governments, which were also experiencing a slow economic growth. All these developments led toward the arguments for balancing budgets and reducing deficits and taxes and hence reducing public spending on healthcare.

In the 1980s it was observed that while the public expenditure on healthcare was increasing, the length of stay of patients was declining. This was happening partly due to rapid proliferation of costly drugs and diagnostic procedures etc. However, the reforms closed some hospitals; merged some of them and restructured hospital service delivery to make it less expensive. Due to these new measures, there were pressures to keep patients from entering the system. Similarly there were efforts to create new nursing homes, which would be less expensive for the elderly, but it has grown slower than the closure of hospitals. For the treatment of patients who were discharged quickly, required home care and it was observed that the home care expenditure by the government had doubled during the 1990s. Thus there have been efforts to shift the responsibility of care to the community.

---

[11] For reviewing the experiences of Canada we have referred to Woodward and Charles, 2002; Angus, 1992; Angus Reid Group, 1999; Baer, 1997; Canadian Medical Association, 1998, 1997a, 1997b; Fooks, 1999; Hurley, Jeremiah, Lomas, Jonathan and Bhatia, 1996; Hurley, Goldsmith, Lomas, Khan and Vincent, 1997; Kent, 1998; Lomas, 1997; Lomas, Jonathan, Woods, John and Veenstra, 1997; Ryten, Thurbar and Buske, 1998.

A new office called the Canadian Coordinating Office for Health Technology Assessment was created in 1989 by the federal, territorial and provincial ministries of health which collects; analyses and disseminates information on the cost and effectiveness of a technology and its impact on health. In the 1990s its mandate further increased to conducting and managing pharmaceutical-product economic assessments. Off late it has been engaged with rationale use of drugs.

Similarly provinces have come out with legislations to make health professional more accountable to society and to regularize the emerging professions like midwifery, physiotherapy and nurse practitioners. Further under the provincial health insurance most physicians were remunerated on a fee-for-service basis. However as the cost was going up the provincial governments removed some services from the insurance coverage and these services were made available though the private sector.

To check the growth in number of physicians, the medical school enrollment was reduced by 10 percent and the immigration policies, which restricted the number of physicians from outside the country, were strictly implemented. Earlier the provincial drug plans used to cover the elderly, the poor and catastrophic drug costs and these were adding to costs of public drugs plan. To address this, the availability of drugs was reduced to those of known effectiveness. Similarly efforts were made to regulate the prices of patent medicines by the federal government. Decentralization measures have tried to give more authority to the regional level for planning, management and for funding decisions.

Thus reforms in Canadian healthcare system have tried to introduce market mechanisms to make it more 'efficient' and 'effective' in achieving its targets.

United States of America[12]

According to the World Health Organisation in 1997, 55.9 percent of American health expenditures came from private sources, whereas in other OECD countries except Mexico and South Korea, the private healthcare expenditure was in the range of 10 percent to 30 percent. Further in US, government financed health insurance was available to a small section of its population compared to other OECD nations[13]. While historically the regulation of healthcare in US had been not strong enough, since the Reagan era the deregulation of healthcare has been emphacised. Further the role of charity and philanthropy has been on gradual decline in second half of the 20th century.

The public hospitals and health facilities in US were expected to function within the framework of the market system but to a large extent the American healthcare institutions have always been dominated by voluntary community based organizations. The voluntary health insurers begun as non-profit community based entities but at a later stage many of them shifted to for-profit status. Gradually over the years for-profit insurers have dominated the market. Similarly many public hospitals have been acquired by the private sector. Thus in US the trend has been toward increasing privatisation.

Instead of a single payer system of financing in countries such as Canada, UK and Sweden, in America there are a variety of payment mechanisms. In terms of health policy making in US, except for the enactment of Medicare and Medicaid, federal legislation on the healthcare system has not resulted in major systemic changes. Therefore in case of US the private sector has played a dominant role over the years and in recent times, with mergers and acquisitions of private players in health sector, the market mechanisms were in full play.

---

[12] For reviewing the experiences of USA we have referred to Wessen, 2002; American Hospital Association, 2000, 2001; Anderson and Poullier, 1999; Blau and Marshall, 1987; Blendon, 1975; Enthoven, 1985a, 1985b; Evans, Tandon, Murray and Lauer, 2002; Ginzberg, 1991; Gray, 1991; Haber, 1999; Hellander, Himmelstein and Woolhandler, 1994; Himmelstein, Lewontin and Woolhandler, 1996; Mcpherson, Wennberg, Hovind and Clifford, 1982; Perry, Seymour and Thamer, 1997; Wennberg and Gittelsohn, 1973; Woolhandler and Himmelstein, 1991; WHO,2000.

[13] Wessen, 2002.

Eastern Europe[14]

Here we would be discussing about the health sector reforms in Czech and Slovak Republics, Hungary, Poland, Croatia and Slovenia.

Czech and Slovak Republics

In 1990 the *Czech and Slovak Republics moved from a controlled socialist structure to an insurance-based, fee for service model.*[15] This was due to the report of the Health Reform Task Force constituted in late 1989. *The payment of hospitals and physicians on a fee-for-service basis was introduced in Czech republic in 1992.* Membership was made compulsory for its citizens and the contribution was 13.5 percent from the members. With the separation of Czech and Slovak republics in 1993, this insurance system became autonomous, *collecting premiums and disbursing payments without direct government involvement.* After the creation of two republics, the general Health Insurance Company of Czech Republic, which was a publicly financed private firm, became the primary insurer covering 8.5 million or 83 percent of its population. The remaining 1.8 million populations who were mostly government employees like, police, army, bankers, miners and large individual firms were covered by sickness funds.

However this new system was a burden on the GDP, which was found to be unsustainable and it was also the time when the economy was moving through an inflationary phase. Thus the healthcare expenditure in 1993 was more than 50 percent compared to 1991 figures, in Czech Republic. To meet these additional expenditures, individual contributions were about 30 percent. Premiums were collected from 95 percent of the employers and 60 percent of the self-employed. In terms of effort toward privatisation, about 50 percent of doctors and 40 percent of clinics have been privatised.

---

[14] For reviewing the experiences of Eastern European Countries of Czech, Poland and Hungary, Croatia and Slovenia we have referred to Ackerman, 1994; Albert, Bennett and Bojar, 1992; Avah, 1995; Bodenheimer and Grumbach, 1994; Chinitz, 1995; Deppe and Oreskovic, 1996; Dorozynski, 1996; Hayo, 1997; Hebrang, 1994; Kalman, Massaro and Nemec, 1994; Karcher, 1996; Maynard and Bloor, 1996; McKee, Bobak, Kalina, Bojan and Enachescu, 1994; Smolen, 1992; Wloch, 1993.
[15] Oreskovic, 2002.

Hungary

The second largest country in Central Europe with a population of over 10 million in 1996 had a GDP growth of 2 percent. After 1948 a centralized healthcare system was developed, *consisting of three levels of care: physicians (primary), polyclinics and hospital care*. However in 1990s with the collapse of former Soviet Union, the Health Insurance Act was introduced in 1992, which formalized the separation of health insurance funds from the state budget and it also established a managing committee to be chosen by national election. This new fund paid for health services and sickness benefits and was underwritten by the government. In terms of premiums collected, employees paid 4 percent and the employers paid 23.5 percent of their pre-tax salaries. The employees also paid 4 percent toward a solidarity fund, which was a contribution on behalf of the unemployed.

Further this new act established a network of family physicians and made possible the *free choice of general practitioners and the pediatricians*. However the companies and those individuals who could not fully pay their contributions due to economic hardship, either the reimbursement payments were withhold or the assets of companies were seized. The private health insurance was introduced in late 1990s, which was aimed at higher-earning portion of the population.

Poland

Poland was the first country to adopt market economy in Central and Eastern Europe in early 1990s. However the growth rate in GDP declined by 17 percent from 1990 to 1993. As the economy was in transition phase, the healthcare expenditure experienced a negative growth of 4.8 percent during 1991 to 1994. Prior to the introduction of economic reforms the healthcare system in Poland was financed and planned by the central government. The preventive aspects of the healthcare were also closely linked with the curative aspects.

The reforms in health sector was based on a document which was the outcome of an international conference on health policy being organized in Poland by the Ministry of Health and Social Welfare, which was cosponsored by WHO, World Bank and Project Hope. The reasons cited for health sector reforms were, deteriorating healthcare services, poor health status and patient dissatisfaction with the existing system etc. Hence efforts were made to make the healthcare system more 'effective' and 'responsive' to the local needs.

After the initial period of indecision at the highest level of the Polish government, National Investment Funds was *created to start a mass privatisation program* in different sectors of the economy. While the privatisation of pharmacies had started in 1989, in case of the polyclinics only 10 percent had been privatised. The Social Democratic government, which was very concerned about extensive privatisation and wanted a national health service being funded by the state, lost the 1997 elections. Many attribute this loss to the effort toward recentralisation of the healthcare facilities by the Social Democratic government.

Thus the countries like Poland, Hungary and the Czech Republic started health sector reforms in the provisioning and the funding of their healthcare systems. It has put forward the concept like 'freedom of choice', signifying that the responsibility of healthcare rests on an individual. However the introduction of market mechanisms has allegedly weakened the referral system as the patients have direct access to the specialist of their choice. Unlike the earlier system, the ministers of health and finance did not have control over the level of expenditure in insurance funds, which was driven by the market. While the introduction of compulsory health insurance has increased healthcare expenditures in total, the poor have been unable to pay their contributions and hence have been left out of this process. This has further created problems of risk adjustment, financial distribution between sickness funds, increasing burden of contributions and as a result increasing evasion of contributions in the initial phases.

Croatia

Croatia in the 1990s was one of the most open economies in Central Europe. It had a population of 4.5 million and services sector accounting for 60 percent of its GDP. The health sector reforms in Croatia were part of the larger economic reforms, which tried for structural adjustment. There had been effort toward developing a healthcare system, which would be compatible with market economy and resembling the models of developed European countries. The introduction of Health Insurance Act and Healthcare Law, created a new compulsory health insurance scheme for the entire population. The other mechanisms of financing were funds allocated in budgets for certain types of healthcare and certain groups of the population. These were people who could not pay health insurance contributions, like the children, pregnant women and persons above 65 years of age.

Besides there were voluntary health insurance schemes for those who could pay in private sector and there were compulsory forms of healthcare service which the employers had to pay directly, like the occupational diseases and accidents for workers.

While the per capita income in Croatia declined from US $5,106 in 1990 to $2,079 in 1992, the health share of GDP declined marginally from10.6 percent in 1991 to 8.5 percent in 1992. It was being said that the health reforms in Croatia in a short period could contain costs and could improve the health status of its population. According to one estimate in October 1998, 10,000 Croatian enterprises were insolvent and if these were forced to close under new bankruptcy law than it would make 1,50,000 people as unemployed. Besides there were many Croatian firms which were not paying for their insured employees and the Croatian Institute of Health Insurance, which operates the health insurance in Croatia was in debt for US $115 million in 1997. Thus by the year 1999, the Croatian Health financing system was facing a severe financial crisis.

Slovenia

With a population of 2 million and a per capita GNP of $9,161 in 1997, Slovenia was the most prosperous country in Central and Eastern Europe, with the services sector accounting for 60 percent and the industry accounting for 32 percent of its output. The heath care reform was introduced in March 1992 when a new healthcare law was accepted. The reform measures introduced were a national insurance scheme compared to the earlier budget financing, creating contracts between providers and the national insurance plan and a possibility of independent contracting with the national insurance plan.

In the economic front while the government followed a policy of fiscal prudence; however the social expenditures increased in 1990s. Whereas the healthcare expenditure was 8 percent of the GDP since 1991 to 1998, the actual health expenditure increased by 51.8 percent during this period due to the growth of per capita GDP. As the primary care providers and the specialists were paid according to a fixed number of points for service, the primary care givers had an incentive to refer and the specialists had an incentive to accept referrals. Due to this new law, the number of consultations per person per year increased significantly. Health insurance cards were introduced in 1998 by the Health Insurance Institute of Slovenia. Simultaneously health professional cards were distributed to the doctors, medical nurses, pharmacists and other workers. Off late the institute was trying to evaluate the health insurance card project to better implement the health insurance scheme.

Therefore we have seen that the countries of Central and East European countries, which were going through a transitional phase in the 1990s were seeking alternative methods of funding for health services like, introduction of user fees, private health insurance, community based financing and general taxation etc. However since the insurance in these countries is employment based, it would be increasingly difficult for the poor, elderly, unemployed and the chronically ill to afford insurance coverage.

Russia[16]

With the collapse of former Soviet Union in 1991, reform measures were undertaken in it's under funded healthcare service, which was known as Soviet Socialized Medicine. Untill about 1960s the healthcare services in Russia was one of the better performing sector in its economy. It was symbolic of the welfare aspects of the Soviet state. It was the first country in the history of the world, which made a constitutional guarantee of universal entitlement to free medical care to the entire population as the responsibility of the Soviet state. Thus provisioning and financing of healthcare became the responsibility of the state. There was no private sector. The entire manpower in the health sector was state employees. The other significant features of the Soviet systems were, health policy was closely integrated with national planning, the health system was highly centralized and the preventive aspects of healthcare were a significant aspect of the health system.

However the new Russian federation that came into existence in 1991, while emphasizing that all citizens have right to free healthcare, it

[16] For reviewing the experiences of Russia we have referred to Field, 2002; Burger, Field and Twigg, 1998; Cohen, 2000; Ellman, 1994; Farmer, 1999a; Friedman, 2001; Garrett, 2000; Godbeng and Kishovsky, 2000; Mckinlay, Mckinlay and Beuglehole, 1989; Preker and Richard, 1995; Rimashevskaia, 1993; Sheiman, 1997; Shishkin, 1999; Smith, 1999; Woolhandler and Himmelstein, 1985.

suggested that the financing could be from variety of sources. On the other hand the broad reform measures suggested were: decentralization, introduction of health insurance, market mechanisms and competition among the various players. Further the provisioning and the funding aspects of healthcare were separated. For the regional insurance funds, a 3.6 percent tax of the salary fund for every enterprise of the region was levied.

The evidence suggests that the new insurance scheme has not succeeded and the growth of private insurance companies has been quite slow. It was also been observed that funds available for various regions have differed significantly.

Israel[17]

By the year 1994 Israel had four private not-for-profit sick funds, which offered voluntary comprehensive health insurance and it covered more than 95 percent of its population. Significantly apart from the curative and acute hospital care, preventive community care was also been covered under this insurance scheme.

The health sector reforms in Israel were initiated with the passage of National Health Insurance Law in 1994. This new law aimed at universal health insurance coverage, promotion of equity, defining a universal benefit package, creation of multiple providers, to improve the quality of care and *to free the ministry of health from operational responsibilities*. Since 1980s the private health insurance market has grown rapidly in Israel. An analysis of healthcare expenditure pattern in 1994 showed that 27 percent of the national health expenditure came from the central budget, 22 percent came from the employers, 21 percent by sick fund membership fees and 25 percent from payments for services and medicines. In the 1990s while the share of government expenditure to healthcare declined, the share of membership fees increased and out-of-pocket payments remained unchanged. It has been observed that the household healthcare expenditures in Israel increased by nearly 50 percent from 1986/87 to 1992/93.

---

[17] For reviewing the experiences of Israel we have referred to Gross and Anson, 2002; Chernichovsky and Chinitz, 1995; Chinitz, 1996, 1994; Gross and Harrison, 2001; Gross, Rosen and Chinitz, 1998; Shirom, 1995; Twaddle, 1996; Yishei, 1982.

The larger causes for reforms in health sector of Israel were same as in other countries like the reevaluation of the welfare state and its underlying ideologies. The rising costs of healthcare and the welfare measures had exceeded the economic growth and the government was unwilling to increase taxes. At the same time the public healthcare was criticized as inefficient and in many cases it was termed as wasteful expenditures and in its place new terms like *cost containment, accountability, competition and pluralism* were used. Further to introduce reform elements other countries initiatives were studied. Thus the *recommendation to transform hospitals into competing legal entities resembled the hospital reform in Britain.*

Argentina[18]

Since 1940s the healthcare services in Argentina was based on the concept of welfare state. However the beneficiaries were some selected sections of the society like trade unions having closer ties to the state apparatus. These trade unions were given the task of managing the sickness funds, which was created out of compulsory contributions from the employers and employees and from the state subsidies. The rest of the population got health services either through participating in mutual aid institutions or through the public services, which were expanded during 1946 to 1952.

The public healthcare services were divided into national, provincial and municipal jurisdictions, which were intended to serve the poorer sections of the society. However as the sickness funds were controlled by the traded unions it became difficult for risk pulling so that all the working class population could be covered for necessary healthcare. From late 1950s onwards the sickness funds started only the financing of healthcare services and the responsibility of provisioning of healthcare was left to the professionals, which was earlier being done by the sickness funds through remuneration of professionals in its own hospitals and ambulatory clinics since 1940s.

In the late 1950s the professionals created their local, provincial and national confederations, thus taking charge of the services being provided by their members and the management of the respective contracts. As a result liberal medical practices like, choosing a physician of patient's

[18] For reviewing the experiences of Argentina we have referred to Belmartino, 2002; Acuna, 1994.

choice, professional autonomy, user fees and the promotion of curative care were promoted. While the sickness funds and the private sector provided services to the working population and the large part of the middle class like the businessman and the professionals, the public subsystem provided free healthcare to the population outside the labor market. Therefore while the sickness funds and the private sector were catering to the population living in urban areas, the public subsystem catered to the population living in semi-urban and shanty towns characterized by unavailability of adequate infrastructure.

In the late 1960s the private health insurance associations begun to develop but maintained a limited presence till 1980s. These were promoted by professional groups or private hospitals. In the 1980s the Argentine economy faced serious crisis of foreign debt and fiscal crisis at home. This had a deep impact on the social sectors like healthcare. To address the ills of the economy, reform measures were introduced and simultaneously reforms were introduced in the health sector.

Some of the reform measures were like, making it compulsory for every worker to channel his or her contributions to the *obra social* or sickness funds associated with respective trade unions. The idea was to generate greater efficiency among the sickness funds through introducing competition among themselves. Secondly, to help the hospitals and health centres to generate resources, it was made mandatory for the sickness fund to pay for the services, their members had utilised from these institutions. Further the choice of joining different sickness funds was left to the workers to be decided. However the efforts to deregulate the sickness funds from trade unions could not succeed.

Mexico[19]

The healthcare system in Mexico had been a public-private mix in financing and delivery of healthcare services. With 98 million population it was the second largest country in Latin America and also a middle-income country with a GNP of $ 4,410 in 1999. The healthcare system in Mexico had developed over the years with the patronage of the state. Prior to getting independence in 1921, the healthcare in Mexico was mainly

---

[19] For reviewing the experiences of Mexico we have referred to Arenas, Cervantes, Dantes, and Rubi, 2002; Cassels, 1995; Cleaves, 1987; Donabedian, 1980; Frenk, Dantes, Cruz, Freeman, 1994; Hsiao, 1994; World Bank, 1993, 2000.

being provided by the Catholic Church, which created various nursing homes and hospitals. After getting independence the healthcare system was based on the concept of welfare state. With the growth of industrial economy in 1940s, institutional mechanisms were created to provide healthcare to the most organized sector workers and by 1960s this provision was also extended to the working class population. Along with these public healthcare institutions, there were individual and group private practitioners who catered to the small section of a population with a high socioeconomic status.

The healthcare reforms initiated in 1980s was intended to check the disorderly growth of medical care in both public and private sector. It also aimed at addressing the problem of access to healthcare for all. The reforms during 1982-1988 increased the space for the private sector and gave it legitimacy as an important aspect of healthcare. Prior to the 1980s, the Mexican state used to contract most of the physicians active in the medical labor market. However since 1993, with the influence of international agencies, efforts were made to crate pluralistic systems in healthcare in the model of medical care institutions in USA.

The 1984 general health law tried to establish a national health system according to which the public institutions had to cater to needs of the uninsured population, which was 35% of the total population; the social security institutions and the social services were supposed to cover 59% of the total population and the remaining 6% were to be covered by the private services. Further the decentralization process was created in 1987, which created a number of health agencies in different parts of Mexico with autonomy for financial management and healthcare delivery. Efforts were also being made to create managed care institutions for those sections of the population who could pay for their health insurance; thus creating 'freedom of choice' for the users, which would increase the efficiency of entire social security system.

Chile[20]

Since 1920s the Chilean system of healthcare was based on the state responsibility for the public health. The Sanitary law in 1918 established the public responsibility for sanitation and preventive health programmes.

[20] For reviewing the experiences of Chile we have referred to Jara and Bossert, 1995; Reich, 1995; Grindle and Thomas, 1991; Bossert, 1994.

With the creation of National Health Service in 1950s this trend was further strengthened. It utilised the social security contributions and general tax revenues to provide healthcare through public hospitals and clinics. This was possible because at that time a coalition of political parties known as Popular Front was in favor of a democratic socialist state intervention in the social sector.

With the introduction of market mechanisms in Chile in early 1980s, health sector reforms were also introduced. In the 1980s decentralization of primary care and privatisation of health insurance mechanisms were introduced in the health sector. In the 1990s the public-private partnerships were encouraged more and this further strengthened the increasing role of market in Chilean healthcare.

Australia[21]

According to the many observers, the modern Australian healthcare system had been influenced by one- the requirements for public services for the needs of soldiers and felons who were servants of the crown, two- private services for wealthier sections and three- charitable or volunteer services for the poor and sick. Thus the development of Australian healthcare system had been influenced by colonial settlements of the white population. The free settlers were expected to develop land and commerce without any dependence on the state. Therefore all immigrants were seen as 'assets' and this also reflected that the state would take minimal responsibility for the well being of its citizens.

In this context the healthcare system in Australia has developed as a mixture of public and private sector involvement. The national healthcare delivery system, which was financed mostly by the general taxes, had provisions for free healthcare for public patients in public hospitals. Another important feature of Australian healthcare system was the Medicare Levy introduced in 1984 to generate additional revenues for healthcare. Thus the medicare Levy has increased from 1% in 1984 to 1.5% of the taxable income by the year 1997-98. According to one estimate the medicare levy was generating 20% of the commonwealth health expenditures in Australia.

---

[21] For reviewing the experiences of Australia we have referred to Stewart and England, 2002; Australian Institute of Health and Welfare, 1995, 1998a, 1998b; Duckett, 1984, 2000; Gardner, 1995, 1997; Harris and Harris, 1998; Schofield, 1995.

Near about fifty percent of the private sector has been owned by for-profit organizations. Many of them had been listed in the Australian stock exchange and with substantial overseas shareholdings from Southeast Asia and the United States of America. The rest of the fifty percent of the private sector was being owned by not-for-profit organizations, mostly the Catholic Church. These not-for-profit healthcare institutions enjoyed various tax exemptions. The health insurance existed in both for-profit and not-for-profit private organizations.

In 1973 Health Insurance Act tried to introduce universal access to healthcare, which was opposed by the medical profession on the ground that it was interference in the realm of medical autonomy and professionalism. Thus by 1978 the universal health insurance scheme was almost abandoned and by 1983 private sector was subsidized to create voluntary health insurance schemes. Thus in 1984 while 50% of the Australians were covered by private insurance scheme Medicare, by the year 2000 the number declined to 32.7%. The Medicare system reimbursed about 85% of the cost of medicare. The idea was to prevent patients from overuse of the system and to make them aware about the cost of care. Over the years due to high fees of insurance those having least need for it were just giving up.

The introduction of medicare scheme had increased the cost of healthcare in general and the in-patient care in particular. The effort by the National Health Strategy of 1990s to contain the increasing healthcare delivery cost had not succeeded much. In the 1990s it had been observed that a large section of the population who had the private health insurance used the state public hospitals. One explanation has been that the patients were reluctant to pay extra private hospital charges.

China[22]

The healthcare reforms in China were closely related to the economic reforms introduced in 1979. In 1949 when the Peoples Republic of China

---

[22] For reviewing the experiences of China we have referred to Anson, 2002; Berrios, Koponen, Huiguang, 1997; Chen, Hu, Lin, 1993; Dezhi, 1992; Dong, Bogg, Rehnberg, Diwan, 1999; Henderson, Jin, Akin, Li, Wong, Ma, He, Zhang, Chang, Ge, 1995; Hesketh and Zhu, 1997; Huang, 1988; Kan, 1990; Lawson and Lin, 1994; Lennart, Dong, Wang, Cai, Vidon, 1996; Liu, Hsiao, Eggleston, 1999; Normile, 2000; Popkin, paeratakul, Ge, Zhai, 1995; Shi, 1993; World Bank, 2000; WHO, 2000; Yip, Wang, Liu, 1998; Zhou, Hou, 1999.

was established, the health indicators like IMR and MMR were very high and the healthcare service were very weak. Most of these services were located in urban areas and they were privately owned. The rural population mostly had to depend on the traditional healers.

The first five year plan introduced in 1949 laid out the policy that the healthcare should be provided to workers, soldiers and the farmers through publicly financed and owned healthcare services. It tried to integrate the traditional Chinese medicine with Western medicine, gave priority to prevention of communicable and infectious diseases, aimed at creating mass movements for eradicating these diseases and emphasized the aspects of personal hygiene and benefits of nutrition. These policy goals were implemented in second and third five year plans.

With the creation of a communist state, the government confiscated private capital and land. In the health sector the private institutions were also handed over to the government and the doctors in private practice were gradually recruited by the growing public sector. As a result by 1962 only 3.2% of the doctors were in private practice compared to 56.5% in 1950. By the end of 1950s these policies improved health status of the population and also had created a well-developed health network for the rural population.

The Cultural Revolution from 1966 to 1977 introduced by Mao Ze-dong led to near about 20 to 30 million loss of lives. This was an effort to speed up industrialization and allocating most of the resources and rural manpower for this purpose. During this period the remaining private sector in healthcare was banned, the research in higher medicine was abandoned, hospitals were closed, and the number of health facilities declined by 33%. While there was a decline in the total number of healthcare personnel by 5%, the number of nurses and midwives increased by 25% during this period. Thus on the one hand while the urban healthcare institutions were adversely affected, the rural healthcare institutions continued to grow. The barefoot doctor scheme was introduced and 2 to 4 barefoot doctors served a population of 1,000 to 3,000. During the first three five year plans the rural cooperative insurance schemes were introduced and later these were made compulsory during the Cultural Revolution.

These initiatives made the healthcare accessible to all the rural population and all the rural and urban population were entitled to at least one health insurance scheme. However the Cultural Revolution ruined the economy and with the introduction of economic reforms in 1979, collective agriculture was disbanded and land was distributed to families according to household size. Due to this changed policy the cooperative medical schemes collapsed in rural areas. As the medical insurance was left for the farmers' choice the collection for the premiums failed. The private ownership of land created a wealthier section in the villages; those preferred the county or city hospitals. As the demand for barefoot doctors declined, their standard of living also started falling. The fee-for-service scheme was introduced for the village doctors. Further the cost of running the county hospitals and the township health centres was left on the user fees. This closed down many of these institutions and also many of them reduced the number of staff and beds.

With the increasing privatisation of healthcare in rural and urban areas, the cost of out-of-pocket health expenditure has also gone up since 1980s. However efforts have also been made to improve the quality of care by introducing licensing procedure for the village doctors and establishment of pharmaceutical standards. Thus along with the change in the larger economy of China, the changes were also introduced in the health sector in terms of financing, provisioning and manpower.

Zambia

Zambia got independence in 1964 and it inherited a medical system biased toward the urban and copper mining areas. The healthcare services during the colonial period were free from the public sector. However due to its bias toward urban based tertiary care, it was out of reach for a large section of the population. Since independence an effort was made to address this anomaly in the healthcare through a state led intervention in health services.[23]

In the 1980s Zambia faced economic crisis with falling copper prices, which was its primary source of income, and the rise in oil prices. This forced the Zambian government to approach the IMF for a loan under the structural adjustment programmes. In 1987 the government of President Kaunda tried to cancel this process but could not succeed. Thus with the SAP introduced in the economy, it affected the health services structure in

[23] "Health Sector Reforms in Zambia: Implications for Reproductive Health and Rights" by Priya Nanda, Centre for Health and Gender Equity, working papers, October 2000.

the country. Due to the cost containment measures introduced in health sector, the per capita health expenditure by the government declined by 30% in 1992 compared to the year 1982. This led to shortage of drugs and medical supplies and further one-third of the senior medical personnel left their jobs and most of them went abroad. Child mortality and infant mortality increased during this period and 1980s also saw the emergence of malaria and HIV/AIDS, which further increased pressure on the under funded healthcare in Zambia.

The health sector reforms introduced aimed at providing cost effective and quality healthcare through introduction of essential health package.[24] It further emphasised on the primary and preventive care rather than on the high-tech tertiary and curative care. As a cost sharing mechanism user fees were introduced in 1992-93. Although exemptions were there for the poor and the vulnerable, in practice these were not fully implemented. While the healthcare expenditure increased from 5.7% in 1991 to 13.7% in 1997 to the total government budget, the allocations were made according to the priorities identified in the health sector reforms.

The Indian scenario[25]

In India the reform initiatives have to be seen in the larger context of economic liberalization in the nineties. In the health sector over the years India was able to develop a network for healthcare provisioning in primary, secondary and tertiary levels of care. The private sector had been allowed to grow in the mixed model of economic development followed by India. Even the private practice by government doctors had been allowed in many states. Initially in the years after independence the idea was to focus on the preventive care supported by the curative care. However over the years the developments in the health sector followed a path where the health services structure grew mostly in the urban areas and with a focus on the curative aspects. With the abolition of import duties on high-tech equipments in the eighties, the curative care had moved more

[24] The six major thrust areas of this package were, maternal and child health, malaria, family planning, HIV/AIDS/STDS, Tuberculosis, Water and Sanitation. - Ibid.

[25] For reviewing the experiences of India we have referred to Baru, 2002, 2000, 1998; Banerji 1985; Baru, Nayar and Gopal, 1996; Baru and Sadhana, 2000; Berman, 1995, Bhat, 1993; Cassels, 1996; Gill, 1996; Gough, 1979; Government of India, 1946; Jayal, 1999; Nanda, 2000; Omvedt, 1981; Patnaik, 1999; Price, 1989; Qadeer, 1985; Twaddle, 1996; World Bank, 1996, 1993.

toward a high-tech care and as a result the cost of care had increased much more in the nineties than the earlier decades.

Therefore we could say that the changes in the health sector in India have occurred due to:

1-The inherent needs of the country at large and of the state governments.
2- Policy interventions at the Central and the State government levels.
3- It has occurred also due to the influence of World Bank through its various projects and specifically through its State Health Systems Development Projects.
4- The larger phenomenon of economic reforms have also changed the perceptions among the political parties and among the middle class, who were the main beneficiaries of economic reforms and they argued that except at the primary level care, the state should not get involved in secondary and tertiary level care.

Classification of reform elements[26]

Here we would be discussing about eleven states[27] where reforms have been initiated. We would be making a distinction between the initiatives, which could be mentioned as systemic changes, and the initiatives, which could be mentioned as health sector reforms using our new definition of health sector reforms.

---

[26] Here we have classified various initiatives by different state governments in India in terms of 'health sector reforms' and 'systemic changes' according to the new definition we have given in this book. In Chapter V we have classified health sector reforms and systemic changes in the context of Orissa and Chapter IV has specifically discussed about State Health Systems Development Projects and Orissa Health System Development Project as major reform elements.

[27] Punjab, Rajasthan, Gujarat, Himachal Pradesh and Uttaranchal, Andhra Pradesh, Kerala, Madhya Pradesh, Delhi, Tamilnadu and Tripura. These states have been selected as mentioned in the Proceedings of Workshop on "India's Health System: Role of Health Sector Reforms" held on September 4-5, 2003 at India International Centre, New Delhi, India. This did not include the states like West Bengal, Karnataka, Orissa and Uttar Pradesh, which have accepted the State Health Systems Development Project funded by World Bank as we have discussed about these initiatives in Chapter IV in detail.

Systemic changes

Systemic change means that a system trying to respond to new situations to remain efficient. It becomes necessary because the earlier arrangements were not able to respond to new challenges and hence some changes need to be made in the earlier set up. So let us first look at those initiatives, which have been mentioned as reforms but more appropriately could be termed as systemic changes.

Decentralization

This was about bringing the primary health centers under the *control*[28] of Panchayati Raj Institutions. Thus the *Punjab* government had thought about giving the supervisory, administrative and financial powers to the Panchayats over the PHCs. Similarly block health office has been created in *Gujarat* from where one person would act as an interface between the district and the block PHCs[29]. This person would also intermediate about implementation of the national programs. In *Himachal Pradesh* Parivar Kalyan Salahkar Samities or PARIKAS have been formed at all the three levels of Panchayati Raj Institutions. At all these levels the Panchayat president was also the president of PARIKAS. Funds under family health awareness camp and Mahila Swasthya Sangh had been given to these *samities*. Also the state government had tried to make aware the PRIs about health related programs. On the other hand *Kerala* was an exception, where the healthcare institutions along with the funds have been handed over to the PRIs for a *responsive* healthcare system. In Tripura PRIs have been involved in the implementation of national health programs.

Changes in the drugs system

This systemic change has been widely quoted following its successful implementation in Tamilnadu and this was later implemented in different aspects by Orissa, Rajasthan, Himachal Pradesh, Andhra Pradesh, and Delhi governments. Although it has been identified as drug reform it was in fact a systemic change. Under this an essential drugs list, centralized purchase, use of generic drugs, rationale use of drugs had been incorporated. It needs to be mentioned that the changes in the drugs

---

28 This nature of control varies from state to state.

29 The personnel were expected to help the district authorities about planning, implementation and review of activities related to block PHCs.

system has been limited to only the government healthcare institutions. The widespread private sector has not been covered and this was a major flaw of this initiative because the utilisation pattern[30] across states both for in-patient and out patient care shows that private sector was accessed by maximum number of people.

Others

This category includes a variety of initiatives by different states to strengthen their healthcare delivery systems. Some of these initiatives were: Introduction of mobile health clinics, reviewing the performance of all hospitals on a monthly basis etc. by Punjab government. Training of personnel to fully utilize the available manpower in Orissa[31]; Giving some financial power to the medical officer in charge at the block level for petty maintenance in states like Himachal Pradesh and Orissa; Creation of hospital advisory committees for greater autonomy and accountability at hospital level in Andhra Pradesh; Grouping of CHCs in Gujarat to make available the expertise of specialists; Integration of ISM and H practitioners for better implementation of national programs in Himachal Pradesh; Establishment of Emergency Obstetric Care in remote and inaccessible areas in Gujarat to address the high maternal mortality rates; Creation of ZSS in states like Himachal Pradesh and Orissa for better functioning of district societies; Introduction of Disease Surveillance mechanisms as it was the case of Orissa, Kerala and Himachal Pradesh; At the national level the change in population policy from MCH to RCH in the 1990s.

The above list was not an exhaustive one, however these have been some of the initiatives those had been taken by many states and identified as health sector reforms. Here it has been argued that these changes were meant to improve the existing healthcare system, which was an integral part[32] of any system.

---

[30] See for example the National Family Health Survey I and II figures.

[31] In case of Orissa these were Lab Technicians. It needs to be mentioned here that if the existing staffs are trained to fulfill the shortage of staffs than that initiative could be termed as a reform initiative for it talks about the use of existing staffs efficiently. This issue has been discussed in chapter V where Orissa experience has been analysed.

[32] Any system tries to incorporate changes in it keeping in view the new challenges it faces in its day-to-day functioning so that it retains its relevance. However there is a thin dividing line here, which suggests that we need to separate the health

Health sector reforms

Now let us have a look at the initiatives, which could be termed as health sector reforms according to the definition that we have provided.

Introduction of user charges

User charges have been introduced in all the states, which have implemented the State Health Systems Development Project funded by World Bank. The rationale of this project has been to focus more on secondary level care so that the states could invest their limited resources in primary level care. While creating facilities like addition in terms of beds, equipments and specialist care, it has tried to impose a price for it. The argument was that those who could pay for it should be charged and introducing user charges would deter people from unnecessarily using healthcare facilities, just because they were available free of cost. However the difficulty lies in when the matter comes about exempting the poor from user charges[33]. User societies have also been created at the district level for management of funds. It has been ensured that the money generated in one institution was spent in that institution only. However the International experience and the experience from states show that the collection from user charges were very low and hence it was good to the extent that the money generated helps in petty maintenance. It was not sufficient enough to run an institution.

User charges have also been introduced by states like Himachal Pradesh by creating institutions like Aspatal Kalyan Samities at Zonal and District and sub divisional hospitals level. These Samities were also engaged in generating resources through community financing. Similarly Medicare Relief Society in Rajasthan[34] had been created to collect user charges at district, sub district and at CHC level.

---

sector reforms from systemic changes. Although the private sector has existed in healthcare prior to the 1980s in many countries, still the space the state has been providing to the private players in health sector since the decade of eighties is unprecedented for last two centuries.

[33] This issue has been discussed in detail in Chapter V.

[34] It needs to be mentioned that Rajasthan was one of the states where the State Health Systems Development Project was going to be implemented as part of phase II of this project.

Contracting out services[35]

Another reform initiative has been contracting out or out sourcing of services in secondary and tertiary level institutions. The services, which have been contracted out to the private sector were security, sanitation, ambulance services, and dental services in *Punjab*. The IEC activities in *Gujarat*; Cleaning in *Orissa*; Scavenging, laundry and diet in *Himachal Pradesh*; Sanitation, laundry and diet services in *Uttaranchal*; Security and cleaning in *Andhra Pradesh*; Cleaning, laundry and security in *Rajasthan*; Diet, catering, laundry, security and IEC in *Tamilnadu* and maintenance of hospitals in *Tripura*.

Public private partnerships

This aspect has taken various forms in different states. For example some states had tried to hand over the PHCs in remote areas to the NGOs, as it was the case of Orissa and creation of pay clinics in medical colleges or leasing out operations and maintenance of hospitals, as in case of Punjab etc. In Gujarat Initiatives have been taken toward providing primary level care to the urban population, through community based health volunteers; to address the shortage of specialists in medical services private doctors have been appointed in some institutions; one PHC and three CHCs have been handed over to NGOs etc. and handing over one PHC each in the tribal areas in Andhra Pradesh to NGOs. In Himachal Pradesh medical treatment by government employees were reimbursed if it had been availed in select private institutions. On the other hand Tamilnadu had involved the business groups in adopting a local PHC or sub center or a district hospital to 'improve their performance'.

Setting up private institutions

Encouragement to the private sector for establishment of medical colleges in Andhra Pradesh and Orissa and to create training institutions for paramedics by the private sector in Andhra Pradesh, were some of the initiatives in this direction. Rajasthan on the other hand had allowed private sector to provide medical education and training.

---

[35] Here we have mentioned it as a separate reform initiative. However the initiatives taken under this sub heading could also be included under the category of public-private partnerships.

Contractual paramedics and doctors at the district level

This has been created in the states of Rajasthan, Orissa and Andhra Pradesh. It needs to be mentioned here that while the states like Himachal Pradesh have made the paramedics as district cadre[36] they have not made their appointment contractual. In states like Uttaranchal, ANMs and medical officers were appointed on a contractual basis in remote areas. Similarly in case of Orissa contractual doctors could be appointed by CDMOs to fill the shortage of staffs at periphery[37] level institutions.

These were some of the initiatives by the state governments in India which has been classified here as health sector reforms. However our definition of reforms in health sector has kept a wider scope for inclusion of any other private initiative or increasing space for the private sector as a reform initiative in healthcare.

Conclusion

The review of existing definitions with regard to health sector reforms showed that they were trying to include all the changes being taken by various states in the decade of 1990s within the health sector as an element of reform. This was creating a definitional confusion and hence also in classification of this phenomenon. According to our new definition, health sector reforms were an effort by various states to increase the space for the private sector in health care since 1980s. Using this definition we have identified different reform measures being carried out in various countries of the world. In the context of India we have made a distinction between health sector reform measures being carried out in different states and the phenomenon of systemic changes.

We have said that the term *health sector reforms* have been broadly associated with the concept of Structural Adjustment Programmes. It was part of the 'reform measures' being followed in the social sector of different country economies. The elements of market were also introduced to the health sector and the focus was mostly on the healthcare services and the financing aspects.

---

[36] However Orissa had made the district cadre for paramedics as contractual in nature.
[37] At the PHC level institutions.

Describing about various country experiences from Europe, North America, South America, Russia, China, Australia, Africa and India, we have shown that the phenomenon of health sector reforms were carried out since the beginning of 1980s. It was part of the reform measures being introduced in the larger economy, which tried to give a larger role to the institution of market, and at the same time tried to reduce the role of the state as a regulator, which promotes fair competition among the private players. Therefore as the allocation of resources was reduced in the social sectors, health was seen as an individual responsibility. Similarly the concepts like 'efficiency' and 'effectiveness' were introduced in the health sector. It was argued that the limited available resources need to be used efficiently to achieve maximum output. This was to be done through reorganization of the existing healthcare services, introducing private managerial practices, increasing users choice through encouraging private sector in provisioning of healthcare, cost cutting measures through focusing resources more on the selective primary level care, reducing the budgetary expenditure on secondary and tertiary levels of care etc. To generate resources for the health sector it encouraged private participation through introducing private or community insurance mechanisms and by introduction of user fees etc.

Our review of various country experiences showed that while the process of health sector reforms have been documented, there have been very few evaluative studies about this phenomenon.

However concerns have been raised about this new understanding of healthcare, which places the responsibility of good health on an individual. In this new approach interlinkage between various levels of care and the inter-sectoral aspects[38] of healthcare has been missing. Further it has been criticized on the ground that it promotes a unified model of healthcare and in that process neglects various country contexts. It also emphasizes on curative care and neglects the preventive aspect, which is such an important element of raising health status in developing and under developed countries. Therefore it has raised apprehensions in many quarters that years of gains in health sector could be undermined due to the introduction of market elements. This has got serious implications for the health status of the poorer sections of populations in various countries adopting health sector reform measures.

---

[38] Here various levels of healthcare suggests about primary, secondary and tertiary levels of care. The inter-sectoral approach places health within the framework of socio-economic and political developments of a country.

CHAPTER TWO

METHODOLOGY

Conceptualization

The cutback on public spending on health was a global phenomenon of the 1980s and 1990s. During this period the public sector was seen as insignificant and any investment in it was assumed as wasteful expenditure. The eighties saw the thrust on privatization as the solution for the inefficient functioning of the public sector. Economists, Public Health scientists and even the United Nations contested this unquestioning faith on the process of privatization. However the need to selectively invest in public health services was emphacised by institutions like World Bank. There was also the question about improving the public health systems. The dominant view was to restructure the public institutions through the introduction of market mechanisms in order to improve efficiency and cost-effectiveness.

The context

In the decade of eighties and nineties India and many other developing countries took loan from International Monetary Fund (IMF) to deal with the fiscal crisis. The World Bank had recommended for cutting back on public expenditures in social sectors and this affected investments in health sector across developing countries. The negative impact of SAP, in terms of increase in unemployment and poverty and reduction in health status among the poor in different countries has been observed by various studies. The focus of health care reform as could be seen from Cassels definition has only been on health services financing. It does not include other components like wages, employment, food security, housing, water supply etc., which play a crucial role in improving health status of populations. Studies which have tried to review the experiences of privatization of health care in both developed and developing countries show that the principles of equity and universal access was undermined by adoption of a market model in achieving health targets.[1]

The role of World Bank

The Structural Adjustment Programmes[2] suggested by the World Bank in the eighties and nineties had an impact in health sector at the global level, across different continents. The World Bank document titled 'Financing Health Services in Developing Countries'[3] was one of the first to argue for a change in the role of government in terms of financing. It argued about introduction of user charges in government health care facilities, involvement of NGOs in generating resources and decentralization of planning. The nineties also saw a shift in pattern of international funding in health care. Until the eighties bilateral agencies were the dominant player in terms of health funding and in this type of arrangements individual countries had the freedom to chose their priorities according to their own historical contexts. However due to the fiscal crisis generated by oil shock in the late seventies the number of bilateral funding in health sector declined across the developing countries and World Bank emerged as a major financier for health care in the decade of nineties. Due to this nature of change in the funding, the developing countries had very little choice for bargaining in terms of their priorities[4].

The World Bank funding came along with certain conditionalities. In the case of countries from Latin America and Africa this was the scenario[5]. The experience from these countries show that the reform measures suggested by World Bank gradually crippled the public structures of

---

[1] See for example Creese: 1994; Reich: 1995; Banerji: 1993; Qadeer: 1994; Baru: 1998, 2002.

[2] These were meant for opening up of the economy to the world market, reducing the role of the state to be the regulator of the economy and to a large extent increasing the role of the market.

[3] The World Bank, 1987.

[4] The emergence of World Bank in the nineties as the single largest financier of health services for developing countries has replaced the bilateral donor agencies, which played a substantive role in the eighties in health sector. But unlike the bilateral donor agencies, which were only supportive of specific health sector interventions, the World Bank also decides the priority areas of interventions.

[5] In the eighties the World Bank had emphasised on blanket privatization for the health sector in Africa and Latin America, which created adverse impact on the health status of these countries. For example, the child mortality and morbidity for most age groups rose, suggesting inequities of access to health care.

provisioning and an alternative structure also could not come up. For example the introduction of user charges generated very few resources in countries like Zambia.[6]

The World Bank (1993) annual document titled *Investing in Health* argued for improving government spending on health, which would help the poor. This document has been seen as a blueprint for reforms in the health sector of developing countries. To attain these objectives it suggested some measures like reduction of government spending in tertiary sector and in specialist training, introduction of user charges in government hospitals, introduction of essential clinical package to make the health care system more 'efficient' and 'effective'. For improving the management services in the government health care structure, it suggested measures like decentralization of administrative and budgetary authority and contracting out of services. In a way this document suggested *a greater role for the private sector* in tertiary and specialist training. By asking for introduction of user fees in government hospitals for the affluent sections, it was suggesting that these institutions become financially independent in the long run.

The World Bank in its 1993 report[7] for developing countries had mentioned the broad outline for health sector reforms. These measures were:

" 1- Cutback on tertiary medical care in the public sector.
2-Private sectors to play a more prominent role in providing care.
3-Introducing cost recovery mechanisms in the public sector.
4-Implementing an "essential clinical package for primary level care."[8]

The reasons for the growth of World Bank as the single largest financier in health sector were: one- To protect the vulnerable sections from adverse impact of SAP and two- The World Bank's effort to be seen as addressing the problem of inadequate investment in the social sector.[9]
In the eighties the World Bank had emphasized on blanket privatisation for the health sector in Africa and Latin America, which created adverse impact on the health status of these countries. For example, in Child mortality and morbidity for most age groups rose, suggesting inequities of access.[10] The dominant philosophical approach for the health sector reform

[6] P. Nanda, 2000.
[7] World Development Report, 1993.
[8] World Bank, 1993. Ibid-214.
[9] Baru; 2002.
[10] Creese, 1994.

in the nineties was the utilitarian perspective, which tried to maximise output with least input. This perspective had certain inbuilt assumptions regarding issues of efficiency, quality and effectiveness of public and private provisioning.

The new perspective placed more faith in private and voluntary sectors. The inherent assumptions were that the private sector was more efficient, cost-effective and could provide better quality care than the public sector. These assumptions were not based on any empirical evidence. Baru has suggested that there were methodological problems in evaluation and drawing comparisons of quality and efficiency between public and private health care. For example, the public sector by its very nature tries to provide universal access to health care and also it provides a range of services. The basic motive has been to provide everyone a healthcare system without taking into account one's ability to pay. On the other hand the private sector is motivated by profit. As various studies show that private sector goes to those areas where it could have profit. There is a tendency among private health care sector to concentrate on developed regions. They provide a limited range of services to make their venture a profitable one. Also their focus is on curative rather than on preventive health care. The patterns of financing and investments also differ between the public and private sector and thus making comparisons in cost of care a difficult job. Further studies on quality of services in private sector were problematic due to its heterogeneous nature.[11]

Different country experiences show that the reforms in health sector seem more interested in cutting costs and reducing state involvement in health care. Thus it undermines the principles of equity and universal access, which are essential for public health. In this backdrop the present study intends to look at implications of health sector reforms for the health services system in a state like Orissa from a systemic view. A systemic approach looks at linkages between various levels of providers, inter-sectoral approach to health and rational use of technology. It locates the healthcare and health status of a community within the socio-political and economic context of a society.

---

[11] Baru: 1998.

Why Orissa

Socio-economic background

Orissa was chosen as a field of study because of several reasons. According to 1991 census of India, Orissa's population compared to the total population of India was 3.74 percent constituting 316,597,36 in numbers. Out of its total population, Scheduled Castes constituted about 16.20 percent and Scheduled Tribes constitute about 22.21 percent. Thus together, scheduled castes and scheduled tribes constituted about 38.41 percent of Orissa's total population. These two sections constituted the bulk of the poor in Orissa and lived in remote and hilly areas. Almost 81% of the SC/ST population was landless laborers with very little assets.[12] The large number of scheduled tribes in the state also results in different understanding of notions of good health. This cultural difference was a significant barrier for promoting universal health care. As a result in tribal areas it has been observed in many cases that while health care infrastructure was available, utilization was very low. Also women from these two groups suffer from disadvantages of income, caste and gender discrimination in every aspect of life.[13]

In terms of literacy rate total literacy was 49.09 percent. Out of this male literacy was 63.09 percent and female literacy was 34.68 percent.[14]

The census figures showed that more than half of Orissa's population was illiterate. Significantly female illiteracy was more than 65 percent of its female population[15]. Coupled with this, near about 48 percent of Orissa's total population lived below the poverty line[16]. As we know from various studies that health status of a population was determined by overall socio-economic conditions. Therefore if near about half the percentage of total population was living below the poverty line that means malnutrition was very high among its population. This could have an adverse impact on the health status of Orissa's population.

---

[12] Census of India, 1991.

[13] Orissa Vision 2010: A Health Strategy, February 2003.

[14] Census of India, 1991.

[15] Census of India, 2001.

[16] The poverty line in India has been conceptualised by the Planning Commission of India in terms of Calorie intake per day. While for rural areas it has been fixed at 2400 Kilo Calories per person per day, for urban areas it has been fixed at 2100 Kilo Calories per person per day.

Orissa was also a state where the growth of private health care in terms of hospitals and beds had actually declined during 1973 to 1996. Here public health care services were utilized by most of the population. Therefore the health sector reforms that advocates more roles for private health care, and introduction of user charges for secondary and tertiary levels of care in public sector, has serious implications for a state like Orissa.

Epidemiological situation in the state

Communicable diseases like malaria, tuberculosis and leprosy continued to be major public health problems in the late twentieth century Orissa, apart from filariasis in the coastal districts. According to one estimate more than 60 percent of the diseases prevalent in Orissa were water related. Communicable diseases like diarrhoea and dysentery, worm infections and typhoid were present throughout the year. The state still shared largest number of deaths due to malaria in India. Malnutrition continued to be a major public health concern. The data from NFHS II showed that while 54 percent of the children under age 3 were underweight, 44 percent were stunted (height/age) and 24 percent were wasted (weight/height).

According to one estimate Non Communicable Diseases or NCDs constituted 22 percent of morbidity in the state and 16 percent due to accident and injuries. Besides, diabetes, cardio vascular diseases, chronic bronchitis, asthma and mental illness constituted major NCDs in the state. Apart from these, natural disasters like floods, droughts and cyclones in the coastal areas create havoc and increases morbidity and mortality among the large sections of its population.[17]

Health care services structure[18]

Before proceeding further let us have a look at the organizational chart of health care services structure in Government of Orissa. The Ministry of Health and Family Welfare was the nodal ministry for the health care services in the state. At the top of the hierarchy was the Minister of Health and Family Welfare. Under him/her was the principal secretary to the

---

[17] NFHS II, Orissa.

[18] The structure means that all the elements constituting the structure should be working toward achieving a common aim. However in later chapters we have discussed as to how the structures created by for example OHSDP, has bypassed the line departments of the Health Directorate, Government of Orissa.

government of Orissa, Health and Family welfare department. There were four secretaries to assist him. They were in the hierarchical order of Additional, Joint, Deputy and Under secretaries. Apart from these four secretaries, the project director OHSDP or Orissa Health Systems Development Project was of the rank of Additional secretary. There were six technical directors who directly come under the Principal Secretary. These directors were mostly from the health care services cadre and hence having a medical background. These six directors were Director of Medical Education and training or DMET, Director Health Services or DHS, Director Family Welfare, Director of SIHFW or State Institute of Health and Family Welfare, Director Drugs control and Director of IM and Homeopathy.

In terms of functions the Medical and Nursing colleges comes under DMET. The Health care services cadre comes under the DHS. The Director of Family welfare looks after the Family Welfare program in the state. The role of SIHFW has been to recruit and train staff for different health programs in the state. It has recently been given the status of Regional Training Center to train health personnel from Jharkhand and Chattishgarh apart from Orissa.[19] The Chief District Medical Officer or CDMO who was in charge of a district comes directly under the control of DHS. Director Drugs Control was the nodal agency for checking the quality of drugs in the private sector in the state through its drugs inspectors. It also issues licenses to Private health care sector in the state. At the district level ADMO Public Health, ADMO medical and ADMO Family Welfare assist the CDMO. The CHCs and PHCs come under the control of CDMOs. The director of Health and Family Welfare controls 30 CDMO's in 30 districts of Orissa[20].

As per norm while CHC's cater to the services of more than one lakh population in a block, the PHC's cater to the services in a block having less than one lakh population. At the CHC level there was a Medical Officer in charge who was a junior class I officer. Then there was a second medical officer who was a class-two grade officer. Then there was a pediatric specialist and a Gynecologist. At the PHC level there was a Medical Officer in charge, who was a class II officer and a second medical officer who was also a class II grade officer. Each CHC/PHC had under its control 4 to 12 Primary Health Center New or PHC new institutions. PHC

---

[19] This was known from interview with a certain official in SIHFW, Bhubaneswar.
[20] See annexure 1.

New was a single doctor medical institution previously known as Dispensary or Additional PHC or subsidiary health center or mobile health unit. Each PHC New had under it 4 to 6 sub-centers. One female health worker or ANM who was assisted by one health worker male were supposed to be in each sub-center. A supervisor supervises them who in turn were accountable to his/her sector medical officer at PHC (N). An Anganwadi worker[21] who was given charge in a village with population of 1'000 also assists each health worker female.

At present the government of Orissa was planning to convert all PHC (N) to PHC and to promote all PHCs at block level to CHCs. At the CHC/PHC level, Departmental Review Meeting in the block and sub-divisional level were held at each month. For the CHCs and PHCs, the Medical Officer in-charge was responsible for all health activities in his/her block. Each health worker female or HFW was also assisted by auxiliary nurse/midwifes, who were non-government health workers.

Utilization pattern

The 42nd and the 52nd rounds of NSS showed that Orissa was a state where there was higher utilization of health care services by both the poor and the rich from the government sectors. This was due to the larger presence of the government sector in health care in the state and also due to the absence of a private sector in a strong way as it has been seen in other states. As per March 2005, Orissa had 158 CHCs, 1349 PHCs and 5927 sub centers. There were in total 181 hospitals. This includes 3 medical college hospitals, 31 District Headquarter Hospitals, 21 Sub Divisional Hospitals and 126 other hospitals.[22] The absence of private sector in the state could be explained by the fact that Orissa was not a developed state. Most of its population lived in rural areas with low per capita income and almost fifty percent of its population lived below the poverty line. Hence the purchasing power of the people was very low. Therefore people would try to look for avenues of health care where they could afford at a lower cost. As the private sector in health care was oriented to make profit, it was not profitable for it to invest in a state like Orissa at a large scale. In these circumstances we could draw an inference that there was very little

---

[21] Who comes under the centrally funded scheme of Integrated Child Development Program or ICDS.

[22] Data collected in the year 2005 from the Directorate of Health Services, Govt. of Orissa.

incentive for the growth of the private sector in the state.[23] As studies by Baru and others have shown that the private sector has a tendency to move to the developed areas or developed regions and it was purely guided by the profit motive. As a result it not only focuses on select geographical areas, it also provides a narrow range of services.[24]

Thus we saw that in case of Orissa the state has played a dominant role over the years in terms of provisioning of health care services. To provide health care to the different sections of the population the health care services structure has also expanded in the state over the years. But still a lot was there to be done. For example field visits to different single doctor PHCs[25] showed that there was absence of doctors and the pharmacists mostly ran these institutions. Many of the single doctor PHCs and the sub centers were run in rented buildings.

All over India it has always been difficult for the state governments for retaining doctors in rural and remote areas, where there is absence of proper transportation and communication and other infrastructure facilities. This problem was also there in Orissa but in an acute form. Apart from other reasons, the major reason was that there has almost always been political interference in posting and transfer policy and according to informed sources it has turned out to be a lucrative industry.[26] However those with bureaucratic or political connection connections while do benefit from this system, it has demoralized the doctors at every level. This has significant implications for delivery of health care at the

---

[23] This was the view of many officials in the state about the absence of a strong private sector in Orissa.

[24] For example the Health Survey and Planning Committee observed, "Of the 47,400 doctors available in the country only about 13,000 are reported to be on the staff of medical institutions maintained by government and other agencies. The remaining medical men must therefore be in private practice. The tendency for the latter is to concentrate in urban areas. For instance in Bengal, the ratio of doctors to the population is three and half times more in urban than in rural areas. In Sind the doctor to population ratio in urban centers being about 49 times that for the rural areas". The committee further noted that 'In Orissa average population served by a medical institution in 1942 in rural areas was 52,548 and in urban areas 15,276'. *Report of the Health Survey and Development Committee, Volume I, Manager of Publications, Delhi; Calcutta, 1946.*

[25] Known as PHC (New). The other staffs were one pharmacist, one ANM and a sweeper.

[26] This was known through interaction with various officials at different levels of the Health Services Structure in the Govt. of Orissa.

periphery level institutions. Many observers were of the opinion that the periphery level institutions have almost 'collapsed'. This has serious implications for accessibility, availability and quality of services as well as performance of various national programmes.

Hypothesis

In this background the present study intended to suggest some hypothesis. They were: 1- The health sector reform process in the long run would undermine the universality of health care which was an essential feature of public health.2- The public health services in the long run would try to withdraw from provisioning of the secondary and tertiary level care, this would weaken the sustainability of primary level care.3- With increasing privatization of health care the cost of care would go up, this would affect the poor most and would also affect their overall quality of life.

Overall objective

To examine the process and experience of Health Sector Reforms in Orissa.

Specific objectives

1. Trends in public financing in Orissa relative to India since mid- eighties.
2.To examine the trends in growth of public health services at the primary/secondary/tertiary level in Orissa during the eighties and nineties.
3. The trends in quantum, source and agencies providing external assistance to the health services system in Orissa during these two decades.
4. To study the perception and experience of bureaucracy dealing with the health sector and the experience of health sector reforms in Orissa.
5. How they perceive the shifts in financing, provisioning and manpower of health services during these two decades and its implications for equity.

Methodology and Design of Study:

This study was designed to examine the process and experience of reforms in the state of Orissa. Due to the qualitative nature of the study, in-depth interview and direct observation were adopted as key methodological tools to interact with the key actors in both the donor agencies as well as in the government. A pilot study[27] was conducted in one of the districts before going to the field with interview schedules. Apart from this the interviews with senior officials of the donor agencies and review of literature of different country experiences did help in preparing the interview schedule and an insight into the nature of problem that might be confronted in the field. An ethnographic[28] approach to the study was adopted to bring out the actors perspective with regard to the process and experience of reforms.

Quantitative vs. qualitative methods[29]

It has always been a subject of debate as to whether to study a social

---

[27] "How does the researcher formulate items in areas where the literature is inadequate? The answer lies in pilot study. …After the literature has been carefully studied and experts consulted, the researcher may still have only a rather vague idea of what are the crucial elements in his problem. A pilot study may then be launched as a step preliminary to the formulation of a schedule". P- 146, *Methods in Social Research by William J. Goode and Paul K. Hatt, McGraw-Hill Company, 1981.*

[28] We have discussed about ethnographic approach in the later part of this chapter. However we can say that ethnographic approach has been traditionally used by Anthropologists. "Anthropology, which was closely linked to colonization, directed its attention to people who were different from the researchers, tending to become above all study of *otherness*. Accordingly Anthropologists have been described as people who chose the *exotic* as their profession. The gap between the ethnological researcher and the people he studied was often accentuated by the fact that the latter were illiterate and lived in a pre-modern, tribal society" p- 219 in *Anthropology and Colonialism in Asia and Oceania ed. By Jan Van Bremen and Akitoshi Shimizu, Curzon Press, 2000.* In recent times the use of ethnographic approach has been used in different contexts apart from using it in closed societies.

[29] In recent times the use of quantitative method has been used as synonymous with scientific method. In this context it is worthwhile to look at the observations in this regard Goode and Hatt had made. They observed, "Science itself rests upon a series of postulates, or assumptions, which are themselves fundamentally unproved and unprovable. We can assert that these postulates are true; but we cannot prove them. They represent those areas in the philosophy of science, which is usually called epistemology." P- 20. Opt. Cited. Similarly Kapil Raj observed in a lecture that, "The kind of people working in one laboratory is different from kind of people working in another laboratory. They compete with each other to certify their knowledge before others. That's why knowledge is local". Dr. Kapil Raj was giving a lecture in SSS II, JNU on 9th September 2005 about how scientific knowledge is generated. He was a visiting professor from Ecole Institute, Paris, France.

phenomenon we should use quantitative or qualitative method.[30] Those who have advocated quantitative methods do so in the faith that there were underlying laws or truths[31] in a social phenomenon just as there were laws

---

[30] For example in December 15-17, 2003 in a seminar on *Monitoring Shifts in Health Sector Policies in South Asia* conducted by Center of Social Medicine and Community Health, JNU, the use of quantitative vs. qualitative method became a subject of debate. While some of the participants were arguing for quantitative methods as valid method of research, others were arguing about the significance of qualitative methods as a tool of data collection in Public Health.

[31] Let us have an interpretation about how *truth* is constructed in different settings, "Is there such a thing as truth? Foucault's main tenet is that societies produce 'regimes of the truth'. This means that every society at specific historical periods produces an all-enveloping 'truth' to which people in that society adheres. This is their 'reality', but it has been constructed and produced by people in that society themselves. The 'truth' therefore is not a universal or everlasting entity; it is a product…. Foucault than goes on to describe the transmission of this truth through a variety of 'discourses'. A discourse is a set of ideas, practices and beliefs, which coalesce to produce an overarching picture of reality. In the eighteenth century, religion was the dominant discourse in European societies through which a 'truth' was constructed. But with increasing industrialization and technological advance, modern societies developed other more powerful discourses: science and medicine. These discourses, with another set of practices, beliefs and sites of operation, produced a new regime of the 'truth'." P-8. See *Social Construction of Community Care ed. By Anthea Symonds and Anne Kelly, Macmillan, 1998.* Similarly Petersen and Lupton argue, "Medical, scientific, epidemiological and social science knowledges are routinely employed as 'truths' to construct public health 'problems' and to find solutions for dealing with them. Professional expertise remains privileged over lay expertise, as is highly evident in health educational advice to populations on how they should regulate their lives to achieve good health. Thus, while the new public health may draw on a 'post modernist' type of rhetoric in its claim, it remains at heart a conventionally modernist approach." By this the authors wanted to say that the search for a single underlying 'truth' still dominates the field of public health as it is being practiced around the world, although volumes of literature has been generated which shows that 'truth' is a constructed category in the field of public health also. P- 8. See *The New Public Health by Alan Petersen and Deborah Lupton, Sage Publications, 1996.* Similarly reflecting on the Habermas's views on this issue, Sambler writes, "Habermas's critique of western science is essentially a critique of ideology. That is, it is critical of 'scientism' of science which attempts to give the impression that science, and in particular those forms of science which can be conducted in controlled settings, is the only form of activity through which knowledge of the world can be developed…One can not study the context of science out of relation to its content or vice versa." P- 39. See *Habermas, Critical Theory and Health ed. by Graham Sambler, Routledge, 2001.*

of the nature. Their point was that because there were underlying laws, it could be discovered through rigorous use of quantitative methods, which could be verified and thus the result would subject itself to test by peers.[32]

On the other hand those who argue for a qualitative method say that 'human beings attach meaning to their actions'.[33] And hence any comprehensive understanding of human action must have a place for the understanding of underlying meanings to it. Commenting on the methods of natural sciences Jurgen Habermas said that while using the methods of natural sciences we have been able to get control over the physical world; however it has its obvious limitations[34].

Those who argue for a Marxist or a Parson's approach to the social phenomenon try to give these interpretations as the power of natural science, which could not be questioned.[35] These have been the dominant interpretations of the social phenomenon. The idea that the study of social phenomenon could be undertaken by using the methods of natural science was based on the desire to make a scientific study of society. However with the critical reflections on universal theories like Marxism or systems theory by Parsons, there was a wider understanding that there were multiple realities.[36] That means there could be various interpretations of the same phenomenon by different individuals. Thus coming to an understanding of reality could happen through *communicative action*[37] and not necessarily with the interpretations by experts in a particular field.

This way of interpretation of the social phenomenon does not necessarily lead to conflict of different interpretations. Rather a decisionistic model could resolve these tensions. For example in case of a policy decision a

[32] Here the term 'peers' suggest a community of scientists, as pointed out by Robert K. Merton in his book *Social Theory and Social Structure.*

[33] As German sociologist Max Weber had famously said in his theory of social action.

[34] See the book by McCarthy, T, titled *Critical theory of Jurgen Habermas,* Published by polity press 1984.

[35] This has been well argued by Foucault in his book *History of Sexuality.*

[36] As advocated by the Post modernist school. The post modernists believe that there was not a single path of progress but there were multiple paths and also multiple goals for progress of different societies.

[37] Again see Habermas in his various writings.

politician could choose from different interpretations of the same phenomenon and the same could be applied for a researcher also.[38]

Arguing a case for a qualitative method in this book, an effort has been made to give the meaning of actors in our analysis of a social phenomenon and in this case to study the perception and experience of health sector reforms from the providers' perspective. While the success and failure of a program or a project could be learned form statistical figures, the internal dynamics, which determined these outcomes, could only be known from the actors' point of view. In the case of process and experience of reforms in the health sector, the *ethnographic method* gives an insight not only to the internal dynamics of inter-personal relationship within the *rationalist bureaucracy*,[39] it also brings out those aspects which would have never come into the open through a quantitative method, although it was vital for a total understanding of the phenomenon intended to be studied.

Due to the nature of the study[40] ethnographic approach was the main tool used in gathering information from the field. However statistical data have also been collected both from the government and donor agencies to give as much comprehensive picture about the phenomenon as possible. In some places qualitative method has been used without giving a quantitative verification and at other places it has been done. It was hoped that the mixture of these two methods would help in bringing the different aspects of reality to the fore.

What is ethnography?

"The growing interest in ethnography stems largely from a disillusionment with the quantitative methods that have for long held the dominant position in social sciences. ...There is a disagreement as to whether ethnography's distinctive feature is the elicitation of cultural knowledge or the detailed investigation of patterns of social interaction or holistic analysis of societies. Sometimes ethnography is portrayed as essentially descriptive or perhaps as a form of story telling; occasionally by contrast, great emphasis is laid on the development and testing of theory"[41].

---

[38] Ibid.

[39] This term has been borrowed from German Sociologist Max Weber.

[40] This book was looking at the perceptions of the providers about the health sector reform process.

[41] Page 1 in "Ethnography: Principles in Practice" by Martyn Hammersley and Paul Atkinson, Tavistock publications, London and New York, 1983.

In this study we have used ethnography as a descriptive method of study to get the actors perspective[42] of their world. Here the actors were the government officials and the officials from the donor agencies in health sector.

> Ethnography is a basic form of social research and it does not have a long social history. But it bears a close resemblance to the routine ways in which people make sense of the world in everyday life. Some commentators regard this as its basic strength and some as a fundamental weakness[43] of ethnography. However once one recognizes the reflexive character of social research, that it is part of the world it studies, many of the issues thrown up by the dispute over positivism become easier to resolve and the specific contribution to be made by ethnography emerges more clearly[44].

The argument of the positivism was that the social phenomenon could be studied as natural phenomenon and hence the methods of natural sciences could be applied in social sciences. However ethnography argues that the character of social research was reflexive in nature and that means when a researcher studies a social phenomenon he or she was also part of that phenomenon and hence the construction of reality depends on inter-subjectivity.

> However there has been some disagreement over whether ethnographic theories can be proved valid, and in fact it seems that they cannot: there is always the possibility that new facts will appear in the future that will disprove them. The most elegant attempt to resolve this problem is the work of Karl Popper who argues that while theories can never be proven true, they can be falsified since only one contradictory example is required for this. On this view the defining feature of science is the attempt to falsify theories[45].

Therefore the argument that the ethnographic theories cannot be proved valid holds true also for other sciences, including the natural sciences. Thomas Kuhn in his *Structure of Scientific Revolutions* said, *the most striking feature of normal research problems... is how little they aim to*

---

[42] Here an inspiration has been drawn from German Sociologist Max Weber according to whom, social action which is oriented to others by their very nature should be the study of social phenomenon.
[43] P-2, opt cited.
[44] Ibid.
[45] P-20 opt cited.

produce major novelties, conceptual or phenomenal. Sometimes, as in a wavelength measurement, everything but the most esoteric detail of the result is known in advance... Therefore *bringing a normal research problem to a conclusion is achieving the anticipated in a new way.*

But the question arises as to what happens when the existing paradigm is faced with a new fact? To this Kuhn says *confronted with anomaly or with crisis, scientists take a different attitude toward existing paradigm, and the nature of their research changes accordingly....* Hence at a given point of time a theory may be able to explain a larger set of phenomenon than other theories and when a new phenomenon was discovered which could not be explained by the old theory than a new theory emerges. This was true in case of both the natural and social sciences. Therefore as the theories change, the method of investigation also changes and hence the dispute over quantitative or qualitative method was totally misplaced. One method may be suitable for a particular kind of study and another for another type of study.

In the present study

To address the objectives 4 and 5 in this study we have used the ethnographic approach to understand the providers' perspective at different levels of the government and the donor agencies with the use of in-depth interview methods.

These interviews were conducted with the help of an interview guide. The interviews were conducted at two levels. One, the key persons at different levels in the Government of Orissa health sector were interviewed. For example in the Directorate of Health and Family welfare, Government of Orissa, all the six directors at different departments were interviewed. Two, in the donor agencies both multilateral like UNFPA, UNDP, UNICEF and the World Bank and bilateral agencies like European Commission and the DFID were covered. These donor agencies were interviewed in both the state and at the central level, where their head offices in India were located.

On the part of the state government it had also instituted some *reform offices* like Policy and Strategic Planning Unit or PSPU with the help of

British funding agency DFID.[46] Other reform office was the Sector Reform Cell funded by European Commission. It was looking after the projects funded by European Commission.[47]

Thus the directors at both the PSPU and the Sector Reform Cell were interviewed. Besides, some consultants and key persons, who have been closely involved with the reform process, were also interviewed from these two reform offices. Interviews were also taken from the director, Orissa Health Systems Development Project or OHSDP, which was being funded by the World Bank and a key official who has been there since the beginning of this project.

Interview was also conducted with the then additional secretary Health and Family Welfare Department, Government of Orissa. While the former health secretary could be interviewed, the incumbent health secretary said that the directors could give a better picture about the reform process and the health minister said that as he was new to his post, he wouldn't be able to reflect much. However the interaction with the additional secretary, Health gave an insight into the current thinking of the government of

---

[46] The role of this agency was being worked out when this researcher was visiting the state for fieldwork. However interviews with the DFID officials and the existing staff of the PSPU revealed that this reform office would help the ministry of Health and Family welfare, Government of Orissa, in Policy formulation and Planning for the overall health services sector. It would also act as a coordinator between the different donor agencies in the state. The staffs were sent in deputation from the Health Department to the PSPU and the entire funding was done by the DFID and this office directly comes under the Ministry of Health and Family Welfare, Government of Orissa. Thus DFID was closely related with the reform process in the state. During the field visit it was observed that, the PSPU officials were quite busy with their plan of presentation for the visiting DFID officials from Delhi. They were literally on their toes. It was found that the current Director of the PSPU was an Indian Administrative Service officer from the state cadre. Apart from directly funding the PSPU, the DFID had a state office, which looked after the broader dimensions of development in the state. Here the staffs were recruited on a contractual basis. There were consultants for different projects. It was found that the consultants from the DFID had easy access to Health Department and to its director and senior officials. Thus DFID was playing a very active role in engaging with the issues of health in the state in collaboration with the government officials.

[47] This office came under the direct control of Health and Family welfare department, Government of Orissa. Similar to the PSPU, the staffs in the Sector Reform Cell were mostly from the Health Department, Government of Orissa. They also had consultants hired on a contractual basis.

Orissa with regard to the issues of health services in Orissa and ongoing health sector reforms process in the state.

In Delhi interviews were also conducted with the donor agencies like World Bank, DFID and European Commission as these organizations were closely involved with the health sector reform process in the state of Orissa.[48]

To address the objective one, Annual Plan documents and the Tenth Plan document of the government of Orissa, RBI reports and CMIE reports were referred. To address the objective two, official published and unpublished documents from the directorate of health services, government of Orissa and from the department of statistics, government of Orissa were referred. To address the objective three documents of the various donor agencies were referred.

Districts chosen

At the district level two districts *Sundergarh* and *Khurda* were selected through *purposive selection*. The idea behind the use of purposive selection was that the districts chosen should have some functioning health care infrastructure. While Sundergarh district was situated in the northwestern part of Orissa, Khurda district was situated in the coastal belt. These districts were among the five most developed districts in the state. The district of Khurda was second most developed district in Orissa and the district of Sundergarh was third most developed one according to one report by National population commission[49].

---

[48] It has to be mentioned here that the Orissa Vision 2010 Document, which was published in the year 2003 by the Health and Family Welfare Department, Government of Orissa, was completed with the inputs from different donor agencies in the state. During the field visit it was mentioned by different donor agencies that the earlier health secretary was quite eager to involve different donor agencies on the issue of health in the state, while the present health secretary was not only ignorant about different issues, but he was also very reluctant to take interest on health issues. The vision document 2010 has identified different features of health reforms, which we have discussed later chapters.

43 The selection of these two districts was based on National Population Commission's ranking of all India districts. The national population commission on the basis of twelve indicators had ranked these districts. The indicators used were: Percentage decadal population growth rate; Percentage of birth order three and above; Percentage of current users of family planning methods; Percentage of girls marrying below 18-years of age; Sex ratio [females per 1000 males];

In these two districts, the respective chief district medical officers as well as the other supporting officers were interviewed in a group interview. In these interviews CDMOs were taking the lead in most of the times. Besides in the Sundergarh district the district headquarter hospital was visited to get a first hand view of the implementation of the user charges. This was also done in case of Capital Hospital, Bhubaneswar where some of the staffs and patients were interviewed to know about their perception of the privatisation of cleaning and the introduction of user charges.

In Orissa at the block level, in some places while the PHCs were headquarters[50] and in other places CHCs were the headquarters. The bed strengths at the block headquarter PHCs varied from 16 to 30 beds. During the field visit to the state it was known that the government of Orissa was planning to convert all the existing PHCs into CHCs and the PHC (New) s into PHCs. The PHC (New) s' were the single doctor PHCs with other staffs comprising, one pharmacist, one ANM and a sweeper. It was found that under a block PHC there were 3 to 5 PHC (New) s' and then there were sub centers where one ANM was placed at each sub center. The ANM was supposed to be accompanied by a multi purpose health worker male. But in these two districts from the field survey it was found that there was shortage of MPHW (M).[51] This was the case all over Orissa.

At the block level the entire health care services structure was studied. Thus in each district *two blocks* were selected with *random sampling procedure* to eliminate bias in selection of blocks. An intensive study was done at the block level using interview schedule and in-depth interviews. Interviews were also conducted with two district CDMOs and in each district two PHCs/CHCs were covered. At the PHC level interviews were taken from Chief Medical officers and weekly meetings at the PHC level were attended to get a feeling about the working of the PHC staffs and group discussion and individual interviews were also held with ANMs or

---

Percentage of women receiving skilled attention during deliveries; Percentage of children getting complete immunization; Female literacy rate; Estimated percentage of villages not connected with pucca roads or all weather roads; Estimated percentage coverage of safe drinking water [habitations]; Estimated percentage of births registered. Estimated percentage of deaths registered.

[50] This was in the majority of cases.

[51] Multi Purpose Health Worker (Male).

auxiliary nurse/midwives[52]. At the district level monthly meeting was attended in Sundergarh district, which helped in getting an overall picture of health services in the district. It has to be mentioned here that to attend the monthly meeting the permission of the CDMO was required, which was not possible in case of Khurda district. The monthly meetings were not originally intended to be covered, however in the field it was felt that it might give good first hand information about the functioning of health services in the district. In one of the PHCs of the Khurda district, monthly meeting was attended. This gave first hand information about the actual ground situation in the block in terms of functioning of the health care institutions and the disease burden in that block.

Overall we have looked at the health sector reforms at the district level from systems approach.

Pilot study

Before going for field work in Orissa a two-week pilot study was done in Sundergarh district. During this time one CHC and the district headquarter was visited. One Community Health Center was studied in detailed. Here interviews were conducted with various staffs and the medical officer in-charge about the different aspects of health care that CHC was dealing with. The nature of problems various staffs faced in day to day functioning, the epidemiological challenges of the CHC concerned, the overall atmosphere of work in that CHC and the idea about reform initiatives in health sector they had etc. was covered. In the district headquarter the CDMO was interviewed on a range of issues like the strengths and weaknesses of the health care services structure in the district, whether the CDMO was aware of health sector reforms process in Orissa and whether he was involved in that process, what were the reform initiatives taken in the district etc. A detailed statistics of the health care services structure of the district was also collected from here.

Once this much data was gathered it was used as a feedback in preparing the interview guide. However as we have mentioned earlier with each interview our interview guide was improved or modified according to the

[52] At the PHC level in weekly meetings all the staffs under that block PHC gather and discuss about various health issues and immediate public health challenges in that block.

emergence of new facts. The pilot study also helped in getting an idea about the structure of health care services at different levels in Orissa.

Sampling

As time and resources were limited in nature, sample was used to study the universe[53]. And in case of a study like the present one, which was not only interested to explore the field but also to get an academic degree and hence sampling had to be used.

Sample Size

In any kind of research sample size has been emphacised to ensure that the *universe* being studied has been adequately represented. The size of the universe varies according to the nature of the study. However in the zeal to give representativeness to the sample size the larger question of *nature of study* has been found to be neglected in most of the studies[54]. As we have observed that our overall objective tried to examine the process and experience of health sector reforms in Orissa, therefore the nature of study suggested that the data to be collected was qualitative in nature and hence

---

[53] "Ideally the researcher would like to observe the entire population to add more weight to the findings. Limited resources, time and money frequently preclude a study of the entire population. Subsequently, a subset of some predetermined size must be selected from the population of interest" p- 118. *Research Techniques for the Health Sciences, Second Edition, James J. Neutons and Laurna Rubinson, Allyn Bacon, 1997.*

[54] Reflecting on the sample size, Neutons and Rubinson observed, "The determination of the sample size usually perplexes many researchers because they often have no conception of a minimally adequate sample size. They need to understand that correct sample size is dependent on both the nature of population and purpose of the study. An ideal study would have a sample large enough to represent the population so generalization may occur, yet small enough to save time and money as well as to reduce the complexity of data analysis." They further added, "It is a popular misconception that a sample is a small carbon copy of the original population, identical in every way.... One can never be certain of representativeness unless the entire population is used. An obvious deduction at this juncture is that larger the sample, the greater the likelihood of representativeness i.e greater the heterogeneity, the greater the necessity for a larger sample. For populations in which there is no heterogeneity on a variable (of complete homogeneity), a sample size of one would suffice" p- 125. *Research Techniques for the Health Sciences, Second Edition, James J. Neutons and Laurna Rubinson, Allyn Bacon, 1997.*

the sample size need not had to be large like a quantitative study. The size of a sample also depends on the homogeneity and heterogeneity of the universe to be studied. If the universe to be studied was homogeneous then even a sample size of one is sufficient. However this is a theoretical possibility, in actual field it would most probably be heterogeneous in nature.

Nature of the Universe

However the sample size also depends on the nature of universe to be studied. In this case the universe of study was the health bureaucracy in both government and donor agencies who were closely involved with policy formulation and its implementation. Besides we have interviewed key officials who have been involved over the years, while the initiatives for health sector reforms were being taken in Orissa. To get a comprehensive picture of existing health care services officials with more than fifteen years of field experience in Orissa were also interviewed.

Different officials interviewed

The table below gives a picture of number of officials contacted and numbers interviewed at the central, at the state and at the district level. While both the donor agency and government officials were interviewed at the central and state level, at the district level only the officials from the government departments were interviewed.

Table: 2.1 Number of Officials contacted and interviewed

Actors (Central level)	Numbers contacted	Numbers Interviewed
Bilaterals like EEC, DFID	3	3
World Bank	2	2
MOHFW	3	1
Actors (State level)		
Health and Family Welfare Department, Govt. of Orissa.	17	16
OHSDP	3	3
Bilaterals like EEC and DFID	5	4
UN agencies, Orissa	5	4
Orissa state level academics	1	1
Total	39	34
District Level:		
CDMO's and allied staff	8	8
Block PHC MO's	8	8

Source: Field work, 2005.

Note: MOHFW- Ministry of Health and Family Welfare, EEC- European Commission, DFID- Department for International development of UK, OHSDP- Orissa Health Systems Development Project.

The table shows that at the central level out of 5 donor agency officials contacted 5 were interviewed and among the 3 MOHFW officials contacted only one could be interviewed. Similarly at the state level in Health and Family Welfare Department, Government of Orissa, out of 17 officials contacted 16 could be interviewed. In the OHSDP out of 3 officials contacted 3 were interviewed. Among the bilateral agencies like EEC and DFID and the UN agencies out of 5 officials contacted 4 were interviewed in each case. Finally from the state level academics one person was contacted and one could be interviewed. In total out of 39 senior officials contacted at the central and state level, 34 could be interviewed. At the district level among the CDMOs and allied staffs out of 8 officials contacted, 8 were interviewed. At the block PHC level out of 8 medical officers contacted, 8 were interviewed.

Sample Techniques

To identify the officials in the government and in donor agencies both purposive selection and snowball sampling was used.

Purposive selection

In purposive selection, 'the researcher employs his or her own discretion to select the respondents who best meet the purposes of the study. This is a great advantage to the experienced researcher who can apply prior knowledge and skill.'[55] Thus officials were interviewed who were closely involved with the health sector reform process in the state of Orissa. This list was prepared also with the help of snowball sampling.

Snowball sampling

'This is a multistage technique that literally *snowballs*. In the first stage of snowball sampling, a person possessing the requisite characteristics is identified and interviewed. This person then identifies others who may be included in the sample. The next stage is to identify these persons who in turn identify still more respondents who can be contacted and interviewed in following stages.'[56] The requirement to use snowball sampling arises when the respondent to be studied or interviewed are not known easily. For example in the case of study of prostitutes, they are not identified in public. As a result a researcher interested to study their problem would have to use a snowball sampling method. In our case the personnel to be interviewed were mostly technical experts in their fields and hence to identify them snowball sampling was a useful tool. Thus few officials of the donor agencies in Delhi were identified in the initial stage and once interviewed; they were requested to mention other interviewees who could be approached for interview. Similarly in Orissa once some of the officials were interviewed, they referred to some other officials. This was the case about all the officials at Bhubaneswar, the capital of Orissa. At the district level the concerned officials were interviewed without using snowball sampling. Here these officials were identified directly by visiting these institutions.

---

[55] P-125, Ibid.
[56] P-125, Ibid.

Techniques used for data collection

Interview guide

Interview guide consist of a set of broad outlines while conducting an interview. It is never exhaustive in nature in an open-ended interview technique. In this study different interview guides were used for different officials from the government as well as from the donor agencies. Before the interview a set of questions were prepared keeping in mind the broad and specific objectives of our study and specifically what objective a particular interview would address. For this an intensive Internet search about the department in which a particular official was to be interviewed was carried out and other relevant documents were referred. Once an interview guide was prepared it was rechecked several times before giving it a final shape. As we have mentioned earlier that most of the interviewees were interviewed more than twice, these interview guides were also modified after each interview. While an ordering of questions was there in an interview guide, it had almost in all the cases to be rearranged when the actual interview was going on. It needs to be mentioned here that while an exhaustive list of interview guides were prepared before going to the field; it was also modified to a large extent in the actual field interview.

Field notes

Field notes were used in collecting data during field visit. 'Field notes contain anything and everything that observer feels is worth noting.'[57] Brief notes were taken during the interview itself. Notes were also prepared at the end of everyday about the day's developments. Thus the gaps in writing during interviews were filled up by memorizing the event. The field notes were both descriptive and reflective in nature. The descriptive aspect looked at the timing and date of interview, the place of interview, the name of the interviewee and about the surrounding place. By asking probe questions, by cross checking with other interviewees and wherever written records were available were referred, to verify the data collected through interview. The reflective aspects looked at this researcher's impressions about the larger picture the interviewees were trying to provide and about the overall work atmosphere etc. It needs to be

---

[57] *Research Techniques for Health Sciences*, Second Edition by James J. Neutens and Laurna Rubinson, Allyn and Bacon, 1997.

mentioned here that all the interviews were conducted during office hours at various office premises. This was true both in case of government and donor agency officials.

Tape recorder

Prior consent of the interviewees was taken before using the tape recorder. Tape recorder was used because most of the respondents were senior officials in either the government and donor agencies. And as these interviews were on technical questions, it was thought as appropriate to use tape recorder so that not a single important point was missed. These records were transcribed regularly. While most of these interviews were conducted by using tape recorder, in some places the interviewees felt uncomfortable in the presence of a tape recorder and hence in these cases it was not used. Here field notes were used in the presence of the interviewee and also at the end of the interview the gaps were filled up by recollecting from memory. Later when the same interviewee was met for second time these opinions were cross checked again by asking probe questions. In most of the cases a respondent was interviewed for at least three times and this includes senior officials of the government and donor agencies.

Group interviews

This was conducted only with the ANMs at the four block PHCs, which were covered intensively. These interviews were taken during the weekly Saturday meetings at the PHC level when all the ANMs gather at PHC headquarter to discuss about their field challenges. In all the cases interviews were conducted at the end of their weekly meetings within the PHC premises. Questions were posed and it was suggested that anyone could respond and in many cases on a single question many of them responded. Questions were framed with regard to their knowledge of various national programs, day to day field challenges etc.

Direct Observation[58]

Direct observation was used to understand the culture of work atmosphere in both the government and donor agencies. By the culture of work

[58] Direct observation is one of the important tools in an ethnographic approach to get a better understanding about the actors' perspective.

atmosphere we could say how the office was organized, what was the office arrangement, what was the surrounding of the office, the cleanliness in and around the office, whether the staffs were gossiping in official hours, whether the staffs were in their place during official hours, the arrangement of files and the morale of the staff etc. For example in government offices of Orissa, maintenance of files was manual in nature and not well maintained.

Most of the staffs in the Directorate of Health were observed to be either gossiping or most were not in their desk at official hours. Records of health statistics were not maintained properly. It was as if cleanliness was the last thing one could expect from a government office. There were lot of people moving around to get their work done and in some instances it was clearly observed that the staffs were responding to only certain selected people whom they either know or who had come with the direction of an influential person like a minister or an MLA. While the official work time was from 9 am to 5 pm, the staffs used to come to the office around 11 o'clock and would start their day with a cup of tea and after relaxing for half an hour or so would start work. In between gossiping would be a common feature. By the time it was 12.30 pm, the staffs would start leaving for their lunch and they would come to their desks at 3pm to 3.30 pm and by the time it was 5 in the evening they would start leaving. Only time when the staffs were getting active was when the officer in charge was either asking for a file or when the officer was supposed to visit them. The combination of all these factors was making the whole atmosphere very depressive.

Contrary to this the surrounding of the donor agency offices was quite neat and clean. They were located in institutional areas or prime areas in the cities and this was true both in the state of Orissa and in their Delhi offices. The staffs were in their desks during office hours. There was no gossiping, files and records were maintained in computers and information was easily available. The offices had enough space and they were looking clean and properly lighted contrary to government offices, which were not properly cleaned, were congested and with many dark places. The atmosphere was looking very professional and the staffs were quick to respond to any request. The office buildings of the donor and multilateral agencies were also looking new and this suggested that the renovation work was done regularly.

At the district level the CDMO offices were well maintained in the two districts covered. The staffs were present and they were also quick to respond to any query. This may have been possible because of the instructions from the CDMO concerned. However the picture at the block PHC level was quite different. The medical officers in charge were not at all happy with their current positions. The PHC buildings were in bad shape in three cases out of four covered. While the beds in PHCs were available, during the field visit not a single bed was found to be occupied in the four block PHCs covered. The medical officers interviewed had their own private practice. In one block PHC the medical officer in charge was found to be absent most of the time and was busy in his clinic located in a nearby town. During the meeting with the CDMO concerned it was found that the CDMO was aware about this issue and had communicated his message to the medical officer. While some medical officers had their own clinics, others were doing private practice from their official residences. The problems at the PHC level when raised before the higher officials, it was known that they were very much aware but were helpless about it. There was consensus that the political will was lacking to correct these lacunaes.

Direct observation was also used in two cases at the two districts. In Khurda district, the monthly meeting at the PHC headquarters level was attended when all the staffs under that PHC gather to share their achievements during the last month and their likely targets for the next month. In Sundergarh district, the monthly meeting at the CDMO's office was attended with the permission of CDMO, Sundergarh. Here all the medical officers in charge of block PHCs had gathered to discuss the specific challenges their blocks faced along with the CDMO and his allied staff. In both these cases while their proceedings were going on this researcher was present noting down the proceedings and the issues those were raised. In the fist case the meeting had continued upto four hours and in the second case the meeting had gone upto three and half hours.

Structural constraints

The issue of structural constraints is significant in analyzing the implications of health sector reforms. The different aspects of structural constraints, which have been analysed in the context of present study were, the constraints within the health care services structure in Orissa, like the shortage of staffs at various levels, difficulties of retaining MOs and other staffs at periphery level institutions, inter departmental coordination, problem of inadequate training[59] etc; In terms of donor agencies, the lack of donor coordination, difficulties for the Health and Family Welfare department in writing reports for different donors, in case of OHSDP the alienation of the Line departments etc; in the context of health sector reforms the lack of wider consultations; the involvement of indigenous services providers for referrals to nearest block PHC; the declining presence of private health care over the years and paradoxically the growing perception of government officials at various levels of health care services in favor of private health care; and the effort by the government to increase private participation in a state where public sector was the dominant health care provider and where near about half of its population lived below the poverty line and less than 15 percent of the state's population lived in urban areas with scheduled castes and scheduled tribes constituted about 39 percent of its total population.

Duration of field visit

In total eight months were taken for field study starting from December 2004 to July 2005. First two months were used in Delhi to contact and interview the senior officials of donor agencies and another four months were used for field study in Orissa. Then again coming back from Orissa another two months were spent in interviewing the donor agency Officials at Delhi. In Bhubaneswar itself near about two months were spent and in Sundergarh and Khurda districts one month each was spent. Here it needs to be mentioned that because at the district level the monthly meetings were to be attended it took a lot of time to wait for those meetings. Then there were weekly meetings at block PHCs to be covered so that group interviews with ANMs could be possible. On an average minimum three times one block PHC had been visited.

Secondary sources

Data was also used from secondary sources like official records, published data of Directorate of Health Services, Central Bureau of Health Intelligence data, National Family Health Surveys, Census reports, Working Papers, Reports of donor agencies, Unpublished documents, Journals, Books etc.

---

[59] Like the MOs were mostly trained in curative care whereas they were supposed to respond to the requirements of preventive care.

Chapterisation

The book has been divided into eight chapters. They are:

First Chapter: It has discussed about review of literature. Here national and international experiences on health sector reforms have been documented.

Second Chapter: It has dealt with conceptualization, objectives and the methodology used in this study.

Third Chapter: It has given an overview of the health care services structure in Orissa. It has focused on the objective:
a-To examine the trends in growth of public health services at the primary/secondary/tertiary levels of care in Orissa during the eighties and nineties. It has also given a brief description about the growth of health care services structure in India.

Fourth Chapter: It has analyzed the SHSDPs and the OHSDP in the context of Structural Adjustment Program in India. Here we have interpreted OHSDP as a major reform initiative in Orissa. In this context we have described about some aspects of the process and experience of reforms in Orissa.

Fifth Chapter: This chapter gives a comprehensive picture about the process and experience of health sector reforms in Orissa. It has mostly dealt with objective: perception and experience of health bureaucracy dealing with HSR. It has also analyzed the perception of health bureaucracy about the shifts in financing, provisioning and manpower of health services during these two decades and its implications for equity.

Sixth Chapter: It has looked at the two study districts in terms of their socio-economic background and the process and experience of reforms.

Seventh Chapter: Here we have looked at the financing, structure and utilisation of health care services in Orissa, and some major states in India. Here we have also looked at the objectives: a-The trends in quantum, source and agencies providing external assistance to the health services system in Orissa during these two decades. b- We have also analyzed our first objective which has looked at the trends in public financing in Orissa, relative to India.

Eighth Chapter: This was the final chapter dealing with discussion and conclusion.

Annexure: 1

Organizational Chart

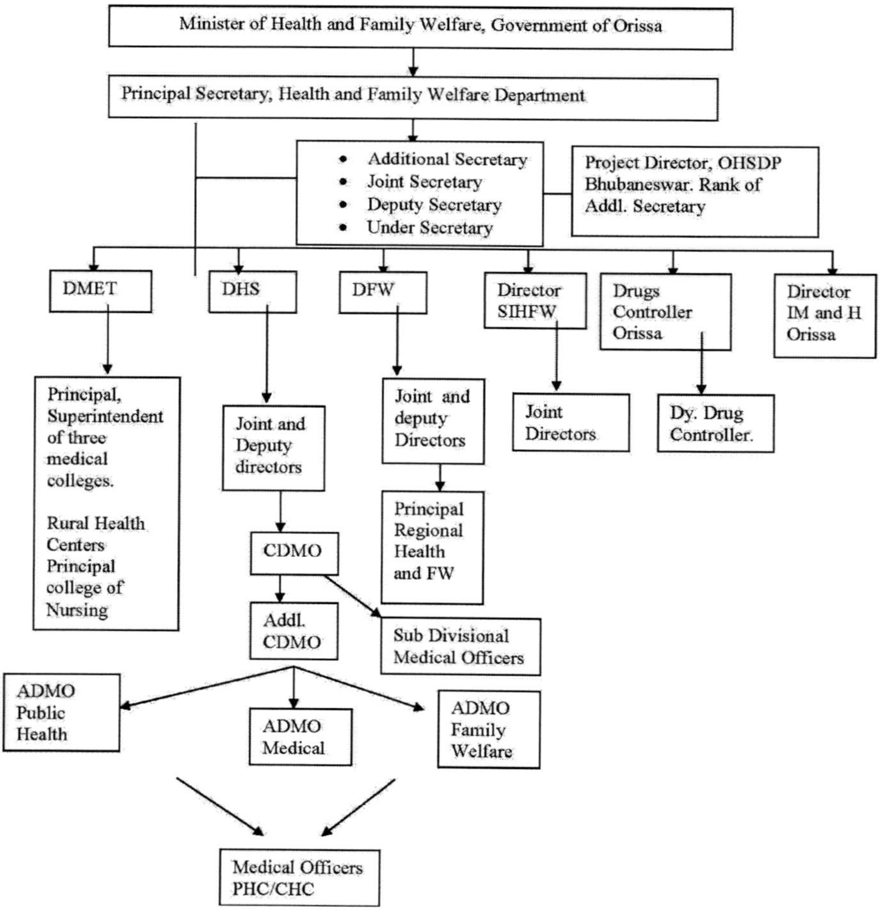

Source: http://orissagov.nic.in/health/organogram.pdf as on 23.06.2006.

CHAPTER THREE

OVERVIEW OF HEALTH CARE SERVICES IN ORISSA

Introduction

In this chapter we have discussed about the health care services structure in Orissa compared to India over the years.[1] In case of India we have begun with the evolution of public health care services sector since independence. We have also described in brief about improvements in health status over the years, the shifts in epidemiological pattern over the years and about the health care infrastructure created since 1951 till the year 2000. Before describing about the health care services structure of Orissa, we have given a comparative picture of health indicators of Orissa and India in recent times. In case of Orissa we have described in detail about health indicators over the years and the epidemiological shifts since 1980s etc. Along with the improvements in health status over the years in Orissa, we have also discussed about the family planning program in the state; because it was one of the national programs, which has supposedly been implemented successfully in the state. In infrastructure, in the allopathy system we have provided a picture of growth of public health care services structure in Orissa over the years, in terms of growth of institutions and beds and the number of registered medical practitioners since the beginning of health sector reforms in the state[2]. In the allopathy

[1] While this chapter has been primarily intended to give an overview of health care services in Orissa, a brief evolution of health services in India has also been provided here, because in chapter VII we have given a comparative picture of growth of private health care across major states of India since 1980s. Therefore to understand the growth of private sector, it was important to give the background to the development of growth of public health care services in India. Further in case of India the growth of private health care institutions has been closely linked with the government policies toward the public health care services over the years.

[2] This cut off period was 1996 when the House Committee was formed to assess the then existing health care facilities in Orissa.

system we have also analysed the then existing vacancy in various posts and we have presented a picture of number of sub centres having government buildings out of the total strength. Besides we have discussed about existing institutions, beds and number of registered manpower in the Indian System of Medicine in Orissa to give an overall picture of ISM and H system in the state.

In case of Orissa it has been observed that in remote and difficult areas the health care services personnel refuse to stay. Besides in these periphery level institutions the infrastructure maintenance has been a problem[3]. In this context we have discussed about the unserved and under served areas[4] of Orissa. Although our analysis was based on not so comprehensive report of the government of Orissa, it did provide an insight about the challenges of operating periphery level institutions in an efficient manner. Along with analysis of unserved and underserved areas, we have presented a comparative picture of availability of Sub centres, PHCs and CHCs in tribal Orissa, in terms of their required numbers, actual presence of these institutions and the gaps still required to be filled. Finally drawing from the field interviews at different levels we have discussed about the strengths and weaknesses in the health care services structure in the state[5].

---

[3] This was the observation of a senior donor agency official in Delhi.

[4] The unserved and underserved areas have been defined in the later part of this chapter.

[5] It needs to be clarified here that in chapter VII we have also given a comparative picture about the growth of private and the public sector in terms of institutions and beds. Whereas in this chapter we would be discussing about the growth of public health services in Orissa over the years. Therefore it might give a perception about repetition or that the subject matter discussed in chapter VII could have been discussed in this chapter. However there was a strong reason for not doing this. In chapter VII we have argued about the implications of reform elements for the health care services in terms of equity and universality. So we have analysed the trends to see whether there has been an increasing presence of private sector in different states, including Orissa or not since 1980s? Because we have defined health sector reforms as any initiative by a state to increase the space for the private sector while reducing the role for the public sector. Therefore it was important to look at whether the reforms in health sector were undertaken keeping in view the actual growth of private sector in different states or the reforms in health sector had been carried out in a uniform manner?

Evolution of public health services in India

The leadership of the Independent India had committed itself to principles of universality and a nationalized health services system. They had a vision for the self-reliance in the economy through public and private sector participation. The leading industrialists at that time were of the opinion that the private sector was not strong enough to invest in different sectors of the economy and specifically in infrastructure. Therefore they requested the government to invest heavily in infrastructure in the initial phase and the idea was that once these infrastructures were in place the private sector would take over. Hence it was quite clear that since independence India had adopted a model of economic growth where along with public sector the role of the private sector was also recognised.

In case of health care, the private players were present more in the form of individual private practitioners. When the Bhore committee gave its report based on the then existing health status of Indian population, it suggested the central role for the state in developing health care infrastructure. Significantly it also suggested the inclusion of the private sector in achieving the health targets of newly independent India. However the Committee had suggested the abolition of private practice by government doctors. But as the public sector could not grow in subsequent years, the legitimacy of private sector increased and abolition of private practice by salaried employees were largely unsuccessful.[6]

The survey of the health status of then Indian population showed that the communicable diseases were the major reasons for morbidity and mortality of vast sections of the population. The IMR and MMR were also very high at that time. Looking into these aspects the Committee had suggested a three-tier structure of health services with greater emphasis on primary and secondary levels of care. However over the years more funds flowed toward secondary and tertiary levels and this resulted in weak growth of the primary level care. The investments were also more in the urban areas than in the rural areas. Therefore the real growth for health services was during the sixties, but the level of investment was very low.[7] The Bhore committee had suggested an annual investment of 12% of GDP

---

[6] Baru, R, Private Health Care in India, Sage Publications, 1998. Also see Jesani & Anantha Ram: 1993.

[7] Banerji, Debabar, "Poverty, Class and Health Culture in India", Vol. 1, Prachi Prakashan, New Delhi, 1982. And Qadeer, I., "Health Services System in India: An Expression of Socio-Economic Inequalities", Social Action, July 1985.

in the health services sector, which could never materialize due to resource constraints and lack of political will.

While the investments in health sector were required more in the preventive aspects compared to the curative care, the opposite happened over the years. Therefore the structures of provisioning, reflected the needs of the then emerging middle class. From 1940s onwards the development of health services in India could be divided into three phases. The first phase comprises post- independent period upto the seventies. This period witnessed the growth of health services in the public sector. Though investments were meager an effort was made to build a network of services in both rural and urban areas. In the second phase that was during the late seventies to late eighties there were cutbacks in public spending and concessions given to the private sector. During this period India took loans from IMF and World Bank. The third phase saw the investment by Non Resident Indians in super specialty hospitals in cities like Hyderabad. This was also the period when the government of India liberalized norms for importing costly equipments from abroad. Besides many private players were given land in concessional rates to operate their hospitals on a profitable basis in cities like Delhi, with the condition that 25 percent of their beds would be reserved for below poverty line people. However none of these private hospitals have respected this agreement.

Improvements in health status over the years[8]

With the growth in public health care services over the years, with declining poverty, increase in urbanisation and a rising economic growth, it was expected that the health status of the population of India must also have improved. So let us have a look at the health status of Indian population since 1950s. The table below gives some comparative figures of life expectancy, crude birth rate, crude death rate and IMR rates since 1951 to the year 2000.

[8] It was important to clarify here that it was not being argued here that the improvement in health status was dependent only on the improvement in health care services. For while the health care services do play an important role, it terms of providing curative and preventive care, the health status of a population to a large extent depends upon the socio-economic and political contexts.

Table: 3.1 Improvement in health status over the years - 1951-2000.

Indicator	1951	1981	2000
Demographic changes			
Life Expectancy	36.7	54	64.6(RGI)
Crude Birth Rate	40.8	33.9(SRS)	26.1(99 SRS)
Crude Death Rate	25	12.5(SRS)	8.7(99 SRS)
IMR	146	110	70 (99 SRS)

Source: National Health Policy 2002.
Note: RGI- Registrar general of India, SRS- Sample Registration Survey.

The figures show that life expectancy has increased from 36.7 in 1951 to 54 in 1981 and 64.6 in 2000. This was a remarkable achievement over the years. Similarly the crude birth rate has decreased from 40.8 in 1951 to 33.9 in 1981 and further declined to 26.1 in the year 2000. The crude death rate has also decreased at a faster rate form 25 in 1951 to 12.5 in 1981 to 8.7 in the year 2000. In the year 1951 India had infant mortality rate of 146 per 1000 population, which was very high. However it could reduce IMR to 110 in 1981 and further to 70 by the year 2000.
These indicators show that India has improved its human development indicators since independence but there were many milestones yet to be achieved.[9]

Controlling communicable diseases over the years

The table below gives a picture of India's achievement in terms of its control of major public health challenges like malaria, leprosy, small pox, guinea worm and polio.

[9] In the form of Millennium Development Goals.

Table: 3.2 Communicable diseases: achievements over the years - 1951-2000.

Epidemiological Shifts	**1951**	**1981**	**2000**
Malaria (cases in million)	75	2.7	2.2
Leprosy cases per 10,000 population	38.1	5.73	3.74
Small Pox (no of cases)	>44,887	Eradicated	
Guinea worm (no. of cases)		>39,792	Eradicated
Polio		29709	265

Source: National Health Policy 2002.

There has been a public health assumption that with the change in the development pattern of a society, the disease pattern also changes. Hence it has been argued that while the developing countries suffer from communicable diseases, the developed countries suffer more from non-communicable diseases. Therefore the question arises as to what have been the epidemiological shifts in India[10] since 1950s? Whether India has been able to control the communicable diseases, which have been its major public health challenges since Independence?

The above table shows that while small pox and guinea worm had been eradicated by the end of 20th century, the other communicable diseases like malaria, leprosy and polio have been brought under control, significantly.

Infrastructure and manpower

Health services infrastructure is an important indicator of the outreach of preventive and curative services in a country. It shows on an average

[10] Because at the time of Independence the economy of India was heavily dependent on agriculture, however over the years with the state led investment in industries and the growth of services sector led by IT in 1990s, has reduced the share of agriculture in total GDP. Along with this the percentage of people living in urban areas, which is widely perceived as a development indicator, has also increased near to 28 percent by 2001.

whether the people have access[11] to primary, secondary and tertiary levels of care. The manpower in health care services is an integral part of improvement in infrastructure. The table below gives a picture of infrastructure and manpower created since 1951 upto the year 2000 in India. It contains data on sub centers, primary health centers and community health centers, dispensaries and hospitals, the combined public and private beds, allopathy doctors and nursing personnel.

Table: 3.3 Infrastructure and manpower created since 1951-2000.

Infrastructure	1951	1981	2000
SC/PHC/CHC	725	57,363	1,63,181 (99-RHS)
Dispensaries &Hospitals (all)	9209	23,555	43,322 (95–96-CBHI)
Beds (Pvt. & Public)	117,198	569,495	8,70,161 (95-96-CBHI)
Doctors (Allopathy)	61,800	2,68,700	5,03,900 (98-99-MCI)
Nursing Personnel	18,054	1,43,887	7,37,000 (99-INC)

Source: National Health Policy 2002.

It shows that the number of PHC/CHC/SC has increased from725 in 1951 to 57,363 in 1981 to 1,63,181 by the year 2000. This was a big increase in terms of absolute numbers. When it comes to dispensaries and hospitals, these increased from 9209 in 1951 to 23,555 in 1981 to 43,322 by the year 2000. Similarly private and public beds were 1,17,198 in 1951, which increased to 5,69,495 in 1981 and it further increased to 8,70,161 by the year 2000. In terms of medical personnel, doctors increased from 61,800 in 1951 to 2,68,700 in 1981 and it further increased to 5,03,900 in 2000. The nursing personnel also increased from 18.054 in 1981 to 1,43,887 in 1981 and it further increased to7, 37,000 by the year 2000. Therefore there were significant increase in number of doctors and nurses in absolute terms over the years.

---

[11] Here the term 'access' suggests the physical availability of health care services to the people. It is important to mention here that even though the health care infrastructure may be physically available in a particular area, people may not be accessing it due to poor quality of services, economic or cultural reasons or due to ignorance of the presence of these institutions.

Thus in terms of infrastructure, India has improved a lot since the time of independence. However national averages mask inequalities across regions and different sections of the population[12]. In this context health and health service indicators between Orissa, which is a poor state and India becomes important.

Health indicators of Orissa relative to India

The table below has shown the differences in health indicators of Orissa compared to India, in terms of various criteria like, rural-urban differences, total fertility rate, perinatal mortality rate, neo-natal mortality rate, post-natal mortality rate, still birth rate, crude birth rate, crude death rate, infant mortality rate, doctor population ratio, ANM population ratio, nurse-bed ratio, nurse doctor ratio, maternal mortality rate etc.

Table: 3.4 Health indicators of Orissa and India.

As per Sample Registration System Report		Orissa	India
1	Mean age at marriage (female) 1996-SRS		
	Total	19.6	19.4
	Rural	19.5	19
	Urban	20.4	20.7
2	Total Fertility Rate		
	Total	3.3	3.5
	Rural	3.4	3.8
	Urban	2.5	2.7
3	Perinatal Mortality Rate		
	Total	63.1	42.5
	Rural	68.8	43.4
	Urban	49.1	38.7
4	Neonatal Mortality Rate (1997-SRS)		
	Total	65.3	47.7
5	Post-natal Mortality Rate		
	Total	32.8	26
	Rural	33.6	27.5
	Urban	26.1	19.6

[12] Like scheduled castes, scheduled tribes, women and children and the urban poor etc.

6	Still-Birth Rate		
	Total	14.4	8.9
	Rural	13.6	7.3
	Urban	21.6	15.2
	As per Sample Registration	System Bulletin	
7	Crude Birth Rate 2002		
	Total	23.1	25
	Rural	23.6	26.6
	Urban	19.5	19.9
8	Crude Death Rate 2002		
	Total	9.8	8.1
	Rural	10.3	8.7
	Urban	6.3	6.1
9	Infant Mortality Rate 2002		
	Total	87	64
	Rural	91	69
	Urban	56	40
	Other Ratios		
10	Doctor Population Ratio 2001	1: 7462	1: 1916
11	Bed Population Ratio 2001	1: 2663	1: 1451
12	A.N.M Population Ratio 2001	1: 5178	
13	Nurse Bed Ratio (Calculated on Hospital & CHC beds 2001)	1:6	
14	Population Served per Medical Institution 2001	1: 21679	
15	Area served per medical Institution 2001	1: 92 sqm.	
16	Nurse Doctor ratio 2001	1: 2	1: 5.1
17	Paramedics Population Ratio	1: 1672	
18	M.M.R (Per one lakh birth)	367	407

Source: Website of the ministry of Health and Family Welfare Government of Orissa and Field Work, 2005.

The table shows that the mean age at marriage for female population in Orissa was higher than all India average. Interestingly while the rural population of Orissa had a higher mean age of marriage for females, the urban population of Orissa had a lower mean age of marriage for females compared to all India average.

In terms of total fertility rate or TFR, Orissa was showing better result with 3.3 compared to 3.5 for India. Here in both the rural and urban Orissa had a much better TFR rates than the urban and rural India. Thus it shows that although Orissa has a large number of its population living below the poverty line, it has managed to move closer towards population stabilization measures. This area needs further research because various studies show that the poor have a tendency for more children as they see children as economic assets, who can help in increasing the family income. May be due to the focused state intervention Orissa could achieve this.[13]

In terms perinatal mortality rate, Orissa was far behind India on an average, as well as in both rural and urban areas. However it seems that the gap between rural Orissa and rural India was much more than the gap between urban Orissa and urban India. The neonatal mortality rate of Orissa was again higher than India. In terms of post-natal mortality rate Orissa was behind India and this was the case for both rural and urban Orissa when compared to rural and urban India. While Orissa on an average had stillbirth of 14.4, India had 8.9; thus both urban and rural Orissa fare below urban and rural India. However the gaps between urban Orissa and urban India were much more than the gap between rural Orissa and rural India.

The crude birth rate of Orissa was 23.1 and it was 25 for India. However rural Orissa shows lower CBR than rural India as compared to the gap between urban Orissa and urban India. However the crude birth rate of urban Orissa was lower than rural Orissa. The figures for crude death rate or CDR show that while Orissa had CDR of 9.8, India had CDR of 8.1. Both the rural and urban Orissa lagged behind rural and urban India. In both the cases urban CDRs were less than rural CDRs. Infant mortality rate for Orissa was very high when compared to all India. Thus while India had IMR of 64, Orissa had IMR of 87. Here also the gap between rural Orissa and rural India was much more than the gap between urban Orissa and urban India. In both the cases, urban areas show better results than the rural areas.

In terms of doctor population ratio, India shows better result than Orissa. Thus while Orissa had one doctor per 7462 people, India had one doctor per 1916 people. This was a big gap. Bed population ratio also showed that India was far ahead of Orissa. In case of Orissa while there was one bed per 2663 people, it was one bed per 1451 people for India. However the nurse doctor ratio also showed that Orissa was in a better situation than

[13] In the later section of this chapter we have tried to explain this phenomenon by referring to field interviews.

India as a whole. Thus while Orissa had one nurse per two doctors, India had one nurse per 5.1 doctors. Finally in terms of maternal mortality ratio or MMR Orissa showed better result than India.

Health indicators of Orissa over the years

In the above table we have compared some basic health indicators of Orissa with India. In the table below we have looked at the differences in health indicators of Orissa since 1980s to the year 2000 to see the trends. The table has shown the health indicators like infant mortality rate, maternal mortality rate, under 5 mortality rate, crude birth rate, crude death rate, total fertility rate, couple protection rate, percent of children in the age group of 0-3 remaining malnourished, percentage coverage of pregnant women with TT, percent of institutional deliveries and percent of children aged 12-24 months fully immunized.

Table: 3.5: Health Indicators in Orissa since 1980s.

Indicators	1980	2000	Source
IMR	143	97	SRS 1999
MMR	738 (1992)	367	SRS 1999
U5MR	131 (1992)	104.4	NFHS II
CBR		24.1	SRS1999
CDR		11.1	SRS 1999
TFR	3.0 (1992)	2.5	NFHS II
CPR		39	DHS 1998
% children aged 0–3 years malnourished		54.4	NFHS II
% coverage of pregnant woman with TT		74.3	NFHS II
% institutional deliveries		22.6	NFHS II
% children aged 12–24 months fully immunized		43.7	NFHS II

Note: IMR: Infant Mortality Rate; MMR: Maternal Mortality Rate; U5MR: under-5 Mortality Rate; CBR: Crude Birth Rate; CDR: Crude Death Rate; TFR: Total Fertility Rate; SRS: Sample Registration System; NFHS: National Family Health Survey; CPR: Contraceptive Prevalence Rate; DHS: Demographic and Health Survey.

Source: Meena Gupta, State Health Systems, Orissa, 2002.

The data shows that in 1980 the IMR of Orissa was very high with 143; it got reduced to 97 by the year 2000. However it was still the highest among all the states in India. Similarly the maternal mortality rate in 1980 was 738 per one lakh population; it got reduced to 367, which was more than 50 percent. This has been a remarkable achievement in a span of twenty years. The total fertility rate also declined from 3.0 in 1980 to 2.5 in the year 2000. The under 5 mortality rate was 131 in the year 1980 and it came down to 104.4 by the year 2000, which was still very high. However the crude birth rate was 24.1 in the year 2000, while the crude death rate was 11.1. The couple protection rate was 39 in the year 2000, which was below the national average. On the other hand Orissa had 54.4 percent of children in the age group of 0-3 who were malnourished. Coincidentally this was nearer to the percent of its population living below the poverty line.

Therefore a question arises that with high infant mortality rate, high maternal mortality rate and high under 5 mortality rate and low institutional delivery of 22.6 percent, how the population of Orissa was nearing towards stabilization than other states? Because near to 48 percent of Orissa's population lived below the poverty line[14]. The urban population was only about 14 percent of its total population. That means most of its people depended on agriculture for their livelihoods. Further 38 percent of Orissa's population comprised of scheduled castes and scheduled tribes.[15] In these communities cultural barriers exist for utilisation of health care facilities apart from lack of accessibility and availability of health care facilities.[16] At the same time in Orissa the government was the major provider of health care services across the state, both for in-patient and out-patient care. And from the field visit it was also very clear that doctors and paramedics refuse to go to the rural and tribal areas or even when they were posted, they do not visit their institutions at all or visit rarely. In these circumstances, how could the state reduce its total fertility rate to 2.5?

One explanation was that floods in the coastal districts and droughts in the central and western districts frequently visit the state; as a result large number of deaths occurs. Then there were communicable diseases like malaria, which were endemic in northwestern districts of Orissa and every year mortality rate was very high due to malaria. There were districts like Kalahandi, Bolangir and Koraput, which were in news for droughts and

[14] This was according to the 2001 census of India.
[15] Ibid.
[16] This was the view of most of the officials in the state.

hunger deaths. These in a combined way reduced the growth rate of population. Thus it was not only due to successful family planning campaigns in Orissa, but due to these various reasons, population growth rate was declining compared to other states in India. However population control measures[17] introduced in the state also had an important role to play in this regard.

Family welfare[18]

As in other states of India, in Orissa also family welfare has been synonymous with population control. And in population control methods the female sterilization was the main method. This was observed during the field visit in two districts. At the block PHC level it was observed that the ANMs had been given targets of female sterilization for each month. Although in pen and paper it was written that the ANMs would decide after consulting the community about the number of male or female sterilization, in practice it was the medical officer in-charge in a block PHC who decided the target and that too only for female sterilization.[19] This was observed during the attendance of weekly meeting at one of the block PHCs at Khurda district. Later interacting with senior officials at the state capital it was found that female sterilization was one of the most 'popular' practices for population control all over Orissa. Although in late nineties RCH or reproductive and child health has been introduced in the state as in other states of India, for the ANM at the village level, the priority was to control population through female sterilization.

---

[17] Rather than using the term 'family welfare' we have used 'population control' because for the personnel at the district level the term 'family welfare' was synonymous with 'population control'. Infact interacting with the senior state officials it was clear that despite having loftier goals of family welfare, it has been primarily seen an important national program to control growth rate of population. Because the importance of population in development never figured in our discussions with these officials. For them 'population growth was a problem which needed to be controlled as soon as possible.

[18] A section on family welfare has been included here along with health indicators of Orissa because Orissa has been a state where they have been able to reduce the total fertility rate nearer to population replacement level. Therefore what could be the possible reasons?

[19] Of course the provisions for male sterilization were there but it was more of a voluntary nature.

As we have mentioned above that the declining growth rate of population in Orissa was due to a variety of factors apart from adopting focused family planning approach. As one of the senior officials in the state observed "High incentive oriented activity cannot be sustained, as it has happened in Family Welfare for 50 years. Once the incentive is withdrawn the scheme will collapse. Orissa's growth rate in population has come down; this may be due to family welfare method like spacing, due to natural calamity, due to diseases contributing to death rate. Perhaps our effort in Family Planning programme is not balanced."

While on the one hand there was decline in the growth rate of population[20] and on the other hand IMR rates were very high in Orissa,[21] coupled with a high Crude Death Rate.[22] This was a very contradictory phenomenon because studies from elsewhere has shown that people opt for family planning if they were sure that their existing children would survive in coming years. Therefore what were the reasons for such a high IMR rate? Responding to this question one senior official in the Health and Family Welfare department, government of Orissa said, "One reason as to why IMR is not coming down is that peri-natal deaths are more and contributing to maximum deaths. However vaccine preventable deaths are low".[23] He further added "All our attention should not have got diverted to immunization… WHO, UNICEF, Government of India all these organizations focused on immunization, on mobility, infrastructure etc. for a long time. There was belief that vaccine preventable diseases were leading to major deaths and hence all the resources were channelised for immunization programme. But now it seems that malnutrition, diahhroea, malaria and underweight are major cause for peri-natal deaths." Therefore while the Immunization program did help in preventing infant and child deaths, it could not reduce the infant mortality rates, as there were other

[20] As per 2001 Census-Provisional of India, the annual growth rate of population in Orissa was 1.59 percent compared to 2.13 percent for India. In terms of decennial growth rate, in 1981-91, the population growth rate of Orissa was 20.06 percent as compared to 23.86 percent for India and during the decade 1991-2001, the decadal population growth rate of Orissa declined sharply to 15.94 percent as compared to 21.34 percent for India. Similarly while the Crude Birth Rate was 24.1 for Orissa in 1999 as per SRS, the figures for all India were 26.1.

[21] As per Sample Registration Survey in the year 1999 the Infant Morality Rate of Orissa was 97 as compared to 70 for all India.

[22] As per SRS 1999 the crude death rate of Orissa was 10.6 compared to all India figures of 8.7.

[23] Neo-natal deaths were low.

significant reasons like, malnutrition, underweight, diarrhoea and endemic malaria in certain districts of Orissa.

Continuing with his narrative the official said, "The causes of peri-natal deaths like unsafe delivery, pre maturity, low birth weight and respiratory tract infection are preventable. These are happening because antenatal check up is not done properly and risk pregnancies are not detected. As a result maternal death rate is high. We are realizing this after so many years of concentration on immunization. Ante-natal check up and safe delivery should have been given equal importance". Off late to address the requirements of safe delivery and to prevent maternal deaths the government of Orissa had introduced training of block level medical officers for short-term anesthesia courses.

In tribal districts and in rural areas the government health care machinery has almost collapsed and the traditional practitioners or quacks have taken their place[24]. The effort by institutions like the World Bank to involve the traditional practitioners in referrals in tribal districts brought this fact to the limelight that the pregnancy related deaths were the major causes for maternal mortality rates, specifically in tribal districts. Therefore the indigenous service providers have also been involved in tribal districts to refer the risk pregnancies to the nearby PHCs.

It was being argued that the state has been able to reduce the total fertility rate from 3.0 in 1980 to 2.5 by the year 2000. This was not entirely due to family planning methods. Even it could be argued that family planning methods have played a very small part in moving the state towards population stabilization[25]. Here we could say that due to the feudal and patriarchal nature of the social set up in Orissa, female sterilization has been widespread. Off late the reproductive and child health programme has replaced the maternal and child health programme of the early nineties. "However lofty the ideals of RCH may be but until the situation at the block PHC level has not changed, nothing significant is going to happen"[26].

---

[24] This was an observation from interacting with officials at various levels in the state and with the donor agencies. We have discussed about this aspect in the later sections of this chapter.

[25] This aspect has been discussed above.

[26] This was the view of many senior officials interviewed at various levels in the state. We have discussed about these structural issues in the later section of this chapter.

Giving explanation from another aspect, a senior official of a donor agency in Orissa said, "One of the reasons that the institutions like block PHCs are not functioning well in Orissa is that the panchayats are very weak unlike in West Bengal. As a result accountability of the staff at this level is lacking."[27] Here the respondent was emphasizing about the importance of strong panchayats at block levels to ensure the effective functioning of periphery level institutions. While this argument seems quite logical, it was surprising that in our interviews with senior state officials, the officials from donor agencies as well as with the officials at district level, the idea of involvement of panchayats for effective functioning of block level health institutions hardly figured.

Prevalence of some major diseases over the years in Orissa:
How Orissa has performed in controlling its major communicable diseases since 1980s? The table below gives a picture of three major communicable diseases like malaria, tuberculosis and gastro-enteritis in Orissa since 1980 till the year 1997.

Table: 3.6 Prevalence of major diseases in Orissa

Year	Malaria		Tuberculosis		Gastro-enteritis	
	SPR%	PF%	Prevalence rate per 1000	Old cases as percentage of total	Case fatality rate	Prevalence rate per 10000
1980	10.4	75.3			12.2	0.9
1986	11.2	80.0	2.08	55.5	10.6	1.5
1990	8.7	84.7	2.30	55.3	10.3	3.4
1994	10.2	85.6	2.23	57.2	7.2	4.1
1997	10.3	86.4	2.52	65.3	-	-

Source: State Bureau of Health Intelligence, 1998 and Director Health Services, Government of Orissa.
Note: SPR – Slide Positive Rate. PF – Percent of plasmodium falciparum cases in total number of positive cases.

It shows that for malaria, SPR percent had almost remained same over the years, with a marginal increase in the year 1986 and a decrease in the year 1990. By the year 1997 the SPR percentage came nearer to the 1980 level. On the other hand, the PF percentage has increased over the years steadily.

---

[27] This was also the view of some senior officials at the state and at the district level.

Thus malaria continues to a big challenge for Orissa. One of the reasons for high SPR percentage and high PF percent may be that the block PHCs and the single doctor PHCs were not well equipped to face the situation. During the field visit one monthly meeting was attended in the Sundergarh district, which was highly endemic region for malaria. It was found that the medical officers' in-charge of block PHCs' were disagreeing with each other about the treatment protocol of malaria, specially the PF cases. It was resolved with the intervention of ADMO public health,[28] who said that WHO has given clear guidelines to the state and it should be followed. If this was the case with medical officers' in-charge at block PHC levels, then what happens at the PHC (N) s, which was single doctor PHCs? And what about the ANMs who were supposed to be directly in touch with the community to distribute tablets and make people aware about preventive measures on communicable diseases?

In case of tuberculosis, the table shows that the prevalence rate has increased since 1986 till the year 1997. It had decreased slightly in 1994 when compared to the year 1990. Thus in 1986 the prevalence rate per 1000 was 2.08 and it increased to 2.52 in 1997. Similarly old cases as percentage to the total cases have increased over the years. Thus in 1986 there were 55.5 percent old cases as percentage to the total cases, which increased to 65.3 percent. In case of gastro-enteritis the prevalence per 10,000 populations has increased over the years. However, the case fatality rate has decreased over the years.

In tuberculosis the prevalence rate and the old cases as percent to the total, show that it has increased over the years. What could be the probable reasons for this? During the field visit, one weekly meeting of a block level PHC was attended in Khurda district. Incidentally this PHC was nearer to Bhubaneswar[29]. In the meeting the medical officer in charge of that PHC told the ANMs to get ready with readymade answers for different communicable diseases and RCH as a team from Delhi was expected to visit them. They were told, "Suppose they ask you that you do not have a sub center building then how do you manage? Then you say that we are working from a rented building. Please do not say that you live in Bhubaneswar and rarely visit your field!" Then he went on to tell them on what to answer for question on RCH or for immunization. He also reminded them of their weekly routines. And finally he said, "With these

[28] Even not by the district malaria officer!

[29] The distance from Bhubaneswar was 30 kilometers only.

answers the team from Delhi will return happily and everything will be alright."[30]

The buildings of sub centers were in a dilapidated condition like many of the PHC News' and the block level PHCs. ANMs hardly visited the field. The supervisors interviewed said that they faced lack of transportation facilities as a result they had to travel through bicycle. The government did not provide any fuel cost to them. And the numbers of lady supervisors were very few. The male workers who were supposed to help the ANMs very rarely visited their fields. Therefore it was hardly surprising that the national programmes like malaria and tuberculosis were a failure in the state.

Coupled with this the transfer and postings of doctors have been politicized in the state. Those with proper connection get postings in urban areas like Rourkela and Bhubaneswar. "They pay regularly to their superiors and to the political bosses to stay in their posts. Even in RGH Rourkela[31], there are biddings for posts and the highest bidder is allowed to stay".[32] And therefore "there is demoralization of doctors at all levels in the state".[33] We have discussed this issue in the later section of this chapter in detail.

Heath care infrastructure in Orissa

As we have discussed above that the existence of health care infrastructure is an indicator of level of curative and preventive services available for the population of an area. It is also an important development indicator. The table below gives an overall picture of health care infrastructure in Orissa in the beginning of 21st century.

---

[30] It needs to be mentioned here that this researcher was not allowed to sit inside the small hall where this meeting was going on, however standing from outside the conversations at the meeting could be clearly heard as the medical officer in charge was literally dictating to the ANMs about the possible answers to probable questions.

[31] Rourkela Government Hospital, Rourkela, it was located in Sundergarh District.

[32] This was the view of an MO in-charge of a block PHC in Orissa.

[33] This was the view of a donor agency official who had the experience of working for 22 years in the health care services in Orissa.

Table: 3.7 Health care Infrastructure in Orissa

Institutions	Numbers
Capital Hospital	1
Medical Colleges	3
District Head Quarter Hospitals	30
Sub Divisional Hospitals	21
Other Hospitals	125
CHCs	157
PHCs	184
PHC (N)	1168
MHUs	14
Total	1703
Health Sub Centers	5927

Note: CHC was Community Health Center with 16 beds as a norm; PHC was Primary Health Center with 6 beds as a norm, PHC (N) was a single doctor institution catering only for outdoor patients. MHU was Mobile Health Unit. As per norm one PHC (N) has to be opened for a population of 20,000 in tribal areas and 30,000 in non-tribal areas. Out of 1168 PHC (N) institutions created the required number of posts for 49 PHC (N) could not be sanctioned hence these were not functioning. It had been observed that the CDMOs were recommending for opening of PHC (N) institutions without verifying the norms fixed by National Health Policy.

Source: Health and Family Welfare Department, Government of Orissa. Field Work, 2005.

It shows that there was one Capital Hospital, which was located at Bhubaneswar, the capital of Orissa. Besides there were three medical colleges, 30 district head quarter hospitals, 21 sub divisional hospitals, 125 other hospitals, 157 community health centers, 184 primary health centers, 1168 PHC (N) single doctor institutions and 14 mobile health units and 5927 sub centers.

Health and manpower ratio in Orissa

Health and manpower ratio is an important indicator of people's access to health care. If this ratio is not maintained upto a norm then not only the people suffer from access and better quality care, the health personnel also remain over stressed. The table below has given a picture of doctor-population ratio, doctor nurse ratio, nurse-bed ratio and female worker[34]-population ratio.

Table: 3.8 Health and manpower ratio in Orissa

Indicator	Ratios currently
Doctor-population ratio	1:7560
Doctor-Nurse ratio	2:1
Nurse-Bed ratio	1:6
Nurse population ratio	1: 16,000
Bed Population ratio	1:2500
Population served per medical institution	1:21700
Health worker population ratio	1:5200

Note: For health worker population ratio the all India norm was, 1:5000 in the plains and 1:3000 in tribal areas.
Source: fieldwork, 2005.

The analysis of the table shows that in terms of doctor-population ratio, there was one doctor per 7560 people. The doctor-nurse ratio shows that there were two doctors per one nurse. In terms of nurse-bed ratio, Orissa had one nurse per 6 beds. In terms of nurse population ratio, it was 1 nurse per 16,000 people. This shows that there were acute shortages of nurses in the state. One senior official of nursing in the Health Directorate of the government of Orissa was of the view that "Doctors are dominating at every level of health care services". The official mentioned about the fact that there was not a single joint director of nursing in Orissa. The bed population ratio shows that there was one bed available for 2500 people. Further one medical institution served 21,700 people and there was one health worker available for 5,200 people. This suggests the stress level the health institutions had to face if they were actually utilized, as many of these institutions were inaccessible and also due to inadequate services provided, very few people utilized their services.

Medical education in Orissa

The medical education available in a state is an important indicator of availability and sustainability of tertiary level care on a long-term basis. Reflecting on the medical education over the years in Orissa, one senior

[34] Female worker here refers to ANMs.

official in the Ministry of Health and Family Welfare, government of Orissa said, "Orissa has been a state where the state run medical colleges have been there since 1950s. The private sector has neither the resourses nor the expertise to open a medical college and it was also due to the stringent norms by MCI[35], it has been difficult to open private medical colleges"[36]. The table below gives a comparative picture of number of medical seats in the three government operated medical colleges. It needs to be mentioned here that, over the years Orissa has had these three medical colleges. They were SCB medical college, Cuttack, MKCG medical college, Berhampur and VSS medical college, Burla.

Table: 3.9 Medical education in Orissa

Institutions	Undergraduate. MBBS	Post Graduate. MD, MS etc.	High Specialty MCH, DM.
SCB Medical College, Cuttack.	107	110	4
MKCG Medical College, Berhampur.	107	65	
VSS Medical College, Burla.	107	67	
Total	321	242	4

Source: Orissa Vision 2010, A Health Strategy, February 2003, Published by Health and Family Welfare Department, Government of Orissa, Bhubaneswar.

The table shows that for undergraduate courses all these three colleges had 107 seats each. For the post graduate courses SCB medical college had highest number of seats followed by VSS medical college Burla and the MKCG medical college Berhampur. For high specialty courses like MCH and DM, there were only 4 seats in SCB medical college Cuttack. These three medical colleges have a total intake of 321 undergraduate and 246 postgraduate students per year.

[35] Medical Council of India.

[36] This was the view of a senior official at the Ministry of Health and Family Welfare, government of Orissa.

> Off late medical graduates are leaving Orissa for other states where opportunities are more. They are also going for post graduate courses in other states. Those who join the government service many of them leave soon, as they find it quickly that those who have political blessings only they can survive[37].

In recent times government of Orissa was planning to open three private medical colleges in the state. These were being promoted by Western Orissa Development Council, which was a statutory body under the government of Orissa, Act. We have discussed in detail about this aspect in chapter V.

Growth of allopathy institutions over the years in Orissa

The allopathy system has been the main branch through which the government of Orissa has tried to increase its health care services structure over the years. The table below mentions about the growth of allopathy institutions since 1980 till the year 2000. It shows data with regard to number of hospitals, CHCs, PHCs, subsidiary health centres, medical aid centres, dispensaries and mobile health units.

The table shows that in 1985 the state had highest number of hospitals of 210 and by the year 1992 it had the lowest number of hospitals. Compared to 1980 figures, the state had less than 19 hospitals by the year 2000. Thus we could say that the state had experienced declining growth rate of public hospitals during these two decades.

The trends for CHCs in Orissa show that it has increased over the years from 12 in 1980 to 158 in 2000, which was an addition of about 146 CHCs. The sudden increase in 1989 was because of the DFID projects, which created some UGPHCs.[38]

---

[37] This was the view of a government official who had worked in the government health services of Orissa for 22 years. We have discussed in detail about the challenges of retaining medical graduates in government services in Orissa in the later section of this chapter.

[38] Upgraded PHCs.

Table 3.10 Growth of allopathy institutions over the years

Year	Hosp.	CHC	PHC	PHC (N)	SHC	MAC	Disp.	MHU	Total
1980	200	12*	314	0	64	70	217	14	879
1981	200	17*	314	0	64	70	217	14	879
1982	202	17*	314	0	103	70	216	14	919
1983	202	17*	314	0	103	70	216	14	919
1984	209	17*	314	50	103	70	216	14	943
1985	210	17*	314	198	240	66	195	10+2$	1087
1986	192	17*	314	200	215	54	169	10+2$	1154
1987	186	17*	314	346	213	56	173	10+2$	1156
1988	193	17*	314	519	188	47	151	10+2$	1253
1989	181	50	285	612	175	39	125	12	1386
1990	181	75	219	612	171	38	140	12	1448
1991	181	75	219	612	171	38	140	12	1448
1992	176	110	232	626	172	38	139	12+15&	1520
1993	177	110	232	642	172	39	142	12+15&	1541
1994	177	111	231	644	172	39	142	12+15&	1543
1995	177	111	231	644	172	39	142	12+15&	1543
1996	180	157	185	700	171	42	150	12+15&	1617
1997	180	157	185	1105	**	**	**	14	1641
1998	180	157	184	1150	**	**	**	14	1685
1999	180	157	184	1168	**	**	**	14	1703
2000	181	158	183	1166	**	**	**	13	1701

Note: * Functioned as Upgraded PHC and included in PHC.
** Converted to PHC (N).
$ First Aid Center
& MHU were functioning under Prime minister's relief program.
Abbreviations:
Hosp.-Hospitals, CHC- Community Health Centre (Including upgraded PHC), PHC- Primary Health Centre, SHC- Subsidiary Health Centre, MAC- Medical Aid Centre, Disp.- Dispensary, MHU- Mobile Health Unit.

Source: Health Statistics of Orissa, 2000-2001, Compiled by State Bureau of Health Intelligence, Directorate of Health Services, Orissa.

Since 1988 the number of PHCs declined till 1991 and again increased slightly for next two years and from there it experienced gradual decline till the year 2000. Thus in terms of absolute numbers the total number of PHCs declined from 314 in 1980 to 183 in 2000 which was less than 131 in total. The reasons were that these 131 PHCs were upgraded to UGPHCs which has been shown as CHCs in the table. Therefore it could be said that the trends for CHCs and PHCs in Orissa need to be seen together. Therefore overall these institutions have remained almost same from 1980 till the year 2000.

There was no concept of PHC (N) s in Orissa till 1983. These were single doctor institutions operating under a block PHC. The idea was that in remote areas the people should have access to primary level care. The figures show that the number of these institutions increased from 50 in 1984 to 198 in 1985 and over the years it continued to grow and by the year 2000 the number of PHC (N) s in total was 1166. Therefore from zero in 1980 to 1166, that's a big gain. This suggests that the idea of providing PHC (N) s to people in remote areas has appealed to various political parties over the years[39]. How ever, these were the institutions where the absenteeism of medical officers was found to be acute.

The SHCs[40] Subsidiary Health Centres were single doctor institutions and the total numbers of SHCs were 64 in 1980, which increased to 240 in 1985 and gradually declined since then to 171 in 1996. The MACs or the Medical Aid Centres as well as the dispensaries were single doctor institutions, which remained same till 1984 but were later renamed as PHC (N) s.

The Mobile Health Units remained same from 1980 till 2000, except during 1992 to 1996 when additional MHUs were functioning under Prime Minister's relief program. The Mobile Health Units have been used mostly in the tribal districts. And it was surprising that their number has not increased over the years.

Thus broadly we could say that the decline of hospitals over the years in Orissa was a matter of concern. Similarly the block level institutions like CHCs and PHCs have almost remained same and effort has been made to strengthen these institutions over the years. However the single doctor institutions remained as a major challenge for the health care services structure in the state. At the same time the need for increasing the number of Mobile Health Units has been felt like never before.

---

[39] This was the view of various interviewees during field visit to the state.

[40] SHCs or Subsidiary Health Centres had a staff structure of one medical officer, one pharmacist, one ANM and a sweeper. This structure was same for Medical Aid Centres also.

Growth of sub centres from sixth plan onwards in Orissa

The sub centers have been an integral part of connectivity between the block PHC and the community of that block. The success of national programs also depends on the efficient functioning of sub centres. Therefore let us have a look at the trends in growth of sub centres in Orissa from sixth plan onwards. The table below gives a picture about the number of sub centers created in Orissa from 1981-95 till the year 2001.

Table: 3.11 Sub centres in Orissa since 1981 till 2001.

At the end of Sixth Plan (1981-85)	At the end of Seventh Plan (1985-90)	At the end of Eighth Plan (1992-97)	As on 31.03.2001
4127	5927	5927	5927

Source: Health Statistics of Orissa, 2000-2001, Compiled by State Bureau of Health Intelligence, Directorate of Health Services, Orissa.

It shows that the number of sub centres in Orissa was 4127 at the end of sixth plan period of India. It increased by more than 1800, at the end of seventh plan period to 5927 in total.[41] However, there were no new sub centres created since then till the year 2001. However the increase in the total number of sub centres in itself does not ensure the improvement in the quality of these institutions. In the later section of this chapter we have discussed about the actual functioning of these institutions in Orissa.

Sub centres functioning without government building

Now let have a look at the sub centres functioning without a government building. Because where there were no government buildings, it was assumed even by the senior officials of the state that these sub centres were not functioning at all![42]

---

[41] During the field visit to the state in March 2005, it was known that the total number of sub centres was 5927 as on 2001.

[42] This was noted from interviewing various government and donor agency officials in the state.

Table 3.12: Sub centre building position in Orissa.

Total sub centres	Sub centre in government building	Sub centre in rented building
5927	2542	3385

Source: Fieldwork, 2005.

The table shows that out of the total 5927 sub centres in Orissa only 2542 had government buildings. That means only 42.88% of the sub centres had government buildings and the remaining 57.12% of the sub centres had no government buildings. In these circumstances how could various national programs succeed in the state? Also what about the reporting by ANMs for disease surveillance program in the state?[43]

Growth of beds in Orissa

The number of beds available also suggests the improvement in health care services in a state in terms of access to in-patient care for the people. The table below gives the trend in the growth of number of beds in allopathy institutions of Orissa since 1980 till the year 2001.

The table shows that while the number of hospitals declined during these twenty years the growth of hospital beds increased from 7954 in 1980 to 9512 in 2001 and it reached to 10,046 during 1989 to 1991.

In case of Orissa, the growth of beds in CHC/UGPHC and PHCs has to be seen together. Therefore while the number of PHC beds has decreased over the years, the number of CHC/UGPHC beds has increased over the years. Therefore while in 1980 there were 2172 beds in total in these block level institutions, it increased to 4128 beds by the year 2000-2001.

In terms of other beds or beds in PHC (N) institutions the figure was nil, till 1994-95 and it started with 138 beds in 1995-96, which declined to 122 in next year. The figures show a further increase to 146 in 1997-98 and it remained same till 2000-2001. The total number of beds increased over the years from 10126 in 1980 to 13786 in the year 2000-2001.

[43] We have discussed about this aspect in chapter V.

Table 3.13 Growth of beds in Orissa (allopathy)

Year	Hospital Beds	CHC/UGPHC beds	PHC beds	Other beds **	Total
1980	7954	*	2172	0	10126
1981	8052	*	2172	0	10224
1982	8092	*	2328	0	10420
1983	8092	*	2328	0	10420
1984	8414	*	2328	0	10742
1985-86	8884	*	2708	0	11592
1986-87	9061	*	2708	0	11769
1987-88	9107	*	2796	0	11903
1988-89	9474	*	2846	0	12320
1989-90	10046$	0	2561	0	12607
1990-91	10046$	0	2411	0	12857
1991-92	9321	1125	2411	0	12857
1992-93	9355	1604	2227	0	13186
1993-94	9355	1604	2227	0	13186
1994-95	9355	2082	2221	0	13658
1995-96	9450	2966	1110	138	13664
1996-97	9427	3018	1110	122	13677
1997-98	9512	3024	1104	146	13786
1998-99	9512	3024	1104	146	13786
1999-2000	9512	3024	1104	146	13786
2000-2001	9512	3024	1104	146	13786

Note: * Beds of upgraded PHC included under PHC
** Other beds include beds in PHC (N).
$ Inclusive of CHC beds.
- Reduction in PHC beds in the years 1995-96 and onwards was due to conversion of PHCs to CHCs.

Source: Health Statistics of Orissa, 2000-2001, Compiled by State Bureau of Health Intelligence, Directorate of Health Services, Orissa.

Registration of medical and para–medical professionals in Orissa

The increase in the number of registration of medical and paramedical professionals in a state is an indicator, which suggests that these personnel are optimistic about the future of health care services in that state. On the other hand if the number of new registrations decline than it suggests that the health personnel do not see a better prospect in future. In case of Orissa it has been said that the state was facing the shortage of nursing personnel. Therefore what was the reality in the context of Orissa?

The table below gives a picture of registration of medical and para-medical professionals in Orissa from 1996-97 to 2000-2001. As the health sector reforms in Orissa have been initiated since 1996 with the formation of the House Committee, it was interesting to see the trends in the registration of medical and para-medical staffs during this period.

Table 3.14 Registration of medical and para –medical professionals in Orissa

Name of the registering authority/ Categories of Professionals	**1996-97**		**1997-98**		**1998-99**		**1999-2000**		**2000-2001**	
CMR, Orissa	No. Reg.	Cum. total	No. Reg.	Cum. total	No. Reg.	Cum. total	No. Reg.	Cum. total	No. Reg.	Cum. total
Medical Graduates	295	12911	338	13249	360	13609	329	13938	302	14240
B.D.S	9	182	19	201	16	217	30	247	10	257
CNM, Orissa										
Staff Nurse	382	5371	393	5764	56	5820	282	6102	472	6574
ANM	229	5869	108	5977	114	6091	80	6171	296	6467
LHV	0	110	0	110	0	110	0	110	0	110

Note: CMR, Orissa- Council of Medical Registration, Orissa; CNS, Orissa- Council of Nurses and Midwives, Orissa.
Source: Health Statistics of Orissa, 2000-2001, Compiled by State Bureau of Health Intelligence, Directorate of Health Services, Orissa.

The table shows that while the number of new medical graduates registering every year has declined during these years but in terms of total numbers the medical graduates registering with CMR, Orissa have increased over the years. In terms of absolute numbers the number of BDS registrations has increased over the years. The figures for Staff nurse show that in terms of absolute numbers the total number of staff nurses registering with Council of Nurses and Midwives, Orissa has increased over the years.

The figures for ANMs show that in 1996-97, 229 new registrations were there which declined to 108 in next year. The number of new registrations increased to 114 in 1998-99 and in the following year the number of new registrations declined to 80. By the year 2000-2001 the new registrations increased to 296. Therefore in case of ANMs also the total number of new registrations has increased over the years.

The table shows that there were no new registrations for the post of Lady Health Visitor or LHV since 1996-97 to 2000-2001 and the total number of LHV registered with the CNM, Orissa has remained at 110. This was because the post of LHV has been abolished in the 1990s.

Therefore, overall trends show that, the number of new registration for medical and paramedical staffs have increased over the years in Orissa. That means these personnel were willing to work with the state government. However it was due to the faulty policies[44] of the government that these health personnel refuse to work within the health services system in the state.

Shortage of various staffs

Now let us have a look at the categories of staffs where Orissa was facing shortages.

[44] We have discussed about this aspect in the later section of this chapter.

Table 3.15: Vacancy in various positions in Orissa

Various Posts	Sanctioned Strength	In Position	Clear Vacancy	% In Position to the total
Sr. Class I	278	233	45	83.81
Jr. Class I	486	388	98	79.83
Class II Specialists	824	610	214	74.02
Asst. Surgeon	2629	2382	247	90.60
Staff Nurse	2244	2154	90	95.98
Pharmacist	2040	1984	56	97.25
MPHW (M)	4911	3392	1519	69.06
MPHW (F)	7121	6768	353	95.04
MPHS (M)	1605	740	865	46.10
MPHS (F)	1052	1005	47	95.53
Radiographer	128	91	37	71.09
Lab. Technician (Pathology)	445	418	27	93.93

Source: Field Work, 2005.

The table shows that among the various categories of posts, the staff nurse, pharmacists, multi purpose health worker female and the multi purpose health supervisor female were more than 95% in position compared to their sanctioned posts. Similarly assistant surgeons and the lab technicians were more than 90% of their sanctioned posts. Therefore in these categories of posts the state was not facing acute shortages.

On the other hand in the category of multipurpose health supervisor male, the state was facing serious crisis, because the in-position staffs in this category was less than 50 % of the sanctioned strength. This would seriously affect the supervision aspect of the sub centers. The next category of concern was multipurpose health worker, male, where the in-poison staffs were less than 70% and as a result the functioning of health sub centers would be badly affected.

This was followed by radiographers with 71.09%, class II specialists with 74.02%, junior class I with 79.83% and the senior class I with 83.81% of in position staffs to the total sanctioned staffs in these categories. The shortage of class II gynic specialists would have serious implications for the maternal and child health. Similarly the shortage of junior class I posts would affect the functioning of PHC level institutions and finally the shortage of senior class I posts would affect the smooth functioning of CHC II institutions which acts as a first referral units in Orissa.

It needs to be remembered that the above figures were average for Orissa in general and there were inter-district and intra-district variations in shortage of staffs. Because it has been observed that the different categories of staffs refuse to work in remote and difficult areas.[45] Therefore apart from the vacancy of various categories of posts it was also the case that even where there were posts that were in-position in pen and paper, in reality these did not function for most part of the year.

ISM and H services in Orissa

Indian System of Medicine and Homeopathy has been sidelined in Orissa as it has occurred in other states of India. The table below gives a picture of, number of undergraduate medical colleges in this stream, number of graduate medical colleges, number of hospitals, number of beds, number of dispensaries, and number of registered medical practitioners under this system.

Table: 3.16 ISM and H services in Orissa

Sl. No.	ISM and H network	Aurveda	Homeopathy	Unani
1	Number of Undergraduate medical colleges	6	6	-
2	Number of Graduate medical colleges	1	1	-
3	Number of hospitals	5	6	-
4	Number of beds	203	175	-
5	Number of dispensaries	519	460	9
6	Number of registered medical practitioners	4133	4885	13

Source: Orissa Vision 2010: A Health Strategy, February 2003, Health and Family Welfare Department, Government of Orissa, Bhubaneswar.

[45] We have discussed about this aspect in the later part of this chapter.

The table shows that under this system Aurveda had 6 undergraduate medical colleges, one graduate medical college, 5 hospitals, 203 beds, 519 dispensaries and 4133 registered medical practitioners. Homeopathy had 6 undergraduate medical colleges, one graduate medical college, 6 hospitals, 175 beds, 460 dispensaries and 4885 practitioners. Unani had only 9 dispensaries and 13 registered medical practitioners. There was no medical college or hospitals or beds under the Unani system in Orissa.

A comparison between Aurveda and Homeopathy shows that both had similar numbers of graduate and under graduate medical colleges. While Aurveda had 5 hospitals, Homeopathy had 6 in total. However the number of beds and dispensaries in Aurveda were more than total number of beds and dispensaries under Unani. On the other hand the number of registered medical practitioners was more in Unani than in Aurveda.

Growth of beds under Indian System of Medicine and Homeopathy, Orissa

Now let us have a look at trends in the hospital beds available in the ISM and H system in Orissa. The table below gives a picture of number of Homeopathic and Ayurvedic Hospitals in the state since 1995-96 till the year 2000-2001.

Table 3.17 Number of beds Under Indian System of Medicine and Homeopathy, Orissa

Year	Homeopathic Hospitals beds	Ayurvedic Hospitals beds
1995-96	125	203
1996-97	125	203
1997-98	125	203
1998-99	125	203
1999-2000	125	203
2000-2001	125	203

Source: Health Statistics of Orissa, 2000-2001, Compiled by State Bureau of Health Intelligence, Directorate of Health Services, Orissa.

It shows that the number of beds in Homeopathic hospitals in 1995-96 was 125 and the total number of beds in Ayurvedic hospitals was 203 in Orissa. The figures have remained same till 2000-2001 without any variation. Therefore the figures suggest that the Homeopathic and the

Ayurvedic hospital beds have remained stagnant since the second half of 1990s.

According to one senior official of the Directorate of Health, Orissa, this system has been sidelined in the health care services structure over the years and these institutions did not come in the purview of ongoing health sector reforms in the state. It needs to be mentioned here that there was no Unani hospital in Orissa; only Unani Dispensaries existed in the state.

Registered ISM and Homeopathic practitioners in Orissa[46]

Now let us have a look at the number of registered ISM and H practitioners in Orissa. These figures also in a way suggest the present condition of ISM and H services in the state. The table below gives a picture of registered practitioners for Indian System of Medicine and Homeopathy in Orissa.

Table 3.18 Registered ISM and H practitioners in Orissa.

Ayurveda	Unani	Siddha	Homeopathy	Total
3810	16	0	4955	8781

Source: Health Statistics of Orissa, 2000-2001, Compiled by State Bureau of Health Intelligence, Directorate of Health Services, Orissa.

The table shows that in the ISM and H systems of health care, the number of practitioners in Homeopathy were 4955 in total, which was the highest, followed by the Ayurvedic practitioners with 3810 in total. The total number of registered practitioners in Unani was only 16 as on 01.01.2003. However there were no registered practitioners for Siddha system of medicine in Orissa. In total there were 8781 ISM and H practitioners in Orissa, which was 162% less than the total number of registered medical graduates in Orissa.

[46] It needs to be mentioned here that the data with regard to number of beds and registered practitioners in Ayurveda and Homeopathy have varied in the two different documents of Orissa government. One was the Orissa Vision Document, 2003 and another was the Health Statistics of Orissa, 2000-20001. One of the reasons could be that the Orissa Vision Document was published two years later than the Health Statistics document and during this period the figures might have changed actually. There was also another possibility of misprinting of these data.

Unserved and underserved areas

Out of 30 districts in Orissa there were many areas which have been facing shortage of manpower, and infrastructure had been almost non-existent at PHCs, PHC (N) s and at sub centre levels in these districts. Unserved and underserved areas have been identified as "Those socio- economically backward areas, which do not have access to health care services from the existing government health infrastructure …In specific terms these areas are: where post of MO, ANM, LHV etc have been vacant for one year; PHC is not equipped with minimal infrastructure, performance on critical RCH indicators is poor."[47]

Now let us have a look at the figures given in the below table.

The table gives a picture of 15 districts of Orissa where blocks had been identified as Unserved or underserved areas. If we make a comparison between these 15 districts, the figures show that Kalahandi had the worst scenario with 13 blocks identified as unserved/underserved and 28 sub centres as unserved and 61 as underserved. The figures show that Baleswar, Cuttack, Keonjhar and Bargarh were better performing districts compared to Nawrabgpur, Nayagarh and Jajpur where maximum number of blocks has been identified as unserved or underserved. In between these two extreme groups of districts were Sambalpur and Angul.

[47] "Underserved and Unserved Areas in 17 Districts of Orissa for RCH Service Delivery Intervention, Documented by NGO Cell, Government of Orissa, Health and Family Welfare department" 2004.

Table: 3.19 Unserved and Underserved areas

Name of the District	Total number of blocks	Total No. of PHC/CHC	No. of block PHC/CHC, UGPHC and PHC (N) Underserved or Unserved	Total number of sub centers	Number of Sub Centers Unserved or underserved
Bargarh	12	PHC-52 CHC-5.	PHC/CHC- 4, PHC (N)-3.	187	26
Balasore	12	PHC-74 CHC- 6	PHC- 5	250	8
Cuttack	14	PHC-62, CHC-4	PHC-3, UGPHC-1, PHC (N)-1	299	14
Keonjhar	13	PHC-47, CHC-6	PHC-3, CHC-6, UPHC-1.	213	19
Boudh	3	PHC-13, CHC-Nil	*	59	21
Khurda	10	PHC-6, CHC-4	6 underserved blocks out of 10	186	*
Puri	11	PHC-44, CHC-4	6 underserved blocks out of 11.	221	*
Jagatsinghpur	8	PHC-18, CHC-2	6 blocks out of 8 as underserved	182	9
Jajpur	10	PHC-59, CHC-5	5 blocks out of 10 as Unserved/underserved.	235	10

Nayagarh	8	PHC-34, CHC- 4	7 block PHC/CHC/UGPHC as Unserved/underserved.	150	21
Sambalpur	9	PHC-35, CHC-5	PHC- 4, CHC -3, UGPHC- 1.	142	17
Mayurbhanj	26	PHC-89, CHC-13	8 blocks identified as Unserved/underserved.	521	12
Nawrangpur	8	PHC-41, CHC-5	6 blocks identified as Unserved/underserved.	222	*
Kalahandi			13 blocks as Unserved/underserved	*	28- Unserved 61- underserved.
Angul	8	PHC- 33, CHC- 3	PHC/PHC (N) and CHC- 8	146	8

Note: The PHC institutions also include PHC (N) in many of the districts. The * mark suggest that data not available. The column 4, which describes about Unserved and Underserved block PHC headquarter institutions. The above table mentions about only 15 districts. The remaining data of three districts were not available in the original document.

Source:"Underserved and Unserved Areas in 17 Districts of Orissa for RCH Service Delivery intervention, Documented by NGO Cell, Government of Orissa, Health and Family Welfare department" 2004.

The data collected for unserved and underserved PHC/CHC/UGPHC/PHC (N) and the sub centres of these 15 districts were difficult for comparison. The first reason was that the format of reporting for unserved/underserved areas had varied among different districts. While some of the districts have mentioned about particular PHC/CHC and sub centres as unserved or underserved areas, others have reported in general terms, like number of blocks unserved. Further these data have been compiled on the basis of reports submitted by the CDMOs and many of the districts seem to be under reporting. For example, figures for Jajpur district show that while 5 out of 10 blocks were unserved or underserved, only 10 sub centres were unserved/underserved out of 235 sub centres in the district! In the same logic the figures for Mayurbhanj, Nayagarh and Jagatsinghpur could be questioned. Another aspect was that if the disaggregated data had been provided for these districts in terms of PHC/CHCs and sub centres, rather than reporting that 'this many number of blocks as unserved', than it would have given a better picture for not only understanding the real situation but it would also have provided basis for concrete action.

Further there were districts like Nawarangpur, Puri and Khurda, where the numbers of unserved/underserved sub centres have not been reported. Similarly in case of Boudh the data for unserved PHC/CHC had not been provided.

In spite of having all these lacunaes in data collection, this was a first of its kind of effort to collect data with regard to unserved/underserved block level institutions in Orissa. These data had been collected to involve NGOs in delivery of RCH services in these unserved/underserved areas by using the existing government health care institutions in these places.[48] This was part of the Mother NGO scheme or the service NGO scheme under the RCH program of government of India.[49] So the question arises as to whether this was an indirect attempt to handing over the block level institutions, where there have been absenteeism among the staffs, to the NGOs?

---

[48] "Underserved and Unserved Areas in 17 Districts of Orissa for RCH Service Delivery Intervention, Documented by NGO Cell, Government of Orissa, Health and Family Welfare department" 2004. The unserved/underserved areas were: where the post of MO, ANM, LHVetc have been vacant for more than a year and the PHC was not equipped with minimal infrastructure and the performance on critical RCH indicators were poor.

[49] Ibid.

Availability of Sub centres, PHCs and CHCs in tribal Orissa

Tribal areas in Orissa mostly come under the category of 'remote and difficult' areas in the state. As the tribals in Orissa constitute about 22% of its population and hence to improve the health status in general, the availability and efficient functioning of health care institutions in these areas become that much significant. While the debate about the institutions available in tribal areas has been in terms of their efficient functioning, it has rarely figured in terms of availability of health care institutions in these areas. Therefore let us have a look at the availability of Sub Centres, PHCs and CHCs in terms of their requirements in tribal areas of Orissa.

Table: 3.20: SCs/PHCs/CHCs in Tribal Orissa

Sub Centers			PHCs			CHCs		
R	P	A	R	P	A	R	P	A
2634	1865	70.80	507	461	90.93	118	60	50.85

Note: R- Required number of Sub Centres, PHCs and CHCs, P-Presence of these institutions, A- Achievement in terms of Percentage to the required numbers.
Source: Health Statistics of Orissa, 2000-2001, Compiled by State Bureau of Health Intelligence, Directorate of Health Services, Orissa.

The table shows that in case of sub centres in tribal Orissa, while the required number was 2634, only 1865 sub centres existed. Similarly in case of PHCs, out of the required 507, 461 of these institutions existed and in case of CHCs out of the required 118 in total only 60 existed.

Therefore while the presence of primary health centres were more than 90 percent of the required numbers, it was in case of the sub centres and community health centres, where these institutions were present in 70.80 percent and 50.85 percent respectively. Therefore in terms of periphery level institutions in tribal Orissa, it was the sub centres and the CHCs, which required urgent attention.

Strengths and weaknesses in the health care services structure[50]

In this section we have discussed about the strengths and weaknesses in the health care services structure in Orissa. While in the earlier sections we have discussed about the trends in health care services over the years, here the actual functioning of this structure has been looked at.

Cadre structure in Orissa

An interview with a senior donor agency official, it came to the front that the health care cadre structure in Orissa was not a pyramidal one. As a result there were very few incentives for promotion to a higher level. The official had said, "There are cases where people in a district after 20-22 years of service have got a promotion and it is a demoralizing case for them". However when this was asked to a senior official in the health directorate the response was, "This is not true. Infact people are not interested to work at the district level."

When the same question was asked to a senior official in the Orissa government he said, "Here norms for cadre promotion in next stage is not done. Earlier they went on increasing class II posts, without creating new class I posts. New institutions like PHCs were created at the block level. This increased class II posts. But proportional promotional posts were not created. Financial constraints have also been there." Therefore while class II posts were created the proportional class I posts were not created. As a

---

[50] It was really surprising that the observations of the Bhore Committee which was made in the 1940s about the then existing health care services in India had so much relevance in the context of health care services structure in Orissa in 2005! For example reflecting on the quality of services, the Committee had observed, "During our tours in the provinces we noticed that in most dispensaries and out-patient departments of hospitals, the time devoted to patients was so short as to make it perfectly obvious that no adequate medical service was given to the people.... In addition medical officers in charge of many dispensaries, have for long periods, been out of touch with modern medical practices without an opportunity to work in a well conducted hospital, such as the better class institutions located at the headquarters of districts.... Other defects include unsatisfactory conditions in regard to the design of, and accommodation in, medical institutions, considerable overcrowding in wards and grave insufficiency of the nursing staff." Opt Cited. In the following sections as we proceed we could see the relevance of this observation, if applied in case of Orissa.

result the incentive for promotion was not there and the few class I posts were filled up by those personnel who had any higher-level connection[51].

Interviews with the medical officers at the Primary Health Center level one fact which came to the front was that, there was hardly any transfer or postings policy for medical officers in the state. Therefore the postings and transfer of the doctors in the state was politically motivated. Hence who was posted in a remote area was sent there for the rest of his or her career. It has led to a situation where in remote and rural areas the post of a medical officer remains vacant for most of the year.

To address this situation the government of Orissa came out with a scheme under which those who aspire for a Post Graduate Degree, they have to go for a mandatory one year posting in remote or rural areas. The idea was that it would help in addressing the shortage of doctors in these areas. However interactions with government officials in the state revealed that this has not happened in reality, although it is being shown as a 'success' in government documents. A senior official in the state said, "While on pen and paper it is a success story, on the ground it has not worked." He cited the example of Koraput district "where two lady doctors were posted. One was married and another was not. They had to travel three kilometers up to a hill by some private vehicle and then they would be reaching their PHC. So what they used to do was that they would be going two days in a week and stay there for two to three hours only. The concerned CDMO had the knowledge but he simply gave them a certificate that they had successfully completed their field responsibility. The situation is not different in other districts, as my interaction with CDMOs has confirmed this."[52]

It was quite surprising that rather than trying to implement a fair posting and transfer policy it was decided to bring in legislation to show that the government was doing some serious work. Another consultant to the Orissa government reflecting on this issue said, "There are vested interests in transfer and posting policy. Infact it has become a lucrative business. For example a doctor posted in the Capital Hospital[53] will try to remain there by paying regularly to the politicians. And it has happened many

[51] This aspect we have covered in different sections of this chapter.

[52] This official was currently on deputation to OHSDP. He was earlier with DFID in Orissa.

[53] Capital Hospital is located at Bhubaneswar.

times that suppose the money has not reached the politician at the end of the month, than the doctor has been transferred the next day!"

Inadequate training

Students in medical colleges are trained for clinical services. Whereas, if a person joins the government medical service than he or she has to look after the preventive aspects more than the curative aspects. However there is a contradiction here, "A doctor in society is recognized for his or her clinical skills and not for preventive aspects. Hence it has been observed that even the CDMOs have their own clinics, where they spend their quality times. Not only that, a CDMO coming from a particular discipline thinks along those lines and as a result the health care structure in the district suffers.[54]

So could we say that creation of two separate cadres would help? "However to create two cadres is not easy. What stage you will create two cadres?[55] In a PHC two cadres are not required. It may be required in a little higher side. A proposal has been given to the government, one for the clinical cadre and another for the Public Health cadre. However the public health cadre is not popular as one does not see any promotion here" said one senior official.

The official further added, "At first promotion, that is at the Junior Class I level, two cadres can be created. Both cadres will have same opportunity for career growth. However every clinician also needs managerial skills." Therefore consultations among the senior health officials of the state were going on with the donor agencies like World Bank and DFID. However emergence of some concrete policy initiative was looking very remote.

Challenges at PHCs, CHCs and sub centers

The challenges at these levels could be divided in terms of the medical officers' challenges and the challenges the paramedics face. First we would look at the medical officers' situation.

---

[54] A senior official in government of Orissa had given this opinion.
[55] One for clinical aspects and another for preventive or Public Health.

The doctor

"Why a doctor being educated by the state, in state's money is reluctant to serve in rural areas? The issues involved here are the availability of doctors in target institutions and the second is the lack of motivation among them. If a doctor is forced in this condition, than he will be physically present but will remain a non-performer. Consultants from abroad might come, but they are not going to the grassroots level to implement the programme,"[56]said one senior official in the state.

The official further said, "Most of our institutions are not manned by doctors,[57] which hampers delivery of quality services to the people. Even if all the facilities are available but provider is absent, than everything is futile. On the other hand there are many institutions where all the staffs are present. But the question is, whether services delivery system is on expected level there. Which is not the case? Here also programme implementation is not at the desired level. Mere physical presence does not improve situation. Doctors trained in medical colleges are tuned for curative services. A doctor is recognized for diagnosis and treatment. But in PHCs and CHCs, curative service is not the priority. There the preventive and promotive service is most important. But the doctor thinks that his responsibility is only for curative services. Hence doctors do other activities[58] as compliance, rather than feeling any involvement. He does not see his role as a public health person."

Continuing with his narrative the official said, "Twenty five to twenty years back doctors were staying in rural areas. In rural areas there was no electricity, not a single graduate in the village[59], no entertainment facilities and a dispensary with three to four staffs. So what motivated doctors at that time? The motto was not money but to serve people. First two-three months used to be very painful. People were illiterate but very affectionate. Even in husband-wife quarrel people used to ask the doctor to intervene. But now a day's people are not going. Why there are so many vacancies…? …Doctors are available. You are posting 300 people as

---

[56] This was an interview with an official of government of Orissa, who was currently on deputation at OHSDP with having 22 years of experience of working at different levels of the health care services.

[57] The official was referring to the fact that doctors remain absent at the periphery level institutions in Orissa.

[58] Here it means preventive and promotive services.

[59] With whom the doctor could at least interact in his or her leisure hours.

assistant surgeons. But how many are joining services and how many have completed one year? Out of 300 only 120 joins and within a year only 40 people are left. What is the demotivating factor? Reason is there is no clear transparent transfer policy. When a person joins say Malkangiri[60], if it is guaranteed that after 2-3 years of service one will be posted in a better place, it would change the situation dramatically. …Difficult areas will always be there. You can not make all the areas cosmopolitan areas." This was a significant observation by this official. For structural constraints like difficult areas would always be there. However the challenge is to create a confidence among the different levels of staffs that the system is sensitive to their difficulties and it is also transparent in terms of implementing laws.

But then the question arises as to how to address this situation? Responding to this query the official said, "There needs to be gradation of institutions in terms of difficult areas, semi-urban, urban and cities. See for example, in flood affected areas people are working in such difficult conditions as it is for a temporary period. It should be made *legal* that if a person serves at least for 2-3 years than he or she would be posted in a better place. Due to the lack of transparent transfer policy, anybody can be posted anywhere and through political connection people can get desired places. Hence there is a need for a sound transfer policy" said the official.

The official further added, "If you are placing a doctor with 15 years of service, having children studying in high school, in remote areas, he will remain absent from the institution. Hence at the joining stage, doctors should be placed at remote areas. This issue of transfer policy has come up many times but it has not materialized. This requires political commitment."

Continuing with his narrative the official said, "When newspapers report about vacancies of doctors in remote areas, politicians jump for quick fixes…. What the working environment does, what the head of the unit does, has very deep impact. Suppose a doctor gets involved in an area, it takes six months time to get fully acquainted with your own staff and people and after six months you are leaving that place![61]Than why should

[60] Malkangiri was one of the most backward districts of Orissa with most of its population being tribal.

[61] The official was referring to mandatory pre-PG rural scheme, where any doctor aspiring to do a PG course had to serve in remote and difficult areas for one year, if they are selected for the course.

one go there in pre-PG training course? People are joining, getting a certificate but they are not doing work. They are posted to show in pen and paper that vacant posts are being filled up.

The earlier strategy was that, a person working in a rural area, who have achieved various targets and the CDMO/SDMO certified that the doctor was a good performer, than a 5-10% weightage was given in PG selection. This was a concrete gain for a doctor. This strategy was changed in last 5-6 years. Almost every year there is new rule for PG selection and hence nobody is sure as to what will happen to the rules next year.... See everybody is concerned about his own career. If it is taken care off and whatever strategy adopted is continued, it will work." Therefore the existing system was quite insensitive to the requirements of various levels of health personnel. Besides, policies were made without going into the root causes of the problem.

Absenteeism among doctors

It was observed during field visit that at the block PHC level all the doctors were absent most of the time. And at the "PHC (N) level the doctor is absent permanently and the pharmacist is taking his or her place."[62] When this researcher had visited three PHC (N) s, in Khurda District and the three PHC (N) s in Sundergarh district the doctor was absent in all the cases. They were either engaged with their clinics or were simply in their home. The pharmacist was found to be in four places and in another two places only the ANMs were present. While visiting one of the block PHCs in Khurda district, the medical officer in charge was found to be absent. And this PHC was nearer to the capital, Bhubaneswar. Hence a question arises if this was the case of a PHC, which was nearer to the state capital, than what about those that were placed in remote areas?

In the remote and difficult areas all the staffs remain absent in most of the days. And as a result the whole region remains out of reach of the government health care services and hence the national programmes were the first casualties in these places. As one medical officer in a PHC said, "The CDMO, as he is also a doctor, hence any negligence by an MO in-charge of non-attendance of doctors at PHC (N) is not acted upon by the CDMO. Hence a non-medico like an IAS should be at the top level of administration in a district".

[62] This was the view of an official in SIHFW, Orissa.

The infrastructure

One of the PHCs of Khurda district, when visited it was found that the medicines for Pancha Byadhi Chikitsa[63] were not there. It was observed that the PHC building was in very bad shape. The medical officer in charge said that in rainy season his quarter gets wet. The room where an X-ray machine was kept had leakage in the roof. "There is no separate operator for the X-ray machine and the government expects the medical officer to operate the machine, which is not possible."[64] It was also observed that the single doctor institutions or PHC (N) s were in very bad shape. In many places these buildings were looking very dirty and broken in some structures.

The paramedics[65]

"In the transfer and postings of paramedics, the political and bureaucratic influences work just like it is there in the case of medical officers,"[66] said one senior official. When asked that if the transfers and postings are made as a law will it restore the morale in the cadre?[67] Responding to this question the official said, "In a democratic framework like ours such legislation won't be passed. In many cases buildings do not exist for sub centers or say an ANM has to travel many villages. In this scenario they take the help of their MLAs,[68] who in turn asks the CDMO to change the posting of that ANM." The official further added, "My twenty three years of experience from being a doctor at a PHC than gradually becoming a CDMO and than joint director at the directorate, what I see is that at every level, there is shortage of manpower and resources in terms of drugs,

---

[63] The five disease programmes for which, medicines were supposed to be available free of cost. A list of diseases was prepared, and out of that five were identified on the basis of incidence, hospital attendance, cost and ease of treatment. These were malaria, leprosy, diarrhoea, acute respiratory infection, and scabies.

[64] This was the view of the medical officer in charge of one of the PHCs' visited.

[65] The paramedics were Pharmacists, Nurses, Laboratory technicians and ANMs etc.

[66] This interview was taken from an official who was working as a consultant in the Sector Reform Cell, which was funded by the European Commission. This official was earlier CDMO of two districts in Orissa with twenty-three years of work experience at different levels of health care services structure in Orissa.

[67] This question was asked with reference to both the transfers and postings for medical officers as well as for the paramedics.

[68] MLA stands for member of legislative council.

equipments. However the challenge is to work with these limited resources."[69]

Elaborating his point further he said, "The purchasing power of rural Orissa is very low compared to say rural Punjab. In terms of fiscal crisis[70] Punjab might be in deeper crisis than Orissa, but for their health care people do not depend on their state government. The per capita expenditure on health in Orissa is Rs16 to Rs17. Untill and unless Orissa becomes a rich state, it won't be able to allocate more resources to the frontline institutions like PHCs and sub centers. The peripheral level institutions are in a crisis." Therefore here the official was giving a different explanation for the lack of a transparent transfers and postings policy for paramedics. The reasons identified were the democratic set up of India and the economic backwardness of Orissa.

Talking about the different reform offices, the health secretariat and the directorate of health services the official said, "We people sit in AC rooms and talk big things but the frontline workers[71] face the real challenges and their condition can be ameliorated when Orissa becomes a rich state." However he cited another issue of concern. He said, "In a year there are three to four changes at the level of directors than it becomes difficult for any continuation of a policy or programme."[72] Therefore along with economic backwardness, there was also the issue of frequent changes at the level of directors, which hampers in implementation of any program and hence it also affects the expected policy outcomes in the long run.

The ANMs

The auxiliary nurse/mid wife works in the sub center and is the link between the Primary health center and the community. Implementation of the national programmes also depends on them apart from looking after the day to day health needs of a community.[73] They also report any outbreak of diseases, encourage pregnant women for safe delivery,

---

[69] He said that for delivery a medical officer might not have equipment.

[70] Fiscal crisis is a situation where the expenditures of a government are more than its revenue, forcing the government to borrow either from domestic or external market and thereby again increasing its burden.

[71] He was referring to Paramedics.

[72] In fact one senior DFID official in Delhi had also cited this as a major problem.

[73] Here community means the group of villages that an ANM is given charge about.

distribute iron and folic acids to the pregnant and lactating mothers, immunize the children and look after the reproductive needs of a community.

However in the field it was found that the situation was entirely different. If one looks at the number of sub centers having building of their own, than from the statistics itself a lot of disturbing things emerges.[74] There were many sub centers, which did not have a building of their own. In these cases an ANM was supposed to take a rented building for which, the money paid was very meager. So what happened was that in pen and paper they stay in a rented building but in reality they do not. "Even where buildings are there the ANMs do not stay there. The reasons are that many of these buildings are at the outskirts of the villages. There are sub centers, which have been built in burial grounds! And some have been built in high up in the hills in hilly districts".[75] Responding on this issue, a senior official of a donor agency in Orissa said, "For sub centre buildings you can not purchase land. Money is sanctioned only for constructing the building, which is done in a government land, which generally is available outside or in the outskirts of a village. Hence most of the sub centres are located in these places. Another reason is that as with the sanction of government money; say in January, the sub center has to be built up by March, so to negotiate with the villagers[76] within this short period is not possible."

The official further added, "Even when the sub centers are inside the village and that village is nearby a town area or say the ANM's husband works in the town or her children study there, then she opts for up and down to the sub center, rather than staying there." But is there any possibility to curb this phenomenon? Responding to this query the official concerned said that he had no clue. Thus what the official was trying to say was that the answers to these structural issues were not so easier. However one medical officer in charge of a PHC said, "If the ANMs are provided with one assistant than it will make the RCH program successful. It is not about increasing the money of the existing ANMs but to increase the personnel to cover all the areas".

---

[74] The Directorate of Health Services, Government of Orissa, publishes the statistics.

[75] This was told by one senior official in the Directorate of Health Services, Government of Orissa.

[76] For providing land within the village.

It was observed that while the PHCs, PHC (N) s' and the sub centers were the frontline organizations for success of any programme; they were the most neglected ones in terms of infrastructure, manpower and resources. Lack of motivation among the staffs was very much visible. The workload was unacceptably high on the sub centers.[77] "The lacunaes are well known to the CDMOs and the higher authorities in the directorate but there is a deep cynicism in the system. The CDMOs want to present a rosy picture and the staffs below the CDMO cooperate with him."[78]

Responding to a query about these structural issues a senior official in the state said, "The Orissa government's view is that there is lack of resources in the state".

CDMO's challenges

A question was asked as to what are the challenges of a Chief District Medical Officer? Responding to this one senior official in the government of Orissa said, "There are acute shortage of manpower, doctors and paramedics. CDMO himself is not motivated. He himself is part of the system. The lack of manpower is problem at every level."

Not only that the CDMOs also face the difficulties of coping with the public health[79] issues. Hence a senior official of a donor agency in Orissa said, "It has been seen that many CDMOs are busy running their clinics, rather than taking interest in the health care of the district, which requires leadership skills and an inclination for public health."

Another official in the Health and Family Welfare department was of the view that, "If a gynecologist is made as CDMO or as director of a department at the health directorate than he is not equipped to handle his new job and at the same time the state looses a specialist which this person could have provided." Therefore this was also a technical issue which needed an urgent attention.

---

[77] One ANM covered four to five villages and in some cases six to eight villages by walking. They were supposed to cover these villages every week.

[78] This was the view of a senior official in the Directorate of Health Services, Government of Orissa.

[79] Here public health has been used as promotive and preventive health care.

This aspect was also mentioned by the CDMOs interviewed in the two districts. They said that they had learned their public health skills by being in the PHCs and CHCs.

The other reasons

Giving an explanation from another aspect a senior health official who had been closely associated with IEC activities in the state said, "Even if health care delivery network is very strong in Orissa, there are areas where health care institutions are not accessible to the people like in tribal, hilly and remote areas. Here other alternative strategies need to be devised."

He further added, "The other big factor is the mismatch between expectations of the public and the availability of services. There should be complementarities between people's expectations and the services available. Electronic media raises expectations. People know much more. To match these expectations a PHC cannot provide all the services that people expect from them. It is a good sign that people expect more. But it has to be judiciously communicated to the people that at least for some services they should pay.[80] These things should be transparent to the people."

The Official further added that, "What services are available in which institutions should be made transparent. This has to be more in case of tribal and hilly areas as here the presence of quacks is more. On the other hand access to information on available services is lacking in certain areas. Hence here the demand is low as the people are ignorant. Here the barrier is physical communication, low economic status, illiteracy or ignorance. Here let the health institutions go to people in the form of mobile health units, like in tribal areas. Certain work on this aspect[81] is now being done by OHSDP. In many instances people are not aware of diseases they are suffering from. People should be informed correctly about what drugs are available and where".

---

[80] This support for private participation even at the PHC level was found to be widespread across the different levels of health care delivery structure in Orissa. In one PHC the medical officer in charge said that if people could spend on drinks (he was referring to the fact that tribals drink regularly) than why they could not spend on their medicines? This element of support for increasing privatisation of health care has been discussed in the chapter V on reform experiences in Orissa.

[81] Like providing Mobile Health Units.

Ensuring quality health care

Besides being the above mentioned factors affecting the quality of health care there were some other aspects which were although not directly involved with the health services sector, still they had an impact on the quality of care. Thus one senior health official in the state said, "Quality of health services can not be ensured unless other aspects like literacy and economic status is not improved. It has to be a multipoint approach to improve health care delivery system. A joint action plan is needed.[82]The planners should understand that there is need for a holistic and not vertical approach.[83]Whatever money comes all the programmes should run simultaneously. Hence there is need for inter-departmental coordination to raise health standards along with literacy and economic status."

Elaborating on this point the official concerned said, "Funds coming to education, agriculture, or industrial sector, all these have a health component. For example if agricultural and industrial workers are not healthy than how will they do their work? In corporate and private sector they take care of health of their officers and staff. But still we[84] have not thought health sector as a productive sector." Therefore there is need for adoption of an inter-sectoral approach to improve health care quality.

Further the different PHCs visited during the fieldwork, it was told that average patient load per day were 100 patients; at the same time all the doctors were not present regularly. This also definitely affected the quality of health care.

Summing up

What were the strengths of health care services in the state? Replying to this question one former senior official said, "In Orissa unlike in many other states[85], everybody uses the government sector, because people who are rich are able to discriminate quality at a better level. Now if tomorrow there are lots of private sector hospitals and everybody goes to the private sector…this has happened in private schools. So the government school

---

[82] The official was referring to inter-sectoral approach to health.

[83] Vertical approach looks after a single programme from top down manner of implementation, with having separate manpower to implement it.

[84] The official was referring to the mindset of the health policy makers and those who take decisions with regard to health in the state.

[85] Where private sector has a presence.

standards are going lower and lower. When I was in Orissa, a person came from Hyderabad and said he had private hospitals and wanted to open one in Bhubaneswar…he came and told me that he went to the Capital Hospital and he said that best specialists were there and the poor had access to them…. If the rich do not go to the government hospital than the standards will fall. The poor don't know standards…the doctors can do anything. The doctors can give them very poor level of care, because there is no awareness and there is no voice. Whereas if both using… the rich and the poor, the standards can be maintained." This was a very important observation. Drawing a parallel with private schools the official concerned said that when the rich and influential sections moved out of the government schools the standards started falling in these institutions. Because the poor were not aware about the standards that need to be maintained nor could they pressurize the institutions hence they won't be able to ensure a minimum standard alone. In case of health services sector in Orissa both the rich and the poor utilize the government institutions because they were the only one those exists. This was one of the strengths of health care services in the state. So if tomorrow private hospitals and private clinics starts coming up then it would affect the quality of care in government institutions.

Conclusion

In this chapter we have given a comparative picture of health care services structure in Orissa viz a viz India. We have seen that the evolution of health services in India initially saw the growth of public sector since independence till early seventies. In the second phase that was during the late seventies to late eighties there were cutbacks in public spending and concessions given to the private sector. The third phase saw the investment by Non Resident Indians in super specialty hospitals in cities like Hyderabad. This was also the period when the government of India liberalized norms for importing costly equipments from abroad. Besides many private players were given land in concessional rates to operate their hospitals on a profitable basis.

Apart from a large section of Indian population being poor, the communicable diseases were the major public health challenges in India at that point of time. The IMR and MMR were very high at the time of Independence. Therefore the Bhore Committee had suggested a three-tier structure of health services with greater emphasis on primary and secondary levels of care. However over the years more funds flowed toward secondary and tertiary levels and this resulted in weak growth of the primary level care. The focus was also more toward the urban areas rather than the rural areas. This might have been due to the emergence of new middle class as a result of green revolution.

In terms of various health indicators, it was observed that India had achieved significant milestones in terms of crude birth rate, crude death rate, IMR and Life expectancy since independence. Similarly in terms of epidemiological shifts, it had eradicated small pox and guinea worm by the year 2000 and had gained significant controls over polio, malaria and leprosy. In terms of infrastructure created there were significant gains in terms of sub centres, PHCs and CHCs created since independence. The total number of public and private beds had increased significantly. In terms manpower doctors and nursing personnel had increased manifolds.

A comparative picture of health indicators of Orissa and India brought to the fore the divides in health status in rural and urban areas as well as between Orissa and India. The trends in health indicators of Orissa since 1980s showed that it had achieved a low growth rate of population despite having half of its population living below the poverty line, the highest infant mortality rate in India and about 85 percent of its people living in rural areas. Close analyses showed that it was not only due to the focus of family planning programs over the years but there were other factors like the burden of disease and resultant death rate, deaths due to natural calamities like floods, droughts and cyclones etc which reduced its growth rate of population. On the other hand, the high rate of IMR, in spite of immunization program running over the years was a puzzle. The reasons cited was that the focus to reduce IMR was only through immunization by all the agencies involved and the other aspects like nutrition, the safe delivery and ante natal check ups were neglected.

In terms of communicable diseases, the figures show that while Orissa could achieve a certain level of control over gastroenteritis since 1980s, malaria and tuberculosis cases actually increased during this period. One of the main factors for this was that the periphery level institutions like PHCs and sub centres had almost become non functional in the state. The analysis of health and manpower ratios showed that there were inadequate staffs in all the categories of personnel in Orissa.

In terms of medical education the state had only three government run medical colleges operating. However there were proposals to create more private medical colleges in coming years. While the allopathic system has grown over the years in terms of number of beds, institutions and manpower, the India System of Medicine has experienced a stagnant growth over the years in Orissa. While total number of sub centres had grown over the years, by the year 2005 more than 57% of the sub centres in the state were functioning without any government building. Therefore these periphery level institutions were really at a crisis.

Among the vacancy positions in various categories of posts, Orissa was facing problems in the category of class II specialists, junior class I and senior class I posts. These were crucial shortages because these personnel were manning the posts at PHCs and CHCs. However the acute shortage was among the category of MPHW (M), followed by MPHS (M) and the radiographers. The shortage in health worker, male and in health supervisors, male had implications for effective functioning of sub centres and their proper supervision and which in turn had implications for successful implementation of various national programs. The vacancy in the post of radiographer had implications for quality care at the PHC level institutions.

The figures for unserved and the underserved areas showed that the health care institutions and manpower were unevenly distributed in different parts of Orissa. In remote and difficult areas, it has been observed that the health care institutions were understaffed due to the absenteeism among the staff members. In the tribal areas the institutions which required immediate attention in Orissa were the CHCs and the sub centres.

In terms of strengths and weaknesses in the health care services structure in the state, it was clear that the cadre structure in Orissa was not properly managed over the years. For example in many cases it used to take 20 years for a person to move from block level to the district level. This was a huge demoralizing factor for the health personnel's. It had also created problems at the level of CDMOs and technical directors at the directorate of health, where the tenures were very short. As a result it was hampering the effective implementation of various health programs in the state. Secondly the staffs were inadequately trained in public health at all levels. While the medical officers had been trained for curative services, their main task at the periphery level institutions like block PHC, which was their first posting, was the preventive aspects. So whatever one learned it happened at the PHC level directly and it was all depending on one's own effort. Hence it has been observed that even the CDMOs with a specialization in a particular area prefer to concentrate on that area only and it was told that most of the CDMOs were giving most of their times in their clinics rather than in the district health care services. Besides in our society a doctor is recognized for curative care. This problem was seen to be pervading even at the senior technical directors level. While the problem has been well identified any concrete policy steps have not been initiated still now.

Similarly the single doctor institutions known as PHC New in Orissa have been functioning without the medical officer in most of the cases. It has been observed that generally the pharmacists were running these institutions. There have been suggestions that as these institutions cater to outdoor patients and hence they do not require medical officers and even a pharmacist was enough to run these institutions. The important thing mentioned was that these institutions should be sending referrals in time. One of the major problems was that the medical officers were refusing to stay in periphery level institutions. The reason was lack of a transparent transfers and postings policy. However rather than addressing this structural problem the state government had initiated schemes like, mandatory pre PG scheme and the training of medical interns with the guidance of CDMOs etc. And because these schemes were not addressing the structural issues, they have literally failed to make any impact on the ground. The major problem identified was that there was lack of political will for bringing in structural changes in the health care services in the state.

The problem of ANMs was more acute. While the male worker existed in pen and paper it was observed during field visit that they hardly visited the field. It was left to be done by the ANMs. It needs to be remembered that the success of the national programs depends upon the success of the ANMs in doing their duties in a satisfactory way. In Orissa in most of the places government buildings were not there. That means these sub centers were not functioning at all because even where government buildings were there the ANMs refused to stay there, because these places were located at the end of the village or were in burial grounds! Compounding the problem was the kind of daily abuses the ANMs had to face in their daily activities in the field from the villagers. This had a very negative impact on the RCH activities. It was also the case that many of the ANMs were hardly aware of the various national programs, which they were supposed to carry out in the field. The training of ANMs was also inadequate. Therefore the problem was multi pronged. During the field visit it was observed that while the officials at various levels understood the problem they felt helplessness about doing anything about it. Further the creation of contractual district cadre for paramedics had not solved the problem of absenteeism of ANMs in remote and difficult areas.

To improve the health status of a population along with improvement in health care services, there was necessity to improve the economic and social status of the people. However our interaction at various levels in the state showed that this inter-sectoral approach to health was missing.

The main strength of the health care services in Orissa was that for in-patient and out patient care both the rich as well as the poor utilized the government services. This has ensured that these institutions function at a certain level of quality care. However as the support for increasing private participation grows in the state among the key actors, like the state government and the donor agencies, it would be really difficult for the poor and the marginalized sections to get an effective and quality health care from government institutions.

CHAPTER FOUR

SAP AND HEALTH SECTOR REFORMS IN ORISSA

Introduction

India opted for the liberalisation of its economy in 1991. This was due to the balance of payments crisis that the country faced at that time. With the liberalisation process in the economy the role of market was given a greater share and along with this the role of Indian state also changed. The concept of welfare state changed to the state having more of a regulatory role while creating an atmosphere for greater competition among the private players. This larger trend in the economy was also reflected in the social sector and within it the health sector has also been influenced by this process.

The involvement of the World Bank in the health sector began with population and nutrition programs during the late seventies and early eighties. It was with the Structural Adjustment Programmes or SAPs in Africa and Latin America, the World Bank and IMF moved into policy issues concerning health financing, which advocated state withdrawal from social sector. This approach was described as their agenda for reform of the health and allied sectors. The privatization policies in health were to increase the role of market in curative services, reduce public investments in health, introducing cost recovery mechanisms in public institutions through user fees and community financing. The emergence of World Bank as a lead financier of health care also promoted concept of a unified model of development.

In this chapter we have discussed in general about the role of World Bank in the health sector of India, in terms of its involvement through population and nutrition programs and the disease control programs in the early 1990s and with a particular emphasis on the State Health Systems Development Projects in the late 1990s. Before discussing in detail about the Orissa Health Systems Development Project, an overall picture of ongoing donor agency led various health projects in Orissa have also been discussed. Broadly the SHSDPs and the OHSDP have been contextualised within the framework of 'fiscal crisis' debates. The other areas of involvement by the Bank like public-private partnerships, introduction of user fees, new ways of financing health care in terms of health insurance, training of Indigenous Service providers, etc. have also been discussed.

SAP and the disease control programs in India

Due to adoption of Structural Adjustment Program or SAP there was a huge cutback in public expenditure during the early nineties in the health services sector. This resulted in fall of central grant for disease control programmes. The poorer states, which depended more on central outlays, suffered the most. Some of these cutbacks were restored during 1992-93 through World Bank loans for specific disease control programmes. This restoration of cutbacks for communicable diseases was done to offset outbreak of several epidemics resulting in a large number of deaths. The deaths due to plague epidemic in Surat and malaria in western Rajasthan in 1994 were attributed to two reasons, one was the cutbacks for communicable diseases in early nineties and the second reason was declining standards of public health in general.[1]

The central grant for disease control programmes fell from 41 percent in 1984-85 to 29 percent in 1988-89 and further down to 18.5 percent in 1992-93. The poorer states suffered the most as they were much more dependent on central outlays. Some of the cutbacks were restored through World Bank loans during 1992-93 on specific disease control programs. Out of this, 34 per cent increase was attributable for AIDS control and a marginal increase for TB and blindness control programs. There was a marginal increase for malaria during 1993-94 but spending for other communicable diseases registered a decline. Some of these cutbacks were restored after a large number of deaths occurred due to outbreak of communicable diseases.

[1] See Qadeer et.al, 1994, as cited in Baru 2001.

Restructuring of state level health care

The state health systems project intended to strengthen the state health systems by making them more efficient and cost effective.[2] In order to improve quality, efficiency and effectiveness of public hospitals it proposed for:

"- Cutback of secondary and tertiary spending and channel it into effective interventions at the primary level;
- Contract out ancillary services in public hospitals to private contractors.
- Involve private providers in National communicable disease programs.
- Institute user charges in all public hospitals.
- Encourage private sector growth at secondary and tertiary levels by instituting regulations; and
- Initiate decentralization measures.[3]"

Therefore what these new measures suggested was that the limited resources in the public sector should be used judiciously and hence it advocated for more investment in the primary level care by the state and opening more space for the private sector in the secondary and tertiary levels of care.

The World Bank led reform of the public sector was initiated in 1995 in Punjab, West Bengal, Karnataka and Andhra Pradesh, which opted for state sector adjustment loans. Both the India country Document 1991 and World Development Report 1993 had articulated the need to limit the role of public sector and to encourage the private provisioning of medical care.[4] They argued for cutback in secondary and tertiary levels of care, which could be channeled into the primary level care. The state health systems project was based on this understanding.

While ten state governments had submitted project proposals for the SHSDPs, West Bengal, Karnataka, Andhra Pradesh and Punjab were chosen on the ground that "they capture the heterogeneity of this country in terms of epidemiological profiles, levels of economic development, health services development, and political structures."[5]

---

[2] World Development Report 1997.
[3] Ibid P-223.
[4] See Baru 2001.
[5] Interviews with a senior official of the World Bank, New Delhi.

The State Health Systems Development Projects

Now let us look at the state health systems development projects, which were primarily intended to strengthen the secondary levels of health care in various states.

A brief history

Describing the brief history about the State Health Systems Development Projects a senior official of the World Bank said, "First came Andhra Project, which was State Health Systems Project-I. Then came Karnataka, Punjab and West Bengal, which was known as State Health Systems Project-II. This was a single project. After that came Orissa, which will end by march next year and then Maharastra, which will close in August this year, than UP and Uttaranchal, than Rajasthan and Tamilnadu, which has just begun." Therefore projects in six states were nearer to completion and in another four states it had just begun. So was there any similarity among these projects? To this the official said, "All these projects were similar in nature. But the new ones, Rajasthan and Tamilnadu are different from old projects."

Replying to a question about how many SHSDP projects have been completed and how many were ongoing the official said, "At present four projects have finished. Ongoing projects are Orissa, Maharastra, UP, Uttaranchal, Rajasthan and Tamilnadu."[6] Thus the four projects finished were in Andhra Pradesh, Karnataka, Punjab and West Bengal.

Rationale of SHSDPs[7]

When asked about the rational of SHSDP, the official said, "In the early 1990s, before the Andhra Project had started, the World Bank was looking at what are the areas that the Bank should look at. It had prepared a report on the basis of its earlier activities. Before that historically the World Bank had been funding mainly population programmes like family planning and family welfare. We did what we call India Population programmes, under this there were nine different projects. Then we supported the nutrition

[6] Thus in six states the State Health Systems Project was going on at that time.

[7] State Health Systems Development Projects. Here we have described about the World Bank's involvement in earlier health projects in India in brief and hence a separate section for it has not been added in this chapter.

programme, the ICDS[8] programme of the country". Therefore at the initial phases the World Bank was involved with population and nutrition projects in India.

"Besides that after this report was produced, we said that we would support individual states to develop and upgrade their health systems across the state. So it was a kind of reform from the states' perspective but it was looking at state health systems development and Andhra[9] was the first one. And based on the discussion and analysis with the states it was found out that the primary level care had relatively good resources from the national programmes, from the Family Planning programme and the disease control programmes. Tertiary level care was supported by the individual states because it is important; secondary level care was not receiving enough resources and enough attention, even the hospitals those were there, over time nobody had given them maintenance budget. So, over time they had deteriorated. So that was the need of that state at that time," said the official. Hence after the analysis of the then existing situation in different states it was concluded that the primary and tertiary levels of care were funded well but the secondary level of care was neglected and so it was decided that an intervention was required at this level.

Continuing with her narrative the official said, "So one of the things we did in these states was upgrading those secondary level facilities or the *first referral level facilities*, looking at what is it or what is the kind of services a district hospital should provide… So rationalizing *what kind of services* a CHC should provide or what kind of services a sub district or area hospital[10] should provide and what kind of services a district hospital should provide. Then discussing with states that to providing such kind of services *what kind of manpower* it is important to place there. Then looking at *what kind of equipments* would be required and wherever there were gaps say in equipments to be funded then we also set up systems for equipment maintenance, equipment repairs, those kind of thing were never there." Therefore three things were focused at the secondary levels of care. They were rationalizing the kind of services a secondary level institution should provide; the required manpower for providing these services and the third was to make available the required equipments in these institutions.

---

[8] Integrated Child Development Programme.
[9] Here Andhra means Andhra Pradesh.
[10] Area hospitals were generally 30-bedded hospitals.

"So across the states what we did was to support the *health care waste management* because while these projects were going on the Supreme Court ruling came in the form of bio medical rules. Before that it was not existed. Than we started supporting *Health Management Information Systems* or HMIS *mainly hospital based* but computerization, looking at the data, validity of the data and finally looking at how the data collected at the hospital level could be used for management purposes," said the official. Another two aspects covered were health care waste management and supporting HMIS for utilisation of data generated at the hospital level.

However the hospital data was also used for other purposes. Elaborating about different aspects focused by SHSDPs in different states the official said, "We also went beyond that in some of the states where using the data there was grading of hospitals. So there was a kind of performance grading of hospitals, which finally led to a part of quality improvement or quality assurance. That we did across states. Than we looked at entire human resources issues in the states. As resources are a constraint, what kinds of resources are required like training of doctors, nurses and technicians etc? Then we looked at the services norms, so rationally what should be the referral system? A person should be referred from where? Where should a service be available? How is the referral follow up and referral loop completed? Then equipments, maintenance and repair and the whole issue of quality assurance came up.

At the same time we had dialogue with the states about increasing the total resources for the health sector,[11] from total budget and also relative to that the total amount that goes to the primary and secondary levels relative to the tertiary levels… that we have not had too much success in too many places, because all the states themselves went through financial crunch because of the fifth pay commission. So, that…[12] we could not push. But that much we could bring to their knowledge… But what we did look at was that they[13] in some ways maintain the drug budget; maintain the maintenance budget… issues like that."

---

[11] This was about states themselves increasing their budgetary allocation for health sector.

[12] Here the official was referring to states incapacity to increase overall budgetary allocation for health sector.

[13] Here it refers to states.

On defining the secondary level care

But how does the Bank define the secondary level care? To this the official responded, "It goes from the CHC[14] usually till the district hospital. And there is a wide range between them because different states have different nomenclatures. So it usually ranges from 30 bedded to 400 bedded institutions."

Selection criteria of states for SHSDPs

What were the selection criteria of states for State Health Systems development Project? To this question the official said, "Selection *criteria has changed over time*. When the project begun the selection criteria was, *which states were really interested and which states were committed to some level of health sector reforms* and they were asked to send proposals. Because the Bank[15]funds, only when a proposal comes either from a state or from the central ministry and then it is forwarded through the department of economic affairs to the Bank and then the Bank reviews it. Our criteria now, in recent times has changed because now we are looking at…. because we did two years back a study which looked at Millennium Development Goals and what it will take India to achieve the Millennium Development Goals and that study is basically showing that there are certain states and even in certain states there are certain districts which are lagging behind and if those states do not achieve Millennium Development Goals, India itself may not be able to achieve Millennium Development Goals. So our focus is on working with those states on a long-term basis like Orissa, Rajasthan, UP… we have not worked in Madhya Pradesh so far but MP[16], Bihar that is our focus." Therefore the selection criteria for states eligible of SHSDP has changed from the states own interest and their commitment to some level of health sector reforms to the assessment of different states by the World Bank about their capacity to achieve Millennium Development Goals. It needs to be mentioned here that after the Millennium Development Goals were agreed upon by most of the countries at United Nations in the year 2000, almost all the donor agencies have shifted their priorities to achievement of these goals in different countries.

---

[14] Which was the first referral unit.
[15] Here the Bank means the World Bank.
[16] MP refers to Madhya Pradesh.

The definition of health sector reforms[17] by the World Bank

But the question arises as to how the Bank defined the HSR?[18] To this the official said, "It was defined, one- in terms of commitment of increasing resources for health sector per say; increasing resources for the primary and secondary level care. Their[19] willingness to look at the whole issue of human resources, how the postings are done? What are the criteria? Is there transparency in that? ...Then there is whole issue of user fees, cost recovery, but exemption of the poor to these facilities. To ensure that the poor are exempted form the services, to ensure that the poor receive all these services. Because studies have shown that in spite of everything, in spite of government services supposed to be completely free, the lowest quintile or the poorest quintiles do not access these services...are not able to access these services. So it was these kinds of issues that at that time we were talking about... and basically a commitment from the states to want to reform, the need for it; for them to justify it and write a proposal for it." Hence from the World Bank's point of view the health sector reforms involved, use of resources judiciously apart from increasing them where required and the state's willingness to remove structural constraints to achieve better health results. The official was of the view that for the World Bank to make an intervention, the states' themselves should feel the need for such kind of changes in the health services sector.

Why the three states[20] were taken as a single project

Coming back to the rational of SHSDP, it was asked as to why the three states of Karnataka, West Bengal and Punjab were chosen initially? Replying to this question the official said, "Because at that time all three states had come up with their proposals. We had just started with our experience of Andhra Pradesh. We thought we learnt a lot from our experience of Andhra Pradesh. All these three states were committed to it and had good proposals and so we went for it." And why was Andhra chosen earlier? To this the official said, "Because it was ready at that time...the government had shown commitment."

---

[17] Here the viewpoint of the World Bank official has been provided about the World Bank's understanding about the concept of 'health sector reforms' because the World Bank considered the SHSDPs as part of health sector reforms.
[18] HSR stands for Health Sector Reforms.
[19] Here it refers to the states.
[20] Karnataka, Punjab and West Bengal.

Reference to Mexico and Vietnam

It was observed that the World Bank had taken the experiences of Mexico and Vietnam in its analysis of the reform experiences in the four states.[21] Therefore a question arises as to why these two countries were specifically chosen for evaluation of SHSDPs in India? Responding to this question the official said, "There was no specific reason. It was just that we wanted to share.... the states had been telling us; government of India had been telling us that they would like international experience. Our colleagues in these countries had experiences and they were forthcoming. They were willing to share it with us and so we thought that it would be useful to share what they had done." So, what were the positive outcomes of reform initiatives in these two countries? "They were basically looking at ways of *community health insurance or exemptions...* so that did relate to what we are doing just right now in this country. But that just gave options. Because one of the things we were looking at is how to ensure the poor from going into debt... from accessing health care services," said the official. Therefore the reference to these two countries was based on the availability of expertise on community health insurance and about exemption of the poor for paying the premiums for these insurance schemes.

"So those are the different kinds of options tried like using *health voucher*[22], health insurance...so we just brought that experience to share with the government here. Health insurance in India is still at a rudimentary stage. So just to tell them what is happening at other places and share it," the official said. The sharing of the experiences of Vietnam and Mexico was significant because this has the potential to create health insurance schemes in India on a large scale, either by the states or by the Indian union. Because more the Indian state withdraws from the financing aspect of health care[23], the more it would look for alternative strategies of financing and one of them could be introduction of insurance schemes for different sections of the population.

---

[21] These four states were, Andhra Pradesh, Karnataka, Punjab and West Bengal.

[22] A piece of paper that may be exchanged for particular kinds of health services.

[23] This has been one of the major arguments of health sector reforms that the state should gradually reduce its role from financing of health care in general by selectively focusing on certain areas of the health sector.

Positive outcomes of reform initiatives

When asked about the positive outcomes of the reform initiatives in the four states where the State Health Systems Projects have been completed, the official said, " One, they did find was that the dialogue among higher state level authorities, in the importance of health resources even if they had not been able to ensure it. They all found that what we had done for HMIS,[24] for health care waste management, for quality assurance, for referral, training of manpower and upgradation of facilities... it's a result of which they have found marked increase in in-patient attendance, out patient attendance, lab investigations, radiological investigation and access to poor and women at these facilities...their data shows that." Thus the initiation of health reforms in these four states increased dialogue among inter-departmental higher state level authorities. This helped in understanding the issues in a better way. According to the official the reforms also helped in improvement of health care facilities, which was reflected in increasing utilisation of services in in-patient and out patient departments. Besides, the access to poor and women had also increased.

However it needs to be mentioned here that while assessing the reforms in health sector, caution should be adopted in terms of what have been the achievements compared to different targets. As the Orissa experience, which we have discussed in the later parts of this chapter, shows that the expected outcomes have not been achieved. The question of exemption of the poor from user fees was very much doubted by even the senior health officials in the state. While the institutions might have been built up it was very difficult to say that these were being accessed by the poor for the simple reason that the institutions might be inaccessible through roads or communication facilities from distant areas or people may not be aware at all about the existence of these institutions.

Health Management Information Systems or HMIS

But what was HMIS? "Because these earlier projects[25] focused on hospitals, mainly secondary levels...so we looked at hospital data, hospital activity data, in-patient, out patient, individual departments output, patient satisfaction, all those. And it was routinely reported but not in a systematic way, so we tried to help them systematize it much more, to computerize it,

---

[24] Health Management Information Systems.

[25] The projects in the four states of Andhra Pradesh, Karnataka, Punjab and West Bengal.

to have actually reports going to managerial level for them to look at and then see what happens to it. So you actually had in West Bengal and Punjab people down from the health minister downwards…these reports are produced every month…going down for these reports in visits and saying ok these are your problems. Why is it? Why you are not performing in surgeries or in this particular area? Are there some genuine problems or what is it because of it…sometimes there were some genuine problems… sometimes equipments not working. Then who repairs the equipment? What is the equipment downtime?[26] So it was all those issues, which earlier were not being asked because data were not being looked at. So we got into the system, looking at data, analyzing it and using it for management purposes. And this I think is one of the biggest contributions of the project." Therefore what the Health Management Information System did was to strengthen the already existing hospital data for better feedback and strengthening the services in these hospitals.

"We tried to build on what was in different states…drug management systems are different in different states…very very different. But what we did support was to look at it regularly, to ask questions when they looked at the data and issues like that" said the official.

But then the question arises as to whether there was any link between management of warehouses for drugs and the Health Management Information Systems? Responding to this the official said, "The data management for drugs through ware housing and the HMIS, they are linked in some states but not all. But HMIS is basically hospital based. So it would look at drug availability but it would not link up to what was happening at the drug warehouse. In Orissa, basically the drug warehouses were supported by DFID and few of our earlier projects. So that link is not there very strong. In Orissa, HMIS has not been successful for many reasons, though they are also now collecting some manual data. All the facilities[27] are reporting on manual data. The computerization part we have not been able to do because of some technical reasons."

---

[26] That is how long the equipment is supposed to function.

[27] The 157 secondary level institutions supported by World Bank as part of Orissa Health Systems Development Project.

Public private partnerships

Introduction of the concept of public private partnerships have been one of the elements of reform formulated by the World Bank. There have been discussions about public-private partnership by the Bank. So what were its different elements? Replying to this question the official said, "The World Bank definitely supports it. When we begun eight or nine years back, in all these projects we talked about public-private partnership…the whole attitude of government was resistance because the interpretation of the word public-private partnership was very threatening…that we are asking them to privatize the public hospitals. But that was not the case. The whole essence of public-private partnership came into because lot of data showed that 70 to 80 percent of services are still provided by the private sector, especially ambulatory care, in-patient care is about 50 percent. And the poor in spite of being poor are not able to access public facilities but go to private facilities of different qualities. *And the private sector here means, right from the unqualified person to the highly super specialized hospital.* So, it's the whole thing. So we were encouraging individual sate governments to look at how they could best utilize the resources in the private sector to their benefit. And the first thing that we begun with…because that was also new to everybody…*private partnership for non-clinical services.* So they[28] began with contracting with the private sector for cleaning of hospitals, for diet, for laundry, for security and there they found extremely positive results. They found that hospitals once contracted out for cleaning services was much cleaner than when it was not. But they could not get rid of class IV, so some of the states innovatively trained class IV for other things. So, their motivation level also increased." Therefore here the official rightly mentioned that by public private partnerships it has been assumed in India, privatizing the public hospitals. So what the official was mentioning was that in case of India already the presence of private sector was large enough and hence there was need for involving the private sector for better achievement of health results like many public hospitals have given responsibility to private parties in the cleaning aspect. However there was another dimension to it. The talk of public private partnership also has included the terms like handing over PHCs to NGOs as it was observed in case of Orissa. And when one looks at these initiatives an impression was generated that private sector was inherently seen as more efficient than the public sector in health care provisioning.

[28] Various states adopting SHSDPs.

Continuing with her narrative the official said, "But the big lesson that we have learnt is that *governments are still not entirely proficient in how to write contracts with the private sector or the NGO sector.* So that is something we have learnt and in our newer projects we are trying to bring expertise for that…how actually you write a contract so that you actually ensure that what you want from the private sector or from the NGO you get it…define the contract in those terms. That is still one part where lot of capacity building is required. So we began with that and told them… ok look at different options. …In remote areas public sector is just not working, can you collaborate with the NGO or the private sector and that is what happened at West Bengal. In West Bengal, in Sunderban areas, which is very remote, where you can go by launches, there we began by collaboration with one NGO and asked that NGO to provide services like out patient, in-patient and finally they found it successful and today they have contracted five NGOs and now they are doing it with their own money because the project is finished. So they are continuing that because they have found that kind of collaboration very useful. So *West Bengal is one of our best examples of NGO collaboration to provide services in remote areas.* Similarly on a smaller scale basis we are encouraging them to look at collaboration with the NGO and the private sector to provide even the clinical services." So here what the interviewee was saying was that in case of West Bengal the handing over of PHCs to NGOs in remote areas of Sunderban have succeeded but when we look at the Orissa experience the same experiment failed. Hence it was important to know that uniform models of private sector participation were not possible in different places.

It needs to be mentioned here that by private sector the official was also including the supposedly non-profit making sectors like NGOs. However the term private sector is widely used as a profit making sector. Hence a question was asked as to whether the official was making a distinction between NGO and the Private sector? Replying to this question the official said, " Distinction in the sense that they are all in the non government sector…distinction in the sense that initially the government to work with the NGO sector and than gradually move on to the private sector. The biggest constraint that is there in working with the private sector is the *lack of regulation.* We don't have regulation. What we would be finally looking at if services were not available…if we were looking at health insurance at 10 facilities, in an area both public and private are accredited and people can go to anybody with say health vouchers. But that is still...we don't even have regulation for the public facilities. Then regulating the private sector and ensuring quality services...because until and unless that is done... The whole definition of private sector is wide. Like in Orissa, we are trying to work with the *informal service providers*, what they call quacks or whatever and trying just to increase their skills a little bit... not giving the medicines but just that the lives are saved. So that if they know the early signs of obstetric emergency or a neo natal emergency or falciparum malaria, they can refer the patient first. And our initial data is showing that referrals from them have improved. But we still have to look at it more." Therefore the official was mentioning about how this large private sector was unregulated and hence the quality of service it provided was very difficult to access. One important observation was that initially the NGOs were being involved and at later stages the private for profit sector would be involved for say insurance schemes, where people could go to these identified places with their health vouchers. Similarly the case of Orissa was mentioned to say that the indigenous practitioners were present in large numbers in the state and they also provide health care to people living in remote and hilly areas and hence rather than putting a ban on them, an attempt has been made in some districts to use them for referrals in cases of complicated pregnancy and malaria. It needs to be mentioned here that this approach toward indigenous practitioners was being widely accepted among the health officials at different levels of health care services in Orissa as well as among the other donor agencies.[29]

The negligence of primary level care

Thus in the SHSDP projects the Bank's focus had been on the secondary level care assuming that once these institutions were well equipped with manpower, medicines and equipments people would use the services available. But "to go to the primary level care people should have knowledge that such facilities do exist and they must have easier transportation facilities"[30] This has been the lacunae of the projects of SHSDPs. They just build up the institutions without looking into the aspects of structural constraints the people might face to use them.[31]

---

[29] This observation was made from interaction with officials at different levels during the field visit to Orissa.

[30] This was the view of another senior official of the World Bank.

[31] See the Proceedings of workshop on India's Health System: Role of Health Sector Reforms, 2003. Bureau of Planning, Directorate General of Health Services, Ministry of Health and Family Welfare, Government of India, New Delhi (in

Therefore a question arises as to why not the Bank's focus was on the primary level care? "Primary level support is there. We support the entire Reproductive and Child Health Programme at the national level…full support we are giving. Our second RCH project is going to the board. Than we support the nutrition programme. That is again at the primary level. Then we support TB, HIV/AIDS and Malaria. So these are separate programmes where we work with the Centre and all that basically go to the primary level because those programmes are implemented at the primary level. *But now in our newer states*[32] *we are also looking at supporting the primary level.* Looking at the gaps and whichever gaps are not being filled even looking at that. That's why when we have discussion with a state, we say that you must ensure that you maintain or increase both the primary plus secondary as compared to the tertiary level budgets b*ecause if we do not look at the primary level the millennium development goals will not be achieved"* said the official. Therefore here an acknowledgement was made that while the Bank has been funding projects like RCH and nutrition where the money directly goes to the primary level care, still the state health systems projects should have taken into account the accessibility of people to these primary institutions so that referrals from here could be sent to the secondary level institutions. Because as we have discussed earlier in this chapter that now achieving the targets of Millennium Development Goals have been the priority of donor agencies like World Bank and without improving the facilities and accessibility to primary level care these targets won't be achieved.

What the SHSDPs Lack

The projects in the four states have come to an end. So from the experiences of these four states what were the areas that you found, where if interventions were made than the output of the project would have been better? Replying to this question the official said, "One, we need is much *more focus on health financing*. How do we ensure that adequate… the state is committed to health and Millennium Development Goals and that adequate resources are provided for it. Then a big big issue is *human resources in health care sector.* Sending doctors and other para medical staff to remote areas from the public sector is difficult…in some places almost impossible and that is where positive way of looking at the private

---

collaboration with WHO). Neither the Orissa Vision Document 2010 mentions about OHSDP as a reform initiative.

[32] Rajasthan and Tamilnadu.

sector, the NGO sector comes in … thus broadening the scope. Then *actually measuring that whatever you are doing, you are increasing access of the poor and utilisation by the poor of health services*, so that actually the full focus of whatever the state does should be improving health outcomes for the poor and the disadvantaged. That focus should be there much more." So the interviewee was of the view that given a chance the SHSDPs would have liked to increase the spending of resources in health care for better achievement of results and in remote areas where it has been difficult to retain the manpower from the public sector and the involvement of NGOs and the private sector should be thought out.

However as the field visit to Orissa show that the main problem why medical officers refused to stay in remote and difficult areas was because of lack of a transparent transfer and postings policy. Hence in states like Orissa where the public sector was the dominant provider of health services and where the presence of private sector was very week it was important to make transfers and postings transparent, so that the remote posts were filled up. And equally important was to understand the fact that in these circumstances if rather than addressing these structural issues a case was being made for involvement of the NGOs or private sector, it won't address the issue[33].

Health financing

As the official concerned mentioned about the need for increasing financing for the health care services, so it was asked as to what could be the different ways of health financing? To this the official said, "The state is there, the government budget is there. So what we need to say is one- if they *free up the subsidies from agriculture and power*, only then they can invest in health and education. So looking at that and having a dialogue at higher level[34] and then looking at other health financing options like health

---

[33] We have discussed about this aspect in detail in chapter III.

[34] At the Central government level. In fact this was an ongoing process for the World Bank. In case of Orissa, a senior official of the World Bank said that with the Bank's suggestion the government of Orissa has put a ban on new recruitment of new staffs in the education and health care services. These would have serious consequences for the health and education of millions of Indians in the coming decades. Now the debate in the economic sector was about reducing subsidies from the agriculture and power sector. This has been a national debate in India and various states and the central government were toying with the idea of reducing

insurance and risk pooling at the community level. So that the poor at least do not go into debt because of …when they need health care and that is something, which we are still looking at. We are also learning. That is why we brought international experience. But it is a gradual process. Even politically to convince governments it is a very sensitive issue." Here the official was giving the viewpoint of the World Bank about the different ways of financing health care by the state when there were limited resourses at its disposal. The official further added that the idea of common health insurance and risk pooling should be explored in Indian context to generate more resources. So it was being argued that if subsidies could be freed up from the agriculture and power sector than additional money could be generated. However these were very sensitive as well as debatable issues for even the European countries were refusing to reduce subsidies in agriculture in WTO negotiations to keep their advantages in agricultural exports. And while in Europe less than 10 percent of people depend on agriculture for their livelihood, in case of India it was nearer to 70 percent of its population and in states like Orissa 85 percent of its total population depend on agriculture as their main source of livelihood. About the question of reducing subsidies from agriculture, USA and Europe were providing their farmers with billions of dollars in subsidies and which has depressed the international prices of agricultural products and harming the poorer countries more. Therefore the arguments for reducing subsidies in agriculture to generate more resources reflect two things, either one was insensitive to the Indian context or one was just trying to implement a uniform model to generate new sources of financing.

Question of fiscal crisis

Fiscal crisis, which puts a constraint on the state's capacity to finance health care and in a federal set up like India the nature of financial relations between the Center and the states have a larger role to play. So if somebody prescribes the state to amend their financing, they have very few leverages. To this concern the official said, "True, there are few leverages. In fact in several states we have done what we call mid-term plans for financing or MPFPs. What has come out is 80 percent of government spending is not flexible because it is for salaries. So the flexibility that you have is about 20 percent. At that flexibility is also

---

subsidies in these two sectors. These initiatives have clear indications that World Ban was playing a significant role in shaping policy decisions in India.

there, but what happens is the finance department has to give that flexibility to individual departments. And what they find difficult is that they say if we give it to the health department then we can't give it to only one department. We have to give that kind of flexibility to all departments and that's where it runs into troubles. And *politically they are very sensitive issues, like you cannot say that ok in that remote area the government PHC will never work. So, let us close it down and transfer those resources to something else. Now, that is a very sensitive area. But if those kinds of decisions are taken and they are beginning to be taken* …even the government is taking those bold decisions and say ok that area we are leaving for the NGOs[35] to do. They are doing a good job let them do it. And our whole thing is to ensure that the poor get services[36], which sector they get it from we will not worry about that, but we will ensure quality. We will ensure regulation…all that. *So the government has to change its role from actual provision to actually looking at more broader issues of policy, regulation, accreditation…those kinds of things.*" Here the interviewee was mentioning about the difficulties the states face in terms of financing for health care. The official was of the view that only 20 percent of a government's spending has flexibility, as the rest 80 percent was given in terms of salaries. Besides, there were structural constraints like working in difficult areas and hence here it was proposed that the remote PHCs could be handed over to the NGOs. Significantly this line of argument was also been forwarded by some of the government health officials in Orissa. However as we have discussed earlier the solution was not that easy. The suggestion that the government should move from provisioning to look at broader issues of policymaking, regulation of the both private and the public sector health care and accreditation of institutions was a significant observation. However in a state like Orissa where the presence of private sector[37] was very small; how could one imagine involving them in remote and difficult areas? On

---

[35] In a state like Orissa NGOs were nearly absent and few of those which existed lack in expertise and resources. After the 1999 super cyclone, lot of NGOs had sprung up and they were asked to get involved with relief and rehabilitation activities by the state government. But there were allegations of misuse and mismanagement of funds and as a result the NGOs were seen with suspicion by the state. In this scenario the talk of giving responsibility to NGOs to the remote and difficult areas means that one was out of touch with reality.

[36] This was like paying lip service to the poor.

[37] We have discussed about the presence of private sector in various states, including Orissa in Chapter VII.

the other hand this line of argument suggests a unified approach of the World Bank.

Has off late effort been made from the side of the Bank to look at the constraints the states face in terms of fiscal crisis to raise their health care expenditure? To this question the official said, "We are looking at it. That's why we have changed our perspective. That's why our newer projects both Rajasthan and Tamilnadu look different a little bit and a new project, which will come for Karnataka, will look very different. Because that is a kind of dialogue we are having. But it's a gradual process." However what was that changed perspective, was not elaborated further.

In case of Orissa, there was Orissa Economic Review Package, which had hardly any linkages with the Orissa Health Systems Development Project. Replying to this observation the official said, "We are trying to. Because in the next phase in Orissa we are trying to really link up with what DFID is doing, what the economic people[38] will be doing and what the health[39] will do and trying to ensure that they have a close link up between them. Because, those are all the lessons that we have learnt." Here the official was mentioning about the initiatives by the World Bank to be taken in the next phase of the OHSDP in Orissa. So there would be interlinkages with PSPU or Policy Planning and Strategic Unit being funded by DFID, which would look at the larger issues of health policies in Orissa. Thus it would work as a think tank. Similarly the loans for OHSDP would be attached with the loans by the state under Orissa Economic Review Package. However here a question arises that the effort to link funding for the second phase of the OHSDP with larger loans by the state from the Bank, would it really be helpful for the health care delivery system in the state? Would it lead to a unified model of health care delivery system? If the World Bank was looking forward to put pressure on the state government through the PSPU, than would it not be equivalent to interfering in the policy making process in the state?

In the first phase of OHSDP, institutions have been built up and people have been manned in these institutions. During the field visit it was observed that the state government was not increasing its share of expenditure each year and hence most likely it would become essential for the state to depend on the World Bank for sustainability of these

[38] Here it refers to Orissa Economic Review Package.
[39] Health refers to OHSDP.

structures. In this scenario the Bank was planning to invest in the second phase of this project. Therefore the question arises as to what kind of control the state government would have on these institutions in future? So could it be said that in the long run these secondary level institutions would be handed over to the private sector because, already user charges have been introduced in all these 157 OHSDP institutions.

Donor agency supported health projects in Orissa

Before we discuss about different aspects of OHSDP, let us have a look at the various donor agency supported health projects in Orissa, which were going on during our field visit. The table below gives a picture of donor agency supported various health projects in Orissa. It gives the list of donor agencies like DFID of UK, World Bank, DANIDA of Denmark, UNICEF, WHO, UNFPA and SIDA. It has mentioned about four different aspects of these projects. These were nature and level of involvement in health, the agency involved, area of operation and the period of operation of these projects.

Table: 4.1: Donor agency supported health projects in Orissa

Nature and Level of Health	Project in Operation	Area of Operation of the Project	Period of Operation
Primary Health Care	DFID Phase III	Bhadrak and Keonjhar	1997 to 2000
Rehabilitation and Reconstruction in cyclone affected areas	DFID	14 district, CHC/Block level PHC - in 130 Blocks and below	2000-2004 in the pipeline
Strengthening of Sector Development of Health care	DFID	30 district	2001-2006 in the pipeline
Secondary and Primary Health Care Project (Health Systems Development Project)	World Bank	156 Institutions all over the State	1998-99 to 2004

Reproductive Child Health	WB/GOI,	State Wide - Sub-project Kalahandi, Koraput, Nawrangpur, Malkangir, Rayagada	1997-2002
Malaria	World Bank through GOI	158 Blocks in 21 districts	1998-2004
Tuberculosis	DANIDA/GOI	Keonjhar, Sambalpur and Mayurbhanj district, 11 district to be include	Dec. 1996-Dec 2001
Blindness	WB & GOI	All districts of the State	1.4.94 to 31.3.2001
AIDS	WB through NACO	All districts of the State	June 1999-2004
Leprosy	DANIDA	Cuttack, Jagatsingpur, Jaipur, Kendrapara in Phase I	1987 - Contd
	DANIDA	Sambalpur, Jharsuguda, Deogarh, Bargarh in Phase II	1991 - contd
	Lepra Mission	State in Phase III	1997 - contd
	Lepra-India	Rayagada, Nuapada, Umerkote	1997 - contd
	WB	Sonepur, Bolangir, Junagarh, Udala Jasipur (MBJ)	1994- - 1999
	Hoina	Phulbani, Kalhandi, Sundergarh, Keonjhar, Boud, Gunupur, Muniguda	1991
	WHO	Ganjam	1983
	SIDA	Ganjam	1983
	UNICEF	Puri	1985
Integrated population Development (IPD) project	U.N.F.P.A.	In the districts of Koraput, Rayagada, Malkangiri, Nawarangpur.	1999-2003ss

Source: Website of the Ministry of Health and Family Welfare, Orissa Government, January 2005.

It shows that DFID was involved in Phase III of Primary Health Care Project in Bhadrak and Keonjhar districts during 1997 to 2000, rehabilitation and reconstruction in cyclone affected areas of 14 districts in 130 block PHCs and below, during 2000-2004 and it was also involved in strengthening of sector development of health care in 30 districts since 2001- 2006. The last two projects of the DFID were in the pipeline.

Similarly World Bank has been involved in secondary health care project to upgrade 156 health institutions in Orissa during 1998-99 to 2004. It was also involved in RCH phase I along with government of India, which was involved across the state and a sub-project was also going on in Kalahandi, Koraput, Nawrangpur, Malkangir and Rayagada. The RCH Phase I went on since 1997 to 2002. Besides, the World Bank was also involved in malaria control programme along with government of India in 158 blocks of 21 districts since 1998 to 2004. In blindness control programme also the World Bank has been involved with government of India, which was being implemented across the state since 1994 to 2001. In leprosy control mission also World Bank has been involved in four districts of Sonepur, Bolangir, Junagarh and Mayurbhanj. The World Bank had also been involved in National AIDS Control Programme through NACO, which was being implemented all over the state since June 1999 to 2004.

DANIDA was involved in Tuberculosis programme along with government of India in 14 districts since 1996 to 2001. It was also involved in leprosy programme Phase I in four districts of Cuttack, Jagatsingpur, Jaipur, Kendrapara since 1987 and Phase II in four districts of Sambalpur, Jharsuguda, Deogarh Bargarh, since 1991 and Phase III in three districts of Rayagada, Nuapada, Umerkote since 1997.

For Leprosy programme WHO had been involved in Ganjam district since 1983, SIDA had been involved in the same district sine 1983 and UNICEF had been involved in Puri district since 1985. UNFPA on the other hand has been involved in four districts of Koraput, Rayagada, Malkangiri and Nawarangpur since 1999.

The analysis of ongoing projects suggested that Orissa has been a donor driven state. This was because of various reasons like; it had almost 48 percent of its population living below the poverty line; the scheduled castes and scheduled tribes in the state constitute about 39 percent of its total population; the state had more than 85 percent of its population living in rural areas, that means economy was predominantly agricultural and the state was frequently visited by droughts, floods and cyclones. Therefore Orissa has been seen as an ideal place for the donors to invest their money and resources. "However due to this donor driven projects in Orissa for a long time, people have become dependent on donors".[40] "To get funds from donors the Orissa government had been approaching them with 'begging bowls' like we are a poor state please help us. But the situation is changing now. In last meeting the Orissa Chief Minister presented his case by saying that we are a reforming state and a performing one too… so the language has changed".[41] Even during the field visit in the state many of the officials conceded that many times they just show poor indicators to get more funds from donor agencies.

However the involvement of donors has not helped the state in addressing its health concerns in a significant way, because donors have always come with some projects of their own, with their own agendas. This has resulted in many donors working in the same programme and even in the same district but without having any coordination among them. There were also different styles of report writing, which makes it difficult to assess the impact of these projects. One senior official of the state was of the view that to avoid this piecemeal approach by donors the state came out with a vision document[42] in 2003. The idea was that the donors could look into the vision document and identify their areas of interest from it and then can work there. This would help in avoiding duplication of work and in better coordination between the Health and Family Welfare department and among the donors. However during the field visit in the state it was found that the situation had not changed at the ground. This aspect has been discussed in detail in chapter V. Now let us have a look at Orissa Health Systems Development Project in detail.

Orissa Health Systems Development Project

The Orissa Health Systems Development Project or OHSDP could be termed as a major reform initiative in Orissa, which was wholly funded by the World Bank, but surprisingly it has not been included as a reform initiative by either the Orissa Vision document 2010 or by the observers of health reforms in the state.

[40] This was the view of a senior official of a donor agency.
[41] This was the view of a senior official of a donor agency.
[42] This refers to Orissa Vision Document 2010.

Aim of OHSDP

It was an Rs415 crore project wholly funded by the World Bank. So what was the aim or what were the objectives of this project? Responding to this question a senior official in the OHSDP, Orissa said, "For strengthening secondary level health care institutions is the aim of this project." Therefore the project intended to strengthen the secondary level institutions in the state. In the earlier sections we have already discussed about what does the Bank identifies as secondary level institutions. And what about the duration of this project? "This project was introduced in 1998. This was a five year project and now has been extended to one year and would be completed by 1st March 2005" said one senior official of OHSDP.

Table: 4.2 OHSDP at a Glance

Project Period: 1998-99 to 2003-04. Date of commencement: 18th September 1998. Date of Completion: 31st March 2005. Project Cost: Rs 415.58 crores. Share of Loan amount: Rs 348.75 crores. Share of Grant: Rs 66.83 crores. Total expenditure upto 15.02.2005: Rs 210.76 crores. Reimbursable amount claimed to World Bank: Rs 163.03 crores. Reimbursement received from World Bank: Rs 141.55 crores.

Source: Fieldwork, 2005.

As the above table shows, initially the project period was 1998-99 to 2003-04, which was later extended to 31st March 2005. The project commenced on 18th September 1998 with the project cost of Rs 415.58 crores. Out of this total amount the loan component was Rs 348.75 crores and the grant amount was Rs 66.83 crores. The total expenditure upto 15th February 2005 was Rs 210.76 crores, out of this the reimbursement claimed to World Bank was Rs 163.03 crores and the reimbursement received from the World Bank was Rs 141.55 crores.

Project institutions

Now let us have a look at the health services institutions, which OHSDP intended to cover. The table shows that in total 157, mostly secondary level institutions have been covered under this project to 'improve efficiency and effectiveness of health care delivery system in these institutions.'[43]

Table: 4.3 OHSDP financed institutions

Project Institutions	Numbers
Number of DHH (District Headquarter Hospitals)	30+2 (One Capital Hospital and another Rourkela Government Hospital)
Sub Divisional Hospital	20
Area Hospitals	19
CHC I	37
CHC II	48
SIHFW (Annex)	1
Total Number of Institutions	157

Source: Fieldwork, 2005.

Out of these 157 institutions, 30 were District Headquarter Hospitals, One Capital Hospital[44], One RGH, Rourkela, 20 Sub Divisional Hospitals, 19 Area Hospitals[45], 37 CHC I institutions, 48 CHC II institutions and the annex of SIHFW or State Institute of Health and Family Welfare, Bhubaneswar.

Components of OHSDP

So what were the components of OHSDP? Responding to this question the official said, "Broadly there were seven components of OHSDP. The different components of OHSDP are:

1- Infrastructure development: Under this 157 institutions are included.
2- The second component was *provision of diagnostic and surgical equipments and furniture.*
3- The third component was provision of ambulances for *mobility support.*
4- The fourth component was *in-service training*. There are three components in it.

[43] Source: CDMO conference Report, 2005, Government of Orissa.
[44] The 'Capital Hospital' was the name of a Hospital at Bhubaneswar, the capital of Orissa. It was not one of the hospitals in the capital of Orissa!
[45] Area hospitals were not below sub divisional hospitals but they were 16, 20 or 30-bedded hospitals in Orissa.

They are:

- i- Induction training for newly recruited medical officers. Here preventive and promotive aspects are emphasised. This goes on for 3-4 weeks.
- ii- Management development programme for health managers. Here the in-charge of CHCs, sub divisional hospitals and the CDMOs are trained. The aim is to develop managerial skills in them.[46]
- iii- Clinical updation training for specialists and clinicians in institutions where advanced treatment is given, as they need training regularly. This is given to clinicians of different disciplines. Earlier this was not done in a systematic manner.

5- The fifth component was *Health Management Information System*. Here the information from the periphery institutions is streamlined and the data is computerized. This helps to make the feedback faster. Under the existing system the data is not collected or forwarded and hence any analysis becomes difficult. Manually to manage this information is not possible now.
6- The sixth component was Disease Surveillance and Quality assurance. Prior to this project, disease surveillance was done just before an epidemic and not as a regular phenomenon. Disease Surveillance is a continuous process and this requires monitoring at every level. Now this system has been fully established.[47]
7- The seventh component was Hospital Waste Management. Now it has been made as a legal requirement. The project is providing technical and financial support."[48]

It needs to be mentioned here that the Health Management Information System or HMIS in Orissa was little different from elsewhere in India. Whereas at other places HMIS was synonymous with hospital data management, in Orissa it has looked at collecting data from periphery level institutions like PHCs and CHCs and processing these to higher

---

[46] It has to be mentioned here that the doctors in medical colleges were trained only for the clinical aspects and the preventive and promotive aspects were generally neglected, which was required in the district, sub divisional and the block level health services structure.
[47] In chapter V we have discussed in detail about disease surveillance mechanism established in Orissa.
[48] The concerned official had a field experience of 22 years in Orissa as a medical officer and was now on deputation to the OHSDP.

levels as feedback. However due to lack of computerization at periphery levels the HMIS initiative has not been successfully implemented so far.

The components of inductive training for newly recruited medical officers and the health management component for senior officials were two very significant steps taken toward addressing the issues of training medical officers for management of PHCs, CHCs, sub divisional Hospitals and effectively taking care of the needs of a district by CDMO. For in medical colleges this preventive aspect of training has been the most neglected one and although different initiatives like, internship training for medical graduates, have been taken from time to time but the situation has not improved at all. Therefore if this initiative by the World Bank succeeds than it would really be a big step forward.

The clinical updation of training for specialists and clinicians was another important initiative because it has been observed that the medical officers hardly keep themselves informed about the latest developments in their respective fields. And most of the time the only way they could get any information in these aspects was from the medical representatives from pharmaceutical companies trying to promote a particular drug. Therefore if specialists were updated with their skills then it would help in strengthening the referral services from the periphery institutions.

The Hospital Waste Management component was another important reform initiative because the public sector health services structures lacked the cleanliness aspect. It was almost becoming synonymous with public institutions that 'they do not maintain cleanliness.'

Motivation for reform in the form of OHSDP

To the question that what was the motivation for initiating a project like OHSDP, the official said, "Any funding agency is interested to provide funds. States decide the priority areas according to health indicators. Orissa has a very poor health status and the state finance is not in a position to cope with the demand. Hence the World Bank was approached. While the priority areas are decided by the group of planners in the state, the investment and expected outcomes and the co-relation between these two are decided by World Bank experts." Thus the official was of the view that while the priority areas were decided by the state government planners, the required investment and the expected outcome was decided by the World Bank.

The consultation process[49]

So the question arises as to whether consultations were held with different levels of health services personnel before initiation of this project? Replying to this the official concerned said, "Consultations were held with health department, urban development department, engineering department, CDMOs, Director Health Services. Thus service providers, planners and policy makers were consulted. When project formulation was done, people below CDMO level were consulted. However there was some opposition from people below CDMO level." Thus mentioning about the consultation process the official was of the view that consultations were held at different levels. However during field visit to two districts, the CDMOs said that they were not at all involved in this process.

Informal service provider programme

One of the major initiatives with the potential to affect the provisioning of health care services was the idea about involvement of indigenous services providers for referrals in remote and hilly areas. Describing about this program one senior official at OHSDP said, "The involvement of Informal Service Providers in health delivery system is implemented in Mathalput block of Koraput district on pilot basis since October 2003. The IPD project has taken over this activity for implementation in other blocks of Koraput and the districts of Malkangiri, Nawrangpur and Rayagada and it would also be implemented in Rayagada block of Gajapati district. Further it is proposed to be implemented in all the tribal blocks of rest of the districts like Kandhamal, Sundergarh, Mayurbhanj, Gajapati, Keonjhar, Kalahandi, Balasore and Sambalpur. The CDMOs of these eight districts are to identify one ISP from each village of the tribal blocks and finalize the list in their ZSS meetings."

Defining ISPs

Before asking in detail about this program how the indigenous service providers were defined was important to know. Responding to this query, the official said, "Informal service providers are those who live in that village. Their main occupation is not medicine. However they advise people in cases like, snake bite, pregnant women, risk pregnancy etc."

[49] We have also discussed about this consultation aspect in Chapter V.

Thus the indigenous service providers were residence of that village where they provided their services in cases like snaking bite, pregnant women and risk pregnancy. It needs to be mentioned that in those remote areas where malaria was endemic, the indigenous service providers were also treating these cases.

Why the programme was started

To the question why the program of ISP training was started, a senior official of the World Bank said, "What we are finding is that people are dying from malaria because they go to the traditional practitioners at village. If the person has got fever, they do what they have to do but in time they do not refer the person or a pregnant lady if she has complications, in time they do not refer. So what we are saying is that we should work with them, involve them and tell them that you are also part of the system. Probably we will make malaria drugs available to them. In some way there has to be some incentive for them also…so tell them… do what you want but tell them that in time please refer… For referrals transportation will be made available… so at least we can avoid deaths. But that is their livelihood, if we ban them they will go underground but they still will be working. So we are saying do what you are doing but please refer in time in case of fever or complications in pregnancy. They also have to be made aware about where health care facilities are available. In tribal districts we are having workshops. The district collector is actually organizing this. We have not even finished the first round. From the little bit of data we are getting, it shows that the number of referrals has increased, which is a good sign." Therefore the official was of the view that if we ban the indigenous service providers they would go underground and it won't solve the problem and hence they need to be involved in referrals to nearby health center and they also need to be made aware about the facilities available in a health center. However the idea of providing them drugs for malaria was a serious matter and concern was shown by officials at different levels about this proposal.

Another senior official at OHSDP, Bhubaneswar said, "The idea was to identify some people in village areas who will be liasioning between community health needs and services institutions. This program was started in 2003 in few blocks of Koraput, Gajapati, Keonjhar and Phulbani districts on a pilot basis. These are tribal districts and are most inaccessible. In these districts the population is scattered and health institutions are widely dispersed. From each district two blocks were identified and from each block one or two informal services providers were selected. These services providers are asked to refer patients to nearby PHC or to the ANM.[50] One follow up program is done in Koraput district and the outcome was very good. However it has to be critically verified in the field and lot of field supervision and monitoring is required for this. In the pilot study it was found that informal service providers were using injections for easy delivery. This was discouraged in workshops. Because of this practice there are lot of deaths of pregnant mothers and their children. In Orissa one can purchase drugs without prescription. This is not possible in Hyderabad."[51]

Therefore the experiment, which was conducted in a pilot basis, had been showing positive results. But the official raised an important policy issue here about the availability of drugs without a prescription and this was one of the major causes of deaths of pregnant women in remote and difficult areas. Therefore there was need for discussion at various levels about the necessity for bringing in legislation in Orissa to make it mandatory that without prescription one cannot purchase drugs.

Nature of the project

When asked about the nature of the project, the official at the OHSDP said, "This is a reimbursable project. The expenditure is through Government of Orissa budget. Money for the project is budgeted in the state budget, hence government of Orissa finance rules are applicable. Any financial loss or fraudulent activity is subject to audit. Government of Orissa makes budgetary support for OHSDP. Along with activities the five-year project money has also been finalized. Implementation plan for the project was done by health department with the help of World Bank."[52] Therefore care was taken to ensure that a parallel system does not arise due to this project. That means the line departments should be the controlling authority of this project because ultimately these departments would have to run these project institutions i.e. once the project period comes to an end.

---

[50] There was a provision that all pregnant women should be registered with the ANM.

[51] Hyderabad is the Capital of Indian state of Andhra Pradesh.

[52] It was important to mention here that the structure of OHSDP was same as in nine other states in India. This was informed by the official concerned.

The official further said, "The loan money is for a particular period. The recurring expenditures are gradually withdrawn from the project. In first year entire manpower budget is reimbursed by the World Bank. Next year the state government has to take responsibility for 25 percent manpower. In the third year another 25 percent and likewise in the last year of the project the state government is sharing 75 percent of the budget and the World Bank reimbursing 25 percent of the project. If it happens like this than in the last year of the project, it won't be difficult for the state government to sustain the project assets."

However this was not happening in case of OHSDP. "In OHSDP, in the first year there was no post created, in the second year there was no post created, in the third year some new posts were created to manage the newly created institutions. Hence salary portion in first and second year was not utilized and in third year it was partially utilized. Therefore if in third and fourth year posts are filled than all of a sudden 75 percent of the burden, the state has to bear, which has happened in this case." Therefore the posts were created in the third year only and due to this implementation process at the end of fourth year the state government had to bear all of a sudden 75 percent of the total cost of this budget. Therefore it has not been possible for the state government to increase its share over the years. However these issues were related to structural aspects of project implementation and hence it would be judgmental to fix responsibility on one party only.

Organizational structure of OHSDP

Once the project had been formulated and the budget amount decided it requires an organisation for implementation of the project. Describing about the organizational set up for OHSDP the official said, "At the top is the Project Management Cell or PMC, headed by Project Director.[53] There are three units in it. These are: Health Unit, Finance Unit and the Engineering Unit." See the picture below.

[53] The Project Director was of the rank of additional secretary and he had been posted on deputation form the government of Orissa.

Figure: 4.1: Project Management Cell

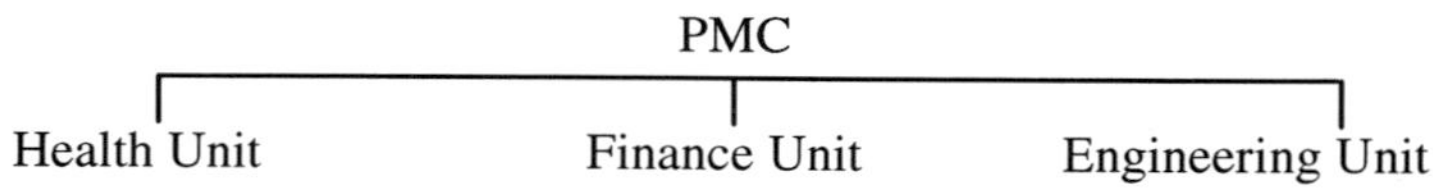

"The project director heads the PMC or project management cell. A joint director heads the health unit. One executive engineer heads the engineering unit and one financial advisor, who is a chief accounts officer, heads the finance unit. In OHSDP maximum components come under the health unit. The engineering unit looks after the construction," said the official.

He further added that under OHSDP, "the key posts are government posts. Consultants and the support staff are on contractual basis, which will terminate with the end of the project. Once the project is over, only the officer on deputation from government of Orissa will remain."

Elaborating about the implementation aspects, the official said, "All the projects are falling under mainly the health and finance units. The implementation is done at the district level. The CDMO reports to the Director Health Services and also to the OHSDP director regarding project implementation."

For the smooth implementation of the project "There are three committees are there in the project. The first is *Project monitoring committee or review committee*. The secretary health is the chairperson and the members are, Directors of DHS, DMET, DFW, SIHFW[54] and the Director OHSDP is the convener. The committee should meet once in every month when the implementation progress of all the project activities is monitored," said the official.

The second was the *steering committee,* "which looks after construction, administrative aspects and expenditures for more than Rs10 lakhs. Chairman is the health secretary; all the directors of the health directorate are its members, and one representative each from the finance and works department. Decisions requiring approval for more than Rs10 lakhs goes

[54] DHS was Director Health Services, DMET was Director Medical Education and Training, DFW was Director Family Welfare and SIHFW was State Institute of Health and Family Welfare.

to steering committee and some administrative and engineering approval go here."

"The third is the policy review committee. This is the highest decision making body. It takes decisions according to the changing circumstances. The Chief Secretary Government of Orissa is the chairman. The members are, Finance secretary, Revenue secretary, Works secretary,[55] Health secretary, Women and Child department secretary and Urban Development secretary."

The official further said, "These are all facilitating bodies for smooth implementation of the project."

The project board

"There is a *project board* where decisions are taken to save time. Its chairman is health secretary. Members are directors from DHS, DFW, DMET, SIHFW and OHSDP and a representative of the finance department," said the official.

But what was the rationale for the project board when already the project management cell and the three review committees were already there? Responding to this query the official said, "In normal course file moves from health to finance department and from there the money is released. As it is a lengthy process, here the project board decides and the money is released immediately and hence it is a quick process."

Reporting from the district level

To the question how and to whom the reports with regard to OHSDP institutions from districts were sent, the official said, "In the monitoring process at the district level, CDMOs report to project directors on various activities on an agreed format. Some are monthly reports and some are weekly reports".

---

[55] Works department looks after construction.

Involving the line departments[56]

However as we have argued earlier that involvement of the line department was necessary for the successful outcome of the project, so what were the steps taken in this regard? Responding to this question the official concerned said, "It is not possible to involve the PMC to monitor every activity and hence line department is also involved. Here the joint directors under DHS and DFW have been allotted districts for supervision. They go to the districts every month. They supervise and monitor all health activities including OHSDP activities."

Status report

Now let us have a look at the existing status of the project in terms of its implementation at ground level. The table below gives the status report of OHSDP. It has looked into the key activities, the targets, achievements of those targets, sanctioned costs, expenditure made till now and what was the percent of this expenditure to the total cost of this project.

Table: 4.4 Status report, OHSDP Figures in Crores

Key activities	Target	Achievements	Sanctioned costs	Expenditure and % to the total cost
Civil Work	157	118	168.5	98.37 (58.37%)
Drugs and Consumables	--	--	16.21	16.21 (100%)
EIF	--	--	36.37	14.28 (39.26%)
Training (Inside Orissa)	2568	911	--	--
Training (outside Orissa)	--	153	--	--
Training	On going activity			

[56] Line departments suggest the regular departments of the Ministry of Health and Family Welfare.

Hospital Waste Management	All project institutions covered
Software activity	210 telephones, 30 each vehicles and equipments provided, 2 computers provided, AMC done in 32 units
Manpower support	1012 posts created and 660 filled on contractual basis. 65 posts created and 25 filled on regular basis. 461 posts upgraded and 90 filled up.

Note: -- means data not available.
Source: Fieldwork, 2005.

The table shows that in Civil Works out of 157 targets, 118 have been completed with a sanctioned cost of Rs 168.5 crores; and in total Rs 98.37 crores had been spent, which was 58.37 percent to the total cost. Similarly for Drugs and Consumables out of sanctioned Rs 16.21 crore 100 percent had been spent. For equipments, instruments and furniture or EIF out of the sanctioned cost of Rs 36.37 crores, Rs 14.28 was spent which was 39.26 percent. For training inside Orissa, out of 2568 targets 911 had been completed and for training outside Orissa, 153 had been completed. The table also mentions that training was an ongoing activity of this project. Hospital Waste Management had been extended to all the 157 project institutions. In terms of software activity, 210 telephones, 30 each vehicles and equipments and 2 computers had been provided. In terms of manpower support 1012 posts had been created and 660 were filled up on contractual basis. Further 65 posts were created and 25 filled up on regular basis and 461 posts were upgraded and 90 posts were filled up.

Posts created on a contractual basis

The table below gives the number of contractual posts created in various categories under OHSDP. It also shows the number of posts filled up and the number of posts yet to be filled up.

Table: 4.5 Posts created under OHSDP (on a contractual Basis)

On contractual Basis	No, of posts created	Filled up	To be filled up
Asst. Surgeon	124	124	0
Specialists	158	0	158
Dental Surgeon	18	18	0
Pharmacist	9	6	3
Radiographer	62	0	62
District Education Officer or DEO	30	30	0
Staff Nurse	535	438	97
Lab. Technicians	40	0	40
Librarian	1	0	1
MPHW (F)	9	0	9
Driver	17	0	17
Total	1012	616	396

Source: Fieldwork, 2005.

The table shows that 124 posts of Assistant Surgeons were created, out of which 124 had been filled up. Similarly out of 158 posts of specialists created, not a single post has been filled up. In case of dental surgeons, 18 posts were created and all the 18 had been filled up. Nine posts were created for Pharmacist, out of which 6 had been filled up and 3 posts were yet to be filled up. On the other hand out of 62 posts of radiographer created, not a single had been filled up. In case of District Education Officer while 30 posts were created, all had been filled up. Similarly 535 posts were created for Staff Nurse, out of which 438 had been filled up and 97 posts are yet to be filled up. However in case of Lab Technicians while 40 posts were created, not a single had been filled up. Librarian also while one post was created; it was yet to be filled. Nine posts were created for MPHW (F), out of which not a single had been filled up. In case of Driver 17 posts were created and here also not a single post had been filled up. Thus in total out of 1012 posts created, 616 had been filled up and 396 posts were yet to be filled.

The analysis of the table shows that the posts of Assistant Surgeons, Dental Surgeons, and District Education Officers had been 100 percent filled up. In case of Staff Nurse and Pharmacists also a large number of posts had been filled up. However, in case of Specialists, Radiographer,

Lab Technicians, Librarian, MPHW (F) and Driver, out of the total posts created not a single had been filled up.

Posts created on a regular basis

The table below shows post created under OHSDP on a regular basis. It gives a picture of total number of posts proposed to be created, the number of posts filled up and the number of posts to be filled up.

Table: 4.6 Posts created under OHSDP (on a regular basis)

On a regular basis	Total posts	Filled up	To be filled up
Nursing sister	7	7	0
Technical Store Keeper	18	18	0
Matron	6	0	6
Asst. Matron	17	0	17
MPHW (M)	17	0	17
Total	65	25	40

Source: Fieldwork, 2005.

The table shows that for nursing sister out of 7 total posts, all had been filled up. Similarly for Technical Store Keeper out of 18 posts, all had been filled up. However, out of proposed 6 posts of matrons, 17 posts of Assistant matrons and 17 posts of Multi Purpose Health Worker (Male) not a single had been filled up. Thus out of the proposed 65 total posts to be created, only 25 had been filled up and 40 posts were yet to be filled up.

Upgradation of posts under OHSDP

Apart from creating regular and contractual posts, some posts were taken up for upgradation under this project. The table below gives a picture of posts proposed to be upgraded for Sr. Class I and for Jr. Class I.

Table: 4.7: Upgradation of Posts under OHSDP

Posts upgraded	Total Posts	Filled up	To be filled up
Sr. class 1	240	31	209
Jr. class 1	221	25	196
Total	461	56	405

Source: Fieldwork, 2005.

Thus out of 240 Sr. Class I posts only 31 had been upgraded and 209 posts were yet to be upgraded. Similarly for Jr. Class I posts, out of 221 posts to be upgraded only 25 posts had been upgraded and 196 posts were yet to be upgraded. This shows that the upgradation of posts would be very difficult for the rest of the project period.

In-service training

In-service training had been an important component of OHSDP. The table below gives a picture of how many number of persons had been trained in different areas like hospital management, nursing management, computer application, media activity and IEC action plan, clinical updation of skills of specialists, skill updation of assistant surgeons, Lab technician training in blood banking, TOT in hospital waste management, district health services management course, induction training of newly recruited medical officers, FMT programme at SIHFW and para medical training at Kalinga Hospital, Bhubaneswar.

The table shows that in hospitals management, 164 persons had been trained and in case of nursing management, 89 persons had been trained. While in computer application, only 39 persons trained, in case of media activity and IEC action plan, 120 personnel were trained. For clinical updation skill of specialists in six disciplines, 92 personnel were trained and for skill updation of assistant surgeons, 171 personnel were trained. In case of Lab technician training in blood banking, 53 persons were trained and for TOT in hospital waste management, 72 persons were trained. In total 78 persons were given training for district health services management course and 61 newly recruited MOs were given induction training. Further 51 persons were trained for FMT programme at SIHFW and 20 para medics were trained at Kalinga Hospital, Bhubaneswar.

Table: 4.8: In-service training, OHSDP

Type of training	Number Trained
Hospital Management	164
Nursing management	89
Computer application	39
Media activity & IEC action plan	120
Clinical updation skill of specialists in six disciplines	92
Skill updation of assistant surgeons	171
Lab. Technician training in blood banking	53
TOT in hospital waste management	72
District health services management course	78
Induction training of newly recruited MOs	61
FMT programme at SIHFW	51
Para medical training at Kalinga hospital BBSR	20
Total	1010

Source: Fieldwork, 2005.

Analysis of different training programme showed that for skill updation of assistant surgeons highest numbers of personnel were trained, out of all the different training programmes followed by personnel trained for hospital management, personnel trained for media activity and IEC action plan, personnel trained for clinical updation of skills of specialists in six disciplines and nursing management.

In terms of lowest number of personnel trained, para medics training at Kalinga Hospital came first followed by, computer application, FMT programme at SIHFW, Lab technician training in blood banking and persons trained in induction training for the newly recruited medical officers.

OHSDP expenditures

The table below gives the expenditure incurred in this project over the years.

Table: 4.9: OHSDP expenditures over the years

Expenditure during	Rs. In Crores
1998-99	05.42
1999-00	05.26
2000-01	34.01
2001-02	27.03
2002-03	25.60
2003-04	57.61
2004-05 upto 15.02.05.	55.83
Cumulative expenditure up to 15.02.05	210.76 or 50.71%

Source: Fieldwork, 2005.

The table shows that expenditure in the first two years were below Rs 6 crores, however it suddenly increased to Rs 35.01 crores in 2000-01 and again declined to Rs 27.03 Crores in 2001-02 and further declined to Rs 25.60 crores in the next year. In the year 2003-04 the expenditure was more than doubled to Rs 57.61 crores and slightly declined to Rs 55.83 crores from 2004-05 upto 15.02.05. In a way we could say that expenditure has increased over the years. In terms of cumulative expenditure till 15.02.05, Rs210.76 crores were spent, which was 50.71 percent of the total OHSDP budget. This shows that although the expenditure in this project has increased over the years almost 50 percent of the money could not be spent. Therefore it could be said that the project had not moved in a satisfactory way and there had been delays at many places.

Proposed expenditure

The table below gives an idea about the proposed expenditure from the year 2004-05 to 2006-07.

Table: 4.10 OHSDP: Proposed expenditures

Proposed expenditure during	Rs. in Crores
2004-05	259.97
2005-06	104.00
2006-07	51.61

Source: Fieldwork, 2005.

It shows that for the year2004-05 the proposed expenditure to be a whooping Rs 259.97 crores and for the following year the proposed expenditure were to be Rs 104.00 crores followed by Rs 51.61 crores in the next year. However if the previous expenditure records were of any indication, these estimates of proposed expenditures seem highly unlikely.

Drugs and Medical consumables

The table below shows the status report with regard to drugs and consumables. It has given different aspects of it like, the provision as per Project Implementation Plan or PIP, orders placed till 15.02.05, expenditure till 15.02.05, procurement in process and the assessment of these expenditures by OHSDP.

Table: 4.11 Drugs and Medical consumables under OHSDPFigures in Rs. Crores

Provision as per PIP	Orders placed till 15.02.05	Expenditure till 15.02.05	Procurement in process	Remarks
29.50	23.41	13.19	11 58	Bill pending with SDMU for balance payment

Note: SDMU- State Drugs Management Unit.
Source: Fieldwork, 2005.

It shows that out of Rs 29.50 crores proposed as per PIP, orders were placed for Rs 23.41crores till 15.02.05, expenditure was Rs 13.19 crores and the rest of the amount of Rs 11.58 crores was in the process for procurement. Therefore it could be said that in this drugs and consumables segment, OHSDP had made good progress compared to other aspects.

Equipments, instruments and furniture

The table below gives financial details with regard to equipments, instruments and furniture under the project OHSDP.

Table: 4.12 Equipments, instruments and furniture

Figures in Rs. Crores

Provision as per PIP	Order placed till 15.02.05	Expenditure till 15.02.05	Remarks
75.72	60.20	27.05	Balance bills pending

Source: Fieldwork, 2005.

The table shows that out of Rs 75.72 crores of provision as per project implementation plan, orders were placed for Rs 60.20 crores till 15.02.05 and actual expenditure incurred was Rs 27.05 crores. Thus in terms of orders placed for EIF, it could be said that this component had made good progress.

Anticipated expenditure under OHSDP

The table below gives an indication of anticipated expenditure under the project OHSDP till 31.03.2005.

Table: 4.13 Anticipated expenditure in OHSDP up to 31.03.2005

Figures in Rs. Crores

Civil works	9.5
EIF	21.5
Drugs	08.00
Salary	7.00
Miscellaneous	3.21
Total	49.21
Grand total	259.97
Anticipated unspent balance as per PIP	155.61

Source: Fieldwork, 2005.

It shows that with Rs 21.5 crores of anticipated expenditure EIF tops the list, followed by civil works with Rs 9.5 crores, drugs with Rs 08.00 crores, salary with Rs 7.00 crores and miscellaneous with Rs 3.21 comes at the bottom of the anticipated expenditure chart. The table further shows that, the grand total anticipated expenditure was Rs 259.97 crores and the anticipated unspent balance as per PIP was Rs 155.61 crores. As we have shown earlier that because of this huge anticipated unspent balance, it could be said that the project had faced many difficulties in its implementation phase.

Proposed expenditure during 2005-06

The table below gives an indication of how the anticipated unspent balance of Rs 155.16 crores would be spent on different activities during the financial year of 2005-06.

Table: 4.14 Proposed expenditure in OHSDP during 2005-06

Figures in Rs. Crores

Balance civil works (8DHH and 1SDH) and refund of security deposit	30.16
Repair and renovation of existing buildings in project and non-project hospitals	37.61
EIF or Equipment, Instruments and Furniture	30.95
Drugs	16.89
Salary and miscellaneous expenditure/ISP workshop	32.00
Maintenance of equipments during 2006-07	08.00
Total	155.61

Source: Fieldwork, 2005.

Out of the proposed expenditure, highest amount would be spent on repair and renovation of existing buildings with Rs 37.61 crores, followed by salary and miscellaneous expenditure with Rs 32.00 crores and Rs 30.95 crores of expenditure in EIF. The fourth largest proposed expenditure would be in balance civil works and on refund of security deposits with Rs 30.16 crores, followed by Rs 16.89 crores of expenditures on drugs and Rs 08.00 crores of expenditure on maintenance of equipments during 2006-07.

Concerns

So the project had been implemented, there was an organizational structure created for implementation of the project and mechanisms for inter departmental coordinations had been created. But was it the case that everything was functioning as planned or there were some areas of concerns too? Replying to this query the official said, "The CDMO conference is done usually twice a year. Here OHSDP activity is also one of the agendas. There is an interaction between the districts." However the official said, "The structure is very good, arrangements are very good, but in real sense this is not happening. For example only 15-20 minutes is given to OHSDP activities in CDMO conferences. Sometimes OHSDP also calls CDMOs and ADMOs[57] in small batches to discuss some issues."

The official further added, "Whether joint directors are giving importance to OHSDP in their districts or not needs to be verified. It began in the project very late.[58] Another aspect is sustainability, which is part of the project. This was agreed at the time of approval of the project. Hence the state government should take appropriate measures to fulfill those commitments."

The official mentioned, "The project objective is to take loan gradually, so that it does not become a burden on the state."

Sustainability of the project

On sustainability of the project the concerned official said, "At present political commitment is lacking in Orissa". He said, "World Bank gives loan to the government of India with 2-3% interest and the government of India gives to the state at 11% interest. This needs to be corrected. Further those who are capable should pay for health services. People will pay only when the credibility of that institution is there. It is after all a question of channeling funds with good governance."[59] This was a very important point mentioned by the official concerned in terms of Centre-state relations in dealing with donor funding. However the significant question was if the government of India gets loan from World Bank at 2-3 percent of interests, than why it charges from the state at 11 percent for passing the same loans? Therefore this aspect needed urgent attention. Another point that the official mentioned was about, charging those who could pay and this was the view of most of the government officials at different levels of health care services structure in the state. Therefore there was need for a

[57] Additional District Medical officers.

[58] The official was referring to the involvement of joint directors in the project.

[59] In fact it needs to be mentioned here that there was support for private participation in health care at every layer of the government health services structure in Orissa.

study, which would look into the users' perspective about user fees all across Orissa. Besides the different aspects should be taken into account, if such a fee was to be introduced across the state. For example, it needs to be ensured that the poor and marginalized sections of the population were exempted from paying fees in reality and not just as a promise to them.

Further the official concerned added, "At present projects are working more or less independently isolating the line department.[60]They are not fully involved. There should be concrete steps to address these issues. External aid if it is to show output should be seen internal by the line department. The line department directors need to be involved. At present when procurement of equipment or construction goes on, inputs do not come from the directors. Now implementation is done by projects and later line directors are consulted. This should be reversed. Formulation and implementation should be done with line department and projects should play as facilitators. In this regard decisions have to be taken by the health secretary and the health minister otherwise line department directors will work as bureaucrats." Further the official added, "Once a project is finished, the assets or manpower created out of it will be left with line directors. Hence, if they are not involved at project formulation and implementation phase, than it will lead to chaos. At present exactly this is happening and it has led toward the alienation of the line department directors. They felt left out of this whole process." Therefore the official concerned mentioned a significant point about the negligence of line department directors in formulation and implementation of the OHSDP project. Therefore some questions need to be addressed in this regard. It was not enough to say that from next time the line department directors would be involved in project formulation and implementation processes. But the questions that should be asked were, why in spite of existing mechanisms for involving the line department directors at every stage, it could not happen? Who were responsible for this? Was it the case that there was something in the project component which was or which would have been opposed by the line department directors? Therefore these aspects need to be dealt with if the project has to show some outcomes.

Then there were also questions about why in CDMO conferences only for 15 to 20 minutes were spent about the progress of this project? While the provisions for Joint Directors in the Directorate of Health to monitor the

---

[60] Line departments refer to the Director of Health Services, Director Family Welfare and Director Medical Education and Training etc.

project in different districts had been there, why it started late and even then questions were being raised about the actual situation in the field? Therefore this aspect also needed a deeper analysis. What were the reasons for which this could not be implemented? Where the structural constraints were there?

Larger issues

The official further added, "In Orissa there is a myth that money is not there. It is rather the lack of political commitment." This was a very important observation from a senior official in the state who had more than 20 years of work experience in various levels of health care services in the state. Infact this was also the observation at different levels in the state as well as from the senior officials of the donor agencies, that political will and commitment was lacking in Orissa, in improving the health care delivery structure in the state.

On the question that, suppose due to reform measures the drug department saves Rs30 crores out of its Rs100 crores budget, than next year Rs30 crores was reduced from its budget. In this situation how could reforms proceed? Responding to this the official said, "This is the real tragedy. Lot of donor money is coming to Orissa but where it is being spent has to be seen. There are lots of wasteful expenditures." This is another important aspect of donor led funding in Orissa. During field visits one medical officer in charge of a block level PHC was of the opinion that "Suppose a program requires Rs 100 to be spent, for this the government of Orissa makes provision for Rs 60, but in case of a donor agency this amount reaches to Rs 160. Because they know that Rs 60 would go to the pockets of different officials!" This was a very honest observation but also serious one too to be taken note of because here the question was about misutilisation or misappropriation of program money. So the reasons need to be looked at. Therefore questions need to be raised as to why out of Rs 160, Rs 60 need to be taken by different levels of officials? So here the structural issues like amount of salary, working conditions, satisfaction at the job etc. for different levels of health personnel needs to be looked at.

To the question of sustainability of project assets once the projects comes to an end, the official said, "This is the real challenge. For example suppose the drug budget of Orissa is Rs4 crores and the World Bank gives another Rs4 crores to address the shortage in money with the condition that from next year the government of Orissa will increase its drug budget by Rs1 crore, so that after four years the state can sustain it. But it is not happening". Than, why the state was drawing money for reforms from the donor agencies? To this he said, "The first thing is that there is lack of political will. The second thing is that donor coordination and plan coordination is lacking at the moment". The lack of donor coordination and also the lack of donor and plan coordination is another important aspect we have dealt with in chapter V in detail.

Further he said, "In other states if a minister does not perform than he is sacked. But here in Orissa one goes on, even if he is inefficient." The official further added, "Seminars and workshops are held but the reports produced out of it remains unutilized. The policy makers[61] do not give it any importance." This was another point to be taken note of because there was lots of money and resources were spent by different governments at the state and central level to conduct seminars and workshops, so that concrete input could be provided to implement a program. However if the reports produced out of these were not utilized then all these effort goes in vein. Therefore question arises as to why these reports lie unutilized? Is it the case that there are structural constraints so large that these findings could not be implemented and hence they lie unutilized? If it is the case than why at all these seminars and workshops conducted at all? Or there could be some other reasons?

Apart from these, another major reason cited by the official was that "However good a project or programme might be, in terms of its formulation, it fails when it comes to the issue of implementation, as they do not look into the aspects of health care delivery system." He said, "The shortage of staff is faced from the Director Health Services to the CDMOs to the doctor at the CHC or PHC level. At the PHC level there are shortages of paramedics and at the sub center level there are shortages of ANMs." He further added, "Because of the arbitrary nature of transfer and postings it will be difficult to find a single doctor who has faith in the system."[62] Therefore what was mentioned here were that the donor agencies do not take into account about the health care delivery structure through which a project was supposed to be implemented and hence from the beginning the failure of the project is almost certain! Therefore

---

[61] By that he meant health secretary and the health minister.

[62] It has been mentioned elsewhere that the transfer and postings were done in a very arbitrary manner in Orissa. This had almost demoralized the cadres at every level. This fact also came out during interaction with CDMOs and the medical officer in charge of block PHCs.

questions need to be asked as to why donor agencies do not take into account these structural issues? Is it because they try to implement a model, which has succeeded at another country?

Conclusion

In this chapter we have discussed about the State Health Systems Development Projects being implemented by the World Bank in India and also we have discussed about the Orissa Health Systems Development Project in the context of India adopting Structural Adjustment Programmes in the nineties. We have learnt that the SHSDPs were initiated with the aim of upgrading the secondary level institutions; from CHCs to district headquarter hospitals, which were mostly 30 to 400 bedded institutions in different states.

Due to the initiation of Structural Adjustment Programmes various states in India faced shortage in funding for various communicable diseases from the centre. However as there were cases of plague in Surat and malaria in Rajasthan, these cutbacks were restored through donor agency funding like the World Bank. The World Development Report 1993 had emphasized the need to reduce public spending from secondary and tertiary levels of care and focusing the limited resources of the state on selective primary level care. Within this framework SHSDPs were introduced to strengthen the secondary level institutions and in the long run to make them self sufficient by introducing mechanisms like user fees.

The first group of states where SHSDPs were introduced was Andhra Pradesh, Karnataka, Punjab and West Bengal. These states were chosen on the ground that they represented the heterogeneity of India, in terms of its economic and political structures. These were followed by Orissa, Maharastra, UP and Uttaranchal. The latest group of states to be included was Rajasthan and Tamilnadu. While the projects in first four states had been completed, it was going on in remaining states.

In the early nineties, the World Bank was involved with population programs, like family planning and family welfare and in nutrition programs like the ICDS in India. However after assessing its past activities, the Bank decided to upgrade the state health systems in different states of India. Their internal analysis showed that while the primary level care in India was supported by national programs like family planning and the disease control programs and the tertiary level care was mostly catered to by different states, it was the secondary level care which was the neglected area. As a result the secondary level institutions were not getting their annual maintenance budgets. This had affected the first level referrals.

Therefore the first thing that was done by the Bank was to identify the kind of services a secondary level institution like a CHC or a district hospital should provide. Hence an effort was made to rationalize the services available in these institutions. Once the services were identified, then the required manpower and equipments were also decided accordingly. Part of this project was introduction of health care waste management, under which cleaning aspect was privatized and health management information system was introduced, which tried to utilize the existing hospital data so that the limited resources could be used efficiently. In some states hospital data was also used to grade different hospitals in terms of their performance. The idea was that the grading of hospitals would improve the quality of care. In states like Punjab and West Bengal the hospital data generated was used as a feedback to upgrade the services.

Along with this an effort was made to identify what kind of personnel should be trained for these institutions and to rationalize the referral system. Further the states undertaking this project were asked to maintain the drugs and maintenance budgets systematically. So that the issues like where the resources were spent and whether these were spent judiciously could be analyzed.

The criteria to select the first group of states for SHSDP projects was that the states should show a level of commitment for health sector reforms and they had to be genuinely interested in this project. However in the later stages the criteria changed to those states of India which would be lagging behind in achieving the targets of Millennium Development Goals. We need to mention here that in recent times, most of the donor agencies all over the world have shifted their focus on achieving the targets of MDGs in various counties.

Further to evaluate the SHSDPs, the experiences from Mexico and Vietnam in terms of their community health insurance schemes were looked at. This was a significant development because the idea was to generate new sources of financing and to ensure that the poor were exempted through introduction of health vouchers.

While the officials interviewed claimed that the SHSDPs had introduced dialogue among various senior state officials, the Orissa experience suggested that the line departments were not consulted or were consulted very late in the implementation of this project. While the senior officials interviewed at World Bank were quite optimistic that this project had increased access for the poor and women, the officials in Orissa were very skeptical about this aspect. According to them, one of the major challenges of introducing the user fees was about exempting the poor in reality.

Along with the implementation of SHSDPs, the World Bank was also trying to encourage state governments to initiate public private partnerships and it begun with non-clinical services. The idea was to utilize the services available in the private sector effectively. One aspect of this was to give the cleaning aspect of various public health institutions to private parties. It was found that neither the government of India nor the states had the expertise to write contracts with the private sector. In terms of handing over PHCs in remote areas to NGOs, while it succeeded in Sunderban areas of West Bengal, the same experiment could not succeed in Orissa. This suggests that a unified model should be avoided. However one of the challenges of working with the private sector in India was that there was no proper regulation for it and as a result there were no quality checks for the kind of services in provides. Another significant initiative in this direction was about involving informal service providers in referrals in cases of obstetric emergency or a neo natal emergency or falciparum malaria cases. The idea was that the policy of putting a ban on ISPs could not succeed and hence why not involve them in referrals.

The World Bank has been funding for various national programs in India like RCH, HIV/AIDS, Tuberculosis and Malaria, where the money basically went to primary level care. This was one of the reasons that SHSDPs focused on secondary level care. However the experiences from different states were showing that referrals from primary level care to these secondary level institutions had not improved. The reasons were, like people were not aware that such kind of facilities did exist and secondly there were no transportation facilities available for the people. Therefore in the next group of states like Tamilnadu and Rajasthan, the World Bank would also support the primary level care because it has been realized that without improving the primary level care the MDGs won't be achieved. The experience from SHSDPs also suggest that health care financing needed more emphasis in terms of use of existing resources efficiently and generating new sources of financing, in terms of introducing various insurance mechanisms. For increasing public investment in health sector, the World Bank was involved in a dialogue with the centre and state governments to reduce subsidies in agriculture and power. However these were very sensitive issues in a democracy like India. Besides when the developed countries like US, Japan and countries from Europe were refusing to reduce subsidies they provide to their farmers, in WTO negotiations, how far it was justifiable to argue that a country like India should reduce subsidies on agriculture?

Another aspect which was emphasized was about utilizing the existing manpower efficiently. Here it was said that as in remote and difficult areas the medical officers and the other staffs from government were refusing to stay, why not involve the private sector. Therefore the argument was that the government should shift its role from actual provisioning of health care to issues of policy, regulation and accreditation. On the part of World Bank they were trying to interlink the question of fiscal crisis which various states have been facing, with increase in health financing from the Bank. In case of Orissa the Bank was planning to link the Orissa Economic Review Package with funding for health sector. However this has policy implications in the form of people's representatives loosing their capacity to take independent decisions with regard to deciding priority areas of health interventions.

Our analysis showed that Orissa had a large presence of donors since 1990s. However multiple donors and their multiple projects have not really helped in meeting its various socio economic challenges. Rather it has created problems of donor coordination and in many cases the donor led projects were not matching with the health priorities being identified by the state in its vision document 2010. In this backdrop the World Bank led OHSDP project need to be analyzed.

During interviews, senior officials of the World Bank were of the view that because the government of Orissa was interested for OHSDP project, it could be proceeded with. The OHSDP was intended to strengthen the secondary level health care institutions in the state. The different components of this project were infrastructure development, provision of equipments and furniture, mobility support, in-service training, HMIS, ISP training, disease surveillance and quality assurance and hospital waste management.

While mechanisms were created for consultation process with the line department directors and the CDMOs in project formulation, implementation and monitoring, in reality the line departments were totally sidelined. This had implications not only for effective implementation and monitoring but also about the sustainability of the project institutions created. Further the state government was not increasing its share of expenditure each year as it was formulated in the beginning of the project. This was due to the fact that only in the third year of this project some posts were created, as a result all of a sudden in the third year the state had to bear the 75% of the total cost which was not possible.

Under this project while total number of contractual posts created was 1012, the regular posts were only 65. Out of the total contractual posts while 616 had been filled up, in case of regular posts only 25 had been filled up. The total number of contractual posts created suggests that the elements of private sector were being introduced in these secondary level institutions. Therefore if tomorrow the state was not in a position to provide funding for these institutions, then these staffs would have to go or alternatively, services in these institutions would have to be privatized. Hence it seems that in the long run the secondary level institutions might get cut off from the primary level institutions for referrals. This has serious implications for equity and universal access to health care.

The larger issues about donor funding that came up was that while the World Bank provided loan to government of India at 2-3% interest rates, the same loan was being passed to the states at 11% interest rates. This was putting a heavy burden on the state governments. However it was the lack of political-will, which was the biggest stumbling block in bringing about required changes in the health care system of Orissa.

CHAPTER FIVE

THE PROCESS AND EXPERIENCE OF REFORMS IN ORISSA

Introduction

In this chapter we have discussed about the experience of reforms in health sector in the state of Orissa. While in chapter IV we have discussed about health sector reforms in the form of OHSDP, here we have also classified health sector reforms in Orissa according to our new definition. Further this chapter has analyzed our broad objective of 'process and experience' of health sector reforms in Orissa. Here the interviews with the health bureaucracy of the Orissa government at different levels and the perceptions of donor agency officials in Delhi and Bhubaneswar have been reflected.

Among the various donor agencies interviewed, there was a consensus among all these players that the state has to create more space for the private sector in the delivery of health care. In terms of thinking at the top level it was quite clear that these organizations had set their priorities in terms of achieving the targets of Millennium Development Goals.[1] These were targets to be achieved by the year 2015. The World Bank has identified the means to achieve these goals in the field of health. The 1993 document of the World Bank titled *investing in health* has acted as a frame of reference for the donor agencies in Orissa. This has happened against the backdrop of annual documents of the World Bank, which have off late advocated an increasing role of state in health care provisioning and financing.[2]

---

[1] The larger goals of development as identified and prepared by UNDP or United Nations Development Programme known as Millennium Development Goals.
[2] See the World Development Reports published by the World Bank annually since the year 1993 to 2004.

The background

There were two events, which were supposed to have started the systemic changes as well as the reforms in health sector in the state of Orissa in late 1990s. One was the formation of a House Committee of Orissa State Legislature, which looked into different aspects like; rising of resources for the ailing health care sector, introduction of user charges in medical colleges and district hospitals and on the issue of abolition of private practice by government doctors. The second event was an evaluation by the UK development agency DFID about its earlier two projects in Orissa.[3]

However the single connecting thread to these separate events was the effort to privatize the health services sector in the state. For this to happen there was a wider atmosphere of economic reforms initiated by the central government and various fiscal measures being adopted by the state government. Hence reforms in health sector need to be contextualised in the framework of economic reforms.

Now let us have a look at some of the reform initiatives being taken in the state.[4] The two events that helped in bringing the systemic changes had also acted as a catalyst for reforms in the health sector in Orissa. Therefore the process of reforms in the state had been closely associated with the systemic changes.

Health sector reforms

Let us first see the elements of health sector reforms being introduced in Orissa.

---

[3] Gupta Meena: *State Health System: Orissa*, November 2002, ICRIER, New Delhi.

[4] The various reform measures in health sector in Orissa were drawn from Meena Gupta's Paper, from Orissa Vision 2010 document and with various interviews with donor agencies and the State government officials. Further according to the new definition we have given in our present study, other initiatives in the Orissa health sector has been identified as reforms for the first time in this study and many initiatives which have been interpreted as 'reforms' by other studies have been excluded in our classification, because these failed to fulfill the criteria of reforms according to our new definition.

Creation of PSPU[5]

The Policy Planning or Strategic Unit has been started with the initiative of DFID[6] of UK in Orissa. The entire funding was being done by the DFID. This unit would act as a think tank for the Ministry of Health and Family Welfare, government of Orissa. It would help in programme design, implementation, monitoring and revision of health initiatives by the health department. Although the entire funding of this institution would be done by the DFID, its entire expenditure would be shown in the regular government budget. The staff would be both from the government as well as from outside.

During the field visit it was observed that this unit was trying to define its role and hence was at the level of conceptual formation. The DFID and the government of Orissa have been trying since 2002-03 to make this unit fully functional. However as building any institution takes time, the PSPU has also been taking its own time. Interestingly it was also known as the 'Reform Office'. Through interactions with a senior World Bank official it was revealed that the World Bank was also trying to play a greater role through this agency. Therefore once this unit becomes functional, the World Bank would have a more decisive effect on the policy-making aspects with regard to health sector in Orissa. Also it would be for the first time in the state that donor agencies like DFID and the World Bank would be playing a direct role in health policy making.

OHSDP

There has been another major reform initiative in terms of the Orissa Health Systems Development Project or OHSDP, which was wholly funded by the World Bank but surprisingly it has not been included as a reform initiative. In Chapter IV a detailed analysis of OHSDP has been made along with the State Health Systems Development Projects. This project carried a lot of significance because of two reasons. One was the involvement of the World Bank. Because the World Bank has got tremendous influence in economic policy making in India and as well as in

---

[5] It refers to Policy Planning and Strategic Unit, Government of Orissa.

[6] During field visit senior officials of the Health and Family Welfare Department, Government of Orissa observed that the construction work of medical institutions such as District Headquarter Hospitals, Sub Divisional Hospitals, CHCs, PHCs were mostly taken up by DFID and OHSDP in Orissa.

the health sector, specifically after the 1991 economic liberalization by India. The second reason was the amount of money being involved in this project was quite big and in all the 157 institutions[7] being upgraded under this project; user fees have been introduced to meet the maintenance expenditures.

The structures have been created in all these institutions. There has been some training of staffs in different categories undertaken in this initiative. The creation of contractual posts and the training of contractual staffs, introduction of user fees in these institutions were part of reforms in the health sector. Due to the amount of funding which has gone into this project, it would act as a force multiplier for increasing the reforms in the health sector. The World Bank was also planning to do a second phase of this project.

The Sector Reform Cell

The European Commission in the state was funding this office. It was part of the Health and Family Welfare Ministry, Government of Orissa. The European Commission was entirely funding this office and the expenditure incurred by this office was shown in the regular Health Budget of Orissa. This cell was created with the purpose that "Each of the non-SHS participating States[8] would create or so designate an existing body as the *State Health & Family Welfare Sector Reform Cell or* SH&FWSRC. This Cell was created with the idea that it would have the mandate, authority and autonomy to drive the sectoral reform process and to take all actions necessary in pursuance of that objective. The SH&FWSRC was supposed to be chaired by the Principal Secretary or Secretary in overall charge of the H & FW Sector of the State[9].

Thus the Sector Reform cell was to be created in those states where there were no State Health Systems projects going on. Thus it could be assumed that this Sector Reform Cell in Orissa was created with the assumption that the state would not go for an OHSDP project in future. It was also assumed that SHS projects would create an institution, which would

[7] These institutions were mostly secondary level institutions, however the three medical colleges and the Capital Hospital, Bhubaneswar was also included.
[8] Here the term SHS refers to State Health Systems Development Projects being financed by World Bank in different states of India.
[9] P-1 of ECTA Working Papers, 1999/22, "The Sector Reform Cell" March 2000, European Commission.

facilitate the reform process in a systematic way. Further the Sector Reform Cell was to be created to drive the sectoral reform process through an institutional mechanism, because in the absence of institutional mechanism, 'reforms tend to become a series of individual initiatives, sporadic in nature and fragile.'[10]

Further clearly identifying its domain of action it was observed "The SRC is additional capacity of the State Department of Health & FW for generating, prioritizing, advocating and assessing reform proposals in the health & family welfare sector across the State. Reforms would cover State-wide as well as district-specific aspects/activities, including donor supported activities."[11] Therefore the Sector Reform Cell was supposed to generate, prioritize, advocate and assess various reform proposals in the health sector of a state and also in different districts within a state.

Ironically the role identified for SRC would now be fulfilled by DFID funded Policy Planning and Strategic Unit or PSPU in Orissa, although the scope of PSPU was little bit larger.[12] Therefore during field visit to the state, the senior officials at SRC Orissa said that the main aim of this office had been to implement the health projects of European Union in Orissa. It was also observed that this office was engaged in selecting NGOs who could be involved in various health related IEC activities in the state. It was also engaged in selecting NGOs who could be given responsibility to operate single doctor PHC institutions in the state. Off late this office had come out with a draft plan about public private partnerships in the health sector of Orissa. There were people both from the government as well as from outside government of Orissa, working as consultants.

Handing over PHCs to NGOs

It was introduced on a pilot basis to see whether this new arrangement works out or not. This measure was introduced in 1997. In remote and difficult areas it has been difficult to manage the PHCs, as the medical

---

[10] Ibid.

[11] Ibid.

[12] As we have mentioned above that the PSPU intended to act as a think tank for Ministry of Health and Family Welfare, Government of Orissa. So it would mainly focus on larger policy issues, including health sector reforms. Therefore the creation of PSPU had clearly marginalized the Sector Reform Cell in increasing its influence in shaping the future health policy making in Orissa.

officer in charge remains absent for most of the time. There was also problem of maintaining the morale of the other staffs in these institutions. As a result the essential primary health care services were not available to the people in these areas. To address this situation, Government of Orissa came out with this innovative idea. Under this scheme one or two single doctor PHC institutions or PHC (New)'s were handed over to the NGOs. However it could not succeed due to the lack of resources and expertise on the part of the NGOs[13].

NGO Coordinator

The state government had also created a post of NGO coordinator, who would directly help the health secretary in coordination of different NGOs across the state. The NGO coordinator had been given charge of identifying mother NGOs[14] in the state who could be involved in various health programmes in the state. During the field visit it was told that these NGOs would be involved in implementation of National Rural Health Mission. Interestingly, while the NGO coordinator had been provided with an office in the Health Secretariat, no support staffs were provided and most of the time the office of the NGO coordinator used to remain closed.

It needs to be mentioned here that the NGOs in Orissa were involved after the 1999 super cyclone for relief and rehabilitation measures in the coastal districts on a large scale for the first time. However there were allegations of corruption against the NGOs. Therefore now even the government officials see them with suspicion[15]. Further the NGO sector in Orissa was also very weak. There were no activists NGOs in the state. Except some grassroots level NGOs, they hardly did exist anywhere in the state. In this scenario the idea of involving them in the implementation of National Rural Health Mission seems quite surprising.

---

[13] This was the view of senior officials of Health Directorate as well as of the officials from donor agencies.

[14] The mother NGOs were very big NGOs, under whom some small NGOs work or these NGOs had to be the bigger one's in terms of their operation in one district or in more than one district.

[15] This was the view of one of the officials dealing with NGOs at Sector Reform Cell in Orissa.

Introduction of user charges

This was introduced in 1997 in medical college hospitals, all district level government hospitals and in the Capital Hospital, Bhubaneswar. The idea was to generate some funds for maintenance of equipments and furniture in these institutions. User charges have been introduced with the exemption for people living below the poverty line. For which services or for which diagnostic categories user charges would be charged, has been left for each institution to decide. For the district level hospitals, the money collected through user charges was kept in a fund under the Zilla Swasthya Samities or district health societies. After the 'success' of introduction of user fees at various district level hospitals, Government of Orissa was trying to introduce it to the sub divisional level hospitals. The user fees had been interpreted as a success story by the officials interviewed at various levels. They were of the opinion that for petty maintenance of health institutions it had helped them a lot. However the questions with regard to exemption of the poor, the total amount of money collected compared to the total annual budget of an institution and users perception etc. need to be studied in detail.

Creation of contractual district cadre for paramedics

Earlier the paramedical staffs were recruited by the state government and were assigned to different districts. However the staffs from coastal areas were unhappy to be posted in Western Orissa or to the interior parts. As most of the paramedics were female they had also the difficulties of staying away from their families. To address this situation Government of Orissa created district cadres for paramedics, where to be a paramedic in a district one had to be from the same district. However these staffs were now recruited on a contractual basis. One senior official in the Directorate of Health Department, Orissa was of the opinion that the creation of contractual posts would make the staff work better as they don't feel the responsibility to work when they are in a permanent post. However another senior official of the nursing department in the Health Directorate, Orissa was of the opinion that it had acted as demoralizing factor for the cadres.

Privatizing cleaning in government hospitals

Initially it was introduced in the Capital Hospital, Bhubaneswar and later it has been extended to three medical colleges and to some district hospitals.

In these institutions government was no longer recruiting new sweepers. However the old staffs were retained and after their retirement no recruitment was done to fill these vacancies. Hence the idea was to give the cleaning aspect to the private sector.

Multi-skilling of health personnel

This reform measure was introduced to utilize the existing capacity of the Lab technicians fully. Before the introduction of this new measure, a lab technician for TB used to look after only the TB slides and not for malaria or leprosy. This was thought to be a waste of human resources and also as unnecessary expenditure to recruit another lab technician for the same lab. This measure was introduced in 1998 all over the state. One of the purposes of this initiative was to *cut costs* and use the existing resources efficiently and the utilisation of manpower *effectively*. Because this initiative talks about cutting costs and using resources effectively within the larger frame of fiscal austerity by the state government, it has been included as a reform initiative.

Orissa Economic Review Package

This was not a reform initiative; however it has acted as a catalyst for health sector reforms in Orissa. The government of Orissa had taken loan from the World Bank under the Orissa Economic Review Package. Earlier it was named as Orissa Economic Revival Package. The aim of this Review package was to help the state of Orissa reduce its fiscal deficit[16]. Under this measure the state government has banned any new recruitment either in health or in the education departments. It has to be remembered here that in Orissa, the government was the dominant job provider. Unlike western states[17] like Maharastra and Gujarat, there was lack of a vibrant private sector, due to historical reasons in Orissa. In this scenario, people look upon the state as the sole provider of job opportunities. By adopting the World Bank policy of ban on recruitment, the state in most probability would ruin the education and health sector, which were already in a collapsing state. The sectors like education and health need more

---

[16] Fiscal Deficit of a state suggests that its expenditure is more than its revenue. So, the fiscal austerity measures suggest that the state should be able to meet its expenditure through generating new income and cutting costs and by reducing the wasteful expenditures and subsidies in the social sectors like health and education. The idea is that the subsidies should be better targeted to the poor and the needy.

[17] Of India.

personnel unlike other sectors.[18] The World Bank's unified policies have already created havoc in countries of Sub Saharan Africa, where the basic health care structure got destroyed and now the HIV/AIDS was threatening to wipe out a generation of entire population in these societies.

Through interactions with senior officials in World Bank it was known that the World Bank was able to push for health reform in the state due to leverage they got with the state government through this package. It needs to be mentioned here that there was an element of secrecy about the nature of agreement between the government of Orissa and the World Bank officials about the nature of this package. This secrecy was emphasised both by the state government officials as well as from the World Bank. This particular aspect was seen as a matter of serious concern by many observers who say that while on the one hand the World Bank talks about transparency, in its own functioning it prefers to remain opaque.

There were other measures, which have been termed, as 'reforms', but has not been included here as 'reform'. We have termed these as systemic changes, according to our new definition of health sector reforms.

Systemic changes

As we have already discussed that systemic change was a response by a system to remain effective for a new situation. Let us have a look at the different initiatives for systemic changes taken by the state of Orissa.

Disease Surveillance programme

This was a major initiative taken in terms of surveillance of diseases in Orissa. Earlier the data related to outbreak of diseases were collected in an irregular fashion. Therefore timely interventions were not possible. However the situation changed after the 1999 super cyclone in Orissa. "With the help of World Health Organisation and Medicines Sans Frontiers and UNDP, Disease Surveillance Programme was started in 1999. Initially reporting was done on a daily basis. The UN volunteers

---

[18] For example if the higher education were not well funded, then where would the teachers for secondary education come from? And if secondary education were not well funded where would the teachers for primary education would come from? This was the view of a technical committee meeting which was held at National Institute of Educational Planning and Administration, New Delhi in the month of August 2004.

were placed at the block level and later moved into the district level[19]. The WHO was providing the technical expertise and Medicines Sans Frontiers was helping in streamlining data management system.

However once the severity had reduced, reporting started once in a week for ten diseases[20]. These diseases were identified on the basis of burden of disease study conducted by ASCI or Administrative Staff College of India, Hyderabad in 1997. Except for malaria other diseases were not included, to avoid duplication. Also vertical programmes have inbuilt surveillance mechanisms. Provisions were made that daily reporting would be done during natural disasters or outbreaks of epidemics. To identify the diseases WHO case definitions were used.

This whole initiative got reviewed by the health department[21] and the DFID. Disease Surveillance mechanism initially started in coastal districts and later between January to July 2001, it was extended to the whole state and it was funded by the DFID. A second evaluation was done by DFID in 2002," said one senior official in the state who had been closely associated with this program. However later the World Bank also provided some funding for this initiative under its OHSDP project.

Unique features

About the Disease Surveillance Program the official further said, "The unique features of this initiative were, one- reporting at sub center level and two- entire rural health machinery was being involved. The report goes from sub center to the block PHC level and from there it goes to ADMO public health at the district level. From there the report is sent to the State Disease Surveillance cell, which is chaired by joint director public health.

Earlier there was a monthly communicable diseases statement report for 17 diseases and it was done at the upwards to the block PHC level. At the end of every month a pharmacist used to send a monthly report from block

[19] One volunteer each for 10 districts and another two volunteers in two blocks. So 12 volunteers in total were provided by UNDP.

[20] Like snake bite, skin infections, diarrhoea, acute jaundice syndrome, suspected malaria, suspected meningitis, measles, acute respiratory infections, unusual syndromes etc.

[21] Here it refers to Ministry of Health and Family Welfare, Government of Orissa and DFID of the Orissa unit.

PHC to the district level. There were no definition of diseases nor there were records maintained as to how this data was compiled." The official said, "The incubation period for many communicable diseases is 10 to 15 days and hence one month was not enough to check any outbreak... In this entire process OHSDP also joined hand in 1997. They provided hardware in terms of providing computers to districts, data entry operators at the districts and at the state surveillance cell. They also provided the software component in the form of Health Management Information System, which was developed by TCS[22]. It was put in place in 30 districts and in the state disease surveillance cell. All information at district level was computerized. Reports were sent by e-mail from 20 of the districts and another 10 by fax. Also there are well defined deadlines."

Further the official added,

> Every Saturday ANMs bring reports to their sector level meeting at block PHC. One paramedic was to send the report from block to the district level. This was arranged by OHSDP. The paramedic concerned was given some honorarium. This was withdrawn in April-March 2003 and from then onwards the report was sent by phone or fax.

The official further added, "At the district level, there is a post of Assistant Health Officer who investigates outbreaks of epidemics and to analyse data on a regular basis. The data entry operator compiles the data, enters in the computer and takes print outs and transmits it to the state level. Thus ADMO Public Health, Assistant Health Officer and the data entry operator act as a team at the district level... In fourteen to sixteen districts data analysis is done once in a week. The government of Orissa is planning to introduce in all the districts the post of Assistant Health Officer or AHO. The existing AHOs get training at National Institute of Epidemiology, Chennai according to WHO guidelines. Besides the OHSDP has supplied vehicles and mobility support for the disease surveillance programme."

The official said, "Most of the Health Systems Development Projects has an inbuilt disease surveillance component. However this component has not done well in other states. Three things, adequate training, technical support[23] and facilitation are required for its success."

---

[22] Tata Consultancy Services.

[23] Which was at present being provided by the World Health Organisation in Orissa.

About the training of the staff for this program the official said, "In the last round of training 4600 to 4700 medical officers and 15,000 paramedics were trained in periphery level health services.[24] The team at the district level was given technical support by UN volunteer doctors.[25] One UN volunteer is at present managing two districts. Later on one volunteer at the state level will manage all the districts. At present there is one WHO health coordinator is there at the state level for this disease surveillance programme. Due to this programme we have now data of last four years."

Mentioning about the State Surveillance Cell the official said, "Here weekly meetings are held every Friday when the technical committee constituted by Joint Director Public Health, State Surveillance medical officer, State Epidemiologist, an expert from WHO or UNDP and another health consultant from OHSDP held their meeting."

The introduction of disease surveillance mechanism in the state was being seen by many as a success story. However there were some questions, which need to be answered satisfactorily before we could make any judgement about this program. The first and a major question were about the aspect of ANMs' collecting data from the field. As we have discussed earlier that the periphery level institutions in Orissa had almost collapsed, so how the data collected in these circumstances could be relied upon? During the field visit it was also observed that due to structural constraints, the ANMs used to visit the fields rarely and many of them were found to be ignorant about various national programs. Therefore even if an ANM has collected some data with regard to different diseases, could it be said with certainty that the diseases had been identified correctly? So was there a gap in this program in not identifying this structural problem?

New Drugs Policy

The basic driving force behind this new initiative was to cut costs and to make available quality drugs to the people who utilize government health care services. The new drugs policy was introduced in 1998 and it was from the adoption of Tamilnadu model. The principal features of this policy were: central procurement of drugs, adoption of an essential drugs

[24] Periphery level health institutions were CHCs, PHCs, PHC (New) s and Area Hospitals and sub centres etc.

[25] UN volunteer doctors were mostly fresh medical graduates with willingness to work in Public Health. They were attached to ADMO Public Health and the CDMO at the district level.

list from WHO and shifting from brand drugs to generic drugs. After these new measures the drugs were purchased at the central level through an open tendering system and distributed to the districts. This helped in reducing corruption to a great extent. Thus with the new drugs policy the cost of drugs got reduced and the quality of drugs available in the government run health services institutions improved.

It has to be remembered that these initiatives in the drugs sector was applicable only for the government health care sector. WHO had conducted an impact study of this new drugs policy in the state and their study found that drugs were available in more than 85 percent of the government institutions.[26]

Pancha Byadhi Chikitsa scheme

The above term in Oriya means treatment for five diseases. This scheme was introduced in 1999 and it had identified five diseases like, *leprosy, malaria, acute respiratory infections, scabies and diarrhoea,* which would be treated free of cost at any government institution[27] and medicine would also be provided free. After doing an epidemiological study it was found that these diseases were the major reasons for more than 70 percent of morbidity and mortality in the state. Hence this scheme was introduced.

Petty Maintenance for Buildings at PHC headquarters

Here Rs 10,000 per year was to be given to the Medical Officer in-charge at the block headquarter PHC to spend for petty maintenance expenditures in his or her own discretion. This has not been included as a reform measure in this study because this initiative tried to improve the functioning of a government periphery level institutions and it did not fulfill our definition of reform.

Mandatory Pre-PG rural service

Under this scheme any medical graduate aspiring for a PG degree from any government medical college must serve for one year in rural and remote areas after getting selected for a PG course. This was introduced to

---

[26] This was revealed by senior officials involved in new drugs policy of Orissa.

[27] Starting from a sub centre to PHC, CHC, Sub Divisional Hospital, District Headquarter Hospital and Medical Colleges.

address the absence of doctors in rural and remote areas in periphery level institutions like PHCs.

Internship training for medical graduates

This scheme was introduced in the year 2000 to train medical graduates for Social and Preventive Medicine course under the guidance of a CDMO. This new measure was introduced to give exposure to the medical students about how the periphery level institutions like PHCs and CHCs function at the grassroots level. This was a revised course curriculum for the medical students to give them a comprehensive training about the preventive aspects of health care.

Creation of Zilla Swasthya Samities[28]

Earlier there were different societies for different diseases like malaria, TB etc to manage them at the district level. Funds were also maintained separately. However to improve the better management of different societies, it was decided to amalgamate all these societies and to create a new society in its place with District collector as the chairman and the CDMO or Chief District Medical Officer as the secretary. This scheme was introduced in 1999. This new scheme also aimed about making effective the district level societies. For example if the funds under TB had been almost zero and there was a case of TB outbreak in the district, then under this new mechanism, funds under other head could be transferred to meet the demands of the situation and later when the funds for TB comes, it would be transferred to the head from where it was drawn. This facility was earlier not available. Interacting with officials at different levels in the state it was learnt that creation of ZSS has helped a lot in addressing emergency situations.

Criteria for reform elements

In this study we have defined health sector reforms in terms of an element of private participation in the changes introduced in health sector in the state. Using these criteria we have selected the above elements as reforms and those, which could not fulfill these criteria, has been termed as systemic changes. However in both the cases we have looked at the structural constraints in implementation of these new initiatives.

---

[28] See the structure of ZSS in the annexure of this chapter.

The above criteria of selection of different initiatives as reform or not has significant repercussions. For example the new drugs policy could not be accepted as a reform initiative. Why? The reasons were that all the three new elements introduced in the drugs sector in Orissa, namely, central procurement of drugs, adoption of an essential list from the WHO and shifting from brand names to generic names, were basically measures aimed at improving the quality of drugs available at *government institutions* and reducing the cost of drugs purchased by the government from the private parties to be made available at government institutions. Hence here hardly any element of 'reform' according to our definition was there. However this new drugs policy by the state government could be termed as a measure towards *improving the system of drugs supply* while ensuring the *quality drugs* being supplied to the public from a government health institution. These changes could at best be termed as *revisions* by a government department to improve its performance and to respond in a better way to the needs of the public. On the other hand terming these initiatives as 'reforms' was not appropriate.

Any system tries to respond to the new challenges that it faces in its day to day functioning. With due course of time many of its elements, which were created with a particular set of purposes in mind, are not able to respond to the new challenges and hence these elements need to be replaced by other elements which could cope with the new challenges in a better way. Those changes, which have been termed as reforms, were in fact an attempt to make the system respond to the new challenges. However terming these changes as a reform initiative was problematic.

The process and experience of reforms

In this section we would be discussing about the process and experience of reforms from the field interviews with government officials as well as from the donor agencies in Delhi and in Bhubaneswar, the capital of Orissa. In the context of Orissa it was clear that to understand the process and experience of health sector reforms, we need to also look at the processes which initiated systemic changes, because at the policy making level these were not separate processes.

On the process of reforms

Talking about the process of reforms in health sector in Orissa, one former senior official from the government of Orissa said, "We undertook broad reforms. There are large reforms and there are small reforms. These reforms are changes in the system rather than temporary change. A much better system of health care was the intended outcome. The quality of health care was intended to be changed. With these objectives the reforms were started." Therefore the changes introduced were not temporary changes and they were intended to improve the quality of health care available in the government health care institutions.

Two events

The official added, "There were a lot of interests in the reforms. DFID has been supporting health programmes in Orissa since 1980s. But at that point of time … the state evaluation showed that while structures had been put in place, quality had not improved. That was because certain systems were faulty. There were some clear problems in certain areas. They identified three areas called three M's…medicine, maintenance and mobility. Medicines…generally availability, cost appropriateness etc. Maintenance of vehicles, of buildings, of equipments etc. which had broken down. Mobility…there was not enough money for TA, for supervision." Therefore the initiatives for reforms in health sector started with these changes. Although these changes were systemic in nature they paved the way for reforms in the health sector.

What the interviewee was trying to say was that the UK funding agency DFID was involved in the infrastructure projects in the state since early 1980s.[29] Although investments were made in the building of primary health centers and sub centers in different districts, the maintenance was in bad shape. Hence a stock of the then existing situation was taken by DFID. The second event was, "The Orissa Legislature set up a house committee. They also found various problems in the health sector. So the time was ripe for health reforms. When I joined in 1996 as health secretary, I thought that situation was right to introduce a number of reforms because the political atmosphere was also there and various evaluation reports had also come up. One of the things in any reform… because you have to study the situation, plan it out… all that…but there is also the other side of it. If you don't start…then you plan, you examine, you study and by the time you start, may be you get transferred. So there is nobody then to champion that. So my feeling was that small or big, the study should be done very quickly and the reform should be started very quickly. Of

[29] At that time it was known as ODA or Overseas Development Assistance.

course the situation had to be studied about what would work and what would not work.

But I do not think that the study should be very detailed or over a period of time, because by that time the momentum is lost and the person who is pushing it may have been transferred. Every reform has to have a champion. Reform will never be brought about if you are not passionate about it. If you think that let's do something, ok… we will have it…five different people will decide…it never happens. Reforms have to have a champion in my view and that champion has to push it very hard. So, since tenures are uncertain in the states and you can never be sure… once you got your department that you will stay there for a certain period of times…two years…three years…four years, long enough to study it, examine it and then initiate it. My view was that we should take opportunity as and when it comes and with some preparation you should start. With this in mind I had taken up various reform initiatives in the state."

Therefore the observations of the respondent here were very significant because here the respondent was mentioning about the constraints of initiating reforms in a democratic set up like India could occur, where a bureaucrat could be transferred at any moment. Therefore even if an initiative had been taken it would just remain there and when a new person comes in nobody knows what might happen. Thus on the one hand to initiate reforms one need to study the ground situation because then only one could expect that the initiatives taken could have an impact in the field. But on the other hand the relationship between a bureaucrat and a politician in Indian context was such that if one goes for an intervention which was supported by well researched study then by the time the findings were published, the person who might have taken the interest in these reforms would get transferred. But here the question arises that why this kind of situation occurs at all? Was it the case that there was no consensus among the political leadership for reforms in health sector? Therefore from what the respondent was talking about it seems that reforms in health sector in Orissa were initiated half hazardly. Or could we say that in a democratic set up like India it was very difficult to start a reform process with broad political consensus?

On preparing the vision document

But how the vision document was prepared in the first place? Was their wider consultations held?[30] "It was entirely in-house. It was not done by donors. It was entirely written by us. Then after it was ready, we gave it to the donors also and to various government departments in the state and we did all kinds of consultations.....We had consultations with doctors association, nurses association, multipurpose health workers association and other group workers...why things are not functioning as far as they are concerned or are not functioning as they should? So all this we did. Then we redrafted the document many times and then we prepared the vision document, which we got approved by the cabinet[31]. But the vision document was also drawn up from my seven years of being in the health department and from the reform experiences. All this was used to form the vision document," said the official. Thus the vision was prepared by consulting various levels of health officials within the government of Orissa health services structure. This document could also draw from the years of experience of various officials at various levels before it was passed by Orissa cabinet.

Here the respondent was mentioning about the wider consultation process held with different stakeholders in the health care system of Orissa. However these consultations were not systematically held and were selectively conducted by the top officials from Health and Family Welfare Department, where the need for the consultation was felt from a particular section. Because from the interviews with CDMOs in two of our study districts it was revealed that there was no consultation with them and they also had said that they had no knowledge that other CDMOs were consulted about the reform process initiated in Orissa.

Need for a vision document

But the question arises as to what was the necessity for introducing a vision document? "What we did after that was...you know the vision document sets out what needs to be done. There are a number of donors also working in Orissa and we wanted to present this vision document to them. Then what we thought was that once we have a vision document,

[30] This question was asked because one of the senior donor agency officials had claimed that donor agencies were consulted prior to the creation of Orissa vision document 2010.

[31] Here the term 'cabinet' refers to the Orissa state cabinet ministers.

then donors don't come out with their own programmes. Prior to that particular donor says 'I am interested in women's health so I will have a programme on women's health.' Somebody else come up and says, 'no I am interested in upgrading hospitals, as buildings are very bad… so let us have hardware, like your equipments need upgraded etc.' Somebody else comes up and says 'we will build ANM centers.' So each donor used to come with its own interests, which was partly dictated by its own mission.

But what we thought was that it was not always what we needed. And therefore once you put a vision document, which lists out all the things that the state needs, then the donors can read that document and can say, 'ok my interest is in this part.' They don't come readymade with an idea that I want to work on women's health. They will look that 'yes women's health is a problem and that's my interest and I will support.' Somebody else looks at the document and says, 'communicable diseases are an important part I am interested.' It's not that they come in and the state accommodates…ok you want to have programme for AIDs… we will support or you want to have programmes for tuberculosis…you want to have programme for building sub-centers… Instead of that what's the state's requirement and the direction in which the state wishes to move... What is it the state wishes to achieve? Where does the state wishes to be in certain number of years and how does it wish to do that? What is the path it wishes to take and then any donor who wishes to work in the health sector can read the document and say, 'well this part of the document concern my mission statement, my objectives, therefore I will work in it.' Or 'this part of it reflects my interests, which is poverty alleviation and by doing this health programme we feel that poverty will be addressed.'

So by making the document we spell out how the state wants to do and then donors who wish to support can come in…can support any part of that document. That was the intention. *It will not then be donor led but it will be state led.*"

So here by explaining the rationale of a vision document the official was mentioning about the way donor agencies function in a state like Orissa. These were practical difficulties about coordination of donor interests with the interests of a particular state. Because each donor have their own mission statements and accordingly they try to implement their programs to achieve some targets. But the state also has its own priority areas where it needs to intervene. Therefore if a vision document of a state was there then the donors could choose from this document and accordingly go for an area of their interest. This was an important initiative by the state of Orissa because the idea was that the democratically elected state government had a better understanding of the realities of Orissa health sector and hence if they come out with a vision document then it would not only help in donor coordination but it would also help the state in better utilisation of its limited resources in terms of priority areas of interventions.

"Of course there are many things also beyond that. *If you have too many donor programmes, it becomes very difficult to manage because each one has their own reporting system.* You know, DFID has their own reporting manner, DANIDA will want in a certain periodicity or in a certain pattern. EU will want in a certain pattern. So each one has different criteria," said the official. Therefore this different reporting pattern also puts burden on the state to provide data about the impact a particular intervention might have made, to a particular donor agency.

> What we also hope would happen[32] is then everybody supports the Orissa health plan, which is part of the vision document and without saying that, 'I am supporting the TB programme and you report to me about the TB programme.' ...I am supporting let's say family welfare programme or immunization programme and you report to me on that. Instead of that they look at the vision document and say that yes we will support this and this... but individual reports will not go. *This is called sector wide programme, where everybody supports the sector but not specific parts of it...may be its specific but not segmented with different norms of reporting. That's an ultimate kind of hope because the management of so many different donors, so many different kinds of reporting, and so many different kinds of programmes is very difficult. Each one starting at a different year, some going on for five years, some for seven years, some in three districts, some in eight districts... you know all kinds of combinations... all kinds of programmes.*

Therefore here the respondent was trying to put the point in a very straightforward manner. It was suggested that if all the donors would support the vision document and choose their areas of intervention from this document then it would not lead to overlapping of programs and the present system of different types of reporting for different donors, which takes a lot of time won't be required. During the field visit it was observed

[32] This hope was based on the publication of Orissa Vision Document 2010, which was supposed to act as a guideline for donor agencies operating/interested to work in Orissa.

that donor agencies had taken up few districts to present their success story as a role model, which could be replicated by the state in particular, and also by the adjoining states. Their aim was to show some results. But they were not functioning to fulfill the larger health goals of the state.[33]

Continuing with her views the official said, "So if you have one document first of all they will select what you think as important and what you have put up and ultimate objective is that then they don't have individual donor problems. They support the health sector. The report will go to all of them, one common report; because they have to of course meet... their constituency...money is coming from their taxpayers. Therefore they will have to show to their taxpayers that this is what we have done. *So some kind of reporting is required. But we don't have to have different kinds of reporting to different donors.* So this will ultimately happen...not an easy thing. But certainly the state could say that this is where we want to go. This is where we want to go in medical education. This is where we want to go to family welfare, in child health, in infant mortality, in communicable diseases, in aurveda, in traditional medicines and homeopathy. All these things and taking into account the problems that the state has...certain constraints the state has. For instance the state has a problem in getting enough doctors...don't have enough graduates...they do not want to go to remote places. We had taken up many reforms to address that but this is a long-term thing and not something, which you can do today and feel that it is solved. It's a major problem. What do you do about things that ANMs stay in their fields they are posted...? So we looked into the constraints of the state. We looked into what could be done and we looked into the needs of the state and then prepared the vision."

Hence if a single report was prepared by the state and then it was circulated among the donor agencies, it would fulfill their criteria of showing some outcomes of the money they had invested and it would also be helpful for the state concerned. The interviewee was also mentioning that in case of Orissa the vision document 2010 was prepared keeping in view the structural constraints of the state, like where the strengths of the health services in the state was, which areas would require more attention,

---

[33] For example the work of UNICEF and UNFPA in Orissa fall in this category, where they were trying to intervene in certain selected districts to show results to their own funding sources as well as to the state governments. The whole point was about making their presence in the state a legitimate one. But in this process the larger picture was being missed.

which areas would require more time for achieving any health outcomes etc.

Reasons for formation of the House Committee

The formation of House Committee in the Orissa legislature in 1996 had been mentioned as the factor, which paved the way for initiating reforms in health sector in the state. So the question arises as to why this house committee was formed at that time? "The House Committee[34] also made recommendations on the attendance of doctors and cleanliness of hospitals etc.... Health is something, which affects everybody and in Orissa unlike other states, most of the health is government provided or most of the health providers are government institutions. Very few private hospitals... at best few mission hospitals. In Cuttack and Bhubaneswar also big hospitals are few. They are mainly small nursing homes...now Kalinga hospital is there. So private health care is practically missing...ok ...individual doctors are there. In the rural areas individual private doctors are hard to find. The government doctors who are there mostly do the private practice.... Because health is generally provided by the state and health affects every human being, every citizen of the state. Hence it is natural that people get agitated with any problem in health...quality not so good... and people's representatives...MLAs[35] reflects the people's wish and therefore this committee was formed. So the climate was right for change and we took that opportunity to bring about a large number of changes," said the official.

This was a very significant observation. The officials said that Orissa was a state where the presence of private sector was almost non existent and in cities like Cuttack and Bhubaneswar there were small nursing homes and only few big hospitals exist in these cities, otherwise it was the government sector which was having presence everywhere. Therefore it was quite natural that when this government health system was not functioning in certain aspects than the people's representative had to raise the issues of availability and quality of care in Orissa Legislature.

For our purpose it was important to notice that the argument for more private participation in Orissa health sector by the donor agencies as well as by the government health officials at different levels of health services

[34] Of Orissa Legislature.
[35] Members of Legislative Assembly in the state.

structure in Orissa, misses this important point that Orissa was a state where not only the government sector was the major provider of health care, the presence of private sector was almost negligible even in cities like Bhubaneswar, the capital of Orissa. Therefore the question arises as to whether the arguments for creating more space for private sector were influenced by a uniform model of reforming the health sector?

New Drugs Policy[36]

In case of Orissa the first thing, which was thought to be requiring urgent attention for intervention was the then existing, drugs policy. This was mentioned as a priority area requiring intervention by the DFID report at that time. The new drugs policy in Orissa has also been widely appreciated and has been termed as a success story. So the question arises what were the changes made in drugs policy at that time? Responding to this the official said, "Now in this system what happened…we were ordering but it was being verified in the district level. So at the state level we were telling the districts that we have ordered one lakh of these tablets for you and it is being delivered by such and such persons and we also test the quality. Once it goes to the district, the district sends us the sample. It is not that I am not taking samples, which the manufacturer gives…may be he is giving me few good samples…I am saying it very good…. It is going to the districts and districts are sending the samples to us. If the district feels that it's the bad quality and…that they are sending and we are testing it. Now, if I send one lakh tablets of a particular kind, until the district certifies that…yes, one lakh tablets have been received then I am not making the payment. Main advantage of this system is that…one; you don't have multiple points of ordering and multiple points of payments, which lead to increase in costs. Suppose I am a drug supplier, if I have to get 30 different orders for 30 districts[37] and then for three medical colleges…then 33 orders I have to get. Then every order will be small and the interior districts will be very small. So I will not go at all…why should I take the trouble of sending small quantities there? Because I will go to Cuttack, I will go to Khurda, I will go to Berhampur[38] and I will say you

---

[36] While in the earlier section of this chapter we have discussed about the new drugs policy in brief, here we have discussed about the process involved in formulation of new drugs policy in Orissa.

[37] It needs to be mentioned here that Orissa had 30 districts in total.

[38] Cuttack, Khurda and Berhampur were among the developed districts of Orissa.

buy…and I am not bothered about whether Malkangiri[39] gets or not. Because profit is very less and what happens when there are 33 different purchasers… There are so many drugs. Now which drugs to buy, it was up to the CDMO… Now… the CDMO does not have the time to write to 50 different people.[40] So what would happen is that, one particular drug…suppose I am the supplier of one particular drug or two drugs and I go to the CDMO…give me contract. So the CDMO thinks that my money will lapse by 31st March and the list was usually ready by let's say December-January. So I have only three months…by the time I order, I won't be able to give the payments. So let me give order to this person or to five people… I don't buy all the medicines that I require and there is no assessment of quantities of medicine."

So what were the changes made in the new drugs policy? First the new system introduced central quality checks. So the drugs were purchased centrally after quality tests by the state government and then they would send the required quantities to districts and ask the districts to report them whether the drugs were of good quality or not. After the districts mentioned that the drugs were of good quality then only the payments were made to the manufacturers. But if the districts mentioned that the drugs were not of good quality then they would send some samples to the state government for further verification. The second aspect was about purchasing of drugs centrally which was in contrast to multiple points of orderings and payments. In the earlier system it was not financially profitable for the manufacturers to send drugs in smaller districts as well as to districts having bad road connectivity and also as their volume would have been very small. So these districts used to suffer due to lack of adequate and quality drugs supply. The new system addressed these lacunae. Thirdly it also addressed the issue of structural constraints the CDMOs used to face in purchasing drugs.

"We changed all that. We reduced the list. Earlier we had huge list of several hundred drugs…. We took the WHO list, got all the doctors, asked them what are the drugs required. We got all the requisitions from the districts and then we came down to the minimum. So first we reduced the list and then made a central drugs list and then made an assessment of the quantities required…then we got the tenders and finalized the bids…then we ordered the medicine…. But we said, so much in Sundergarh, so much

[39] Malkangiri was one of the poorest districts in Orissa with very low health indicators.

[40] About the required necessary drugs in the district.

in Sambalpur, so much in Nuapara, so much in Gajapati[41]…and when they delivered…and they[42] would give an acknowledgement and then we paid. So there is no way of cheating. Because…suppose I have an agreement with the drugs supplier and say that instead of one lakh tablets you give me fifty thousand and I will pay you for one lakh and you give me a kickback…The man at Sambalpur, he is not going to write one lakh when fifty thousand tablets have been given. Is not it? There are so many checks. There are 30 districts and 3 medical colleges. Why would everybody agree to write a false thing? So… there is no way they can tie up with the manufacturer…also because they[43] are not paying. So suppose a manufacturer gives them… instead of one lakh, fifty thousand and they write one lakh…then the manufacturer will not be paid by him; he will be paid by me.[44] So there is no guarantee that the manufacturer will go back to him and say ok, you wrote a higher amount and this is your kickback. Why? Because he does not have any control on him. So, there are checks and balances," said the official. Therefore first the drugs list was reduced by following the WHO guidelines for essential drugs and this was being supported by feedback from districts and various medical officers' opinion about essential drugs required. As payments were made centrally there was no question of misuse of money by the CDMOs as it was earlier the case.

Ensuring quality

But what about the quality of drugs being procured from the manufacturers? Continuing with her narratives the official said, "And then the quality is very important. Earlier what people doing were…they were all ordering, as time was limited. All these small-scale industries were going and they were giving rotten medicines…I mean absolutely third rate. What we did was that every batch of medicine we tested. We got samples from all the districts and the same batch we sent samples to two private laboratories about which nobody knew. If the laboratory says it's good, then it's ok. If they say it's sub standard, then we send the same batch of samples to two more laboratories. If one of them again says it is bad then we ask the supplier to take back the entire batch…. But what I am

---

[41] Sundergarh, Sambalpur, Nuapara and Gajapati were the districts of Orissa.

[42] Refers to the districts. That was when the drug supplier has delivered the medicines in a particular district; the CDMO would give them an acknowledgement of the medicines received.

[43] The CDMOs.

[44] Here it refers to the central purchasing of drugs.

trying to say is, we worked out a full proof system. And the supplier also…they could give us in much lower rates. Why? Because instead of going to 30 districts to collect their money… he goes to Sundergarh and says ok I have supplied so much and my bill is RS 2,500, please give me…How much manpower and how much time he requires to go to all these districts… Once you go the money may not have come, the allotment may not have come or may have exhausted. So they would have to make five trips. And therefore either they do not supply to the small districts or they make their rates very high. Because if I have to go five times to collect that money and I have to go to 30 places to collect the money, that means I will bill it all into my cost."

Therefore in the earlier system it was a cumbersome process for the manufacturers to approach 30 districts of Orissa and as a result it was also not cost effective for them. With the new system for quality checks a well laid out mechanism was created. Once the samples from different districts were received they were sent for quality tests to two private laboratories[45] and if there was any doubts then again this batch of sample was to be sent to two more laboratories and if here also doubts were raised about the standards of medicines then the manufacturer would be asked to take back the entire batch of that medicine.

Continuing with her narrative the official said, "Here what we did was we paid at the central level. So, provided you have delivered, provided they have given an acknowledgement and say that you have delivered… we pay 90 percent and when we get the test report we pay the remaining debts. We also got the system evaluated by Delhi Society for the Promotion of Rational Use of Drugs. They said that it is such an excellent system that it should not only be emulated by other states but also by other countries…. Due to these new initiatives availability of drugs has increased tremendously." So the new system not only ensured the quality of drugs being supplied it also helped in increasing the availability of drugs in government run health institutions.

"The other thing that we did was earlier what was happening…there is a community health center. Let's say they get Rs 30,000 worth of drugs. When they ask for the drugs…so from the district they would say ok you take this and this and it is worth Rs30,000, so you take it. They did not have a chance to choose. So, they cannot say that I want A, B, C, D… and

[45] Which were outside the state of Orissa and their whereabouts were kept secret.

you give me this. The district would just say ok you need Rs 30,000 worth drugs… you take. Whether it was worth Rs 30,000 nobody knows. It may be more… it may be less. But it was not what the CHC or the PHC chooses.

Under the new system we give each of them a pass and we give them a list. Certain lists at primary level, certain lists at secondary level…and then they would write…we want this…we want this and it would go and then that they would be given. And because all these centers where we supplied…monitored over Internet by e-mail. So at any point of time we know how much drugs were available in a particular district store," said the official.

So in the earlier system at the periphery level institutions like PHC or CHC they had no choice from the district headquarter about the type of medicine they required and they had no way to ascertain that they were getting this much amount of drugs. The new system provided them with a pass and a list of medicines they can get from their districts. And as all the drug stores in 30 districts were connected by Internet, the State Drugs Management Unit had information about the quantity and type of drugs available at each of these stores. So if a drug was available then they could not deny it to the particular PHC or CHC concerned. The pass system also ensured that these periphery level institutions could get their share of drugs.

How could new Drugs Policy succeed?

But the question arises as to why in spite of lot of opposition drugs reform[46] could succeed? Replying to this question the official said, "Actually you know, for any change there will be opposition, even if it does not go against the vested interests. They are used to a certain way of doing things and somebody comes and says 'no no this way not correct and actually may be other is better,' but you are used to it and you don't want to change. All change is difficult …is opposed." The official here

[46] It needs to be mentioned here that the interviewee was asked about 'drugs reform' and not about new drugs policy because the 'drug reforms' has been used as a conceptual category in this study and the respondent had termed this new initiative as 'reforms' in the drugs policy. Therefore it was deliberately used to elicit natural response from the respondent, although we have interpreted in this study the new drugs policy as systemic change.

was mentioning about the typical bureaucratic culture in countries like India, which was resistant to any kind of change.

"In drugs we got a major change. There was opposition. Interests were both… those who purchased at the district level and those who supplied…because there was no quality testing, so anything could be given. There was nobody else to check the quantity. I order you, you give me. I order Rs1lakh and agreement with you is Rs50,000 thousand and I sign for Rs1lakh. There is no third person coming. You give me Rs50,000 and I sign for a Rs1lakh," said the official. Thus in the earlier system as there was no checks and balances, at the CDMO level corruption was rampant. Hence when the new system was introduced it was opposed by both the CDMOs and the local manufacturers as both of them were going to loose.

Continuing with her narrative the official said, "… The opposition was mainly from the people who purchased[47] and the small-scale industries that were getting lots of benefits because they were giving sub-standard medicines. But it[48] got approved initially. It's only later that people got to realize that it was hitting them. So initially we had lots of opposition. In the Assembly they said, *we were buying IV fluids for Rs 22 and now they are getting it for Rs 9, how is it possible? It must be just water.* We said saline is only water and salt in a sterile condition! But the rate was high because you were making it very expensive for the person to supply it…We said that no, Tamilnadu gets even cheaper…Their system was better perhaps. We were just starting…So when they realized that availability of medicine was tremendous…. Doctors were also discouraging patients earlier…and would say that you purchase from outside as sub standard medicines were coming. Gradually the doctors found that no…it was of good quality."

Therefore here a good example has been provided about carrying out reform process in a democratic set up like India. So those who were affected by this new drugs policy like the CDMOs and the local manufacturers, they approached their local MLAs to raise this issue in Orissa Legislative Assembly. But when the actual benefits of these new initiatives were argued then this opposition gradually had to yield.

---

[47] Here it referred about the CDMOs.

[48] Here the respondent was mentioning about the new drugs policy.

The same question was asked to a person in Orissa who had been a part of drugs reform in the state. The official concerned said, "There was opposition from group of CDMOs, and few doctors instigated by local medicine shops, some drug companies and from within the department opposition was from the local drugs inspectors."[49] Therefore opposition was also from the local medicine shops and the drugs inspectors who could make money out of low quality drugs from the manufacturers. Another official in the PSPU[50] who had been closely associated with drugs reform said, "Earlier the CDMOs were hand in gloves with the local manufacturers. Now neither the drug budget nor the weir houses have changed but 90% of the resourses are being used. Earlier it was the reverse."

The official further said, "Earlier the local manufacturers were providing very sub standard drugs with almost no quality checks. There were many repackaging industries that would be bringing medicines from Calcutta and Hyderabad and package and sell it where they had 10% profits. These local manufacturers have made lot of money through selling bad quality drugs to the state in connivance of the CDMOs. And they used to spend their holidays in Goa, Calcutta or Mumbai with this ill-gotten money. There was no way to check quality of drugs being supplied".

So there were vested interests and still the reforms succeeded. So when this official was asked for reasons he said, "It's very simple. The total amount of money for drugs in one year is Rs 10 crores. And this includes the money invested by donors like World Bank in the drugs. This is a very small amount compared to say construction of a road, where for one kilometers of construction work, Rs 1 crore is involved. Hence chances of making money are good. The second important reason was that the then health secretary was very much determined that the reforms should succeed".[51] So the new drugs policy could succeed although there was so much opposition because the total amount of money involved was very

[49] The official was giving an example that in case of bandage no supplier was complying with length and breadth. Earlier their profit was 500 to 1000 times. And in case of threads weight had been given so that it could not be manipulated.

[50] PSPU or Policy Planning and Strategic Unit had started as a nodal agency by DFID to work as a think tank for the government of Orissa, for formulation of health policy and for implementation and monitoring of these policies.

[51] The person concerned was a medical officer earlier in the State Drugs Management Unit or SDMU and currently was in the same post in Policy Planning and Strategic Unit or PSPU.

low and because of the backing of then top most official of Health and Family Welfare Department of government of Orissa.

Continuing with the narrative the official said, "Some politicians argued that the state is planning conspiracy against local manufacturers and some even went to the extent that the state will purchase drugs from the multinationals. To this we said that we would give preference to you while purchasing drugs, provided you apply through the tendering process and subject yourself for quality tests. The term quality test was anathema to them. They were not used to it!" Thus adopting a wider consultative process with all the stake holders, like CDMOs, local manufacturers, Politicians etc. and keeping the door open for any suggestion helped in bringing the much needed changes in the drugs available in the government sector.

Borrowing from Tamilnadu model

Whether a part of the Tamilnadu model was adopted for drugs reform initiated in Orissa? Replying to this question former health secretary said, "No, it was the whole of the Tamilnadu model that we adopted. In preparation of protocol we had gone beyond Tamilnadu model. Protocol meaning how you treat a particular disease. Suppose it is diarrhoea, how you treat it? What is the appropriate treatment about which all the experts agree? Then you workout how many people suffer from diarrhoea and what would be the requirement of these medicines which are proposed? Your purchases are also done on that basis. So you can workout a requirement on the basis of the protocol. So the protocol…and we also had five diseases programme.[52] That was an important innovation/initiative that we took."

So while the whole of Tamilnadu model was borrowed, another addition to it was made in terms of introduction of protocol for various diseases in Orissa. Therefore it seems that the new drugs policy was a major systemic initiative taken by the state government in the late 1990s.

The context of health sector reforms

Elaborating about the role of house committee in the state legislative assembly of Orissa, a senior official of DFID in Delhi said, "A son of a

[52] In Oriya called Pancha Byadhi Chikitsa.

member of the House Committee had died in the Capital Hospital, Bhubaneswar, due to lack of essential drugs at right time. And that member was quite an influential person in the state legislature. And because of intervention from him the initiatives for reforms started in the state". This was an important observation from an official closely involved with health sector in Orissa. This reflects one of the unique aspects of beginning of health sector reforms in the state.

"Thus the reforms in the drugs sector started in Orissa in 1998. It was limited only to the government health care services,"[53] said the official. Therefore we could say that to better understand the new drugs policy we could take the year 1998 as a dividing period. So let us look at the pre 1998 period and the post 1998 period.

Pre 1998 period

The system before 1998 was somewhat like this:
"i- The CDMOs used to purchase drugs from different sources in brand names. There were overlapping of drugs.
ii- Earlier there was no open tender system. So the price[54] was very high.
iii- Purchases were from the traders and there were middleman[55] involved.
iv- No control in expiry date of drugs.
v- Difficulties in procuring drugs for smaller districts due to low volume of requirements and the transportation costs on behalf of the manufacturers used to raise the cost of drugs.
vi- There was no need based procurements.
vii- No quality control measures and
viii- All the drugs were procured in loose."[56]

After 1998 scenario

"i- An essential drugs list was prepared with the help of WHO.
ii- All drugs were purchased in generic names.[57]
iii- There is an open tendering system.[58]

---

[53] The availability of quality drugs in the private sector was the responsibility of the Directorate of Drugs Control, Government of Orissa.
[54] Price of drugs.
[55] Those who used to bargain price on behalf of manufacturers and the CDMOs.
[56] Excerpts from an interview with an official who had been closely associated with Drugs reform in Orissa.
[57] The price difference between generic and brand names was 50%.

iii- Essential drugs list got updated in every two years in consultation with district authorities and specialists from all disciplines.
iv- Purchases were made on the basis of requirements.
v- The budget of drugs was divided into 80:20 that means 80% of the drugs budget was used for central procurement and the remaining 20% goes to the periphery[59] for emergency drugs, for oxygen and lab agents and for transportation of drugs from district to periphery.
vi- The drugs were available in competitive price due to bulk purchases and the cost was reduced by 40-50%.
vii- All drugs were supplied in strip or blister packing.[60]
viii- Maximum retail price is not mentioned over the strip and *Orissa government supply not for sale* is printed to avoid pilferage[61]. This was one of the tender conditions.
ix- All drugs are received at the weir house at 5/6th of shelf life.
x- Providing slow moving essential drugs[62] for smaller districts.
xi- Quality control measures by sending samples of drugs to outside state labs.
xii- The entire system has been computerized from the state to the district level and records are maintained on a daily basis."

What the drugs reform[63] lack

While the new drugs policy has been termed as a success story, let us see where gaps lie. The major lacuna was that the private sector in the state was excluded from its purview and it was the Directorate of Drugs Control, who through its drugs inspectors ensured that quality drugs were available in the market. But an interview with a senior official in the Directorate of Drugs Control suggested that there was acute shortage of drugs inspectors in the state. Further an official at PSPU said, "The report

---

[58] Out of 290 items of essential list, 36 items were procured through small scale industries and 254 items were procured through the open tender. And 9% price preference was given to local industries. Because of this in every one crore rupees the state used to loose Rs 9 lakhs approximately.
[59] Here periphery refered to the districts.
[60] For better patient compliance and to ensure the quality of drugs.
[61] Pilferage of costly vaccines like, anti-rabbies, anti snake and saline bottles etc.
[62] For diseases like diabetes and for heart patients.
[63] Here the term drug reform has been used to suggest popular use of the term by the officials of the state government and by the donor agencies. However we have put the reforms in the drugs sector as systemic change in this study.

of the drugs inspector is final and hence there is quite a possibility that they can be bribed by the private clinics or private drug stores to give them a license". Therefore not involving the private sector was a major gap in this new policy.

An official of DFID in Delhi office agreed that without regulating the private sector or bringing the private sector in the domain of reforms it would be difficult to control the quality of drugs available in the market.

However the initiatives introduced in the drugs sector was important for us for another reason because "the government of Orissa rather than rewarding the drugs department for saving drugs it punishes them by reducing the amount saved through reform measures taken. Thus suppose you have an annual budget of Rs100 crore for drugs and through reform measures you save about Rs30 crore than in the next year the drug budget is reduced to Rs70 crore. And the government will tell you that you do not need those extra money".[64] This was a significant observation because in different aspects of health sector the government of Orissa has been introducing the concept of 'effective' and 'efficient' use of resources.

Why private sector was excluded?

As we have said that the new drugs policy only included the government system and the private sector was excluded. Replying to this question one former senior official said, "There was already a system.[65] We have drugs controller. Every state has a drugs controller. And they look into the quality of drugs and there is a drugs control act, drugs and cosmetics act. All that is already established and there is nothing that we can do. I mean whatever we do… as per the act. Like spurious medicines are caught… combination medicines, which are not permitted, medicines being advertised as food supplements… So there is a big infrastructure, there is drugs controller, drugs inspectors. That goes on… All the quality control of those drugs, preventing spurious drugs from coming into the market or preventing higher rates being charged, all that is part of the drugs and cosmetics act." Perhaps what the official was trying to say was that if initially the private sector had covered then it would have been very difficult to manage or implement this new policy on drugs.

---

[64] This was revealed through an interview with a senior DFID official in Delhi.
[65] The official was referring about the private sector.

The official also mentioned that the new drugs policy as it introduced generic drugs in place of brand drugs and as purchases were made in bulk the price of drugs also went low. "…. Why our rates were lower? One is, you buy in bulk. Two, you buy generic drugs and not brand drugs. There is big increase in price because of brand. If you buy Aspirin and not Aspro or Anacin or Disprine, then you get it much cheaper. Because Aspirin is generic drug, Aspro or Anacin are brand names. So… Penicillin, if you buy and if you buy brand names you pay more. So generic drugs…. it is also what WHO prescribes that you buy generic drugs."

Pancha Byadhi Chikitsa

Along with bringing in new drugs policy another major systemic change introduced in the state was the Pancha Byadhi Chikitsa scheme covering five diseases. Continuing with her narrative a former senior official of Health and Family Welfare Department, government of Orissa said, "Through hospitals, primary health centers…the government system is expected to provide health care free, in actual fact nobody quite knows what he or she will get free. Now if a person from a village suffering from diarrhoea goes to the primary health center, then doctor will look at him and then say he needs A, B, C, D… Now out of that he may say A- you will get from the primary health center, B- you will have to pay, C- we will give you part of it from the hospital but after that you will have to buy, D…like that. So, if I am poor and sick, I do not know how much money will go from my pocket… So, what we thought was at least for the common diseases…nobody, no person in Orissa, no patient in Orissa, living in any part of Orissa and going to any government hospital should have to pay for these diseases. So, the person should know, the doctor should know, the health system should know …and also we advertised it widely so that if I am a patient of diarrhoea or if I am a patient of acute respiratory infections, I know that if I go to any government hospital throughout the state, I will be provided free treatment. Not only for the doctor treating but I will also get the medicines." Therefore here the official was mentioning about the structural constraints with regard to utilisation of health care services even when it was available free of cost. So the poor could not be aware about the health care facilities, which would be provided free of cost to them at government run health institutions. Hence this scheme was started to address this unmet need of the poor who were mostly suffering from these five diseases in the state.

"And we made the scheme and we made the protocols for these five diseases. So, the five common diseases, which usually affected the poor people, like *diarrhoea, malaria, leprosy, acute respiratory infections and skin*… We also wanted to include TB and worms later but as a start we selected these five. And what we also said was that if any patient was asked by the doctor…because we can't really be sure that every doctor will give them the free medicine, because sometimes doctors have tie-ups with medicine shops… And will give a prescription and say, *buy it from there...* We said, if anybody has to pay, they will give the prescription and the bill and we will reimburse it and then we will enquire against the doctor…why the doctor had prescribed? Was there a shortage of medicine? Why he prescribed and if he cannot give satisfactory explanation that money will be recovered from his salary," said the official. So the linkages between a medical officer and local medicine shops in many cases prevent the poor from getting the free medicines and to address this aspect they initiated a process of providing a bill and a prescription to the patient, so that if there was any wrong doing on the part of the medical officer then the reimbursed amount would be deducted from the medical officer's salary.

"At the beginning when we started it… when we introduced the drugs system, we not only improved the quality but we gave it an appearance that it had improved. Like… earlier people were given medicines in the health center in loose. You know ten tablets will be taken in a piece of paper, folded up and given to them…no names, no proper packing, no coil packing. We gave in proper packing, coil packing and above it written *Orissa Government Not For Sale.* So if somebody has to be given, it was strip to be given. This was done otherwise they could take to the nearby medical shop. Retail price was cut out and there was expiry date. So that it was clear that it was only to be sold in a government institution," said the official. Therefore under the new system the drugs were properly packaged, levels were put up and it was clearly written that *Orissa Government Not For Sale* so that the drugs could not be sold to the local medicine shops. Due to this packaging and prescription of expiry dates, the quality of drugs available from the government institutions had improved.

But the question arises as to why these diseases were selected for intervention and on what basis? Replying to this question the official said, "Some diseases we know are common, like diarrhoea. Every year lots of people fall in; a lot of our medicines go…. We also discussed with people in the field, when we went to the PHC…malaria we know is common…We also selected diseases which were widespread… but of which we could be sure of giving medicines like leprosy and malaria. Malaria of course we purchase medicines but some medicines come from government of India. Leprosy…the full amount comes from government of India. Respiratory infections and diarrhoea are very common in Orissa. Scabies sometimes, which affect small children and all…so we discussed with doctors in the field. And there were actually seven diseases that were identified. The other two were TB and worms." Therefore to identify these diseases wider consultations were held within the health system of Orissa.

Continuing with her narrative the interviewee said, "You see these affects the poor people. People who sleep in mosquito nets and sleep in air-conditioned rooms don't get malaria. But who don't take protective measures and live in stagnant waters, they get affected. Similarly leprosy not so much but scabies comes from… if you are not particular about some foods, it's very contagious. Then in acute respiratory infections immunity is low, so that's why this was a kind of self-targeting. We know that it affects the poor and we also know it is widespread in Orissa. Because we spend a lot of money on medicines and on treatment…every year in summer and during the rains we have diarrhoea outbreaks. So we selected on the basis…what affects most people and we also found that these diseases made up about 75 percent of the cases, which come to the primary health care." Therefore the selection of the diseases was made after analyzing the epidemiological situation in the state.

Further the official said, "TB and worms we also wanted to add. But for TB there were three different kinds of treatment pattern at that time in Orissa. So, it was all going to be changed to multi drug therapy. But until the entire state followed one system of treatment, we did not want to take it on because our message would get mixed. Whatever we tried to tell people that you must come and you will get this treatment, it would not hold through[66]. Worms…also we thought let's start with five and then worms can be treated in low birth weight babies…Depending on the state we selected this. If I were in Maharastra the diseases selected would have been different or in Gujarat, the diseases would be different. But in Orissa these we thought as most appropriate."

---

[66] Because then it would have led toward widespread abuse of drugs with regard to TB and it would have created conditions for new drug resistant variants of Tuberculosis.

However during the field visit to the four block level PHCs, the medical officers in-charge were of the opinion that the patients coming to the health centre were not aware about their rights under the Pancha Byadhi Chikitsa scheme. Interestingly in all these block PHCs advertisements for this five disease schemes were written in bold letters almost covering one side of a wall!

Consultation process in various reform initiatives

Asked about the consultation process before initiating different reform measures, the interviewee said, "We had brain storming normally with a number of people in the health sector and including some advisors from outside, medical college people etc. But when we made the policy we had consultation with different associations. Some reforms which were personnel based, we discussed among ourselves. Some which were like cleaning of hospitals, we did not have a major consultation but we took the que from the general public's dissatisfaction with the cleaning system and therefore we went in for contract cleaning and the feedback we used as a way to decide and after that everybody wanted it. So obviously it was a popular measure.... So extent of consultation varied."[67] Therefore the consultation process varied from one reform measure to another.

But what about the OHSDP? Responding to this question the official said, "In case of OHSDP what happened was, it was started first in Andhra Pradesh. A large number of states were interested. So they[68] had a workshop in Goa, which all the states attended and after that we had a meeting in Delhi, where each state made its presentations. On the basis of our presentation the World Bank selected Orissa and after that they selected Rajasthan".

However one of the major reform problems in Orissa has been that the government of Orissa was reducing the budget, for example in case of drugs, which has been saved through reform initiatives. In these circumstances how could the reforms succeed? Replying to this the official said, "Any decrease in drugs budget would not be because of reforms. It might decrease because budget has reduced. Let us say for this amount of medicines you need Rs 12 crores and now this year you are able to buy that amount of medicine for Rs 9 crores. So, I will reduce it to Rs 9 crores.

---

[67] According to different reform initiatives.
[68] Here it refers to the World Bank.

This was not so. What may have happened, during my time OHSDP was putting in some money for drugs. Then this total budget remains the same and that could be reduced. I don't know whether it was done or not done because there was some talk about it... So because this money is coming from World Bank already for drugs, so we won't provide Rs 12 crores, so I will reduce four crores as you are getting the same amount from there. It has got nothing to do with reforms. It's also is a temporary thing if they have done it because medicines requirement increases.... If today you have malaria or diarrhoea as a problem after certain years these may not be a problem rather cancer may be a problem and certainly if government is providing health care you are supposed to provide or take care of those diseases. The profile changes from infectious diseases to non-infectious diseases, from communicable to non-communicable diseases and accidents and injuries. That's how the profile changes. And as you develop, you have less of communicable, more of non-communicable and accidents and injuries also. So certainly it's not rationale to say that reforms have led to cut in drugs budget. Because more money was coming from other sources, there were chances that they might have reduced the drug budget."

However as we have discussed above that some of the senior officials were of the view that as cost cutting was one of the priority areas of government of Orissa, the drugs example was a metaphor for the attitude of the government. For example the government of Orissa had taken a policy decision about not recruiting any manpower in near future and this also included health services sector. This perhaps may have been initiated with the objective of reducing the government's spending on the salary component, which was more than 80 percent in case of health sector. On the other hand during the field visit many officials showed concern for the shortage of nursing staffs and ANMs in the state. Therefore a uniform policy on non-recruitment of manpower needs to be relooked. This policy was also one of the reasons behind creation of contractual posts for paramedics at the district level and most of the posts created by OHSDP project were also of contractual nature. So the question arises whether such steps were taken with an idea of implementing a uniform model of reforms in health sector? And would not such a uniform model hamper in actual realization of health goals in the state? Therefore should not it have been reconsidered keeping in mind the context of Orissa?

Contractual doctors

As we have discussed in chapter III, due to the financial crisis the state government had initiated schemes like contractual doctors and contractual paramedics. When asked about the rationale of this scheme, one former senior government official said, "Contractual doctors we had earlier also. Contractual doctors can be recruited by a PHC. But a PHC takes long time. By the time we write to PHC to recruit, let's say 100 doctors, as it's such a long drawn process that we have another 200 vacant.[69] So we were recruiting contractual doctors earlier not by the CDMO but centrally. We were appointing people on contractual basis and posting them particularly in these remote areas.

Contractual doctors are not necessarily a bad thing, because when you get a regular government job then many people feel that *I decide whether to go there or not there.* If you are given a contract only… if you go to Kalahandi then you will work there. Once you get a regular appointment then people will put a lot of pressure, political pressure and say *I will stay in Bhubaneswar, I will work in Capital Hospital* etc. So we had allowed contractual doctors only in the periphery…. Contractual doctors or contractual paramedics are not necessarily a bad thing; in fact people work better, perhaps."

This was an argument from one perspective and it was a point of view supporting the new idea of creation of more contractual posts. On the one hand if used in a limited way then it seems that the appointment of contractual doctors might help the periphery level institutions to address their immediate needs.

However it seems that in periphery level institutions where there have been problems of medical officers and paramedics staying, the entire posting were thought to be made as contractual. And it seems this logic had also been extended to hand over the NGOs to run these periphery level institutions. These were halfhearted measures because we have mentioned earlier that it was a common agreement among the various levels of health care officials in Orissa that if the government was really interested to ensure that the periphery level institutions were not to remain vacant then the first thing they should do was about bringing in a legislation to make the transfer and postings policy of medical officers' a rule. Therefore it

[69] Posts of doctors vacant.

seems that these measures have not been initiated because of vested interests. And therefore the creation of contractual posts alone won't help in resolving the issue, because the structural constraints have not been addressed.

User charges

During the field visit to Orissa, interaction was made with lot of senior officials in the government and in the donor agencies and they all privately acknowledged that user charges were not exempting the poor in reality. It was the rich and influential sections, which were getting benefit out of this. Thus observing on this aspect one former top health official in the state said, "It's a question of implementation. I don't think what you are saying is an uniform issue because in initial years we have been trying to follow…find out…because they have been given slips…so what percent of patients being treated free? And of course there may have been misuse of this for the people who could pay. Usually it would not be… but that's the implementation problem and not the problem of system as such. So if the CDMO or the person in charge of a particular hospital is particular and ensure it…and it's after all we have given clear instructions. Emergency is nothing…national programmes… no charges. It's an implementation problem. In everything there would be implementation problem." Further elaborating her point the official said,

> If you say that you will admit people within the college with certain percentage of marks and you will find somebody with third division has been admitted, and then people say that he is a son of a minister and got it. That's an implementation problem. It's not a problem with the system. In every place system is abused.[70]

These were the candid views of a former official who was closely involved with the process and experience of health sector reforms in the state. The important point here being made was that those who could pay should be charged and if the poor were not getting exempted then it was an implementation issue. The aspect of user fees also has another dimension of users' perspective. But here as we have been primarily dealing with the provider's perspective, hence perception of introduction of user fees was gathered from officials at different levels of health care services in the state. It needs to be mentioned here that there was wider support for the introduction of user fees among the government and donor agency

[70] Here the italics have been provided to emphasise a point.

officials. However it was observed that important question which should have been asked by these officials have not happened. For example, what was the percentage of user fees collected to the total expenditure of an institution? What were the mechanisms to be devised if in reality the poor were not getting exempted? Could the introduction of user fees generate enough revenues in a state like Orissa where near about half of its population lived below the poverty line and near about 39 percent of its population constituted scheduled castes and scheduled tribes?

As we have mentioned earlier in chapter III that according to the senior officials in the state and at district level the CDMOs, the collection of user fees has helped institutions in repairing equipments and furniture, which has helped institutions a lot. Otherwise earlier they had to wait for funds to be available from the state headquarter.

Referral cards

To the question whether there was plan to introduce referral cards by the OHSDP in project institutions in Orissa, a senior official at OHSDP said, "After the analysis of monthly reports on referral cases of project institutions it was found that out of the total cases referred from one tier to other, 50 percent of them were from District Headquarter Hospitals and Sub Divisional Hospitals to medical colleges. Most of these patients were referred in a small slip without detail address, clinical condition of the patient at the time of referral and the treatment offered to the patient."

Further the official concerned observed, "Sometimes cases which could have been managed at lower level health facilities were referred to next higher levels due to lack of knowledge of service providers on clinical protocol and the services available in the nearby health institutions. Therefore most probably a referral card would be introduced in this project." Hence the idea of introduction of the referral card it seems was to utilize the existing resources 'efficiently'.

Private practice by government doctors[71]

The private practice by government doctors has always been a controversial issue in India. Hence many states have banned and allowed it many times. The heart of the controversy lies in the understanding that if a government doctor goes for private practice then he or she won't be concentrating on his or her official job and the real sufferer would be those patients visiting the government institutions. Therefore this issue was raised before one of the former senior officials in the state. Responding to this issue the interviewee said, "We always allow[72]... Only the medical college, they did not allow. Let me modify that. There have been many changes in policy. There was a time when they did not allow; Biju Patnaik's[73] time...I think they banned private practice. Then they found that some amount of money was being made but they were practicing anyway...No... they say some non-practicing allowance was being paid but they were still practicing. So take away the non-practicing allowance and allow them to practice. So there have been many flip-flops. Not only in Orissa, every state has this problem. Every single state in the Indian Union has had this problem. Sometimes they allow, sometimes they ban. If they ban, they say this is the advantage and therefore we will not allow. If they allow then they say, this is the advantage and therefore we will not ban. So I myself don't know whether there is a solution to this but it is a question of ethos of the place. If in certain place you find everybody is doing private practice despite the ban and no action is being taken then everybody falls into that." Therefore here the official was mentioning about the ethos of a particular place and thus if in a particular place most of the government medical officers were going for private practice then others would also follow the trend.

Continuing with the narrative the respondent said, "In case of Orissa, at some points of time it was banned and at some points of time the ban was removed. So in Orissa everybody is allowed to do private practice ...and these changes from time to time. At one point of time everybody is

---

[71] 'Private practice by government doctors' and the proposal to introduce 'referral cards' has been interpreted here as reform initiatives. Although private practice by government doctors had earlier many times allowed as well as banned subsequently; however as this measure was introduced in late 1990s we have included this as a reform initiative.

[72] Here the respondent was mentioning about allowance of private practice by government doctors.

[73] Biju Patnaik was the former chief minister of Orissa.

allowed to do private practice and no non-practicing allowance is given. And at another point of time nobody is allowed to do private practice and non-practicing allowance is given. At still another point of time some people are allowed to do private practice and no non-practicing allowance is given to them, whereas other people are not allowed to do private practice and NPA[74] is given to them. Even when everybody is allowed there are some levels, which are not allowed. Directors[75] are not allowed, superintendents[76]...they don't allow. So it's a mixed thing." This was another aspect of this issue. Hence while some medical officers were allowed private practice, some others were not like, Directors, Superintendents etc.

Observing another important aspect of private practice by government doctors the official concerned said, "Another thing is in a rural area, government doctors are the only doctors and... in the middle of the night somebody falls ill and comes...he will come to the government doctor. The government doctor cannot tell him, *no go away, I will not treat you.* There is no other doctor! Now should the doctor not be compensated for that time? At any time a patient can come to him...now he treats the patient well and if he is good more people will come. Then he should be compensated for the extra hour that he is putting... There I would say that private practice should be allowed." So here the interviewee was mentioning about private practice by government doctors in the context of rural Orissa. Thus in rural areas of Orissa the government doctor was the only doctor and hence if a patient comes after official hours to meet him or her and if the doctor treats him or her then what was wrong in allowing the doctor for private practice? For the doctor was putting extra effort in his or her private times. Therefore in these cases also one could argue that private practice by government doctors should be allowed. But here the important aspects that need to be ensured was that the medical officers engaged in private practice should be attending to their responsibilities in government institutions.

District cadre for paramedics

Asked about her views about creation of district cadre for paramedics the official said, "Earlier ANMs and multipurpose health workers had no

[74] Non practicing allowance.
[75] Here 'Directors' refer to the senior most officials in the Health Directorate of government of Orissa.
[76] In Medical colleges.

tenure and they were transferred to different districts. Hence the Orissa cabinet took a decision for district cadre for paramedics and nurses. There were ten to twelve thousand nurses and most of them were from the coastal areas. There was interference from MLAs. Once you have the district cadre you limit the interference." Thus this decision was taken for operational reasons so that the difficulties that paramedics used to face could be solved to a large extent. As there were ten to twelve thousand nurses from the coastal areas there used be pressure from the MLAs in their transfers and postings and hence once this new system was introduced this interference could be reduced to a large degree.
Further the official said, "The ANMs must live with the community and should know persons by name. Therefore they should not be transferred." This was a very important observation, as the ANMs were supposed to develop contact with their allotted villages[77] and know persons by name and hence they should be allowed to stay in a particular place. This could be mentioned as a very strong point for creation of district cadre for paramedics.

> Similarly there is need for creating separate cadre for medical colleges as all wants to come to Cuttack Medical College. If one is sure that one has to stay in one place than only one will stay in a place. This could be compared with the tenure of IAS officers who are sent to a state for two thirds of their career.

said the official. Hence it was an observation having practical implications. But to bring such a change, political will would be required.

But the real question was whether the creation of contractual paramedics had helped in addressing these structural issues? Responding to the this question one senior official of a donor agency at Bhubaneswar said, " From the coastal areas people are moving to undivided Koraput and joining there as ANMs and through political connection they are getting on deputation to coastal districts… That is one ANM while has joined in Koraput, staying at Jagatsinghpur[78] and drawing salary from Koraput!" Continuing with the narrative, the official said, "The earlier practice was like one[79] would go and join in remote and difficult areas, where it was easier to get a job and from there getting transferred to a coastal district.

---

[77] In Orissa within a sub centre there were 5 to 6 villages were there on an average.
[78] Jagatsingpur is a district located in Coastal Orissa.
[79] Reference to a paramedic.

But now this is not possible in pen and paper but in reality it is happening." Another senior official of health and family welfare department, government of Orissa said, "From coastal areas paramedics are going and registering with the employment exchange in KBK districts[80]. The reason is that although due to the creation of district cadre for paramedics transfer is difficult, they can be deputed to other areas." Therefore it seems that the implementation aspects of the scheme of district cadre for paramedics have been neglected in Orissa.

Increasing role of the private sector

Utilisation patterns in the state shows that both in urban and rural areas maximum number of people go for the public health care system[81]. The presence of Private health care was also very low. There were private clinics and small nursing homes in cities like, Cuttack, Rourkela and Berhampur etc. and there were some private hospitals in cities like Bhubaneswar and Cuttack. However these were very small in terms of numbers and outreach to different sections of the state. One senior official was of the view that "as Orissa has dominant presence of Public health care system, the rich as well as the poor go for it. And as long as the influential sections have a stake in the public health care system the standards will not fall". What the official was saying was that the influential sections are generally aware about the standards of health care, about which the poor are generally ignorant. So as long as they have a stake, the quality of care in the public institutions could be maintained. In fact this has been the case with Orissa.

However interview with government officials at different levels of the health care services structure in the state showed that there was increasing acceptance of the larger role for the private sector in delivery of health services to the people. Senior officials in the directorate of health services in the state were of the opinion that as the government was in a fiscal crisis; increasingly the private sector has to be given a role for fulfilling the gap in resources and the needs of the people. Therefore this perception among these officials about the role of private sector in health care was

[80] KBK districts refers to Kalahandi, Bolangir and the Koraput districts of Orissa, where the phenomenon of drought in most part of the year force people to migrate to neighboring states of Orissa in search of employment and this also results in hunger deaths among the poorest section of the population.

[81] This was evident from both the NFHS I and NFHS II data.

significant. This would act as favorable factor whenever the government of Orissa decides to increase the space for private participation in different aspects of health care.

Other reform initiatives

Now let us have a look at some reform initiatives by the state government, which has significant implications for different aspects of future health care provisioning in Orissa. It needs to be mentioned here that these initiatives have not been identified by the state government as reform initiatives. However we have included these initiatives as reforms according to the definition of health sector reforms given in this book.

Three private medical colleges within five years

According to one senior official in the Ministry of Health and Family Welfare Department, Government of Orissa, "The Western Orissa Development Council[82], has come off with plans for three Medical Colleges with private participation at Rourkela, Bolangir and Bhabanipatna within five years. The council will give Rs 10 crore and free land to the private parties. One GSL trust has been given the task for building medical colleges at Bolangir and Rourkela. One Selvan Trust has taken the charge at Bhabanipatna.[83]

However there was a gap in this initiative. The official said, "The Western Orissa Development Council[84] budget is hardly Rs 40 crores. But to manage a medical college hospital they need Rs 100 crores." Therefore it seems a serious thought has not been given to this whole initiative.

Public private partnerships

There were some initiatives by the state government, which could be termed as public-private partnerships. These were in the form of joint

---

[82] This council was created so that the development of Western Orissa could be undertaken in a focused manner. It needs to be mentioned that occasionally from the Western Part of Orissa one could hear about a movement for separation from Orissa and this movement was known as 'Koshala Movement'. Therefore to address these regional grievances this council was created.

[83] This was the view of a senior official in the ministry of health and family welfare, Government of Orissa.

[84] This was a statutory body.

ventures in medical colleges, joint operation of hospitals and introduction of private pay clinics in government medical colleges etc.

Proposals for joint ventures in three government medical colleges

Further the interviewee said, "Besides some private hospitals like Hi-Tech in Pandhra, Kitts at Shikhar Chandi and ITR in Kalinga Nagar has come up.[85] In the three medical colleges[86] joint ventures are being planned with the private sector. For example an MRI machine costs around Rs 4 to 5 crores. These are planned to be entirely managed by the private parties. The government will provide only space, water and electricity and if the staff is required it will be provided but the private party will do the running cost. There are also proposals like multi bedded hospitals and instruments to be maintained by the private parties but the staff will be of the government. These will be cutting edge hospitals with latest instruments. The proceeds will be shared in mutually agreed way. This is yet to be finalized."

The official further added, "In West Bengal and UP, private parties are running equipments like MRI, CT-Scan etc. and the government provides water, electricity and staff for which certain percent of money is provided to the government. Similarly here the maintenance of instruments will gradually be privatized. Government will provide electricity and water but these will be owned and maintained by the private parties. They will provide their own staff."

Therefore the tertiary aspect of health care was being thought to be handed over to the private parties, as these would be costlier to operate for the government. The idea of providing staff, if needed, along with space, water and electricity, seems quite interesting because the government of Orissa has put a blanket ban on recruitment of any new staffs. So the question arises from where these additional staffs would come from?

---

[85] These hospitals were located in and around the capital of Orissa, Bhubaneswar.

[86] The official was referring to government medical colleges at Berhampur, Burla and Cuttack.

Private pay clinics in government medical colleges

Giving a rationale for introduction of private pay clinics in government medical colleges one former senior official in the Health and Family Welfare Department, Government of Orissa said, "For example even though you have a government hospital and you are supposed to provide free care…ultimately they are used to channel people to their private clinics because in their private clinics they make additional money over and above their salary. So that's one thing. You don't have any expertise[87]…. In a city like Delhi, it's different. You have private hospitals but in Orissa it's not like that. So the best eye surgeon will be somebody in the Medical College. The best kidney specialist or urinary surgeon, they all will be in the government. Now how do you get their services? You go there in the hospital and he will have too many patients. So one thing which was tried when I was there, was to have pay clinics. Now suppose you want to consult a particular doctor …you don't want to line up in the morning and so you want to take an appointment but she is not allowed to see you because she is not allowed private practice. So in the morning and evening every day they hold a pay clinic. So you go to the doctor and you pay. And that money, as he uses hospital premises, he uses the hospital staff, nurses etc… certain amount goes to the user fund and certain amount they are allowed to keep. So you get the attention of the doctor and because you pay the doctor is able to give you an appointment also. It's not that everybody…first come, first serve…doctors get motivated also. So they were experimenting with dentistry," said the official. This was an important point because the official was of the view that as in Orissa specialists were also in the government sector and hence in case of emergencies they had to be allowed for private practice. Extending this line of argument pay clinics had been started in medical colleges in the morning and evening hours when one could visit a particular medical specialist with prior appointment. In this system the medical officer attending a patient was paid some amount of the money, that he or she had generated out of this practice and the rest used to go to the user fund in medical colleges as the attending doctors were also using the services of staffs and nurses in this institution. Therefore in this context the introduction of pay clinics has some justification.

According to another senior official in the Health and Family Welfare Department, government of Orissa, "Private pay clinics at the dental wing

[87] Here the official was referring about the lack of medical expertise outside the government sector in a state like Orissa.

of Medical Colleges have started. During holidays and in the extra times[88] these operate. This has helped in availability of facilities to the patients at lesser price to the market prices. Out of the money collected, 50% of the money goes to the government and rest 50% goes to the doctors and this is subject to income tax. Many people have benefited out of this and they are also getting the services of the doctors of their choice". Hence the pay clinics have been opened in the dental wing of medical colleges and as it was being interpreted as a success, it was most likely that they would start providing other services in coming years.

Joint operation of hospitals

Another aspect of private participation has been the idea about creating new hospitals where both the government as well as the private sector would operate jointly. Thus one senior official said, "Now government is thinking in terms of joint ventures to set up hospital with private participation. They will set up the building and also provide equipments and the government will provide the staffs. There will be joint agreement on running the hospital. There will be pay beds. The scale of proceeds will be decided by mutual agreement." Thus while the building and equipments would be funded by the private sector the government would provide staffs. The concept of introduction of pay beds suggests that these hospitals were thought to be operating on a profitable basis.

Creation of a 600 bedded hospital at SCB medical college Cuttack

The official further added, "At SCB medical college Cuttack, another 600-bedded super specialty hospital for Orthopedics, Pediatrics and Medicine[89] will come up. In this regard the views of DMET[90] and the principal of the medical college have been sought". This hospital would run on a profitable basis.

---

[88] Here the term 'extra times' suggest that these pay clinics operated in morning and evening hours.
[89] 200 bed each for these facilities.
[90] Director Medical Education and Training, Government of Orissa.

Plan to create eight regional diagnostic centers[91]

This was an initiative to strengthen the government health care institutions in tertiary levels of care. Thus one senior official said, "There are plans to start eight regional diagnostic centers at three government medical colleges and five district head quarter hospitals[92]. Each center will be given Rs 3 crores. In total Rs 24 crores has been provided by 11th finance commission. These are expected to run round the clock with facilities like radiology, X-ray, ECG, CT-scan and Ultra Sound etc.

At present for the diagnostic facilities in medical colleges, although diagnostic instruments are there, doctors refer the cases to outside, where for each case they earn Rs 500 from the private institutions. Hence to check this corruption there is need for round the clock diagnostic facilities." This initiative has been taken with the proposal of 11th Finance Commission and hence from the government of India. However user fees would be introduced here for those who could pay. While on the one hand the government of Orissa has taken initiatives and planning to introduce measures for more private participation in tertiary levels of care, it would be interesting to see as to how these regional diagnostic centres would operate in this larger atmosphere.

Other initiatives

There has also been private participation in other fields. In this regard one senior official said, "...Besides Infosys[93] has come up with 150 bedded pediatrics services in the Capital Hospital, Bhubaneswar, where it has spent Rs 2 to 3 crores. But unfortunately the government does not have the resources to maintain it. They have adequate staffs and equipments but they need little bit more money for maintenance." Thus while the new hospital has been created with the private money, for maintenance the government did not have any resources. Therefore it was most likely that

---

91 We have included this initiative as a reform element because while the entire funding and operation of these diagnostic centres would be with the government of Orissa, user fees would be introduced for those who could pay.

92 Out of these five regional diagnostic centres four would be in the district head quarter hospitals of, Koraput, Kalahandi, Mayurbhanj, Sundergarh and the fifth one would be in the Capital Hospital, Bhubaneswar.

93 The well known IT Company in India with head quarters at Bangalore, the capital of Karnataka, India.

in future a private party on a profitable basis would operate this wing of pediatrics service.

Private physiotherapy, speech and occupational therapy colleges

To the question as to whether the government of Orissa had received any applications for establishment of private physiotherapy, occupational therapy and speech therapy colleges, the official said "We have received application for establishment of private physiotherapy, Occupational therapy and speech therapy colleges in the state but no action has been taken."

Opening up new government medical colleges

When asked as to whether the government was planning to open new medical colleges, the official said, "There is no question about opening new government medical colleges, as government does not have enough money. Now the concept of privatisation has crept into the system." Therefore if the need arises in future about the creation of new medical colleges, it would most probably be started with the private initiative.

The emerging pattern

So what was the emerging pattern, out of all these new initiatives for private participation in tertiary levels of care taken in Orissa? For the explanation we need to go back to the arguments being forwarded by donor agencies like World Bank and DFID that more than 50 percent of the budget of the government of Orissa was being spent on the tertiary levels of care, whereas the government should have focused more on primary and secondary levels of care. These new initiative for private participation in Orissa clearly follow this line of argument and the state government was trying to reduce the role of state from the tertiary levels of care.

However the focus has neither shifted to either the primary or secondary levels of care. As we have argued earlier, in case of primary levels of care the government of Orissa had been thinking about handing over the PHCs to NGOs in remote and difficult areas. In case of secondary health care institutions we have seen that under the OHSDP project the 157 institutions upgraded had been introduced with user fees and the government of Orissa was also not increasing its budgetary allocation annually so that at the end of the project the government could take over these institutions. Therefore while the responsibilities for tertiary levels of care were being relinquished, inadequate efforts were being made to invest in secondary and primary levels of care.

Understanding of 'reforms' among the providers[94]

How the term 'reform in health sector' being interpreted by government as well as donor agency officials at various levels in the state of Orissa as well as at the central[95] level? It was surprising that many could not provide any definition of health sector reforms and those who gave a definition, tried to interpret these in terms of a report published by WHO and Ministry of Health, Government of India, which was an outcome of a seminar held at India International Centre, New Delhi in 2003. Interestingly the report itself concludes with the note that the term 'health sector reforms' need to be defined, so that concrete policy initiatives could be taken by government of India and different states and then these could be included in the five year plans of India. While this was the understanding among the senior officials at Bhubaneswar, from district level and below the officials were at loss of words in defining this term. At their Delhi offices while different donor agency officials could give their own definitions, these were not at all helpful in classification of health sector reforms. In most of the cases the definitions given were trying to include almost every single initiative by the state government of Orissa and India since 1990s as a reform initiative.

Due to this lack of a definition of reforms in health sector, whatever new changes in the existing programs had been taken by the state government beginning with the decade of 1990s in health sector, has been interpreted as health sector reforms by influential documents in the state, like the Orissa vision document 2010. While the increasing private sector participation in health sector was not being openly acknowledged by the government of Orissa in public, but through various initiatives it has already started this process. Therefore while most of the officials at different levels of health care may not be aware about the larger picture

[94] Here the term 'providers' suggest about the officials of the donor agencies, government officials at different levels in Orissa and at Delhi etc.
[95] At the Delhi offices of the donor agencies.

but there were some top officials in the government Orissa who did understood what was going on.

Does it suggest that the reforms were not being implemented properly in the state because of this definitional confusion? The answer won't be that easy because the officials at different levels were aware about various initiatives being taken by the Health and Family Welfare department of government of Orissa. Hence they were mostly involved with issues about whether these initiatives would succeed or not. Thus interacting with them, one would frequently come across issues about structural constraints in implementing these new or revised initiatives by the government of Orissa.

Therefore it could be said that the increasing space for private participation in health sector in the state was being pushed in the state with the knowledge of few top officials of the government of Orissa and from the donor agencies like World Bank and DFID and European Commission.

Role of World Bank in Orissa

What about the role of World Bank in health sector reforms in Orissa? It was not that much a clear case that the World Bank was pushing for increasing private participation in health sector in Orissa. Because ultimately it was about the policy decisions that the state government takes, that matters. For example in case of OHSDP, it was the state government, which had approached the World Bank for initiating this project in the state. Besides, after the 1991 economic liberalisation in India, the role of private sector has increased and this has also created an understanding among the politicians and the government officials that the private sector could fill up those gaps, which the public health sector could not address. Therefore a larger atmosphere in favor of private participation in health care does exist among the providers of health services.

On the other hand, it was also the case that the World Bank through its 'Orissa Economic Review Package' and OHSDP project was in a position to put pressure on the state government to bring in increasing role of private sector in those areas, which the World Bank thought as appropriate. There has been an increasing understanding within the World Bank, after years of working in Orissa, that if they want to get their desirable results in health sector, then they would have to link the financing for health projects like OHSDP to larger projects like Orissa

Economic Review Package, which was intended to help the state from recovering from its fiscal crisis.

Therefore it was never the case that only the World Bank has been pushing for increasing private participation in health sector of Orissa. For within the state government there has been a wider constituency, who were directly responsible for health policy making and implementation, which were supporting the increasing role of private participation in different aspects of health care in the state. However what was observed from interaction with both donor and government officials was that this increasing support for private participation was not based on empirical data and was more a question of faith. It was like ‘we have tried and tested the role of public sector in health care, now let us give a chance to the private sector.’

While the solutions for the existing problems in the heath care services structure in the state, was being seen in the private sector, by the government officials, they were not able to explain as to how more private participation would help in overcoming the structural constraints. Therefore in terms of explanations in support for increasing private participation, most of the arguments were coming more from the World Bank who could rely from their international experience. However this raises doubts about implementation of a uniform model in the context of Orissa. To address the shortcomings of the public health care in the state required innovative solutions and not an act of faith in the private sector.

Conclusion

In this chapter we have made a distinction between systemic changes and health sector reforms, in the context of Orissa, using our new definition. It has been argued that the phenomenon of health sector reforms could not be reduced to some technical terms like ‘efficiency’ and ‘effectiveness’, rather reforms in health sector were ideologically driven. It has to be seen in the larger context of economic reforms being introduced in India and the fiscal austerity measures being adopted by various states due to this.

Using our new definition of health sector reforms we have identified elements like, creation of PSPU, the OHSDP project, the Sector Reform Cell, handing over PHCs to NGOs, creation of the post of NGO coordinator, introduction of user charges, creation of contractual district cadre for paramedics, privatizing cleaning in government hospitals, multiskilling of health personnel, plan to introduce referral cards, allowing private practice by government doctors, contractual district cadre for paramedics, introducing contractual doctors scheme at the block level, plan to introduce three private medical colleges, plan to introduce joint ventures in three government medical colleges, introduction of private pay clinics in government medical colleges, idea about joint operation of hospitals, creation of a 600 bedded hospital at SCB medical college, Cuttack; plan to create eight regional diagnostic centers etc. as health sector reforms.

Similarly using our definition we have also identified some of the initiatives by the state government as systemic changes, which were included as reform element by different observers. Thus the systemic changes were: establishment of disease surveillance programme, introduction of new drugs policy, Pancha Byadhi Chikitsa scheme, provision for petty maintenance of buildings at PHC headquarters, mandatory pre-PG rural service, internship training for medical graduates and creation of Zilla Swasthya Samities etc.

Here we need to mention that this distinction between health sector reforms and systemic changes were conceptual categories. This distinction was made to comprehend the phenomenon called 'health sector reforms' in a better way. The factors like the formation of House Committee of Orissa Legislature and the evaluation by DFID of its earlier projects led to an initiative toward a series of changes in health sector covering both systemic changes and health sector reforms.

In terms of the consultative process in various reform initiatives it was clear that selective consultations were held with health services personnel at different levels in Orissa. It was not a comprehensive consultative process. In case of consultation process with regard to OHSDP project, it was observed that only few senior officials were aware about it. The field experience suggests that at the district and block level even the senior officials were not aware about various reform initiatives undergoing in the state. This had implications for effective implementation and monitoring of various programs in the health sector.

We have said that while the Orissa Economic Review Package was not a reform element in health sector, still it had the potential to influence significantly the future health policy making in Orissa. Because the World Bank was planning to make conditional any new funding for health sector with the successful implementation of fiscal austerity measures, which this package was trying to address. While the Sector Reform Cell was only confined to implementing the European Commission health projects in Orissa; through creation of PSPU, the DFID and World Bank were trying to act as a think tank for the Ministry of Health and Family Welfare, Government of Orissa. With the implementation of OHSDP project in Orissa the World Bank had increased its influence in reorganizing the health services system in Orissa like never before. Therefore among the donor agencies the World Bank was playing the dominant role followed by DFID in the Orissa health sector.

However the presence of various donors in different aspects of health care in Orissa had created problems of donor coordination and it was also a burden for the Health and Family Welfare Department to prepare different categories of reports for different donors. To address this issue, Orissa Vision Document 2010 was prepared with a wider consultative process within the government health sector in the state. The idea was that different donors could identify their areas of interest within this Vision document. However this could not bring any change in terms of better donor coordination.

In terms of major systemic changes, the introduction of new drugs policy, which was mostly borrowed from the Tamilnadu model, made changes in the quality of drugs available in government health care institutions and at a cheaper rate. The new elements introduced in this policy were, shift from brand names to generic drugs, adoption of an essential drugs list from WHO and central purchasing of drugs through open tender. This policy reduced corruption between CDMOs and local drugs manufacturers, who used to supply low quality drugs. This system also made available drugs to districts at a cheaper rate which had poor physical infrastructure and located at a distance from Bhubaneswar. One of the major drawbacks of this new policy was that it did not include the unregulated private sector. As there were shortages of drugs inspectors in the state, there were fewer quality checks for the drugs available in the private sector and also there were possibility of corruption by the drugs inspectors. In spite of opposition from a group of CDMOs, local manufacturers and some members of Orissa Legislative Assembly, the new drugs policy could succeed because there was political will and then health secretary was very committed to this process. Therefore for any reforms or systemic changes in health sector to succeed what was needed was a political will and a bureaucratic support in a democracy like India.

Besides, the introduction of Pancha Byadhi Chikitsa Scheme made it mandatory for all government institutions to provide drugs free of cost to patients for five selective diseases of *diarrhoea, malaria, leprosy, acute respiratory infections and skin* diseases in the state. However in our two study districts, the officials were of the view that patients were not aware about their rights under this scheme. The disease surveillance program which was initiated with the help of World Health Organization, Medicines Sans Frontiers and UNDP was another successful systemic change introduced in the state. Later the World Bank also joined in this program through OHSDP. This program had helped the state in collecting epidemiological data systematically.

The creation of ZSS was another successful systemic change being introduced in the state which had helped in better coordination among various district societies and effective utilization of limited resources.

Under the scheme of petty maintenance of buildings at block headquarter PHCs the money supply was not regular and also there were allegations of misuse of funds by the medical officer in charge of these institutions. The mandatory pre-PG rural scheme was not functioning as expected, because it did not address the structural issues like, making the transfers and the postings policy of medical officers transparent. The internship training of medical graduates under the CDMOs also could not succeed because the CDMOs were not strict about it and due to a common apathy towards issues of public health among the health officers at different levels of health services structure.

Among the reform initiatives, one was the introduction of contractual doctors, who could be recruited by the block PHCs with the consent of the CDMOs. The idea was that in a contractual scheme medical officers would work better in remote and difficult areas. However our field experiences showed that only the retired doctors applied for these posts as most of them expected that they won't have to visit their institutions regularly! This was another scheme from government of Orissa, which did not address the structural issues facing the health care services structure in the state.

User charges had been introduced in all the 157 OHSDP institutions, which included the three government medical colleges, the Capital Hospital, Bhubaneswar and the 30 district headquarter hospitals. During the field visit it was known that the state was planning to introduce user charges at sub divisional level hospitals. While the introduction of user charges had helped in petty maintenance of institutions, the question of exemption of the poor from user fees had been sidelined. Some of the senior officials were of the view that it was a question of implementation issue. Further there were plans to rationalize the referral system through introduction of referral cards at the primary and secondary level institutions.

While in the past, government doctors in Orissa had sometimes allowed and sometimes banned private practice, in the later half of 1990s when this was allowed, it became a significant reform initiative. One of the arguments for this initiative was that in villages and remote areas the government doctor was the only doctor and hence if patients approached them in unofficial hours then the doctor had a right to charge fees. Similarly in case of three government medical colleges, private pay clinics were introduced in dental wings, where the doctors were given a share of their treatment. It was argued that as the medical college doctors were the best doctors in the town and hence if some people were not interested to stand in a queue, then they could be given an appointment of a doctor of their choice.

The creation of district cadre for paramedics, addressed to some extent the availability of paramedics in interior districts. However the idea of making the entire cadre contractual was that, the staffs would be willing to work in remote and difficult areas. Therefore it did not address the structural issues like absence of sub centre buildings at many places, the existing sub centre buildings located in end of the villages and many in burial grounds etc. Besides, the lack of motivation among the paramedics was closely linked with the problems of medical officers and the dilapidated conditions of the infrastructure at periphery level institutions.

Further the effort by the state government to introduce three private medical colleges in next five years in Bolangir, Rourkela and Bhabanipatna with the initiative of Western Orissa Development Council was to increase the role of private sector in tertiary level care. However during the field visit it was clear that the council did not have enough money to run these medical colleges. Further the idea of encouraging the private parties to operate costly equipments in government medical colleges, the proposal of joint operation of hospitals and the plan to create 600 bedded hospital, at SCB medical college Cuttack, were other significant attempts to privatize the tertiary level care in the long run. In this wider attempt to privatize the secondary and tertiary levels of care in the state the proposed eight regional diagnostic centers would most probably function on a profitable basis.

Similarly as the government of Orissa was not providing the maintenance cost for the 150 bedded pediatrics wards in the Capital Hospital, Bhubaneswar, created by Infosys and hence in the near future this entire ward could be run on a profitable basis. While there were no plans by the state government to introduce any new government medical colleges, it had received applications for creation of private physiotherapy, speech and occupational therapy colleges in the state.

There was not only this increasing effort by the state government to privatize the secondary and tertiary levels of care, but also the health officials at all the levels of health services structure were in favor of more private participation in different aspects of health care in the state. Their view was that the presence of private sector would bring much needed money, efficient use of resources and improvement in quality of care. However the larger question that was missing was how the poor would have access to health care?

In the next chapter we have discussed about process and experience of health sector reforms in our two study districts.

Annexure 1

ZSS or Zilla Swathya Samiti (Structure)
Chairperson: President Zilla Parisad.
Co-Chairman: Collector.
Chief Executive: CDMO or Chief District Medical Officer.
Members:
ADMO- Medical and Public Health.
DLO or District Leprosy Officer.
DTO or District Tuberculosis Officer.
DIO or District Immunization Officer
Different Societies in the ZSS:
Malaria- Headed by District Malaria Officer.
Leprosy- Headed my District Leprosy Officer.
Tuberculosis- Headed by District Tuberculosis Officer.
NPCB- National Blindness Control Society.
DHH- For user charges.
Note: This structure was applicable all over the state of Orissa.

CHAPTER SIX

REFORMS IN KHURDA AND SUNDERGARH

Introduction

As we have mentioned earlier that for this study we had selected two developed districts of Orissa, Sundergarh and Khurda, to look at the process and experience of health sector reforms. In this chapter we have also discussed about the socio-economic and demographic indicators of these two districts. Besides we have also presented a picture about the health care services structure in these districts. These two districts were selected on the basis of a ranking by National Commission on Population in terms of various socio economic and demographic indicators[1]. Among the 30 districts of Orissa, Sundergarh was ranked 3rd, followed by Khurda at 4th. The first rank was of Cuttack with a composite index of 63.24 and 197 all India ranking followed by Jharsuguda at second rank with a composite index of 63.21 and all India ranking of 199.[2]

Socio-economic and demographic indicators

To improve the health status of a population, apart from the availability of better health care services, the socio-economic and the demographic

---

[1] National Commission on Population, District Wise Indicators, Government of India, 2001. The ranking of 569 district of India were conducted on a composite index and separately for each of the 12 indicators. These 12 indicators were, 1- Percentage of decadal population growth rate, 2- Percentage of births of order 3 and above, 3- Percentage of current user of family planning methods, 4- Percentage of girls marrying below 18 years of age, 5- Sex ratio, 6- Percentage of women receiving skilled attention during deliveries, 7- Percentage of children getting complete immunization, 8- Female literacy rate, 9- Percentage of villages not connected with pucca road (estimated), 10- Percentage coverage of safe drinking water and sanitation (estimated), 11- Percentage of Birth registered (estimated), 12- Percentage of Death registered (estimated).

[2] Ibid.

indicators[3] also play a crucial role. Therefore let us have a look at the socio-economic and demographic indicators of these two districts below. The table shows that in terms of decadal population growth rate Sundergarh was way ahead of Khurda with 161 in all India ranking. However in terms of percentage of birth order 3 and above Khurda was performing much better with 34.70 percent compared to Sundergarh with 44.00 percent. In terms of current users of family planning methods Khurda with 61.8 percent was way ahead than Sundergarh with only 49.20 percent. In terms of girls marrying below 18 years of age, Sundergarh with 17.00 percentage points was a better performing district compared to Khurda with 23.4 percentage points.

The sex ratio of Sundergarh with 957 was much higher than Khurda with a sex ratio of 901. However in terms of percentage of women receiving skilled attention during deliveries, Sundergarh with 48.90 percentage points was much below Khurda with 65.9 percent. On the other hand, in terms of percentage of children getting complete immunization, Sundergarh with 80.20 percent was much better performing than Khurda with 62.8 percentage of coverage. The indicators for female literacy rate show that Khurda with 71.6 percent was much better performing than Sundergarh with 54.25 percent.

In terms of percentage of villages not connected with pucca roads, Sundergarh with 81.71 percent was a low performer compared to Khurda with 75.18 percent. The figures for percentage coverage of safe drinking water and sanitation show that while Sundergarh had 100 percent coverage, Khurda had 90.32 percent of coverage. In terms of percentage registration of births and deaths, Sundergarh was way ahead of Khurda. Finally in terms of composite index, Sundergarh with 209th rank was ahead of Khurda, which had 223rd rank out of the 569 districts in India.

---

3 Demographic indicators in terms of number of births and number of deaths each year etc.

Table: 6.1 Socio-economic and demographic indicators of two study districts

Indicators	Sundergarh		Khurda	
	Percentage	All India Ranking	Percentage	All India Ranking
Percentage of decadal population growth rate	16.26	161	24.79	384
Percentage of births of order 3 and above	44.00	260	34.70	152
Percentage of current user of family planning methods	49.20	258	61.8	113
Percentage of girls marrying below 18 years of age	17.00	145	23.4	187
Sex ratio (Number of Females per 1000 males)	957	205	901	420
Percentage of women receiving skilled attention during deliveries	48.90	257	65.9	166
Percentage of children getting complete immunization	80.20	112	62.8	245
Female literacy rate	54.25	268	71.06	74
Percentage of villages not connected with pucca road (estimated)	81.71	547	75.18	530
Percentage coverage of safe drinking water and sanitation (estimated)	100.00	100	90.32	181
Percentage of Birth registered (estimated)	76.44	200	65.66	257
Percentage of Death registered (estimated)	62.37	187	39.11	327
Composite Index	62.37	209	61.09	223

Source: National Commission on Population, District Wise Indicators, Government of India, 2001.

Now let us have a look at the health care services structure and experience of reforms[4] in the two study districts of Sundergarh and Khurda. Here we would also be discussing about strengths and weaknesses in the health services in these districts.

Sundergarh district: a profile

The Sundergarh district was located in the northwestern part of Orissa, with a geographical area of 9712 square kilometers, which was 6.24 percent of the total land areas of Orissa. It had 17 community development blocks, 9 towns, 4 municipalities, 262 grampanchayats and 7 assembly constituencies.[5] According to the 2001 census of India, it had a total population of 1829,000, which was 4.98 percent of Orissa's total population. It had urban population constituting 34.38 percent of its total population, which was higher than all India average and a population density of 183 per square kilometer. Thus the population density shows that people were scarcely distributed. Further 7.54 percent of its population was scheduled castes and 43.63 percent of its population was scheduled tribes[6] and it had a sex ratio of 957[7]. Therefore maximum numbers of people were tribals in this district. While it had average literacy rate of 65.22 percent, among the scheduled castes the literacy rate was only 43.86 percent and among the scheduled tribes the literacy rate was 37.34 percent.[8] Therefore while the scheduled tribes constituted the largest section of this districts total population, they were at the bottom in terms of literacy rate.

---

[4] Here it needs to be mentioned that we have not asked questions separately with regard to 'systemic changes' and 'health sector reforms' to our respondents at the district level. However in our analysis we have made a distinction.

[5] District Statistical Handbook, Sundergarh, 2001, Published by Directorate of Economics and Statistics, Orissa, Bhubaneswar. Orissa had in total 147 assembly constituencies.

[6] The percentage of scheduled castes and scheduled tribes were based upon 1991 Census of India. All the 17 blocks of this district were tribal blocks.

[7] The sex ratio or females per 1000 males was based on 2001 Census of India.

[8] While the figures for average literacy rate of the district were from the 2001 Census of India, the figures for scheduled castes and scheduled tribes were from 1991 Census of India.

Health care services structure in Sundergarh District

To understand the health care services structure is an important aspect to determine the implications of health sector reforms because if the structures of provisioning perform to an optimum level than different initiatives for health sector reforms would show positive results. Therefore let us first look at the health care services structure in Sundergarh district.

Table: 6.2: Medical Institutions (allopathy) in Sundergarh District

DHH	2
SDH	2
UGPHCs	2
Area Hospitals (Other Hospitals)	3
CHC I	7
CHC II (Under OHSDP)	5
PHC	6
PHC (New)	54
Mobile Health Units	1
Total Medical Institutions	82
Sub Centres	345
No. of Beds	611

Note: DHH: District Head Quarter Hospital, SDH: Sub Divisional Hospital, UGPHC: Upgraded Primary Health Centre. Area Hospital- All these area hospitals were of 6-bedded institutions. In Orissa a PHC or a CHC I were headed by an MO, who was a Class II officer whereas a CHC II was headed by one Class I officer.
Source: Field Work, 2005.

The table shows that, there were two district headquarter hospitals, two sub divisional hospitals, two UGPHCs or Upgraded Primary Health Centres in Hemgiri and Subdega blocks and both were block headquarter institutions. There were three area hospitals[9], CHC I seven[10] and CHC II

[9] They were, in Bankibazar of Gurundia Block, Bilaimunda of Hemgiri Block and Surda of Nuangaon block.

[10] They were in Rajgrampur, Sargipalli, Bargaon, Kutra, Bisra, Lahunipada and Koida and all these institutions were of the same block. Except in Rajgrampur all had Sub Centres and PHC News'. The earlier hospital in Rajgrampur had been converted to a 40-bedded CHC I.

five[11]. The staff structure in CHC I institutions were, one MO in-charge, one assistant surgeon, three specialists (Gynic, Pediatrics and Orthopedic), one pharmacist and two staff nurse. However in Rajgrampur CHC I there were 8 staff nurses. The staff structure and bed strength in CHC II was same, as in CHC I, however under OHSDP the bed strength in Kuarmunda and Birmitrapur CHC II had been increased to 16 beds. All the CHC IIs' were under OHSDP. There were 6 block level Primary Health Centres, 54 PHC News and 345 Sub Centres[12] in the district. In total there were 82 medical institutions and 611 public beds in the district. Among the Sub Centres only 154 had government buildings and the remaining 191 were supposed to be functioning in a rented building[13]. There was one mobile health unit in the Lephripara block.

According to the Orissa government norms there should be one CHC I or CHC II above 30,000 populations and below it a PHC New institution should be there. Under RCH II government of India was planning to introduce one sub centre per 1,000 populations as against the existing norm of 3,000 populations. However it was observed that in many places these institutions were covering population almost double than their mandatory requirements. At nowhere it was found that an institution was serving less number of populations than either the Orissa government norms or the all India norms.

Vacancies in various posts

The existing manpower in different layers of health care services is a significant aspect of effective functioning of health care services structure. Therefore it was important to look at the then existing manpower in terms of different categories in Sundergarh district. The table below gives a picture of different categories of posts in terms of sanctioned strength, in position and clear vacancy.

---

[11] They were located in Mojhapara of Sadar block, Mangaspur of Tangarpali block, Kinjhirkela of Balisankara block, Kuarmunda of Kuarmunda block and Birmitrapur of Kuarmunda block.

[12] For one Sub Centre building Rs 3 lakhs was provided along with 4-5 decimal areas. One Sub Centre building consisted of one – resident building with 2-bed rooms, one-latrine, one - bathroom and one – kitchen and two other rooms, one for office and another for delivery.

[13] Interviews with ANMs made it clear that when the sub centres were in 'rented' buildings it meant it did not function at all!

Table: 6.3 Vacancies in various categories of posts in Sundergarh District

Posts	Sanctioned Strength	In Position	Clear Vacancy
Sr. Class I	11	8	3
Jr. Class I	25	18	7
Class II Specialists	36	27	9
Asst. Surgeon	138	129	9
Staff Nurse	98	97	1
Pharmacist	25	25	0
MPHW (M)	241	220	21
MPHW (F)	430	397	33
MPHS (M)	90	45	45
MPHS (F)	55	54	1
Radiographer	10	6	4
Lab. Technician (Pathology)	29	29	0

Note: MPHW (M): Multi Purpose Health Worker, Male, MPHW (F): Multi Purpose Health Worker, Female, MPHS: Multi Purpose Health Supervisor.

It shows that in terms of the Senior Class I posts, out of 11 sanctioned strength, 8 were in position and 3 posts were vacant. Similarly for the Junior Class I posts, out of the sanctioned strength of 25, 18 were in position and there were 7 vacancies. In Class II Specialists' category, out of the sanctioned strength of 36, 27 were in position and 9 posts were vacant. In case of Assistant Surgeons, out of the sanctioned strength of 138, 129 were in position and 9 posts were vacant. However in case of Staff Nurse, only one post was vacant, out of the total sanctioned post of 98.

As we have mentioned earlier that the Senior Class I officers were heading CHC II institutions and hence if 3 posts were vacant in this category than it suggest that 3 of these institutions or such type of institutions were functioning without a head and as a result the smooth functioning of these institutions must have been difficult. The vacancies in the categories of Junior Class I, Class II Specialists and the Assistant Surgeons suggest that these posts were vacant in PHC and CHC level institutions and hence these required immediate attention. Significantly in the category of Staff Nurse there was only one vacancy.[14]

On the other hand there were no vacancies in the category of pharmacist. While there were 21 vacancies in case of health worker male, there were 33 vacancies in case of health worker female. In case of health supervisors, male, there was 50 % vacancy and in case of health supervisors, female, only one post was vacant. In case of Radiographers there were 4 vacancies out of total sanctioned strength of 10 and finally there were no vacancies in the category of Lab Technicians.

Therefore the broader trends show that, while in the category of pharmacists all the positions were filled up, there were significant shortages in health worker, male and female. As these people are crucial for effective functioning of Sub Centres, their absence could make the people from different areas totally cut off from the nearby Primary Health Centres. Further there was serious crisis in the category of health supervisors, male, where out of 90 sanctioned posts, only 45 were filled up. The supervision work is an important aspect of implementation of various national programs at the block level and hence the shortage of male supervisors was a matter of serious concern. Similarly the shortage of Radiographers was a matter of concern for the district.

Medical institutions (Indian Medicine and Homeopathy) in Sundergarh district

Now let us have a look at the ISM and H institutions in Sundergarh district. The table below gives a picture of institutions under Ayurvedic and Homeopathic system in Sundergarh District.

Table: 6.4 ISM and H institutions in Sundergarh District

District	Ayurvedic System		Homeopathic System	
	Hospitals	Dispensary	Hospitals	Dispensary
Sundergarh	0	32	1	22

Source: Health Statistics of Orissa, 2000-2001, Compiled by State Bureau of Health Intelligence, DHS, Orissa.

[14] Because in Orissa various posts of Staff Nurses have been vacant over the years.

It shows that under the Ayurvedic system the district had no hospitals and 32 dispensaries. In terms of Homeopathic system there was one hospital and 22 dispensaries. There were no Unani hospitals or dispensaries in the district. Therefore under the ISM and H institutions it was mainly the dispensaries existed under the Ayurvedic and Homeopathic system in this district. Therefore it could be said that the allopathic system of medicine was the dominant system of health care that existed in the district.

Block PHC

As we have discussed in chapter II that two block level PHCs/CHCs were covered in the two selected districts of Orissa each. In this way, total four block PHCs were intensively studied. In Sundergarh district we have studied Kuarmunda CHC II and the Hatibari PHC for the purpose of our study.

Kuarmunda CHC II

Now let us have a look at the Kuarmunda CHC II, which was functioning as a block level PHC. This was one of the two blocks selected for study. With a population of 92,427, it had 106 villages, 20 Gram Panchayats and 118 Anganwadi centres and it was divided into 4 sectors. It was located at a distance of 148 Kilometers from the district head quarters and the road connectivity was good. This CHC II existed nearby the bus stand of Kuarmunda town and nearby it there was one market area, one school and the police station. Rourkela the industrial town of western Orissa was only at a distance of 8 Kilometers from this CHC II. The referrals from here were sent to the Rourkela Government Hospital, Rourkela or to the sub divisional hospital, Panposh which was located at a distance of 5 kilometers.

This CHC II was a 16-beded institution and all these beds were functioning. In terms of manpower at the CHC II headquarter; there were three medical officers out of whom one was MO in- charge with orthopedics and gynic specialization, another MO was a gynecologist and the post of assistant surgeon was vacant for last one year. There was one pharmacist, 6 staff nurses and one lab technicians each for malaria and for pathology. In terms of infrastructure, water and electricity were available within its premises. The PHC headquarter building was well maintained and the Medical officers quarters were in good conditions.

Table: 6.5 Kuarmunda CHC II: Sudergarh District

Total population: 92,427.

Distance from the district headquarters: 148 Kilometers. Road connectivity was very good.

Location: Located nearby a bus stand, which was one of the busy routes for transport and communication in the district.

Number of Anganwadi centres: 118

Number of villages in the CHC area: 106

Number of Gram Panchayats: 20

Manpower at the CHC II headquarters: 3 medical officers out of which Gynic- 1, assistant surgeon- 1 and the other person was M/O in charge with O & G specialization. Out of these sanctioned 3 posts only 2 M/Os were there and another post was vacant for last one year.

Pharmacist- 1, Staff Nurse- 6, Lab Technicians- 1 each for malaria and for pathology.

Infrastructure: Water and electricity was available. The PHC headquarter building was well maintained and the MOs' quarters were in good conditions.

Beds: 16

PHC (N): 3. They were at Raiboga, Andali Jambahal and Kadabhahal

Sub Centres: 22. There were 22 ANMs and 8 male workers present and 12 male workers were vacant. (Note: Each Sub Centre is supposed to have one ANM and one male worker). Many Sub Centres have been built in distant areas from villages due to lack of government land.

Sub Centres with no buildings: 10. Raiboga (3), Kadabahal (2), Kumjharia (2) and Kuarmunda (3). (The figures in the bracket suggest about the Sub Centres with no buildings in the respective four sectors).

Sectors: 4. Kuarmunda (6), KumJharia (5), Kadabahal (5) and Raiboga (6). The figures in the bracket suggests about the number of Sub Centres.

Supervisors: 4. While in Kumjharia one male supervisor was there, the remaining sectors had one female supervisor each.

Indigenous medical practitioners: 107, according to an estimate by the CDMO's office in the district in 2004.

Health status: Birth Rate- 19, Death Rate- 6, IMR- 35, MMR- 56, Sterilization achievement: 265 in October, November and January of 2004-05 out of the target 246. (Note: the term sterilization was synonymous with female sterilization).

Source: Field Work, 2005.

The PHC (new) s' were three and they were located in Raiboga, Andali Jambahal and Kadabhahal. These institutions were well connected through all weather roads. These were located near by market and school areas. However the infrastructures in all the three institutions were in a very bad shape and in two of these institutions cleanliness was not maintained regularly. There were no water supply in these institutions but electricity supply was there only at Raiboga PHC (New).

The mandatory manpower for each PHC (N) was Medical Officer- 1, Pharmacist- 1, ANM- 1, Sweeper- 2. In Raiboga and Kadabahal there were no Medical officers and Pharmacists were heading these institutions. Even where the medical officers have been posted, it has been observed that they were absent.[15] During field visit the Andali Jambahal institution was found to be closed.

There were 22 Sub Centres under this CHC II out of which 10 had no building of their own. Even where the sub centres had any buildings, the ANMs were not staying there. They were staying in the towns of Kuarmunda or Birmitrapur etc. While those sub centres, which had no government building, were supposed to function from a rented house, in reality these were not functioning at all. Due to lack of proper road connectivity, the ANMs were supposed to visit their field by walking. While all the 22 ANMs posts were filled up, the number of male workers post filled up was 8 only and the remaining 12 posts were vacant. The male workers rarely used to visit their field. As a result the work load on the ANMs used to be very high. Most of the ANMs interviewed were not aware about various national programmes. The group interviews with ANMs revealed that the focus of their activities was to achieve targets of female sterilization for each month under the RCH and the immunization program. In their visits to respective villages, the ANMs used to face abuses from the village males with regard to RCH and population control measures.

According to 2004 estimate[16] there were 107 Indigenous medical practitioners in this block. In terms of health status in this block, birth rate was 19, death rate- 6, IMR- 35, MMR- 56; Sterilization achievement was 265 in October, November and January of 2004-05, out of the target 246.

Hatibari PHC

The table below gives a picture of Hatibari PHC. It was the second PHC in this district, which was studied for our purpose.

[15] According to the senior officials in the state it was the pharmacist who in most of the cases was heading these institutions in Orissa.
[16] By this CHC II.

Table: 6.6: Hatibari PHC: Sundergarh District

Population: 96,694.

Distance from the district headquarters: 170 kilometers. Road connectivity was good.

Location: Located near the bus stand of Hatibari town.

The staff structure: Medical officers- 2, Pharmacists- 1, No staff nurse, Lab technicians: 1 for malaria and another for RNTCP, ANM- 1, Attendant- 4, Sweepers- 2, LHV (Lady Health Visitor) – 1, Statistical assistant- 1. Staff nurse post is vacant over the years.

Infrastructure: Water, Electricity was available in the PHC headquarter. The PHC headquarter buildings were well maintained and the quarters of the two medical officers were in good conditions.

Sectors: 3. They were at Hatibari (8), Nuagaon (8) and Sorda (10). One supervisor in each sector. While 3 lady supervisors were present, out of 3 sanctioned posts of male supervisors only one was present.

Beds: 6. All functioning.

Patients per day: 100 average.

PHC (N): 3. They were at Nuangaon, Sorada and Loaram. In Nuangaon the post of medical officer was vacant.

Sub Centres: 26. Only 8 had government buildings. For ANMs where government building was not there Rs 70 per month was given and for male workers 5% of their basic pay, which was 5% of Rs 3200, was provided. According to the ANMs this policy was quite discriminatory for them. In fact this was one of the main grievances of ANMs in all the four block PHCs in two districts that we studied.

ANM: 26+1 on deputation. One post vacant.

Male worker: out of sanctioned strength 16 only 8 were present.

Health Status: Birth Rate- 19, Death Rate- 6.62, IMR- 31, MMR- 53.05. (Note: all these figures were for the year 2004).

Epidemiological status: Malaria was endemic in this area followed by TB, Polio and Leprosy. Among the national programs RNTCP, Leprosy and Malaria were doing well in this PHC.

Note: Referrals from here were sent to RGH or Rourkela Government Hospital, Rourkela.

Source: Field Work, 2005.

The Hatibari PHC was catering to the population of 96,694 with 6 beds in total. It was located at a distance of 170 kilometers from the district headquarters and the road connectivity was good. This PHC existed nearby the bus stand of Hatibari town and was also closer to the market area. Besides one school and the police station were also nearby it. Rourkela the industrial town of western Orissa was only at a distance of 25 Kilometers from this PHC. The referrals from here were sent to the Rourkela Government Hospital, Rourkela or to the sub divisional hospital, Panposh.

In terms of infrastructure, water and electricity were available within the PHC premises. The PHC headquarter buildings were well maintained and the quarters of the two medical officers were in good conditions.

The staff structure in the headquarter PHC was: Medical officers- 2, out of which one was MO in-charge. There was one Pharmacist, Lab technicians one each for malaria and another for RNTCP, one ANM, four Attendants, two Sweepers, Lady Health Visitor one and one Statistical assistant. There was no staff nurse present and the post was vacant over the years. In three sectors 3 lady supervisors were present and out of sanctioned post of 3 male supervisors only one was present. A new RCH building had come up in the PHC headquarter under World Bank funding with facilities like one operation room, one labor room, one duty room and two latrines and bathrooms each.

There were three PHC (N) institutions. They were in Nuangaon, Sorada and Loaram. In Nuangaon the post of medical officer was vacant. All these institutions were well connected through road and these were located nearby market and school areas. However the infrastructure in all the three cases was in a very bad shape and from outside these were also looking very dirty. During the field visit only the Nuangaon institution was open and the other two were closed. There was no water or electricity supply in these institutions, except for Nuangaon where electricity supply was there.

Out of total 23 Sub Centres only 8 had government buildings. However the ANMs mostly used to stay nearby Hatibari or Birmitrapur town[17]. There was no water or electricity supply in 8 existing government sub centre buildings. Among the ANMs out of sanctioned posts of 26 one was vacant and in case of male workers out of 16 sanctioned strength only 8 were present. During group interviews with ANMs it was observed that they were not aware about various national programs and most of them rarely used to visit the fields. Discussing about their field challenges the ANMs were of the view that they had to face abuses from the villagers with regard to issues of RCH, HIV/AIDS and population control measures. The focus of ANMs activities were RCH and immunization programs and within RCH, to achieve targets of female sterilization for each month.

[17] Located at a distance of 25 kilometers from Hatibari town and was famous for limestone mines in Western Orissa. Mostly the limestone and the dolomites were supplied from this town to Rourkela Steel Plant in Orissa, to Bhilai Steel Plant in Madhya Pradesh and to Durgapur Steel Plant in West Bengal.

In terms of health status, birth rate was 19; death rate was 6.62, IMR- 31, MMR- 53.05 according to the figures for the year 2004. In terms of epidemiological status: Malaria was endemic in this area followed by TB, Polio and Leprosy. Among the national programs RNTCP, Leprosy and Malaria were doing well in this PHC. Referrals from here were sent to RGH or Rourkela Government Hospital, Rourkela.

Strengths

"As it is an undivided district government wing officers like DMO, DIO, DTO[18], ADMO Medical, DLO and SDMOs were assisting in performing all national programs. We have also got good infrastructure as compared to other divided districts[19]. Significantly when we compare the two of our study block PHCs of Sundergarh with the other block PHCs of Khurda than it was quite clear that the block PHCs[20] at Sundergarh had better infrastructure than Khurda.

Weaknesses

"Shortage of doctors and paramedics, yet to be filled…as it is a tribal district the periphery institutions need to be filled up." Mentioning about the particular areas of concern he said, "Lahunipada, Nuangaon and Koida[21] are the CHCs/PHCs of concern, where staffs are refusing to stay."

Constraints

"As the sanction has to come from higher authority, new postings are less.[22] For paramedics every month vacancy list is sent…first cleared by

[18] DMO refers to District Malaria officer, DIO refers to District Information Officer, DLO refers to District Leprosy Officer and DTO refers to District Tuberculosis Officer and SDMO refers to Sub Divisional Medical Officer.

[19] It needs to be mentioned that before 1995 Orissa was having only 13 districts and later it was increased to 30 districts and the reason cited was that it would be administratively convenient. However there were districts like Sundergarh, which were not divided.

[20] We need to mention here that in Sundergarh district we have taken Kuarmunda CHC II for our study, because this was the block headquarter institution.

[21] These were three different blocks.

[22] The CDMO was referring about the postings of paramedics in the district who were selected on a contractual basis.

government and then only we can recruit on a contractual basis. Only in case of contractual doctors we can recruit without consulting higher authorities." About infrastructure he said, "Except in medical colleges there are hardly any infrastructures in other places." He further added that "but due to political pressure[23] health centres are created, but nobody bothers as to how these will run without infrastructure." He said that some politician wants to open a PHC New because he had promised in the election and hence they put pressure to open an institution without bothering as to how it would function.

Process and experience of reforms[24]

Understanding the process and experience of health sector reforms at the district level was an important aspect to get a comprehensive view about the ongoing reform process in Orissa. However while the CDMOs were to some extent aware about some of the reform initiatives, the MO in-charge at the block headquarter PHCs had hardly any idea about these.[25]

On the consultation process[26]

Whether the CDMO was involved in consultation process before the reforms were initiated in the district? Responding to this query the CDMO said, "There was no such consultation held". That means reform elements were introduced with top-down approach. This has implications for the successful implementation and the sustainability of the reform process.

---

[23] This was a new dimension being mentioned by the CDMO about the lack of absence of staffs in PHC News.

[24] For understanding the reform elements at the district level, we have not made a separate classification for the 'reforms' and 'systemic' changes. That is our questions to the respondents were not classified into these two categories. However for our own analysis we have used this distinction.

[25] Even the CDMOs were not aware that the new initiatives by the state government were a reform initiative or not. While for the purpose of this study we have classified reforms and systemic changes in different categories, the state government in its vision document 2010 had mentioned in detail about the 'reform' initiatives taken by it. So here we were talking about the ignorance of CDMOs with respect to different health sector initiatives, which had been identified by the state government as reform elements.

[26] The wider consultation process before initiating a reform element was important because the implementation and the sustainability of this reform element depends on the various levels of manpower located in different layers of health care services.

User charges

In Sundergarh district user charges were collected at district HQ hospital, Sub divisional hospital Panposh, RGH Rourkela and in Bonai Sub Division hospital. These institutions were upgraded under Orissa Health Systems Development Project or OHSDP. User charges report was sent every month to World Bank funded OHSDP located at Bhubaneswar.

Responding to the question about his views on user charges the CDMO said, "It is a good scheme. A meeting is held every month called *quality assurance meeting* on the need assessment basis. There is a quality improvement group for quality assurance. Report is sent every month to OHSDP." However it was difficult to collect the data with regard to user fees collected in the district for various years form the CDMO's office. In fact this was also true in case of Khurda district.

On the creation of ZSS

Responding to the question about amalgamation of different district societies, the CDMO observed, "The society fund is separate and functioning as earlier and user charges fund is separate. As collector is the head of Zilla Swastha Samiti, under one platform everything is discussed…coordination is good. Decision and implementation is quick due to the creation of ZSS." The CDMO was of the opinion that the creation of ZSS had helped the district in responding to the emergency situations in a better way. For example if there was a sudden outbreak of malaria in the district and there were no funds for it than the money could be withdrawn from say TB account and later when the money for malaria comes, it could be transferred to the TB account. This was not possible earlier. Thus the amalgamation of district societies had helped in common pooling of resources. Besides the bureaucratic red tap had been reduced due to the creation of ZSS.

Training of medical interns

"Generally in the two UGPHC[27]s of Hemgiri and Subdega[28] trainings are held for three months. Students are mostly from the Burla Medical

[27] Upgraded Primary Health Centres. These had built up in the 1980s with the help of funding from UK funding agency DFID.

[28] These Upgraded Primary Health Centres were of 30-bedded institutions. There were in total two UGPHCs in the Sundergarh district.

College. During this training period students are given exposure to the national programs." The CDMO was of the opinion that this present system was better than the earlier system when the students used to visit a nearby PHC with the guidance of a senior professor. However in that system most of the students used to neglect it and the professors also used to give them the required marks.

While the CDMO claimed that this new system was better than the earlier one but an interaction with one of the medical officers who was currently in-charge of a PHC and who had a nine years stint in one of these UGPHCs, suggested that during his stay only one intern had completed the three months course and 'that too because she was from that area'. He was of the opinion that the CDMOs don't put pressure on the interns and generally give them the certificate even though an intern has not attended the training for a single day.

Indigenous practitioners

To the question as to whether ISP training was going on in this district, the CDMO said "The ISPs[29] are in all blocks of the district for referrals to the primary level care. Training is yet to be provided. At present ISPs are being identified in each block." Thus the CDMO was of the opinion that the ISPs were being identified in all the blocks of this district and would be involved in referrals to the nearest PHCs or CHCs. It needs to be mentioned here that Sundergarh has been identified by the state government as a tribal district and as such indigenous social practitioners must be there in large numbers. During the field visit to Kuarmunda CHC it was known that it had identified the total number of ISPs existing in Kuarmunda block.

Appointment of contractual doctors

"If patients are not coming, doctors are negligent. Once you become a popular doctor in your area, programs will follow and you can control your staff, hence treatment is very important"[30]. The CDMO was talking

[29] Indigenous social practitioners. They have been thought to be included in the referral services to the nearby primary level care for complications in pregnancy and for malaria cases in a tribal district like Sundergarh.

[30] This was the opinion of the CDMO to his medical officers in the district as to how to get the participation of people in a block in various national programs.

about filling the vacant posts in PHC New's[31] through contractual arrangement to a group of medical officer in-charge in some block PHCs in the district[32]. Responding to this issue one medical officer in charge of a PHC said that only the retired old doctors were interested for these posts, as they don't have to come regularly! While another medical officer said that at least let them join these posts.[33] In the meeting it emerged that the ANMs were not keeping in touch with the population and they were also not involved in the national programs.

Petty maintenance of PHCs

For the petty maintenance of PHC headquarters money had not come for the year 2005. However the CDMO was of the opinion that the scheme

---

However this could also be possible that the CDMO made this comment to his officers because this researcher was present!

[31] PHC New's were single doctor institutions in Orissa where only outpatient services were provided. Apart from a medical officer, one pharmacist, one ANM and a sweeper were supposed to be there. In needs to be mentioned here that in these institutions the first posting of a medical officer in the government service occurs. However it was in these posts that the doctors were most of the time absent. This was observed during first hand visit to all these PHC New's in the two districts chosen for study. It was the pharmacists who were present in all the cases and they were virtually running these institutions and in one case the PHC New was closed during the visit, whereas it was supposed to remain open. There were many aspects to this problem. From one medical officer's point of view, they find it very difficult to convince themselves to stay in a remote area after having spent their education in a city and they feel it as a punishment posting. Some other medical officers were of the view that infact a pharmacist could effectively run these institutions and there was no need for a doctor and important thing was that in cases of complications they should refer the patients to the block PHCs in time. Off late the government of Orissa has planned to convert these single doctor institutions into PHC category, as it is the norm in other states in India and to convert the existing block level PHCs or CHCs as CHCs. At present in Orissa many block level headquarter institutions were either CHCs or PHCs. It was observed that at the PHC New level in the Sundergarh district the outdoor attendance was 10 to 15% a day and the CDMO observed that where there was less than 20% attendance, which suggested inefficiency of the MBBS doctor.

[32] Here inferences have been made from the monthly coordination meeting held at the Sundergarh District in the month of March 2005 where apart from the senior officials of the district level, the medical officer in charge of all the block PHCs of Sundergarh district were also present.

[33] This conversation happened in the chamber of the CDMO before the monthly coordination meeting was about to start.

had been helpful for the PHCs. It was interesting to note here, what one of the MOs in our study PHC said with regard to this scheme. "Money under this head comes but it is not regular. In my knowledge this amount is being misutilised by the medical officer in-charge of a PHC in most of the cases…" Thus while the CDMO was not forthcoming on the actual working of this scheme, the medical officer in this PHC gave some good insights.

Pancha Byadhi Chikitsa scheme

Responding to the Pancha Bhadhi Chikitsa Scheme, the CDMO said, "This is going on well…Innovative idea of the Orissa government. Quite helpful at the periphery level." Interacting with medical officers[34] in the PHCs of this district it was known that because these diseases were very common among the population, therefore before the introduction of this scheme, they used to provide medicines for these diseases. However due to better drug supply after the new drugs policy they were able to provide the required medicines to the patients. However according to the MOs interviewed many of the patients were not aware about their rights[35] under this scheme.

New Drugs policy

To the question as to whether there was any improvement in the supply and quality of drugs after the introduction of new drugs policy, the CDMO said, "Situation has improved than earlier." This was also the view of medical officers interviewed at different block PHCs.

Mandatory pre-PG rural scheme

This scheme was operational in this district. However one MO was of the opinion that "By giving money to CDMOs, people are getting a certificate that they have done one year service in rural areas. But it is not happening in reality." This MO was of the opinion that rather than this mandatory one-year scheme, "After doing five-year service, one could go for in-

---

[34] Interviews were also taken with medical officers attending the monthly coordination meeting in the district, apart from interviewing medical officers at block PHC headquarters in this district.

[35] We have discussed in chapter V in detail about the rights of a patient under this scheme.

service PG, where one would be getting regular salaries, promotion and the seniority would also be maintained." While the CDMO said that this scheme was functioning well, in reality it was not working.[36]

Handing over PHCs[37] to NGOs

This scheme was applied in one district of Orissa on a pilot basis. However to know the opinion of the CDMO about this scheme, this issue was raised. Responding to this query the CDMO said, "NGOs in India have not gone to that extent to take up those responsibilities. In our district no such discussion[38] has taken place."

Improving health care services in periphery level institutions

As the CDMO was dealing at the grass roots level and has had experience in this district for more than 20 years he was asked about the way out to improve the health care services in periphery level institutions. Responding to this question the CDMO was of the view that "It will take another 20-22 years for the staff to stay in periphery level institutions. The difference between a village and a town is roads, electricity, schools and latrine…until and unless these things are provided…apart from it literacy level has to improve along with economic status of the people. Orissa is a poor state…. Situation is improving… Compared to the time of independence now it is far better". This observation was significant, as it has been noted that there was a kind of helplessness among the cadres and also the policy makers at the top level about addressing the issues of health care services at periphery level institutions. Therefore it was important to understand that the improvement of health care services was linked with the improvement in other aspects of life.

He further added, "At present we cannot provide remuneration to the MOs and other staffs for staying in difficult areas as Orissa is a poorer state". He was giving a comparative picture of Indian Army having a policy of remuneration for those who opt for difficult areas. Therefore these were structural issues and would require a multi sectoral approach to effectively respond to the situation.

---

[36] We have also discussed about this scheme in chapter III and chapter V.
[37] Here the PHCs refer to PHC (N), which were single doctor medical institutions in Orissa.
[38] About the idea of handing over PHCs to NGOs.

OHSDP institutions and staffs in Sundergarh District[39]

The figure shows that apart from the district hospital, sub divisional hospital and RGH hospital, Rourkela, five CHC II level institutions were selected under OHSDP. If one looks at the post of staff nurse, than it shows that all the positions created were of contractual nature. In fact this was the case in most of the posts for staff nurse created under OHSDP in 157 institutions in Orissa.

Khurda district: a profile

The Khurda district was located in the coastal part of Orissa, with a geographical area of 2813 square kilometers, which was 1.81 percent of the total land area of Orissa. It had 10 community development blocks, 7 towns, 3 municipalities, 168 grampanchayats and 6 assembly constituencies.[40] According to the 2001 census of India, it had a total population of 1874,000, which was 5.10 percent of Orissa's population. It had urban population constituting 42.93 percent of its total population which was much higher than all India average and population density of 666 per square kilometer. Further 10.93 percent of its population was scheduled castes and 4.10 percent of its population was scheduled tribes[41] and it had a sex ratio of 901[42]. Therefore scheduled castes were more in number than scheduled tribes in this district. While it had average literacy rate of 80.19 percent, among the scheduled castes the literacy rate was only 47.46 percent and among the scheduled tribes the literacy rate was 28.11 percent.[43]

Health care services structure

The table below mentions about the existing medical institutions in Khurda district.

---

[39] See Annexure 1 in this chapter.

[40] District Statistical Handbook, Khurda, 2001, Published by Directorate of Economics and Statistics, Orissa, Bhubaneswar.

[41] The percentage of scheduled castes and scheduled tribes were based upon 1991 Census of India.

[42] The sex ratio or females per 1000 males, was based on 2001 Census of India.

[43] While the figures for average literacy rate of the district were from the 2001 Census of India, the figures for scheduled castes and scheduled tribes were from 1991 Census of India.

Table: 6.7 Medical Institutions (Allopathy) in Khurda District

Medical Institutions	
DHH	2
SDH	0
Other Hosp	8
CHC I	6
CHC II	1
PHC	5
PHC (N)	59
Total medical Institutions	81
Sub Centres	186
No. of Beds	715

Note: DHH- District Headquarter Hospital, SDH- Sub Divisional Hospital, CHC- Community Health centre includes upgraded PHCs, PHC- Primary Health Centre, MHU- Mobile Health Unit.
Source: Field Work, 2005.

The table shows that there were 2 District Headquarter Hospitals, one at Bhubaneswar and another at Khurda and 8 other hospitals in Khurda District. Thus there were 10 hospitals in total in this district. The CHC I institutions were 6 and the number of CHC II[44] institutions was 1., Primary Health Centres were 5, PHC (N)[45] institutions were 59 and 186 sub centres in total. Out of 186 sub centres only 90 had government building and the remaining 96 were supposed to be functioning on rented buildings.[46] Therefore in total there were 81 medical institutions in the district with no sub divisional hospital or any mobile health unit. There were 715 public beds in total in the district.

Vacancies in various categories of posts

Now let us have a look at the vacancies in various categories of posts in this district.

[44] It needs to be mentioned here that in Orissa all the CHC II institutions were under OHSDP.
[45] The structure of CHC, PHC and the PHC (New) and Sub Centre were same as they were at Sundergarh district.
[46] This data was collected from the CDMO office, Khurda.

Table: 6.8 Vacancies in various posts: Khurda District

Posts	Sanctioned Strength	In Position	Clear Vacancy
Sr. Class I	8	8	0
Jr. Class I	11	10	1
Class II Specialists	63	61	2
Asst. Surgeon	128	123	5
Staff Nurse	119	115	4
Pharmacist	96	94	2
MPHW (M)	186	142	44
MPHW (F)	239	239	0
MPHS (M)	73	39	34
MPHS (F)	27	22	5
Radiographer	3	2	1
Lab. Technician (Pathology)	5	5	0

Note: MPHW (M): Multi Purpose Health Worker, Male, MPHW (F): Multi Purpose Health Worker, Female, MPHS: Multi Purpose Health Supervisor.
Source: Field Work, 2005.

The table shows that in the category of senior class I, multipurpose health worker females and among the lab technicians all the posts were filled up. This was significant because the senior class I posts were mostly in CHC II institutions and this suggests that the first referral units in the district were well functioning. Similarly the multi purpose health worker females are a link between the community and the block PHC and hence when all the posts in this category were filled up, this suggests that the sub centres in the district must be functioning relatively well. The lab technicians are important for diagnosis of malaria and TB cases and their presence to a certain extent contributes enhancing the people's perception about access to effective health care in a health institution.

Similarly in the categories of junior class I, class II specialists, assistant surgeons, pharmacists, staff nurses and radiographers post, there were few shortages. However there were severe shortages in the posts of multipurpose health worker male and the multipurpose health supervisor male. Filling these two categories of posts was significant for effective functioning of sub centres and through these various national programs.

However another aspect of this problem was that even when the various categories of posts were filled up, in itself it was not enough for smooth functioning of various health institutions, because the staffs may not be willing to stay in the remote and difficult areas of the district.

ISM and H institutions in Khurda district

The table below gives a picture of medical institutions under Indian System of Medicine and Homeopathy in Khurda District.

Table: 6.9 ISM and H institutions in Khurda District

District	Ayurvedic System		Homeopathic System	
	Hospitals	Dispensary	Hospitals	Dispensary
Khurda	1	18	1	22

Source: Health Statistics of Orissa, 2000-2001, Compiled by State Bureau of Health Intelligence, DHS, Orissa.

The table shows that in Khurda district there was one hospital and 18 dispensaries under the Ayurvedic system and there was one hospital and 22 dispensaries under the Homeopathic Systems. There was no Unani dispensary. It needs to be mentioned here that out of total 5 Ayurvedic hospitals[47] and out of total 4 Homeopathic hospitals[48] in Orissa one each was present at Khurda district.

Strengths and weaknesses in the health care services structure

Responding to the question about strengths and weaknesses in the health care services structure in the district the CDMO said, "In terms of vacant posts the post of MOs less. While all the PHCs should have three doctors we have only two. However the main problem is that the District Headquarter hospital has been upgraded from Sub Divisional District Hospital, but new doctors have not been employed." He was also of the opinion that out of two hospitals, one at Bhusanpur and another at Odsing, these were manned by only one medical officer each. He further said, "In

[47] The other four Ayurvedic hospitals were one each in Bargarh, Balangir, Ganjam and Puri district. See Health Statistic of Orissa, 2000-2001, Compiled by State Bureau of Health Intelligence, DHS, Orissa.

[48] Similarly the other 3 Homeopathic hospitals in Orissa were one each in Ganjam, Sambalpur and in Sundergarh districts.

the district Head Quarter Hospital, the specialists' posts like radiologist, FMT, Psychiatrist and pathology are vacant."

On the PHC (N) s in the district he said, "In most of the places pharmacists are running these institutions, in place of the medical officer." Therefore he was of the opinion that there should be two medical officers at these single doctor institutions, so that if one MO was absent than another could be available. The CDMO was also of the view that the basic facilities were also missing in these institutions. Another interesting aspect of these institutions in the district was that, "People were asked to select a plot where there would be one MO quarter, one pharmacist quarter and one dispensary quarter could be build up. This has not occurred. Most of the PHC (N) s has not been handed over to the government."

In terms of strength in the health care services structure in the district he said, "The allotted post for MOs were filled up…Medicines and instruments are adequate and all the block PHCs are in good condition." It needs to be mentioned here that during the visit to a nearby block PHC in this district, the medical officer in-charge said that the PHC building required repairing at many places and even his own quarter gets filled up with water in rainy season! However another question arises here and it was about the Orissa governments attempt to convert the existing PHC (N) s into block level PHCs and the existing PHCs and CHCs to CHCs according to the All India pattern. However if the conditions of the PHC (N) s were such that neither the required physical infrastructure nor the required manpower was available and even where there were posts, staffs refuse to be there, then in these circumstances would it be wise to change the designation of these institutions? Therefore would not it be feasible that the existing structures in the state were changed or renamed according to the requirements of the state, rather than changing to the All India pattern?

Block PHCs

Two block level PHCs were studied intensively in Khurda district, they were Balakathi PHC and Mendhashala PHC.

Balakathi PHC

The table below gives a picture of Balakathi PHC under Khurda district.

Table: 6.10 Balakathi PHC, Khurda District

Established: 1982.
Population: 1,09,000.
Distance from the district headquarters: 30 Kilometers. However half of this distance was without pucca or all weather roads.
Location: Located in a nearby market of this block.
Infrastructure in the PHC headquarters: Water and electricity was available. However there were leakages at many places of the building roofs. Maintenance was poor. Even the quarter of the MO in-charge had leakages in the roof.
Sectors: 3. They were at Pahala (5), Balakathi (6), Bhingarpur (7). (Note: The figures in the bracket suggest the number of Sub Centres in each sector.
Manpower:
Medical Officer: 3, One M/o in charge (MBBS), Gynic- 1, Pediatrics- 1.
Pharmacist: 1.
Supervisor: 6. Female- 3, Male- 3. One supervisor for 6 Sub Centres and for one sector two supervisors.
Lab Technician: 1, BEE (Block Extention Educator for IEC activities): 1.
Statistical assistant: 1, Vital Statistics Clerk: 1.
Ward Attendant: out of 4 posts one was vacant.
Sweeper: out of 2 posts one was vacant.
Beds: 6.
Per day outdoor patients: 200 on average.
Sub Centres: 18. Out of which 11 did not have any government buildings. One Sub Centre covered around 8,000 to 9,000 population. While some Sub Centres had 5,000 populations, maximum was 10,000 populations.
ANMs: out of 18-sanctioned strength one post was vacant.
Male worker: Out of 13 posts only 5 were filled up.
PHC (N): 3. They were Balianta, Pahala and Bhingarpur. (Note: PHC News' were only for outpatient services. The structures for PHC (N) s were M/o-1, Pharmacist-1, ANM- 1, Attendant- 1, and Sweeper- 1).
Referrals: To the Khurda HQ hospital or to the Capital Hospital, Bhubaneswar.
Source: Field Work, 2005.

Established in 1982, it catered to the population of 1,09,000. The Balakathi PHC was located at a distance of 30 kilometers from the district head quarters and the road connectivity was very bad[49]. This PHC existed nearby a market area of this block. Bhubaneswar the Capital of Orissa was at a distance of 30 kilometers from here. The referrals from here were sent

[49] This was very significant because although this PHC existed only at a distance of 30 kilometers from the Capital of Orissa, more than half of the road was not all weather roads. Therefore we could say that if this were the condition of a PHC nearby the Capital, Bhubaneswar, what would be the condition in other districts.

to either the district headquarter hospital, Khurda or to the Capital Hospital, Bhubaneswar.

In terms of infrastructure, water and electricity were available within the PHC premises. However there were leakages at many places of the building roofs. Maintenance was poor. Even the quarter of the MO in-charge had leakages in the roof.

It had only 6 beds and average outdoor patients per day were 200. There were three sectors under this block PHC. They were Pahala, Balakathi and Bhingarpur. The staff structure in this block headquarter PHC was, three medical officers in total, out of which one was MO in-charge, one was Gynic specialist and another one was pediatrics specialist. Besides there were one pharmacist, six supervisors, one lab technician, one Block Extention Educator or BEE for IEC activities in the block, one statistical assistant and one vital statistics clerk.

Among the 18 Sub Centres only 7 had government buildings and the rest 11 were supposed to be functioning in rented buildings. Due to lack of proper road connectivity, the ANMs had to visit their field villages by walking. However the ANMs mostly used to stay nearby Bhubaneswar and hence most of them were not visiting their fields regularly.[50] On the other hand interviews with ANMs revealed that they had to face daily abuses from the villagers during their routine visits. The ANMs interviewed were ignorant about various national programs and many of them were of the opinion that their training was inadequate. The focus of ANMs activities were immunization and RCH programs and within RCH the focus was on population control measures through female sterilization.

There were three PHC (N) s, one each in Balianta, Pahala and Bhingarpur. These institutions were located in one corner of a village, with no proper road connectivity. There were no schools or any market nearby these PHC (New) s. There was no electricity or water supply in any of these PHC (New) s. The staff structure in these institutions was same. During the visit to these institutions it was observed that the medical officer in charge was absent and in one case even the pharmacist was not present. These institutions were located in the interior areas with no pucca road connectivity. In rainy seasons due to water logging these institutions almost get cut off from other areas. These institutions were urgently

[50] This was the observation of the supervisors in this block PHC.

requiring some reparation. However cleanliness was maintained in all these three institutions.

Mendhashala PHC

The table below gives a picture of Mendhashala PHC. Established in 1963, it catered to the population of 1,29,00 with an average outdoor patient load of 100 and with a capacity of 6 beds.

Table: 6.11 Mendhashala PHC (Khurda District)
Established: 1963
Population: 1,29,000.
Distance from the district headquarters: 45 Kilometers. However more than half of the distance was without pucca road.
Infrastructure: Water and electricity was available. However the PHC headquarter building was not well maintained. The quarters of the Medical Officers had leakages in the roofs.
Location: It was located nearby a village market.
Manpower at HQ PHC:
Medical Officer: 2, One M/o in charge and another Gynic specialist.
Pharmacist: 1,
Lab Technician: 1.
ANM: 1, Block Extention Educator: 1.
Statistical Assistant: 1.
Ward Attendant: 1.
Sweeper: 2.
PHC (N): 4. They were at Chandaka, Itipur, Patia and Nuabandha.
M/o- 4 present, Pharmacists- 4 present, ANMs- 4 present, Sweepers were present only in two PHC News.
Sub Centres: 21. Out of which only 6 had government buildings.
ANMs: Out of 21 sanctioned strength, 20 were present.
Male worker: Out of 20 sanctioned strength, only 14 were present.
Sectors: 5. Mendhasala (4), Chandaka (3), Kalaram (6), Putrapada (4) and Itipur (4). (Note: The figures in the bracket suggest the number of Sub Centres in each sector.
Supervisors: 7. Out of which 4 were Lady Health Visitors or LHVs and 3 male supervisors. One supervisor for 4-6 Sub Centres.
Beds: 6.
Out door patients at Block HQ: approximately 100.
Referrals: To the Khurda HQ hospital or to the Capital Hospital, Bhubaneswar.
Source: Field Work, 2005.

The Mendhashala PHC was located at a distance of 45 kilometers from the district head quarters. However, more than half of the distance from the district headquarters was without any pucca road. This PHC existed nearby a village market area of this block. There were no schools or police stations nearby this PHC. The referrals from here were sent to either the district head quarter hospital, Khurda or to the Capital Hospital, Bhubaneswar.

In terms of infrastructure, water and electricity were available within the PHC premises. However the PHC headquarter building was not well maintained. The quarters of the Medical Officers had leakages in the roofs. The staff structure in this PHC was two medical officers out of which one was gynic specialist and another was MO in-charge. Besides there was one pharmacist, one lab technician, one Block Extention Educator, one statistician, one ANM but no staff nurse.

There were four PHC (N) s in this block, located in Chandaka, Itipur, Patia and Nuabandha. Among the staffs in these institutions two sweeper posts were vacant in two PHC (N) s. From this one could understand as to how difficult it would have been to run these institutions. Again among these four institutions medical officers were absent; in three of them during field visit and in the remaining one it was closed at a time when it should have remained open. Besides these institutions were located in the interiors of this block with no pucca road connectivity and these were located in one corner of a village. There were no schools or market near by these institutions. There was no electricity or water supply in these institutions. The buildings were in a dilapidated condition.

Out of 21 sub centres only 6 had government buildings. This suggested the gravity of the situation at these periphery level institutions. One sub centre covered 6,000 to 7,000 populations but some sub centres also covered population of 4,500. On an average one sub centre covered around 6-7 villages. As there was hardly any pucca road connectivity, the ANMs had to visit their villages by walking. Whether a sub centre had a building or not, it was alleged by the MO in-charge that most of the ANMs were staying near Bhubaneswar and would visit the fields occasionally. Among the ANMs out of 21 sanctioned posts 20 were present and among the male workers out of 20 sanctioned posts only 14 were present. About the male workers it was said that while the ANMs occasionally do visit their allotted villages, the male workers hardly ever visit the fields. Out of seven supervisors, 4 were lady health visitors and the rest three were male. Here also the ANMs were found to be ignorant about various national programmes. Interacting with ANMs it was clear that two national programs, they focused were immunization and RCH. Within the RCH the focus was on population control measures through female sterilization.

Process and experience of reforms

Now let us have a look at the process and experience of health sector reforms at Khurda district. As we have mentioned earlier that while we held interviews with the medical officers' in-charge at block headquarter PHCs with regard to health sector reforms, it was observed that they had no idea about these reform initiatives and they could only talk about their institutions. Hence it was only the CDMOs in these two districts who could give their views on some of the reform initiatives. At the same time CDMOs were not aware that a certain health initiative by the state government was a reform initiative or not. They were only aware about different schemes.[51]

On consultation process about reforms

Whether in the initiatives for introducing reforms in the health sector he was consulted by the senior officials in the state? Responding to this question the CDMO said, "There was no consultation at the CDMO level."[52] Therefore here also the CDMO was not consulted prior to the initiation of health sector reforms.

---

[51] This was very significant observation because for the successful implementation of the reform initiatives it was important that at all the levels of health care services structure the staffs were aware about various reform initiatives so that a collective effort could be made toward some concrete results.

[52] It was significant because what the CDMO said was that it was not about a single CDMO only, but at the CDMO levels itself there was no consultation about the reforms in the health sector. The same was also the case about consultation at the block level medical officers who act as a direct interface with the community. However it was quite surprising that the senior officials in the state when interviewed were of the opinion that the consultation process involved officials at all levels in the state, including some ANMs! On the other hand one senior official was of the opinion that it was not necessary to have opinion from all these levels as the senior technical level directors themselves have come from same experience over the years through postings at various places. But the question arises that by not involving the rank and file would it be possible for effective implementation of the reform initiatives in the state?

OHSDP institutions

To the question, what were the institutions funded by OHSDP in the district, the CDMO said, "They have helped in the construction of three CHCs and the District Head Quarter Hospital." Therefore out of 7 hospitals to be constructed in the district under OHSDP, the four, which were completed, Banapur CHC I, Balipatna CHC I, Balugaon CHC II and the Bolagarh Area Hospital.[53]

User charges

What were the institutions in the district where user charges were introduced? Responding to this the CDMO said, "Only in the district hospital user charges has been introduced. The services like routine urine check up, ECG, Ultra Sound, and the paying beds have been introduced." On deciding the cost of user charges he said, "The cost of user charges is passed in the ZSS meeting, which is less than market price." And how the below poverty line people were exempted from user fees, to this question he said, "Near about 40 percent of the user charges are not collected and the direct beneficiaries are the BPL card holders. And the doctor treating a patient certifies him/her as a BPL category."[54]

But how far the collection of user charges help in day to day recurrent expenditure of the institution? Is it sufficient enough? Responding to this question, the CDMO said, "Near about 70 to 80 percent of the regular expenditure was collected from user charges." On his opinion about the concept of user charges he said, "User charges should be enhanced. Some charges for outdoor patients should also be there. It should continue."[55]

---

[53] This was the observation by the CDMO during interview. The construction work for the district headquarter hospital was still going on during the field visit.

[54] However interacting with health officials at various levels they accepted that in practice it was really very difficult to exempt the poor from paying for user fees. This was even the opinion of some medical officers in the Capital Hospital, Bhubaneswar.

[55] It needs to be mentioned here that most of the interviewees at different levels in the state were in favor of introducing user fees at different levels of health services structure. Even the medical officer in-charge of the block PHCs were of the opinion that the introduction of user charges would not only help in improving the services available, it would also help in generating resources for regular maintenance of these institutions.

Petty maintenance of buildings

On the question about availability of funds under the petty maintenance scheme where Rs 10,000 per annum was provided to the medical officer in-charge at the block PHC, the CDMO said, "Money comes from the DHS without CDMO's interference to the MO at CHC/PHC level and hence can not say anything." However, interacting with medical officers at block PHCs it was told that the fund under this scheme was not regular.

New Drugs policy

Due to the introduction of new drugs policy, was there any change in the supply of drugs in this district? Answering to this question the CDMO said, "The supply is good, timely and adequate." Interestingly he added, "The quality was same, however it was earlier difficult to procure drugs locally for CDMOs."[56]

District Cadre for Paramedics

The CDMO was of the opinion that even though the paramedics were converted to district cadres, the situation has not improved in this district. He said, "About 70 to 80 male worker posts were vacant in the district." This was a matter of serious concern and this would also affect the work of the ANMs as work load would increase on them. This in turn would affect the effective implementation of various national programs in the district.

Mandatory Pre PG Rural Scheme

The CDMO said that this scheme was not applicable in this district as the remote and the inaccessible areas were less compared to other districts.

Handing over PHCs to NGOs

This scheme was also not implemented in this district. It needs to be mentioned that this scheme was introduced in a block PHC of one district

[56] About the quality of drugs, even the medical officers at the block PHCs were of the opinion that it had improved.

in Orissa on a pilot basis. However the CDMO was opposed to any idea of handing over PHCs in remote areas to NGOs. Because according to him it was the structural issues which were required to be addressed in these remote institutions and hence as long as these issues remain unaddressed, even the NGOs would face similar type of problems which currently the government staffs faced.

On the creation of ZSS

On the creation ZSS in this district the CDMO was of the opinion that, "As resources are in one point, common pooling of resources has helped to meet any emergency situation." Because funds could be transferred from one head to another, under emergency circumstances and later this could be repaid when the money in this head comes. This has given a lot of flexibility to the CDMOs, which was earlier not possible.

Involving Traditional practitioners

On necessity to involve traditional practitioners in referrals, the CDMO was of the opinion that, "Traditional practitioners can do IEC activities…You cannot stop them. Why not regularize them, so that we can have control over them. Now they are functioning anyway… At present no referrals by traditional practitioners occur." This was an important observation by the CDMO because interaction with other senior officials in the state brought to the fore the view that traditional practitioners were going to stay because they have a greater hold over the community and people rely on them, as in times of need these traditional practitioners were always available in contrast to the government appointed medical officers. Therefore innovative strategies should be thought out about involving them to improve the health care services structure in remote and hilly areas.

Training of medical interns

On the question about whether medical internship training scheme was going on in Khurda district, the CDMO said, "The Banapur CHC was selected and students have successfully got trained. They spent 7 days in the district Head Quarter Hospital and the rest of their time in the periphery institution." It needs to be mentioned here that the Banapur CHC was having problem because medical officers were unwilling to stay there and hence provisions were made for contractual doctors. So the question arises how in these circumstances the medical interns could get any first hand experience?

Difficult areas in the district

About the difficult areas in the district the CDMO said that the "Niladri Prasad area which comes under Banapur CHC in Khurda district is very in accessible and recently we have appointed one contractual doctor there."[57]

Structural Constraints and health sector reforms

The vacancy of staff positions in these two districts show that there were severe shortages of male supervisors, multipurpose health worker male and most of the sub centres in these two districts had no government buildings. Besides, the ANMs were not regularly visiting their fields. And the sub centres even where there were government buildings ANMs refused to stay. In case of male workers they rarely visited the fields. Therefore a suggestion was given about appointing another female assistant to the ANMs. For the ANMs where government building was not there, Rs 70 per month was given and for male workers 5% of their basic pay, which was Rs 160, was provided. According to the ANMs this policy was quite discriminatory for them. In fact this was one of the main grievances of ANMs in all the four block PHCs in two districts that we studied. In the entire four block PHCs the ANMs were of the view that they had to face regular abuses from the village males. Further there was inadequate training of ANMs and as a result most of the ANMs interviewed were not aware about various national programs and about the treatment procedures. Besides, the group interviews with ANMs revealed that their focus was mostly on achieving the targets of female sterilization for each month under RCH and to conduct immunization programs. All these structural issues had a strong bearing on the effective functioning of various sub centres and through them various national programs.

The shortage of male supervisors was hampering in the supervision work for the ANMs. Besides the existing supervisors interviewed were of the opinion that as they were not provided any travel allowance for field visits,

---

[57] Giving a very harsh opinion on the contractual doctors at periphery level institutions in Orissa one senior officials in the state observed, "All the contractual doctors have their own NGOs where most of the time they spend rather than being in their posts."

they had to visit their fields by bi-cycle. As a result most of them used to visit their fields very rarely. However there were suggestions by the medical officers for establishing the post of Lady Health Visitors so that they could interact well with the ANMs and so that the supervision work could be possible.

At the level of PHC (New) institutions[58] it was observed that in most of the cases the medical officers were absent and in their place the pharmacists were heading these institutions. Therefore it was suggested that at these institutions pharmacists were enough to operate daily activities. Another suggestion was that instead of one medical officer two medical officers could be appointed in these institutions, so that if one was absent than other would be available. However, this was not a feasible solution because the medical officers were not absent because of work load, rather they were resentful about being posted in a remote and difficult area. However interestingly the government of Orissa was planning to convert these PHC (New) s into block headquarter PHCs according to the all India pattern. Therefore it seems that this was totally contrary to the ground reality. Thus we could say that the reforms have not made an effort to address these structural issues.

Similarly while the district cadre for paramedics' scheme had been introduced, in reality nothing has changed. The idea was that an ANM should live closer to the community and hence they should not be transferred frequently. The medical officers' in-charge at the block headquarter PHCs were very unhappy about their current postings because there was no promotion policy or rather the transfer and postings policy was very arbitrary in nature. This has created a sense of helplessness among them.

Besides the infrastructure from block PHC level downwards were in a dilapidated condition. While the block headquarters PHCs were requiring urgent repairing at many places, in most of the PHC (New) institutions there were no water and electricity supply. There was no all weather road connectivity to these institutions and in rainy seasons many of them used to be cut off from their block headquarter PHCs. One of the CDMOs was of the opinion that due to political pressures the PHC (New) institutions were being created in Orissa. However these politicians never looked that how in a remote place such an institution would function or where the

---

[58] These were single doctor headed medical institutions.

funding would come from to provide for water, electricity or maintenance costs or how could various staffs be motivated to stay in such places.

The sub centers were at worst condition among these three levels of institutions. Those few sub centres where there was a government building, mostly it was used by stray cattles! Further, from the block headquarter PHCs to various PHC (New) s and to sub centres, in most of the places, there were no pucca or all weather roads. As a result supervision work was difficult, the medical officers at PHC (New) s were refusing to stay and the ANMs had to cover their field villages by walking.

Conclusion

Our analysis of the health sector reform process in the two districts of Sundergarh and Khurda showed that there were no consultations held with the CDMOs with regard to health sector reforms. This was a significant lapse in the implementation of health sector reforms because if the officials at the district level were not consulted at the beginning they would feel left out of the process and would not give their commitment to the various reform initiatives.

Similarly it was observed that the medical officers' in-charge at the block PHCs were not even aware that different reforms were being carried out by the state government. However the most surprising thing was that even the CDMOs were not aware that some of the health sector initiatives by the state government were reform initiatives. This was primarily due to two reasons, one was that there was definitional confusion[59] and another was that there was no effort at the level of health directorate to make the CDMOs aware about various reform initiatives in health sector.[60] As a result various reform initiatives were being carried out at the district level as any other routine activities. Therefore it was important that the CDMOs were to be involved for achieving the expected outcomes of the reforms.

Broadly at the district level we could say that three elements of reforms were introduced, according to our definition of health sector reforms. These were, introducing the scheme of contractual doctors, introducing

---

[59] Because any new initiative in the 1990s by the state government had been termed as a reform initiative by the 'Orissa Vision Document 2010'.

[60] This was the observation of one senior official in the health department of government of Orissa.

user fees at district health quarter hospitals and sub divisional hospitals under the OHSDP project and identifying indigenous medical practitioners. While there have been no discussion about handing over PHCs to NGOs in these two districts, still we have presented the opinion of two CDMOs in these districts about this reform element.

At the block level it was observed that contractual doctors have been appointed in the two of our study districts. Only the retired doctors were applying for these posts knowing that they won't have to visit these institutions regularly. This reform initiative did not address the structural constraints a medical officer faces in working in a remote and difficult area, for there was no effort or no discussion about making the transfers and postings policy transparent in case of the medical officers. Therefore this initiative was also not working in reality.

In case of user fees while the CDMOs were very enthusiastic that this had helped the health institutions in meeting their miscellaneous expenditures. They were of the opinion that earlier due to this lack of money they were helpless in repairing minor faults in different diagnostic equipments or for petty maintenance in district headquarter hospitals. At the same it was also agreed that the poor were not getting exempted from paying user charges. However the real matter of concern was that there was no effort at the district levels to ensure that the poor were exempted from paying user fees. Interestingly even the medical officers' in-charge at block PHCs were in favor of introduction of user fees at block headquarters PHCs for certain services. According to one of them if the poor could spend their money on drinks why not pay for their health care services?

There were efforts to identify the indigenous medical practitioners in Sundergarh district so that they could be involved in referrals to nearby PHCs specifically with matters related to pregnancy related complications and in cases of fever, which was most likely to be malaria.[61]

About the scheme of handing over PHCs in remote areas to NGOs both the CDMOs were opposed to the idea. Particularly they were not favorable to the idea of involving NGOs in operation of PHC (New) institutions. Interestingly during the field visit it was observed that the state government was identifying NGOs through the mother NGO scheme to

---

[61] As Sundergarh was an endemic district in terms malaria, in western part of Orissa.

hand over these PHC (New) institutions in remote and difficult areas. This suggests that before implementing this scheme, concerned CDMOs were not consulted.

Various systemic changes introduced in these two districts were: mandatory pre-PG rural scheme, training of medical interns at CHCs under the guidance of CDMOs, the new drugs policy, Pancha Byadhi Chikitsa scheme, petty maintenance of PHC health quarter buildings and creation of ZSS.

The mandatory pre PG rural scheme and the training of medical interns at CHCs under the guidance of CDMOs have also failed in these two districts because of lack of a transparent transfers and posting policy and apathy of senior officials toward the public health aspects. This was also due to the fact that even the CDMOs had their own private clinics where they used to spend their evening hours.

The new drugs policy on the other hand has ensured the availability of quality drugs at various levels of district health institutions and this has also increased the drug use by patients at these various levels in our two study districts. However it was observed that while medicines for Pancha Bhyadhi Chikitsa scheme were available at different health institutions, people were not aware about their rights under this scheme.

For the petty maintenance of PHC headquarter buildings money was not coming regularly to the block PHCs. There were also allegations of misuse of funds under this scheme by the medical officer in-charge in the block headquarter PHCs.

On the other hand the creation of ZSS had helped in better coordination of district funds and the amalgamation of different societies had helped in its effective functioning under the supervision of district collector.

Annexure 1

OHSDP Institutions in Sudergarh District:
District Headquarter Hospital.
Sub Divisional Hospital Bonai.
Rourkela Government Hospital or RGH.
Mojhapara CHC II.
Mangaspur CHC II.
Kinjhirkela CHC II.
Kuarmunda CHC II.
Birmitrapur CHC II
Note: 10 bedded wards in each CHC II with 1- for delivery room, 1- for minor operation, 1- for waste management.

New Staffs under OHSDP in Sundergarh District:
RGH Rourkela: Assistant Surgeon- 5, Dental Surgeon- 1, and Staff Nurse- 9, Assistant Matron- 1, Lab Technician- 1, Technical Store Keeper- 2, Radiographer- 2.
Bonai Sub Divisional Hospital: Assistant Surgeon- 2, Anasthesia Specialist (Class II)- 1, Staff Nurse- 5 (contractual).
Kinjhirkela CHC II: Specialist O&G- 1, Staff Nurse- 5 (contractual).
Mangaspur CHC II: Specialist O and G- 1, Staff Nurse- 5 (contractual).
Birmitrapur CHC II: Specialist O& G- 1, Staff Nurse- 5 (Contractual).
Kuarmunda CHC II: Specialist O& G- 1, Staff Nurse- 5 (Contractual).
District Headquarter Hospital: Matron- 1, Assistant Matron- 1, Lab Technician- 1.
Note: The posts of staff nurse in most of the OHSDP supported institutions were contractual in nature.

CHAPTER SEVEN

FINANCING, STRUCTURE AND UTILIZATION PATTERNS: A COMPARISON BETWEEN ORISSA AND MAJOR STATES

Introduction

We have defined health sector reforms as an attempt by the state to increase the space for the private sector while reducing the role of public sector in different aspects[1] of health care. Therefore question arises whether there was a strong and a well regulated private sector where maximum number of people went for both in-patient and out patient care across various states in India? Whether there had been presence of a large private sector, which inspired the policy makers to take a decision in favour of increasing private participation in health care in Orissa? Whether this private sector was well defined and with mechanisms for quality checks and accountability to the people? Whether existing data showed that the services available in private sector was better in terms of quality and efficiency compared to the public sector Or they[2] were following a unified model in the belief that the private sector was the only answer for all the deficiencies of public sector?

While in chapter III we have discussed about the public health care services structure in Orissa, in this chapter we have discussed about the presence of private sector in Orissa and in major states of India. Therefore a question might arise as why this overlapping of same issue in two separate chapters? Infact it is not at all a question of overlapping. While in chapter III we have dealt with the growth of public health care services in Orissa over the years, in this chapter a comparison between the private and

---

[1] Like financing, provisioning and manpower.
[2] Various state governments in India, including Orissa.

the public sector has been given to see whether the various reform initiatives in health sector[3] were taken keeping in view the presence of a large and growing private sector? In this backdrop what could be the implications for health care for all?

Since handing over secondary and tertiary curative services to markets is one of the important elements of reform, the proportion of private to public sectors at secondary and tertiary levels and its implications for utilisation of services becomes significant. It is in this context that this chapter focuses on financing, structure and utilisation patterns of the public/private sector in Orissa and across major states in India. While on financing we have focused on the public sector and investment by various donor agencies, in structure and utilisation of health care we have given a comparative picture of both private and the public sector.

Growth of private sector

With green revolution, came the prosperity in rural areas, in certain parts of the country. This gave rise to rich and middle peasant classes. The pressure from these sections resulted in some investments being diverted to rural areas.[4] However these pressures had a marginal impact and hence rural-urban divide in service provisioning remained largely unaltered through the seventies. While India could not manage to invest a large amount of resources in the health services sector, it did manage to build a fairly extensive network of services, invested in research and pharmaceuticals and trained personnel for various levels of care. *However lower investments affected the growth of public sector in health services and this was one of the reasons for growth of private sector during the seventies and eighties. This also matched the interests of professionals who were mostly drawn from upper and middle classes*[5].

There were debates in the seventies about understanding the structural inequalities within health sector and keeping the needs of rural India in mind, it was argued that more investment should be made in rural areas. However, the oil shock of late seventies led to the world recession and this had a negative impact on the financial condition of countries like India, as

---

[3] Which have tried to increase more space for the private sector in different aspects of health care.

[4] As cited in Nambissan, G. & Batra, P: 1989.

[5] Also see Private Health Care in India by Rama V Baru, 1998, Sage Publications.

it was a major oil importing country. As a result the government of India was not in a position to increase investment in health care. The 'new middle class' who emerged due to green revolution found the public sector inadequate to meet their needs and in states where private sector was dominant in provisioning, they started moving out of the public sector. This trend had started since mid eighties. But it was more visible in the richer states compared to the poorer ones. As these upper and middle sections moved out of the public sector it affected the public health care provisioning and it also affected the financing and quality of health care services. With the moving out of these sections from public health care provisioning, the state's commitment to the public sector also declined.

In the sixties there was little growth of private institutions at the secondary level of care but the growth of individual private practitioners continued. Hence in India the growth in the private sector could be located in the seventies and eighties and this happened mostly due to emergence of new middle class and the financial crunch the state faced due to the oil crisis of the late seventies. While individual private practitioners were there before independence, in the seventies and eighties a large number of private institutions came in. However these private institutions were confined to better-developed states and in urban areas. At the time of independence there was no debate about either defining a role for the private practitioners or nationalising them, as was the case in some Latin American countries.[6]

Public healthcare financing

With the beginning of health sector reform initiatives, it has been argued that the state should utilize its limited resources in a cost effective manner and one of the examples has been the argument for essential primary health care[7] and reducing the state's expenditure in secondary and tertiary levels of care. It has also been argued that the private health care financing mechanisms should be encouraged in the form of community health insurance.[8] Keeping these debates in mind question arises as to what trends the public health care financing in Orissa and the other states of India show since 1980s? In this context we have discussed about the per

[6] Jara & Bossert: 1995.
[7] By the World Bank annual document titled, "Investing in Health", 1993.
[8] In this context we have discussed in chapter IV about the experiences of community health insurance in Mexico and Vietnam.

capita expenditure on health in Orissa and India since 1950s, trends in public health care expenditure in Orissa since 1980s, a comparative picture of health care expenditure among major states in India since 1980s and finally about the future projections on increasing public health care expenditure in Orissa.

Per Capita Expenditure on health

As our present study has dealt with Orissa as a primary source of study, let us have a look at the per capita expenditure on health of Orissa vis a vis India since the time of early fifties to the early nineties.
The table shows the comparative figures between Orissa and India

Table 7.1 Per capita Expenditure on Health in Orissa vis a vis India in Rs.

Year	Orissa	India
1950-51	0.48	0.61
1955-56	0.70	0.61
1960-61	1.48	2.45
1965-66	3.51	3.41
1970-71	4.90	6.11
1980-81	15.50	17.35
1985-86	25.54	35.52
1991-92	48.48	60.13
1992-93	52.05	70.15
1993-94	52.05	79.44
1994-95	60.40	85.10

Source: Health Statistics of Orissa, Compiled by State Bureau of Health Intelligence (Vital Statistics Section), Directorate of Health Services, Orissa, 1996.

It shows that in 1950-51 the per capita expenditure on health in Orissa with Rs 0.48 was lesser than all India expenditure of Rs 0.61. However in 1955-56 the per capita expenditure on health in Orissa increased to Rs 0.71, while the all India expenditure remained at 1950-51 levels. On the other hand in 1960-61 while the per capita expenditure on health in Orissa increased to Rs 1.48 the all India expenditure was much higher at Rs 2.45. Again in 1965-66 the per capita expenditure of Orissa crossed the all India expenditure. However since 1970-71 the per capita expenditure on health of India has always remained higher than Orissa, although both of them have increased over the years. However the per capita expenditure on health at all India level remained same in 1950-51 and 1955-56 and in case of Orissa, it remained same in 1992-93 and in 1993-94. Overall the per capita expenditure on health in Orissa as well as in India has increased steadily since early 1950s to the early 1990s.

Thus the table shows that the per capita expenditure has increased over the years. On the other hand with the increase in population and the demand for better health care services, at a faster rate, makes us see that the state was not spending enough on health care. Also the average figures won't tell us the discrepancies in this expenditure toward different class, region and gender divides.

Heath care expenditure over the years

One of our objectives in this study had been to look at the trends in public health care expenditure in Orissa since 1980s. The table below gives a picture about the actual health care expenditure in Orissa compared to its total expenditure over the years. It shows that the health care expenditure in 1980-81 was 2.55 percent of the total Orissa budget, which declined for next two years, and in 1982-83 it was 2.07 percent of its total budget. However the share of health care expenditure increased to 2.39 percent in 1983-84 and it saw a sharp decline in next year to 1.57 percent to the total budget followed by an increase to 2.51 percent, which was more than 1983-84 figures. From 1988-89 to 1990-91 the share of health expenditure increased slightly from 2.12 percent to 2.70 percent respectively. In 1991-92 it declined to 1.89 percent.

Since 1993-94 the share of health expenditure increased till 1995-96, with an unusually high expenditure in 1994-95 to 10.22 percent of its total budget. In 1997-98 it saw a decline to 2.55 percent and from 1999 onwards it has seen an increase to more than 3 percent. This may be due to the fact that the investments under OHSDP were counted as expenditure within the Orissa health budget.

Table: 7.2 Health care expenditure in Orissa over the years

Year	Health Care actual expenditure in Orissa (lakhs)	Orissa's Total expenditure (Figures in lakhs)	Health care expenditure as Percentage to the total expenditure
1980-81	634.15	24821.15	2.55
1981-82	592.21	28117.07	2.10
1982-83	623.7	30084.02	2.07
1983-84	782.89	32665.98	2.39
1984-85	639.9	40648.21	1.57
1985-86	1128.89	44877.04	2.51
1986-87	1155.07	56925.77	2.02
1987-88	1226.25	69353.37	1.76
1988-89	1600.31	75219.35	2.12
1990-91	2935	108574.5	2.70
1991-92	1946.69	102973.7	1.89
1992-93	1989.22		
1993-94	2318.29	109473.6	2.11
1994-95	3084.47	30154.24	10.22
1995-96	3641.65	137052.4	2.65
1997-98	5197.72	203713.5	2.55
1998-99	5662.7		
1999-2000	7545.73	248399.5	3.03
2000-2001	8807.77	256206.5	3.43

Note: As there was no publication of 1997-98 Annual Plan document where the data for 1996-97 actual expenditure would have been there. The various figures have been taken from the Annual Plan documents of Government of Orissa, except for the year 2000-2001 for which data was collected from Tenth Plan document, Government of Orissa.

Let us see how the trends in health care expenditure over the years in Orissa would look like in a graph as shown below

Figure: 7.1: Trends in Health Care Expenditure: Orissa

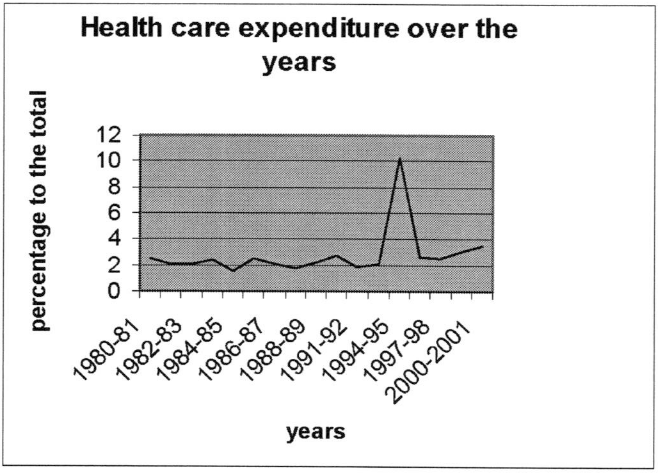

If we look at the graph above, then it is clear that the health care expenditure over the years since 1980-81 has fluctuated. It was unusually high in 1994-95. Therefore before 1999, the health budget was never above 3 percent of the total budget of the state and since 1999 it has observed an increase in health expenditure. Apart from OHSDP investments, the new PSPU office which would be fully supported by DFID, its expenditures would also be counted in the general budget of the state. Therefore in the coming years the health care expenditure might seem to be given a larger share of the total expenditure of Orissa budget.

Health care Expenditure as percentage of total expenditure: A comparative picture

But the question arises that if we compare the public health care expenditure in Orissa with major states of India, than what would be the emerging trend? The table below gives a comparative picture of different states and in various years, in terms of health expenditure as percentage of total expenditure.

Table: 7.3 Health care expenditure as percentage of total expenditure: Comparative figure

State/year	1981	1987	1991	1996	1998	2001	2003	2005
Orissa	5.17	8.50	5.13	5.16	4.82	4.15	3.75	3.90
Andhra Pradesh	5.80	7.88	5.53	4.65	5.44	4.74	3.96	3.53
Uttar Pradesh	4.69	9.08	6.31	6.03	1.74	3.98	3.75	4.49
Tamilnadu	6.18	10.04	6.91	6.29	6.28	4.86	4.10	4.20
Punjab	3.67	10.52	6.73	4.62	4.93	4.54	3.54	3.10
West Bengal	6.30	9.73	8.37	6.43	NA	5.63	4.95	0.93
Karnataka	3.97	8.23	5.40	5.28	5.85	5.11	4.17	3.49
Rajasthan	4.85	14.48	6.50	5.70	7.97	5.16	4.24	3.94
Gujarat	4.38	9.58	5.03	4.70	4.57	3.38	3.21	3.05
Maharastra	4.85	9.38	5.13	4.56	4.29	3.87	3.71	3.51
Kerala	6.56	9.85	7.21	6.53	5.68	5.25	4.74	4.71
J&K	3.79	12.50	5.56	5.50	4.97	4.89	5.30	4.78
Meghalaya	6.25	13.25	6.26	6.19	6.86	5.65	5.88	5.23
All India	1.52	3.95	2.93	2.01	1.75	2.77	2.41	2.42

Note: Up to 1987, data was combined finance and revenue accounts, Controller and Auditor General of India, GOI, respective years. For the year 2001 reference was "State Finance: A Study of Budget of 2002-03, RBI. For the year 2003 and 2005 reference was from Public Finance, November 2004, CMIE. A comparative picture of SHSDP states have been provided along with developed states like Maharastra and Gujarat and also of Meghalaya and Jammu and Kashmir has been for their higher expenditure on health care compared to other states as a percentage to their total budget. In this table the expenditure for sanitation, water supply etc. has also been included in the head of health care expenditure. As a result the figure in this table show a higher health care expenditure of Orissa compared to the earlier table we have discussed above.

Source: "Review of Healthcare in India ed. By Leena V. Gangolli, Ravi Duggal, Abhay Shukla, CEHAT (Center for Equity into Health and Allied Themes, January 2005)."

Trends in Health care expenditure

The figure shows that the health care expenditures increased over the years at a slow pace up to the late 1970s in case of both Orissa and India. However there was quantum leap in per capita expenditure on health in

1980-81, 1985-86 and in 1991-92. This happened in case of both Orissa and India.

Broadly the figures for public expenditure on health care show that in case of Orissa, the health care expenditure was more than 5 percent to the total budget from 1981 to 1996. But from 1998 onwards the percentage of health care expenditure declined over the years till 2003. Thus we could say that in terms of health care expenditure to total expenditure of the state in the 1980s, the percentage of health care expenditure in Orissa was higher compared to 1990s.

The figures for AP show that overall health care expenditure was higher in 1980s compared to the 1990s. In case of UP it shows that the health care expenditure fluctuated over the years and with highest percent of expenditure in 987 and lowest in 1998.

In case of Tamilnadu the figures show that health care expenditure was more than 6 percent from 1981 till the year 1998, but gradually declined to 4.10 percent, by the year 2003. The figures for Punjab show that the health care expenditure fluctuated over the years and it was lower in 2003 compared to 1981.

The figures for West Bengal show the expenditure on health care increased in 1980s but declined over the years in 1990s. The figures for Karnataka show that the health care expenditure fluctuated over the years but the expenditure in 2003 was higher than 1981 figures. In case of Rajasthan the expenditure on health care was higher in the middle of 1980s and 1990s but it was lower in 2003 compared to 1981 figures.

The figures for Gujarat show an increasing trend in 1980s but a declining trend in 1990s. In case of Maharastra the expenditure increased form 1981 to 1987, but a gradual decline over the nineties happened. The figures for Kerala also show the similar trends. In case of J&K the health care expenditure increased significantly from 1981 to 1987, but started declining since then till 2001, followed by a slight increase in 2003. The figures for Meghalaya show a fluctuating trend in health care expenditure over the years.

However the figure for all India show that the health care expenditure increased from 1981 to 1987, but started declining till 1998, but again increased in 2001 followed by a decline in 2003.

Public Expenditure on Health in Orissa: A future assessment

In view of the current trends of public expenditure on health in Orissa what could be the future trends? The table below gives a picture of future public expenditure on health in Orissa. The different dimensions looked at were public expenditure as a share of Gross State Domestic Product or GSDP, share of state public expenditure on health, allocation of resources to different levels of care and public expenditure on health's share to non salary components. It gives a comparison between National Health Policy or NHP targets and current level of expenditure in Orissa.

Table: 7.4 Public expenditure on Health in Orissa

	NHP targets	**Current level in Orissa**
Public Expenditure as a share of GSDP	2% of GSDP by 2010	1.09% (1999-2000)
Share of State public expenditure on health	7% by the year2005, 8% by 2010	5.07% (1999-2000) 6.3% (2000-2001)
Allocation of resources to different levels of care	55% to Primary level 35% to secondary level 10% to tertiary level	51.8% 24.5% 23.6%
Share to non salary component	30%	15% inclusive of user fees

Source: Orissa Vision 2010, A Health Strategy, February 2003, Health and Family Welfare Department, Government of Orissa, Bhubaneswar.

The table shows that over the years the NHP targets were to increase public spending more in the primary and secondary level care and reducing the government expenditure at the tertiary level care. In terms of share of non-salary component to the total health care expenditure, it was 15 percent at current levels and the NHP targets were to raise it to 30 percent of the total health care expenditure. However the debates on reducing expenditure on salary component miss the point that health and education are the sectors where there is more need of human personnel.

Donor Funding in health sector of Orissa

It has been observed that Orissa has been a donor driven state. Therefore question arises as to what role the donor agencies have been playing in the health sector of Orissa since 1980s? In this context let us have a look at the quantum of funding by various donor agencies in Orissa.

Table: 7.5 Donor agency supported health projects in Orissa: Dominant players

Nature and level of health care	Project in Operation	Area of Operation of the Project	Period of Operation	Cost in Rs. Crores
Support to FW Prog.	ODA, Phase I	Three districts *	1981-1986	15.2 ($)
Support to FW Prog.	ODA, Phase II	Five districts *	1989-1994	pd std. 20 #
Primary health care	DFID, Phase III	Bhadrak and Keonjhar	1997-2000	23
Rehabilitation and Reconstruction in Cyclone affected areas	DFID	14 districts, CHC/Block level PHC- 145 in 130 blocks	2000 to 2004 in pipeline	175
Strengthening of Sector Development of Health care	DFID	30 districts	2001 to 2006 in pipeline	200-300
Secondary and Primary Health Care project (OHSDP)	World Bank	156 institutions all over the state	1998-99 to 2004	415
Drug Procurement and Supply	UNFPA	Whole State	In Pipeline	--

Reproductive Child Health	WB/GOI/ UNFPA	State wide Sub Project Kalahandi, Koraput, Nawrangpur, Malkangiri, Rayagada	1997-2002 in pipeline	216 15 35
Malaria	World Bank through GOI	158 blocks in 21 districts	1998-2004	1.5
Tuberculosis	DANIDA/GOI	Keonjhar, Sambalpur and Mayurbhanj, 11 districts to be included	Dec 1996 to Dec 2001	31.95
AIDS	World Bank through NACO	All districts of the state	June 1999 to 2004	80
Blindness	World Bank through GOI	All districts of the state	01.04.1994 to 31.03.2001	68
Leprosy	DANIDA, Lepra Mission, Lepra India, WB, Holna, WHO, SIDA, UNICEF	Cuttack, Jagatsinghpur, Jajpur, Kendrapada in Phase 1 Sambalpur, Jharsuguda, Deogarh, Bargarh in Phase 2 State in Phase 3 Rayagada, Nuapada, Umerkote Sonepur, Bolangir, Junagarh, Udala, Jasipur Phulbani, Kalahandi, Sundergarh, Keonjhar, Boudh Gunupur, Muniguda Ganjam Puri	1987- contd. ---- 1991- contd. 1997- contd. 1997- contd. 1994-1999 1991 1983 1983 1985	26 ---- 31 46 32
Sector Investment Programme, State Plan and District Plan (3 districts)	EC	State Balasore, Bolangir, Phulbani	July 2001 to June 2004	28 –30
Total				1400-1500

Note: * - For the ODA assistance for Family Welfare in Orissa for phase I and phase II we have referred to Gupta Devendra B and Anil Gumber, "External Assistance to the Health Sector and Its Contributions: Problems and Prognosis", Working Paper No. 88, Indian Council for Research on International Economic

Relations, New Delhi, November 2002. In 1997 ODA was replaced by DFID or Department for International Development, headed by Secretary of State with cabinet rank of UK government.
OHSDP: Orissa Health Systems Development Project. # - Refers to Pound Sterling, the currency of UK.
Source: For the remaining data we have referred to an unpublished draft of European Commission titled, "Health Financing in Orissa: A Background Paper to Assist the Development of a Health Financing Strategy", New Delhi, India, 2004.

The table shows that in the 1980s, ODA assistance was mainly in the form of support to Family Welfare Programs in Orissa. These investments were made mostly in the infrastructure development of health care services in the state.[9] Further in the 1990s the investments went for primary health care for maintenance of infrastructure. In the late 1990s after an assessment of their earlier projects in Orissa, DFID decided to support the state government for strengthening of sector development of health care.[10] Interestingly this assessment report also acted as a catalyst for initiation of various systemic changes and health sector reforms in Orissa.

While the World Bank was involved since early 1990s through various disease control programs in Orissa, one of its major investments was made in the RCH project in the late 1990s. However, with the initiation of OHSDP, the major focus of World Bank funding in the state has been on restructuring of secondary level institutions in the state. Our interviews with senior officials of World Bank also revealed that the Phase II of this project would also be started in the state and it would try to include the primary level care along with the secondary level institutions. As we have discussed in chapter V that through this project World Bank was in a Position to influence the health policy making in Orissa in a significant way.

Among the UN agencies, while the UNICEF was involved in Leprosy program since 1980s, the UNFPA was involved in selected districts for RCH program in Orissa. Among the bilateral agencies, DANIDA was involved since 1987 in Leprosy program and since 1996 in Tuberculosis program in Orissa. However since 2005, DANIDA was planning to wind

---

[9] This was the view of senior DFID officials interviewed at their New Delhi Offices.

[10] Ibid. One of the components of this funding provision was to create Policy Planning and Strategic Unit, which would act as a think tank for the Health and Family Welfare Department, Government of Orissa.

up all its activities in Orissa.[11] Finally the European Commission was involved in Sector Investment Program in Orissa since 2001.

The table shows that among the various donor agencies, while DFID/ODA since 1980s till the second half of 1990s was the dominant investor in health sector of Orissa, since late 1990s, the World Bank has emerged as the largest donor. UNFPA was the third largest investor in health sector of Orissa followed by UNICEF. The European Commission came as fifth largest donor investor in Orissa. However after World Bank and DFID, the third most influential player has been the European Commission since 2001, in terms of influencing health policy making in the state.[12] The agencies like UNICEF, UNFPA were the marginal players with little influence in the health policy making in Orissa.[13]

Cost of treatment

As health sector reform initiatives have tried to increase more space for the private sector we need to look at the comparative picture of health care expenditures in private and public sector in both rural and urban areas. This comparison was given to show the cost effectiveness of health care expenditure in private and public sector. In this regard we have presented data, with regard to average total expenditure per hospitalization in rural and urban areas, in both private and public sectors and average household expenditure for treatment per disease episode in Orissa.

Average total expenditure per hospitalization[14]

Now let us have a look at the average total expenditure per hospitalization. The table below has given a comparative picture of average total expenditure per hospitalization in public and private sector, in both rural and urban areas of India.

---

[11] This was revealed through interviewing senior donor agency officials of various donor agencies and the senior officials of government of Orissa.

[12] We have argued in chapter V that with the creation of PSPU the future role of Sector Reform Cell, funded by European Commission in Orissa had also declined.

[13] Ibid.

[14] These figures were for all India.

Table: 7.6 Average total expenditure (Rs per hospitalization) in India

Type of Hospital	Rural	Urban	% Cost of urban health care to rural health care
Public Hospital	2245	2191	97.5
PHC/CHC	740	2461	332.5
Public Dispensary	1887	1977	104.5
Public Sector Hospital	*2080*	*2195*	*105.5*
Private Hospital	4394	5524	125.5
Nursing home	4185	5749	137
Charitable trust	3808	3078	81
Other	3015	1630	54
Private Sector Hospital	*4300*	*5344*	*124*

Source: Morbidity and Treatment of Ailments, 52nd round NSSO, 1995-96, Government of India, 1998.

In terms of the percentage cost of urban health care to rural health care, among the public sector hospitals, the figures show that, the cost of treatment in a public hospital in urban areas was 97.5% of the cost of treatment in a rural area. Among the private sector hospitals, the cost of inpatient care was lower in case of charitable trusts and other institutions in urban areas compared to rural areas.

For other categories of institutions the cost of treatment for inpatient care was lower in rural areas compared to the urban areas. However in case of PHC/CHC institutions the cost of care in urban areas was 332.5% more than in rural areas. On an average the cost of inpatient care in a public sector hospital in urban areas was 105.5% more than in rural areas. In case of private sector hospitals the cost of inpatient care was 124% more in urban areas than in rural areas.

Overall the trends show that, while the cost of inpatient care in a public hospital in rural areas was about 207% less than a private hospital, in urban areas it was less than 243% of treatment in a private hospital. Among all these categories of institutions the cost of inpatient care was lower in rural areas compared to urban areas, except in case of charitable trusts and other private sources, where the cost of care in rural areas was more than in urban areas.

Average household expenditure for treatment in Orissa

What was the average household expenditure for treatment in Orissa in a government and a private hospital? The table below gives a picture of average household expenditure for treatment per disease episode in Orissa, in terms of government or private hospital/clinic and it also provides the data on rural-urban spending.

Table: 7.7 Average Household Expenditure for Treatment per Disease Episode in Orissa

	Urban (Rs.)	Rural (Rs.)
Government Hospital	75	127
Private Hospital / Clinic	109	125

Source: World Bank (1993), India: Public Expenditure Review, as cited in Meena Gupta.

The table shows that in urban areas an average household spends about Rs 75 for treatment per disease episode in a government hospital. However the cost goes up for treatment in the rural areas to Rs 127 in a government hospital. That means a person living in rural areas spends more than his urban counterpart per disease episode in a government hospital. This may be due to the problem of physical accessibility and also due to the problem of economic accessibility.

On the other hand, in a private hospital an average household in an urban area spends Rs 109, while in rural areas it has to spend Rs 125, which was lesser than expenditure in a government hospital. However the expenditure in a government hospital in an urban area was less than expenditure in a private hospital/clinic. Be it a government or a private hospital the average household expenditure was more in rural areas than in urban areas per disease episode.

Therefore in terms of cost of treatment the private sector has been found to be more costly than the public sector in both rural and urban areas. However in terms of cost of treatment per disease episode, it was observed that the cost of treatment in a private hospital or clinic in rural Orissa was less than the cost of treatment in a public hospital or clinic.

Structure of the private health care

To understand the implications of health sector reforms we have analysed the growth of private health care, in terms of number of private medical and health establishments across states; in terms of growth of private hospitals and beds in major states and a comparison of growth of private and public beds since 1980s in Orissa and major states of India.

Private medical and health establishments

The table below shows the non-government medical and health establishments per million populations across major states in India. It has also given a comparative picture of differences between number of private enterprises in rural and urban areas across different states.

Table 7.8 Estimates of non-government medical and health establishments per million populations across major states

State/UT	Estimated number of enterprises		No. of enterprises per million population	
	Rural	Urban	Rural	Urban
Andhra Pradesh	821	4,567	20	368
Assam	43	318	2.4	159
Bihar	1,281	3,269	21	375
Gujarat	1,494	N.A.	64	N.A.
Haryana	N.A.	10,310	N.A.	3,682
Himachal Pradesh	58	37	15	0.008
Jammu & Kashmir	52	122	11	101
Karnataka	1,030	5,588	39	522
Kerala	4,243	4,095	205	871
Madya Pradesh	542	3,354	13	319
Maharastra	7,745	21,052	90	961

Orissa	284	1,337	12	431
Punjab	193	1,124	16	244
Rajasthan	59	N.A.	2	N.A.
Tamilnadu	9,615	10,827	300	681
Uttar Pradesh	729	10,932	8	1,115
West Bengal	6,611	7,944	164	1,805
New Delhi	60	N.A.	133	N.A.
Others	18	3,092	N.A.	N.A.
All India	34,826	87,986	66	553

Source: Government of India, CSO, Enterprise survey, 1983-84 (Government of India 1987) as cited in *Private health care in India* by Rama V. Baru, 1998. P-63-Ibid.

In case of Orissa, while 284 private enterprises existed in rural areas, it was 1,337 in urban areas in terms of absolute numbers. And in terms of private enterprises per million populations, the rural-urban divide becomes very sharp. While in rural areas, there were 12 private enterprises per million populations, it was 431 in case of urban areas. Maharastra was a unique example, where it was clear that while it had the largest number of private enterprises among all the states in India, when it came to private enterprises per million populations it was placed below Haryana, West Bengal and UP.

The table shows that except in Himachal Pradesh and Kerala, all the states have more number of private enterprises in urban areas than in rural areas. In terms of its presence Maharastra had the highest number of private enterprises in urban areas followed by UP, Tamilnadu, Haryana, West Bengal, Karnataka and Andhra Pradesh. However in rural areas Tamilnadu had the highest number of private enterprises followed by Maharastra, West Bengal, Kerala, Gujarat, Bihar and Karnataka. Out of these states, Himachal Pradesh had the lowest number of private enterprises in urban areas and in rural areas Assam had the lowest number of private enterprises.

In terms of absolute numbers, the urban areas of India had 87,986 private enterprises and in rural areas the number was 34,826.

In terms of number of private enterprises per million population in urban areas, Haryana had the highest followed by West Bengal, UP, Maharastra, Kerala, Tamilnadu and Karnataka, Orissa and Andhra Pradesh. On the other hand, Himachal Pradesh had the lowest private enterprises per million populations.

In rural areas, Tamilnadu had the highest number of private enterprises per million populations followed by Kerala, West Bengal, New Delhi and Maharastra. On the other hand, Rajasthan had the lowest number of private enterprises per million populations followed by Assam, UP, Orissa, MP, Himachal, Punjab and Bihar.

In terms of absolute numbers, while 553 private enterprises per million populations existed in urban areas and the figures for rural areas were 66. Thus the above table shows that the private sector had an overwhelming presence in the urban areas compared to the rural areas.

Presence of private enterprises: Trends

Thus we saw that, in terms of presence of the private sector in absolute terms, the states like Kerala, West Bengal, Tamilnadu, Maharastra, Bihar and Karnataka had a significant presence of private enterprises in urban areas. But in rest of the states the presence of private sector was very minuscule in rural areas. Therefore the health sector reforms when advocates for more role of the private sector in health care, then could it be said, that it was motivated by a uniform model of health care?

Growth of Private hospitals and beds in major states

In this section we would be analysing two aspects, one is the growth of private and voluntary hospitals over the years in major states and the second aspect about the growth of private and voluntary beds over the years in these 13 major states.

Table 7.9 Growth of Private and Voluntary hospitals and Beds in Major states

States	1983		1985		1987		1989		1991		1993		As on 01.01. 2000	
AP	266	11,103	266	11,103	266	11,103	266	11,103	841	19,784	N.A.	26,791	2802	42192
Bihar	125	8,447	125	8,447	90	8,519	55	5,536	55	5,536	N.A.	8,519	90	8519
Gujarat	669	16,929	733	16,339	1,211	21,128	1,319	25,093	1,319	25,093	N.A.	33487	2152	36867
Haryana	18	2,566	18	2,566	17	2,558	20	2,772	20	2,232	N.A.	2,232	18	1666
Karnataka	53	6,894	44	6,702	51	7,339	51	7,339	51	7,339	N.A.	9,999	56	9999
Kerala	606	18,203	606	18,203	173	14,309	1,899	44,321	1,899	49,169	N.A.	49,169	1958	67517
MP	N.A.	N. A.	N.A.	N. A.	N.A.	N. A.	N.A.	N. A.	N.A.	N. A.	N.A.	N. A.	NA	NA
Maharastra	682	26,024	945	32,033	1,121	35,296	1,319	35,849	1,319	37,781	N.A.	37,758	3023	42646
Orissa	34	1,408	31	1,227	31	1,227	29	1,306	29	1,301	N.A.	1.306	14	201
Punjab	35	2,913	35	2,913	43	3,466	39	3,781	39	3,782	N.A.	3,782	39	3782
T N	61	8,562	61	8,562	73	9,505	119	10,366	119,	10,366	N.A.	10,366	119	10366
UP	160	12,083	159	12,026	159	12,026	159	12,026	159	12,026	N.A.	12,026	159	12026
W B	126	6,424	126	6,610	126	6,463	129	6,511	129	6,912	N.A.	6,912	134	6701
All India	3022	134266	3,549	139442	3549	144009	6522	177034	6522	180386	N.A.	210987	11330	260669

Note: For each year the first column represents the number of private and voluntary hospitals and the second column represents the number of private and voluntary beds in these institutions.

Source: GOI, Ministry of Health and Family Welfare, Central bureau of Health Intelligence as cited in Private health care in India by Rama V. Baru, 1998. P-65-Ibid. Also from the CBHI data, 2000-2001, Government of India, 2003.

Growth of private and voluntary hospitals

The table gives a comparative analysis of 13 major states in India about the growth of private and voluntary hospitals and beds since 1983 to 2000. It has to be mentioned here that the 1993 figures for private and voluntary hospitals has not been provided for any of the states.

Growth of Private hospitals[15]: Trends

The figures for *Orissa* show a declining trend over the years. In terms of numbers also the presence of private and voluntary hospitals was quite low. It had 34 private and voluntary hospitals in 1983, which further declined to 31 in 1985 and remained so till 1987. Again in 1989 it declined to 29 and remained at that level in 1991. However by the year 2000 the total number of private and voluntary hospitals declined to 14, which was more than 50 percent less, compared to 1991 figures. This was very interesting as with the health sector reforms being initiated in the state, there has been increasing support for the larger role of private sector in health care of the state[16]. The declining trend of private and voluntary hospitals and their low volumes suggest that government health care services were the dominant players in the state.

The trends for all India show that the growth in total number of private and voluntary hospitals was much more in 1990s compared to 1980s. However in percentage terms, while in 1980s the growth in private hospitals was 216%; it was 174% in 1990s. Therefore the growth rate of private hospitals declined in 1990s compared to 1980s. Thus in 1983 it had 3,022 private and voluntary hospitals, which further increased to 3,549 in 1985 and remained at that level till 1987. It again increased to 6,522 and remained there till 1991. However by the year 2000, the total number of private and voluntary hospitals increased to 11330. This was because of the growth of private and voluntary hospitals occurred in primarily three states of Andhra Pradesh, Gujarat and Maharastra in the 1990s.

---

[15] Here the term private hospital refers to private and voluntary hospitals.

[16] This was the perception of various officials interviewed at different levels of health care services in Orissa. The increasing level of support for privatisation of health was not only in the secondary and tertiary levels of care but it was also emphasized by PHC doctors for certain services like utilisation of beds and a minimal charge for medicines available for communicable diseases.

As of 1991 figures, Kerala showed the highest number of private and voluntary hospitals followed by Gujarat and Maharastra with equal number of Private and voluntary hospitals, followed by Andhra Pradesh, UP, West Bengal and Tamilnadu. However, by the year 2000, Maharastra had highest number of private and voluntary hospitals followed by Andhra Pradesh, Gujarat and Kerala. These were also the four states, which had a combined presence of 9935 number of private and voluntary hospitals compared to all India figures of 11330, which was equivalent to 87.68 percent to the total! Among these states, Andhra Pradesh experienced the fastest growth[17] in the decade of 1990s.

Bihar, Haryana, Karnataka, Punjab and Orissa were the states, where the presence of private and voluntary hospitals was very low in terms of absolute numbers. Among these five states, Bihar with 90 private and voluntary hospitals was at the top. Out of these 13 states Orissa had the lowest number of private and voluntary hospitals followed by Haryana and Punjab.

States like Punjab, Tamilnadu, UP and Bihar had experienced a zero growth rate in the decade of 1990s. The states like West Bengal and Karnataka experienced an increase of 5 each private and voluntary hospitals in the decade of nineties. However Orissa and Haryana experienced a decline in number of private and voluntary hospitals during these two decades.

Growth of private and voluntary beds

Now let us have a look at the private and voluntary beds in these 13 states.

In case of Orissa, in 1983 the total number of private beds was 1408, which declined to 1227 and remained so till 1987. The number of private beds again increased to 1306 in 1989 and declined slightly to 1301 in 1991. By the year 1993 again it increased to1306, which was equal to 1989 level. However by the year 2000 there was a decline of more than 1100 private beds to 201 only. Thus while in the 1980s the private beds decreased in the initial phase, it increased in the second half of the decade, but in the decade of 1990s the number of private beds has declined in an unprecedented manner.

---

[17] More than three times from 841 to 2802 in terms of private and voluntary hospitals.

The figures for all India show an increasing growth in private beds, keeping pace with growth in private hospitals since 1983 till the year 2000, except in 1985 and 1987, when the number of private hospitals remained same and there was an increase in private beds. The table shows that there was a stagnant growth in private beds in the decade of 1980s. However it experienced a continuous growth in private beds since 1989 till the year 2000.

The figures for Bihar show that, it experienced an increase in growth of private beds in the initial years of 1980s, followed by a declining growth rate in later part of the decade. With an initial growth in early 1990s, it experienced a zero growth rate in most part of 1990s.

The figures for Gujarat show that except the initial period of stagnation in growth of private beds in the early 1980s, since 1987 the number of private beds has increased till the year 2000 in regular interval.

The figures for Haryana show that the private beds declined in the early part of 1980s followed by an increase in the later part of the decade. However in the decade of 1990s it experienced a decline in growth of private beds.

Figures for Karnataka show that since 1983 private and voluntary beds experienced a decline in growth followed by an increase in the second half of 1980s. In the early1990s it experienced an increase in private beds. However in later parts of 1990s, it experienced a zero growth rate in private beds.

In case of Kerala, the total number of private beds experienced an initial decline in the second half of 1980s. However since 1987 onwards the number of private beds has increased in till the year 2000 with a brief period of stagnation from 1991 to 1993.

The data on Madhya Pradesh or MP was not there; hence a comparison could not be made. The figures for Maharastra show that except the year 1993 it had experienced a continued growth in number of private beds since 1983.

The figures for Punjab show that while the private beds experienced an increase during 1980s, it remained stagnant in the decade of 1990s.

In case of Tamilnadu, while in the decade of 1980s the number of private beds increased, it experienced a zero growth in the decade of 1990s.

The trends in UP was quite interesting. Here in 1983 the total number of private beds was 12,083, which declined to 12,026 and remained so till the year 2000! That means since 1983 there was an initial decline in the number of private beds but since then it has experienced a zero growth rate for next fifteen years.

The figures for West Bengal show that broadly, while in the eighties, in the initial phase the state experienced up and down in the growth rate of private beds, in the decade of 1990s the total number of private beds declined in the state.

Growth of private beds relative to public beds in major states

The number of private or public beds could be taken as an indicator of utilisation pattern of in-patient health care services. The table below gives a comparative figure of public and private beds since 1983 to 2000 over a period of two decades.

Table 7.10 Private beds relative to public beds since 1983 –2000

State	1983		1993		As on 01.01.2000	
	Public Beds	Private Beds	Public Beds	Private Beds	Public Beds	Private Beds
AP	22,722	11,103	22,776	26,761	27586	42192
Bihar	14,078	8,447	20,522	8,519	20522	8519
Gujarat	11,502	16,929	20,708	33,487	22229	36867
Haryana	4,744	2,566	4,796	3,232	5018	1666
Karnataka	21,267	7,779	27,216	9,999	27766	9999
Kerala	24,875	18,203	28,030	49,169	30432	67517
MP	16,127	N.A.	25,310	N.A.	10818	NA
Maharastra	37,790	26,024	34,261	37,758	39350	42646
Orissa	9,988	1,408	13,077	1,306	11668	201
Punjab	11,316	2,913	10,786	3,782	11041	3782
TN	31,574	8,562	37,935	10,366	37935	10366
UP	33,125	12,083	34,267	12,026	34267	12026
WB	42,319	6,424	47,252	6,912	47596	6701
All India	3,29,245	1,34,266	3,65,696	2,10,987	389441	260669

Source: GOI, Ministry of Health and Family Welfare, Central bureau of Health Intelligence as cited in Private health care in India by Rama V. Baru, 1998. P-66- Ibid. Also see the CBHI data, 2000-2001, Government of India.

Public and private beds: Trends

In case of private beds in Orissa, it was clear that it has declined since 1983 till the year 2000. But the percentage decline was very high in 1990s compared to the 1980s. Thus the public beds increased in 1980s but declined in 1990s. In terms of private beds, Orissa experienced a decline over the years but from 1993 to 2000 the decline was more than six times! Among the 13 states that we analysed, Orissa had the lowest number of private beds at 201 followed by Haryana at 1666 private beds and Punjab with 3782 private beds by the year 2000.

Now let us have a look at the all India picture. The figures show that the growth rate in public and private beds was faster during the 1980s compared to 1990s. However by the year 2000 the number of public beds were more than 1,20,000, than the private beds whereas in 1983, the number of public beds were higher by more than 1,90,000 compared to private beds. Therefore over the years the private beds has grown much faster than public beds in India.

As per 1993 figures, Gujarat had the highest number of private beds followed by Kerala, Maharastra and Andhra Pradesh, UP, Tamilnadu, Karnataka, Bihar and West Bengal. Orissa had lowest number of private beds followed by Haryana and Punjab. However as per 2000 figures, Kerala with 67517 private beds was at the top among these 13 states, followed by Maharastra, Andhra Pradesh, UP and Tamilnadu.

Broadly the figures for Public beds show that in case of AP, it increased more in 1990s compared to 1980s and in case of private beds the growth percentage was much more in 1980s than in 1990s. Overall both public and private beds had increased since 1983 to 2000 and the private beds were near to the double of the public beds in 2000.

In case of Bihar, the public beds increased in 1980s but remained stagnant in 1990s. The same trend was also observed in case of private beds. However, here the public beds were near about two and half times more than the private beds by the year 2000. T

The public beds in Gujarat increased at a higher growth rate in 1980s than in 1990s and in case of private beds the trend was same. Here by the year 2000 the number of private beds was much higher than public beds when compared to 1983 figures.

The figures for Haryana show that the public beds increased since 1983 till 2000 and the growth was more in 1990s. Contrary to this, in case of private beds in 1980s it experienced an increase but there was sharp decline in 1990s. By the year 2000 the number of public beds was near about three times higher than private beds.

The figures for Karnataka show that during 1980s the growth in public beds was higher compared to 1990s. But in case of private beds it experienced stagnation in 1990s compared to growth in 1980. By the year 2000 the public beds were near about three times higher than the private beds.

The figures for Kerala show that the public beds have increased marginally since 1983 to 2000. However here the growth rate in 1980s was higher than in 1990s. In case of private beds the growth in 1980s was near about three times but by 1990s it experienced a growth rate of less than 50 percent of 1993 figures. While in 1983 the private beds were lower than public beds, by the year 2000 the private beds were more than double of the public beds.

The figures for MP were a matter of concern. Here the public beds increased in 1980s but declined by more than half by the year 2000. The figures for Punjab show that in 1980s the public beds experienced a decline but increased in 1990s, which was lower than 1983 figures. The private beds increased in 1980s but remained same till the year 2000.

In case of Tamilnadu the public beds increased in 1980s but experienced a stagnant growth in 1990s. The same trend was observed in case of private beds. By the year 2000 the public beds were near about three times higher than private beds compared to 1983, when it was more than three times higher than private beds.

The figures for UP show that, the public beds increased in 1980s and remained stagnant in 1990s. In case of private beds, there was a decline during 1983 to 1993, but remained same till the year 2000.

The figures for West Bengal show that in 1980s the growth rate in public beds was higher than in 1990s. In case of private beds the growth in absolute numbers was higher in 1990s compared to 1980s. However by the year 2000 the percentage of public beds to private beds was higher compared to 1983 figures.

Utilisation pattern

Understanding the utilisation pattern of health care was important to draw the implications of health sector reforms. If the utilisation pattern shows that more number of people were going for private sector for in-patient and out patient care in rural and urban areas across different states and regions, than to some extent[18] it could be justified about the current trend of different state governments in India[19] increasing the space for private participation in different aspects of health care. Therefore let us have a look at the utilisation pattern across different states.

In this regard we have looked at, out patient care by source of treatment, out patient care in government sources among major states, a comparative picture of out patient treatment by public and private providers among major states and utilisation of in-patient care in both rural and urban India.

Out patient care by source of treatment

The table below gives a picture of out patient care by source of treatment in rural and urban areas from 42nd round to 52nd round.

[18] Because here another important point was that even if the poor people were moving to the private health care wherever they could afford, what could be the possible reasons? Was it because of the better quality and low cost health care available in private sector compared to the public sector and the private sector care was more accountable to the people than the public sector health care or that the poor had no option but to go to the private health care due to lack of physical accessibility, availability and deteriorating quality of health care in public institutions?

[19] And this includes Orissa.

Table: 7.11 Percentage distribution of out patient care by source of treatment from 52nd and 42nd rounds

Source of Treatment	Rural		Urban	
	1986-87	**1995-96**	**1986-87**	**1995-96**
Public Hospital	18	11	23	15
PHC/CHC	5	6	1	1
Public Dispensary	3	2	2	2
ESI doctor etc.	0	0	2	1
All govt. source	26	19	28	20
Private Hospital	15	12	16	16
Nursing Home	1	3	1	2
Charitable Inst.	0	0	1	1
Private Doctor	53	55	52	55
Others	5	10	3	7
All non govt. sources	74	81	72	80

Note: The estimates of the 52nd round were based only on the treatments with reported source of treatment.
Source: Morbidity and Treatment of Ailments, 52nd round NSSO, 1995-96, Government of India, 1998.

It shows that among the public sector institutions, the percentage decline in utilisation for out patient care was highest in public hospitals, which declined from 18% to 11% in rural areas and from 23% to 15% in urban areas from 1986-87 to 1995-96. Among the other public sector institutions there was not much variation in utilisation pattern for the out patient care. On an average among the public sector health institutions, the utilisation of the out patient care declined from 26% to 19% in rural areas and from 28% to 20% in urban areas during 1986-87 to 1995-96. Among the public sector health institutions the utilisation of public hospital was highest for out patient care followed by Public dispensary and PHC/CHC institutions in both rural and urban areas.

The figures for the private sector on the other hand show that for out patient care the utilisation patterns increased from 74% to 81% in rural areas and from 72% to 80% in urban areas, during 1986-87 to 1995-96. Among the private health care institutions, for out patient care, the service of a private doctor was utilized most followed by private hospital in both rural and urban areas.

On an average, among the public sector health institutions, the utilisation of out patient care was more in urban areas compared to rural areas in both 42nd and 52nd rounds of NSSO data. On the other hand among the private sector health institutions, the utilisation of out patient care was more in rural areas in 1995-96 compared to urban areas.

Out Patient care in government sources among major states

The table below gives a picture of 15 major states of India about the utilization of out patient care from the government sources in both rural and urban areas from 1986-87 to 1995-96.

Table: 7.12 Percentage of ailments receiving non hospitalized treatment from government sources

States	Rural		Urban	
	1986-87	1995-96	1986-87	1995-96
Andhra Pradesh	12	22	16	19
Assam	40	29	26	22
Bihar	14	13	17	33
Gujarat	28	25	18	22
Haryana	15	13	19	11
Karnataka	32	26	30	17
Kerala	32	28	33	28
Madhya Pradesh	24	23	28	19
Maharastra	21	16	15	17
Orissa	37	38	43	34
Punjab	12	7	11	6
Rajasthan	46	36	52	41
Tamilnadu	28	25	31	28
Uttar Pradesh	*	8	14	9
West Bengal	16	15	20	19
India	21	19	24	20

Note: 1- * Estimate is not available. 2- the estimates of 52nd round were based only on the treatments with reported source of treatment.

Source: Morbidity and Treatment of Ailments, 52nd round NSSO, 1995-96, Government of India, 1998.

Among the 15 states analyzed, Andhra Pradesh was the only state where in both rural and urban areas; there was an increase in utilisation for out patient care from government sources from 42nd to 52nd round. Interestingly the increase was much more in rural areas compared to urban areas in percentage terms. Bihar, Maharastra and Gujarat were the three states, where in rural areas there was decline in utilisation of out patient care from government sources; whereas in urban areas there was an increase in utilisation rate during these two rounds. Orissa was the only state where in rural areas there was a slight increase in utilisation for out patient care in government sources; whereas in urban areas there was a sharp decline by 9 percentage points in utilization rates during these two survey periods.

The remaining states show a declining trend for both rural and urban areas during these two rounds of surveys. Haryana, Karnataka, Kerala, Madhya Pradesh and Rajasthan were the states where the decline in utilisation rate was higher in urban areas compared to rural areas in percentage terms during these two survey periods. Assam was the only state where the decline in utilisation for out patient care, was higher in rural areas compared to urban areas in percentage terms from 42nd to 52nd round of NSSO. Punjab, West Bengal and Tamilnadu were the three states where the decline in utilisation was same in both rural and urban areas in percentage terms during these two survey periods.

A comparative picture shows that Rajasthan, Orissa, Kerala, Karnataka and Tamilnadu were the states where utilisation of out patient care in government institutions was among the highest in India. On the other hand, Punjab, Uttar Pradesh and Haryana were the states where the utilisation of out patient care in government institutions was one of the lowest among these major states of India.

The figures for all India show that the utilisation for out patient care declined from 21% to 19% in rural areas, and 24% to 20% in urban areas, during 1986-87 to 1995-96 in government health care institutions. Therefore the decline was more in urban areas compared to rural areas.

Out patient treatment by public and private providers

The table below gives a picture about the utilization of out patient care in rural and urban areas and the percentage share among the public and private providers.

Table: 7.13 Percentage of Ailments receiving non-hospitalized treatment by public and private providers

States	Rural		Urban	
	Public	Private	Public	Private
Andhra Pradesh	22	53	19	68
Assam	29	27	22	41
Bihar	13	65	33	53
Gujarat	25	67	22	75
Haryana	13	84	11	87
Karnataka	26	51	17	74
Kerala	28	61	28	62
Madhya Pradesh	23	62	19	75
Maharastra	16	73	17	77
Orissa	38	31	34	53
Punjab	7	92	6	91
Rajasthan	36	54	41	50
Tamilnadu	25	54	28	65
Uttar Pradesh	8	83	9	85
West Bengal	15	65	19	72
India	19	64	20	72

Note: The figures are in percentage terms.
Source: Morbidity and Treatment of Ailments, 52nd round NSSO, 1995-96, Government of India, 1998.

It shows that in rural areas of Andhra Pradesh, while only 22% utilized the government health care, 53% utilized the private care. In the urban areas 68% utilized the private sources, while only 19 % utilized the public institutions for out patient care. Similarly in case of Assam, while in rural areas 29% utilized government services, 27% utilized the private sources. However in urban areas while 41% utilized private sources, only 22% utilized the public institutions. Thus in case of urban areas of Assam, the utilisation of private institutions for out patient care was much more compared to rural areas.

The figures for Bihar show that while only 13% in rural areas and 33% in urban areas utlised the public institutions, the majority went for the private providers for out patient care. Similar patterns were observed among the states of Gujarat, Haryana, Kerala, Karnataka, Madhya Pradesh, Maharastra, Punjab, Uttar Pradesh, West Bengal, Tamilnadu and Rajasthan.

Among these 15 states, Punjab was at the top with highest utilisation of private sources for out patient care in both rural and urban areas followed by Haryana and Uttar Pradesh. Along with Assam, Orissa was the only other state where in rural areas the public sector was still the dominant provider of out patient care. However in urban areas of these two states, the private sources were the dominant providers for out patient care. The figures for India show that a majority of people in both rural and urban areas goes for private sources for out patient care.

Utilisation of in-patient care in rural and urban areas

The table below gives a picture of utilisation of in-patient care in both rural and urban areas by type of hospitals in public and the private sectors.

Table: 7.14: Per 1000 distribution of hospitalized treatments by type of hospital during 1986-87 and 1995-96

Type of Hospital	Rural		Urban	
	1986-87	1995-96	1986-87	1995-96
Public Hospital	554	399	595	418
PHC/CHC	43	48	8	9
Public Dispensary	*	5	*	4
All govt. Sources	597	438	603	431
Private Hospital	320	419	296	410
Nursing Home	49	80	70	111
Charitable Inst.	17	40	19	42
Others	17	8	12	6
All Non-government sources	403	562	397	569
All Hospitals	1000	1000	1000	1000

Source: Morbidity and Treatment of Ailments, 52nd round NSSO, 1995-96, Government of India, 1998.

It shows that the utilisation of public hospitals during 1986-87 to 1995-96 for in-patient care declined for both rural and urban areas. During the same period the utilisation of private hospitals increased significantly. However by the year 1995-96, while in rural areas the private hospitals were utilized most compared to public hospitals, in urban areas it was the public hospitals, which were the dominant providers.

In terms of utilisation of PHC/CHC level institutions, it shows a slight increase from 42nd to 52nd round of NSSO data in both rural and urban areas. For all public health care institutions, while the utilisation for in-patient care has declined significantly in both rural and urban areas during 1986-87 to 1995-96, it declined sharply in urban areas compared to rural areas.

Among the private health care institutions, while the utilisation of public hospitals increased significantly from 1986-87 to 1995-96 in both rural and urban areas, the increase was more in urban areas compared to rural areas. However in case of nursing homes while the utilisation for in-patient care increased by 163% in rural areas; the increase was slightly less at 158.5% in the urban areas. Similarly the growth in charitable institutions was 235% in rural areas and 221% in urban areas during 1986-87 to 1995-96. However there was a decline in utilisation of other private sources.

On an average the private institutions witnessed a significant increase in utilisation of in-patient care during 1986-87 to 1995-96 in both rural and urban areas. In terms of public and private sources while in 1986-87, the utilisation for in-patient care was dominated by the public sector, the situation reversed by 1995-96, when the private health care institutions were the dominant providers for in-patient care for both rural and urban areas.

Halfhearted strategies

The National Health Policy 2002 had set a goal of increasing the utilization of public health facilities from current Level of less than 20 percent to more than 75 percent by the year 2010. That means by its own admission the state was agreeing that the public health facilities were hardly utilized by people at large. The reasons were not too difficult to find. The institutions from block PHC downwards have been in a state of desperation. Many of the senior officials of the donor agencies were of the view that these institutions have almost collapsed across India. The problem of ensuring that the doctor and other staffs regularly visit their institutions at these levels has had been a challenge for all the state governments.

With the increasing element of private participation in health care, the focus has also shifted toward curative and high technology aspects of health care. Therefore the target of increasing the utilisation of public health facilities from the present level of less than 20 percent to above 75 percent by 2010 seems just plain talk, because the government does not have any clear strategy in this regard.

Conclusion

Our analysis showed that while the individual private practitioners did exist before independence in India, the growth of private sector occurred mainly in the seventies and eighties due to lack of sufficient investment by the public sector. The newly emerged rich and middle peasant classes, due to green revolution, also saw an opportunity in this private sector growth. The oil shock of the seventies created fiscal constraints for governments around the world including India; as a result with deliberate policy initiatives like liberalisation of import duties on costly equipments etc. private sector was encouraged to grow. During this time many of the NRI doctors also started establishing private hospitals with tertiary level care in southern parts of India. However the growth of this private sector was confined to richer states and in developed regions within these states.

In terms of health care financing our analysis showed that per capita expenditure has increased since independence in Orissa as well as in India. However the average figures do not give a picture of inter state and intra state disparities in terms of actual expenditures. The trends in public health care expenditure showed that since 1980s it had experienced up and down till the year 1994-95. After that it experienced a sudden increase followed by a decline and since 1998 it has shown an upward trend. This may be due to the fact that the money for OHSDP and PSPU were included in the general health budget of the state.

However in terms of percentage of health expenditure to the total expenditure, the figures for Orissa showed that percentage of health care expenditure had declined in 1990s compared to 1980s. In case of India, while the percentage of health care expenditure increased in 1980s, it experienced a declining growth in the nineties and increased slightly in the later years. In terms of future projections, while the NHP targets for increasing health care expenditure by the state were most unlikely to be met by the year 2010, the targets for allocation of resources would probably be achieved. This was because the state government was trying to privatise the tertiary level care and at the same time user charges were being introduced in the secondary level institutions.

Among the donor agencies, World Bank had replaced DFID as the major investor in health sector of Orissa since late 1990s. The third largest investor was UNFPA followed by UNICEF and European Commission. However off late European Commission had emerged as the third most influential player after World Bank and DFID.

In terms of our analysis of the cost of treatment, it was observed that treatment was expensive in urban areas compared to rural areas in public and private sector hospitals. However the cost of treatment in private sector hospitals was almost near to 200% in both rural and urban areas compared to public sector hospitals. On the other hand the analysis of the average household expenditure per disease episode in Orissa showed that in urban areas, the expenditure was much less in a government hospital than a private hospital or clinic. Interestingly in rural areas the expenditure was slightly high in government hospitals than the private hospital or clinic.

An analysis of the presence of private enterprises showed that these institutions were mostly present in urban areas of developed states in India. There were huge gaps in the presence of private enterprises in terms of rural and urban areas. For example in case of Orissa, there were only 12 private enterprises per million populations in rural areas compared to 431 private enterprises per million populations in urban areas.

In terms of private and voluntary hospitals, overall there was growth since 1980s. Among the 13 states analysed, Orissa had the lowest number of private and voluntary hospitals. However interstate disparities were very high, for example by the year 2000 the combined presence of private and voluntary hospitals in four states of Maharastra, Andhra Pradesh, Gujarat and Kerala was 87.68% to the total in India! Among these states while some had experienced positive growth rate, others had experienced a zero growth rate in the nineties. There were states like Orissa and Haryana which experienced a negative growth rate during this period.

In terms of beds, there was growth since 1980s in both private and public sector. However by the year 2000 the total number of private beds was near about two times to the total number of public beds. However there were inter-state disparities in this and in many states the total number of public beds was more than total number of private beds. Among the 13 states, while Gujarat had the highest number of private beds, Orissa was at the bottom. While in the nineties there was decline in the growth of private and public beds in Orissa, the decline was very sharp in case of the private beds.

Therefore, overall trends for Orissa show that the public sector was the dominant provider and the private sector has experienced negative growth rate since 1980s. In these circumstances the creation of a larger space for the private sector by the state government suggests that they were adopting a uniform policy, which placed an unquestioned faith in the private sector.

In case of India as there was no proper regulation and because of the heterogeneous nature of the private sector, it was very difficult to assess the quality of care available in different private institutions. For example even in the capital Delhi where big private hospitals were given public land for free, so that they would reserve 25% of their beds for the below poverty line people, has been openly violated by these hospitals without any penalties imposed on them.

The figures for 52nd round of NSSO showed that both in rural and urban areas, private sector was being utilized for more than 80% of the out patient care. Thus while the utilisation pattern for out patient care had increased for the private sector from 42nd to 52nd round of NSSO, the figures had declined in case of the public sector. However our analysis of 15 major states of India showed that while in some states the utilisation for outpatient care had decline in public sector, other states had experienced a growth during this period. This could be because in these states people had no option but to go to the public sector. Interestingly in some states like Orissa there was an increase in utilisation of outpatient care in public sector in rural areas compared to urban areas.

In terms of in-patient care, private institutions had experienced an increase in both rural and urban areas since 1986. While in 1986-87 the public institutions were the dominant providers of in-patient care, by the year 1995-96 the private institutions were the dominant players in India. However there must be inter-state and intra state disparities in the utilisation of in-patient care.

Studies have shown that in states where the public sector had a dominant presence even the top 20 % of the population utilised the public services for in-patient and out patient care.

Our analysis showed that while the private sector has a dominant presence in some states, it was not so in case of others. Besides there have been rural and urban disparities in terms of presence of private hospitals and beds. In a state like Orissa, the private sector has declined since 1980s and the decline was very sharp in 1990s. Therefore the increasing space being created by the state for private participation in different aspects of health care has serious implications for the access to health care for the poor and the marginal sections.

Orissa presents an example of a state where even if policies were pushed they could not yield the desired results because of historical and socio-political reasons. Here the public sector has been the dominant provider of health care services and the presence of private sector has been very low. As a result both the rich and the poor utilized the services of public sector in large numbers. Due to initiation of reforms in health sector a wider perception among the officials has grown in favor of increasing private participation in health care. Just as in the larger economy the role of the state has got reduced, the same argument was also forwarded to reduce the role of state in health sector.

Thus the reforms initiated by the state government seem to follow a unified model for privatisation of health care irrespective of different contexts[20]. In the ear of globalization where there was increasing flow of goods, information, trade and commerce and of people, while few have got the benefits out of it, a large section of population has not benefited out of this process. This has also been the case of India where the liberalisation of Indian economy has created opportunities for few sections of its population and the vast majority has remained untouched out of this process. In this scenario the proposal for increasing private participation in health care in a state like Orissa would be problematic because it undermines the principles of equity and universal access, which are essential for public health.

[20] As we have discussed in chapter IV and chapter V, in a state like Orissa, World Bank through its *Orissa Economic Review Package* and its *Orissa Health Systems Development Project* has to a large extent influenced the reforms in the health sector. The methods followed have been a unified one in the sense that it assumes that private sector can provide an efficient and effective care, which the public health care services have not been able to provide.

Chapter Eight

Summary and Conclusion

The broad objective of this book was to study the process and experience of health sector reforms in Orissa. Here we have tried to explore the provider's perspective, like the government officials in health sector and the donor agency officials with regard to issues of health sector reforms. The study was conducted in Orissa by using an ethnographic approach. However it was used in a limited way in terms of intensive interviews and observations in the field.

Before documenting about various country experiences we have tried to define health sector reforms as a phenomenon of scientific enquiry. Our main argument was that there was nothing called *health sector reforms* out there in the field. It's a constructed category like any other concept. This very basic understanding was missing in the existing literature. Our analysis of existing literature showed that the term 'health sector reforms' have been accepted as a given category. Therefore as a field of scientific enquiry we have defined the term 'health sector reforms' as *any initiative by the state since the later part of twentieth century, which tries to reduce the role of government in health sector while creating a space for a larger role for the private sector.* Therefore while the private sector existed prior to 1980s in different countries, it never got such an overwhelming support from the state in terms of defining the priorities of health sector in the long run. Our new definition also captures the dominant trends in health sector across the world since eighties. In defining the term health sector reforms we have also looked at those policy initiatives, which could not be termed as reforms but as *systemic changes*. This has helped us in classifying the phenomenon of 'health sector reforms' in a better way. At the same time we have included various initiatives by the state of Orissa as health sector reforms, which were for the first time being classified in such a way. In analyzing the implications of reform initiatives structural constraints were taken into account.

In chapter I we have reviewed the existing literature on health sector reforms in different parts of the world, covering different country experiences. Using our new definition of health sector reforms, we have classified different country experiences in terms of pre reform period health services system in that country, the circumstances in which reforms were introduced in health sector and thirdly to see whether there were any study of outcomes of the reform initiatives. Here also we have included various policy initiatives as health sector reforms using our new definition and also excluded other initiatives, which were termed as reforms in health sector by various studies.

Different country experiences showed that health sector reforms were mostly introduced in the beginning of 1980s and in some countries in the 1990s. These reforms have tried to increase private participation in different aspects of health sector and at the same time tried to reduce the role of public sector. One of the main areas of focus was to reduce the public financing on health and encourage other sources of financing like introduction of private or community insurance mechanisms. In provisioning aspects the private sector also was encouraged in different levels of care. While the terms like 'efficiency' and 'effectiveness' were coined to argue that the limited resources in health sector should be used in a judicious way, the real driving force for the reforms was the neo liberal ideology of encouraging market forces in different aspects of a country's economy. Therefore health sector reforms need to be analyzed in the context of economic liberalisation being followed by most of the countries in the world. There were few studies, which looked into the aspects of impacts of health sector reforms. Those, which analyzed this aspect, have found that the reforms in health sector have increased cost of care and have created inequalities in terms of access for different social groups.

In chapter II we have discussed about the methodology used in this study. While the field of study was Orissa, interviews were also conducted with senior officials of the donor agencies like DFID, World Bank etc. at their New Delhi offices. In the capital of Orissa, Bhubaneswar, senior officials of the Health and Family Welfare Department as well as senior officials from the donor agencies were interviewed. Apart from this, two well-developed districts within Orissa were selected on the basis of purposive selection from a ranking of various districts done by the Population Commission of India. In each district two blocks were chosen on a random basis and thus four blocks were studied intensively. At the district level the CDMOs and his allied staffs were interviewed and at the block level the medical officers' in-charge and the other medical officers in that block were interviewed. At the block level group interviews were conducted with ANMs/Male workers and weekly meetings in these four blocks were attended. In one district the monthly meeting of all the MO in-charge was attended to get better understanding of the functioning of the health care services structure in that district.

Apart from using in-depth interviews as primary sources of data collection, secondary sources like State Bureau of Health Intelligence, DHS, Orissa, CBHI data, the documents from donor agencies, journals and books etc. were used.

In chapter III we have given an overview of health care services in Orissa in comparison to India. Our study of the evolution of health services showed that since independence there was increase in public expenditure on health care till late sixties. However due to the oil shock of the seventies expenditure on social sectors like health started declining and an increasing space was created for the private sector by different mechanisms like liberalizing import duties on medical equipments in the eighties. This process of increasing privatisation was also facilitated by growth of new middle class due to Green revolution and the investment by NRI doctors in super-specialty hospitals. At the same time public investments in health care was more toward secondary and tertiary levels of care, whereas in terms of epidemiological priorities the state should have invested more toward the primary level care.

In terms of health status there were divides in rural and urban areas in case of India and Orissa. In Orissa the major communicable diseases were TB, Malaria and gastroenteritis. While the allopathic institutions had experienced a growth over the years, the ISM and H system had experienced a stagnant growth. While more than 57% of sub centres had no government buildings, most of the categories of vacant posts were at the level of PHCs and CHCs. In the tribal areas the sub centres and the CHCs were requiring urgent attention. The infrastructure at the periphery level institutions was at the dilapidated conditions. The major strength in the health care services in Orissa was that even the rich utilized mostly the government services; therefore a minimum standard was being maintained. In terms of structural constraints, there was no transparent transfers and postings policy for the medical officers and the paramedics. As a result medical officers and other staffs were refusing to stay in remote and difficult areas. Further medical officers were inadequately trained in public health aspects which had affected in their optimum performance in different positions of the health care services. The ANMs were inadequately trained and had poor knowledge about various national programs. Even where there were government sub centre buildings, they were staying in nearby town areas because most of these institutions were at the end of the villages and many were in burial grounds! The male worker was hardly visiting the fields. This had increased work load on the ANMs. Along with this the supervision aspect was very poor. These have serious implications for the implementation and expected outcomes of various national programmes.

Chapter IV has focused on SHSDPs and OHSDP, which were being funded by the World Bank, in the context of Structural Adjustment Programmes adopted by India in the 1990s.

We have included the SHSDPs as major health sector reform initiatives by different states. These State Health Systems Projects were meant to upgrade the secondary level institutions in various states including Orissa. Because the idea was that, as most of the money for national programs went to primary level care and the states mostly focused on tertiary levels of care, it was the secondary levels which were the neglected ones. Therefore the World Bank shifted its focus from population and nutrition programs in the early nineties to upgrading the secondary levels of care in the second half of nineties. While in the first group of states selection criteria for this project was their own willingness to implement it, in the later stages the selection criteria was based on a state's capacity to achieve Millennium Development Goals.

Apart from introducing 'efficient' and 'effective' use of public health care resources, through these projects the World Bank has also tried to introduce various public-private partnerships measures. However our analysis showed that it has tried to adopt a uniform model for all the states and giving an example of, handing over PHCs to NGOs, we have shown that this won't work. While the SHSDPs were meant to increase referrals from primary level care, it did not happen. Therefore in the next group of states like Tamilnadu and Rajasthan, the primary level care would also be upgraded along with secondary level care. Apart from encouraging for new sources of financing health care, through SHSDPs the World Bank was also emphasizing that the state should limit its role only to issues of policy, regulation and accreditation.

The Orissa experience showed that the line department directors were sidelined in the project formulation and implementation phases. Besides, the state government was also not increasing its share of expenditure every year. This had serious consequences for expected project outcomes and in sustainability of the project institutions. With the introduction of user fees, the proposal to create referral cards and by the creation of a large number of contractual posts under this project, an element of increasing privatisation was being introduced in these secondary level institutions. This has the potential to cut off these institutions from primary level care in the long run and this has serious consequences for universal access to health care in a state like Orissa where the government health services were the dominant providers.

In chapter V we have analyzed the process and experience of health sector reforms in Orissa. We have said that in the context of Orissa the process of health sector reforms has to be seen along with the process of systemic changes. The formation of House Committee of Orissa Legislature and the evaluation by DFID of its earlier projects led to an initiative toward a series of changes in health sector covering both systemic changes and health sector reforms in the second half of 1990s. While consultations for reform initiatives were held at different levels of health services personnel, it was not a comprehensive one. While Orissa economic Review package was not a reform initiative in health sector, the World Bank was planning to influence the health policy making in the state to a large extent through leverage gained by this package. Similarly while the PSPU was being created, with 100% funding from DFID, to act as a think tank for the health and family welfare department of government of Orissa, the DFID and World Bank were trying to play a more direct role in the health policy making in the state through it. This raises serious issues about democratic process of prioritizing health interventions in Orissa.

Our analysis showed that in terms of presence of various donor agencies, the World Bank was playing a more influential role in Orissa health sector followed by DFID and European Commission. However presence of various donors had created problem of donor coordination and different styles of reporting for different donors were taking a lot of precious time of the health and family welfare department. In terms of systemic changes while the new drugs policy had reduced the price of drugs and increased its availability in most of the government institutions in the state, the major lacunae was the exclusion of the private sector. There were no mechanisms to control the price of drugs available in the private sector and the mechanisms of quality checks were inadequate. In case of Pancha Byadhi Chikitsa scheme, patients were not aware about their rights in most of the cases. On the other hand the disease surveillance programme had successfully created an institutional mechanism for collection of epidemiological data in a systematic and regular way. However here the major question was, as the ANMs were poorly trained, had limited knowledge about various national programs and they used to visit their fields occasionally, therefore to what extent the disease surveillance data collected through them would be reliable? Similarly the creation of ZSS had helped in better utilisation of districts resources. However the supply of money was irregular under the petty maintenance scheme for block PHCs. The schemes like, mandatory pre-PG rural scheme and the training of medical interns under the guidance of a CDMO were failures because the structural issues like creation of transparent transfers and postings policy and a genuine emphasis on public health were missing.

Among the reform initiatives, the creation of contractual doctors' scheme had not helped in filling the vacant posts in remote and difficult areas. While the introduction of user charges in 157 OHSDP institutions had helped in petty maintenance of these institutions, the poor were not getting exempted from paying user fees as per the provisions under the scheme. The creation of contractual district cadre for paramedics and allowing private practice by government doctors were other examples by the state government to increase more elements of private participation in the health care of the state. However the contractual district cadre for paramedics had not helped in meeting the shortage of these personnel's in remote and difficult areas because the structural issues like providing basic infrastructure and amenities and ensuring a transparent transfers and postings policy were missing. The introduction of private pay clinics in the dental wings of government medical colleges, initiative to create three new private medical colleges and the idea of joint operation of hospitals were other examples of the state government increasing the space for private sector in health care of the state. The broader trends show that there was an unquestioning faith in the efficiency of the private sector in providing quality health care. However the larger question about implications for access to health care for the poor and marginalized was missing.

In chapter VI we have analyzed the reform process in Sundergarh and Khurda, the two developed districts of Orissa. In terms of structural constraints, it was found that most of the sub centres in these two districts had no government buildings. Block headquarter PHCs were requiring urgent repairing at many places. In terms of staffs, there were severe shortages in category of male supervisors and MPHW (M). Apart from this the existing health worker (M) were hardly visiting the fields. This had put a lot of work-load on the ANMs. Besides, the infrastructure at the PHC (N) institutions was in a very bad shape. Medical officers were absent in most of these institutions. In most of the sub centres and the PHC (N) institutions, there were no water or electricity facilities. Further from the block headquarter PHCs to various PHC (New) s and to the sub centres, in most of the places, there were no all weather roads. This had serious implications in terms of health personnel's willingness to stay in these institutions, effective supervision of field staff, people's accessibility to primary health care and in the effective implementation of various national programs.

In terms of reform experiences it was found that there were no consultations held with the CDMOs concerned about various reform initiatives in health sector taken in Orissa. This had serious implications in terms of program implementations, monitoring and in their expected outcomes. Besides at the district level it was observed that neither the CDMOs nor the block PHC medical officers' in-charge had any conceptual clarity about the ongoing reform process. The reform initiatives like contractual doctors' scheme and systemic changes like introduction of mandatory pre-PG scheme and internship training of medical graduates in these two districts were a failure, because the structural issues like transparent transfers and postings policy for medical officers, shortage of staffs at various levels, inadequate infrastructure and a genuine emphasis on public health were neglected. On the other hand, the new drugs policy had improved the quality of drugs available at all the levels of government health care institutions in these districts. At the same time people were not aware about their rights under the Pancha Byadhi Chikitsa scheme. Similarly the creation of ZSS had helped in better channeling of these districts resources. Under the scheme of petty maintenance of PHC headquarter buildings, money was not coming regularly and there were allegations of misuse of funds by the MO in-charge. While the user fees had helped in petty maintenance of health institutions, the poor were not getting exempted as per provisions in the scheme. However from CDMO to the block medical officer, all were in favor of introduction of user fees for more categories of services and at all levels of health institutions. In Sudergarh district they were identifying indigenous medical practitioners to involve them for referrals to PHCs.

In chapter VII we have looked at the financing, structure and utilisation patterns of the public/private sector in Orissa and across major states. We have also given a picture of donor agency funding for health sector in Orissa. In this chapter we have tried to examine whether the health sector reform initiatives were taken keeping in view the dominant presence of the private sector in various states in terms of financing, structure and utilization patterns.

In terms of health care financing to the percentage of total state budget, there was up and down turns in case of Orissa since 1980s till mid nineties. However the upward trend since 1998 may have been due to the implementation of OHSDP and PSPU, as these expenditures were included in the general budget of the state. However the health care expenditure as percentage to the total budget in 1990s had declined in Orissa compared to 1980s. Among the donor agencies, World Bank had emerged as the lead investor in late 1990s followed by DFID, UNFPA, UNICEF and European Commission in the health sector of Orissa. Along with this the World Bank had also emerged as the most influential donor in the state.

In terms of cost of treatment it was expensive in urban areas for both the public and the private sector hospitals compared to the rural areas. However the cost of treatment in private hospitals was almost 200% compared to the cost of treatment in public hospitals. Along with high cost of care the private sector in India and particularly in Orissa, was not regulated at all in an effective manner. This has implications for identifying the quality care being provided in the private sector.

Our analysis showed that the private sector was present mostly in the developed states of India and in the urban areas. In case of Orissa the private sector was mostly located in the urban areas. While there was overall growth in private and voluntary hospitals since 1980s, there were states like Orissa and Haryana, which experienced a negative growth rate during this period. Since 1980s both the private and public beds had grown in absolute numbers. However by the year 2000 the number of private beds was double the amount of public beds. Among the major states analyzed Orissa had the lowest number of private beds.

In terms of utilisation pattern the private sector was catering to more than 80% of the out patient care and even in case of in-patient care the private sector was the dominant provider. However there were inter-state and intra-state disparities in the utilisation pattern of health care. By ignoring these ground realities the health sector reform measures were trying to follow a uniform model across states. Our analysis showed that health sector reform measures were emphasizing 'access to better health care' in terms of 'access to better curative care' and in this process neglecting the preventive aspects, which has a very significant role in improving public health in a poor state like Orissa. By interpreting the concept of 'health' more in terms of an individual's responsibility, the inter-sectoral linkages between economy, existing social structure in Orissa, the nature of polity and health were being neglected.

Therefore in a state like Orissa where less than 15% of its population lived in urban areas, where near about 48% of its people lived below the poverty line, where about 39% of its population was scheduled castes and scheduled tribes and where government was the dominant provider of health care for both in-patient and out-patient care, this could adversely affect the public health care services in the long run and the poor and marginalized sections would be at the receiving end.

Hypothesis tested

Our first hypothesis was that, the health sector reform process in the long run would undermine the universality of health care, which was an essential feature of public health. Our study shows that these apprehensions were true to a large extent. Our second hypothesis was that, the public health services in the long run would try to withdraw from provisioning of the secondary and tertiary level care; this would weaken the sustainability of primary level care. Our study shows that the public health care services were indeed moving away from provisioning of secondary and tertiary levels of care. However to what extent it would affect the primary level care was difficult to predict at this moment. Our third hypothesis was that, with increasing privatization of health care the cost of care would go up; this would affect the poor most and would also affect their overall quality of life. We have found this hypothesis to be true to a large extent.

Difficulties faced in data collection

During the field visit to Orissa it was one of the big challenges to get the required secondary data because the Directorate of Health Services, which was supposed to maintain regular data, did not maintain it. The Health statistics related data was available since 1990 onwards and that too they were not maintained systematically. It was quite surprising that in the statistical section of the Directorate of Health Services, in two registers the information related to manpower was available year wise and that too in terms of addition of personnel in different categories at different levels of health services structure. That means the total number of health personnel existing at different levels was not available year wise! These two registers were maintained manually. Further the statistical division of the Directorate of Health Services was very uncooperative and it was told to this researcher that the person concerned had gone for a leave and would be back within a week. However one month went by and still that person did not turn up. Finally with a signature from the director of health services the files started moving and the required data could be collected.

In terms of the data collected through primary sources like Interview, there were different kinds of challenges in the field because the respondents to be interviewed were mostly the top officials in both the donor and government agencies. They had their own responsibilities and prior appointment was needed for an interview to be possible. In case of donor agencies the respondents were available on the fixed date of interview and hardly there was any change in the last minute. However in case of the persons in government departments, in some cases there were changes in the last minute for scheduled time of interview as the respondents had to attend some important meetings. While the senior technical directors in the Directorate of Health, Orissa were interviewed after much effort, the donor agency officials were not that much difficult to get an appointment with. Overall senior officials were very cooperative in providing information. This was true in both the cases of government and the donor agencies. Only in one case there was difficulty in interviewing a medical officer who was closely involved with drugs reform in Orissa but was unwilling to talk and after getting permission from senior officials this person could be interviewed.

At the district level prior appointments were taken from the concerned CDMOs and during the interview date other senior staffs of the CDMO were also present during the interview. There was not much difficulties faced in collecting the statistical data here. At the block PHC level the medical officer in charge were interviewed without taking prior appointments.

Issues for further research

1- How the official data with regard to health sector is being generated in different countries?

2- The implications of health sector reforms on primary level care.

3- To explore the quality of health care being provided by the private sector.

APPENDIX I

INTERVIEW GUIDE FOR SENIOR OFFICIALS AT THE STATE LEVEL

Interview Guide for the Health secretary Government of Orissa

1-Brief overview of Orissa's health services during the last decade (in terms of provisioning, financing, training, manpower and drugs).

2-Motivations for reforms and the role of donor agencies. Among the donor agencies whom do you think as the major player in the health care sector in Orissa?

3-Why the House Committee on health sector reforms was formed?

4-Why did the Committee focused on the following areas of reform only? Or how did the committee prioritized the areas for reform?

i-Introduction of *user charges in medical colleges and district hospitals.* What is the proportion of below poverty line families using these services? (How the below poverty line families are identified).
ii-Granting greater autonomy to major hospitals. What are the components of grater autonomy? What has been its experience?
iii-Abolition of private practice by government doctors. Has the government been successful in implementing this scheme and what are the hazards faced?

5-DFID suggested reforms in three areas after going through an evaluation of their earlier work. How did the government react to the DFID evaluation? Did they agree with the DFID on the following areas of reform namely:

i- Maintenance of buildings and equipments.
ii- Medicine (a new drugs policy) and
iii- Mobility of Para-medics.

How far have the reform measures had an impact on these areas?

6-There are shortages of doctors and paramedics in the state. The three medical colleges are not producing enough number of doctors. How the state plans to address this situation? Could you please tell us the unemployment level among doctors in Orissa?

7-Health care budget has not increased in Orissa in the nineties and the state is also in a fiscal crisis. In this context how do you visualize about achieving the goal of universal health care in Orissa?

8-In the last decade where has the health sector budget stagnated and where it has increased? (Like in Curative, Preventive, and Family Welfare etc.)

9-The mandatory Pre-PG rural scheme was introduced in the state. How it has performed?
10-What has been the role of World Bank in the health care sector in Orissa?

11-Are there conditionalities attached to loans from the Bank?

12-In "Orissa Economic Revival Package", are there any components of health sector reforms?

13-Whether the Bank is able to put pressure on health sector reforms through this package?

14-There are allegations that the World Bank even though contributes a little in terms of money, it influences in the policymaking. In case of Orissa how far do you think it to be true?

15- Interviews with the donor agencies have suggested that the health services structure in the state is not a pyramidal one, which is hampering in implementation of policies in the long run. What are the constraints faced by the state government in making the structure a pyramidal one?

16-The vision document 2010 talks about introduction of public-private initiatives in the state. But the private sector in Orissa is very small and these are concentrated in urban areas. Further the experience of handing over PHCs to NGOs suggests that it has not worked due to lack of experience and resources on behalf of NGOs. Hence is not it a difficult task?

17-It seems that the reforms are heading towards an idea where the health care cost has to be borne by the people? (For example measures like introduction of user charges and contracting out cleaning etc. and plans for encouraging the private sector). In a state where 47percent of the people are living below the poverty line, how is it going to improve the health care situation?

Interview Guide for the Director of Health Services

1- What are the components of health sector reforms being addressed by your department?

2- As Technical Head and expert of General Health care delivery services of the government of Orissa, in your opinion what are the strengths and weaknesses in the health care services structure of Orissa?

3- As Cadre controlling authority of State Cadre non-Gazetted employees and also disciplinary authority, how do you plan to address the shortages of Para-medics in the state?

4- The introduction of district cadre for paramedics, whether it has helped in maintaining the morale of the cadre?

5. As head executive & Inspector of various health related projects operating in the state, which donor agency in your opinion is the major foreign player in the health sector reforms in Orissa?

6- Whether and how do the donor agencies play a role in influencing health policy in Orissa? (Pathways of influence).

7- As budget controlling authority of primary and secondary health care services of the state, is there any evaluation of the quality of services?

8- As you are responsible for portfolio management including financial restructuring and reformation, what are the financial constraints Orissa is facing for achieving universal healthcare?

9- As appellate authority of district cadre employees under health directorate administration, what are the problems of the district cadre employees and what are your constraints in addressing them? How are you going to overcome these constraints?

10- As you hold key position in Central Purchase of Drugs and Consumables, instruments and equipments, after the introduction of new drugs policy has it improved from the earlier situation? If so, how and what are the areas of improvement? What is the proportion of high tech equipment procured during the last five years? (X-ray, ECG, EEG etc.)

11- As you assist government of Orissa in formulation of Budget, what are the constraints you face in formulating the health budget in the state as the state is in a deep fiscal crisis?

12- As a member of various health related committees and societies under sanction of state government, can you elaborate the role of House Committee on health sector reforms? What are the changes those have occurred after the amalgamation of various societies at the district level?

13- Why the health care cadre structure in the state is not pyramidal in nature. What are the constraints you are facing to address these issues?

Interview Guide for the Director of Family Welfare

1-As the principal objective of the Directorate is to stabilize the population and to provide health services including (Immunization) to both pregnant mother and children, it seems that you have been successful in lowering the population growth rate in Orissa significantly and in Immunization also you have done very good job.

However there is an area that remains unexplained which is that the poor opt for more children for economic reasons and by this logic Orissa should have higher population growth rate than India as a whole. Hence in a poor state like Orissa how your population control strategies were different than other states?

2- In immunization Orissa has done really well whereas other states that started simultaneously with Orissa have not done so well. What are the reasons for this?

3- What role the World Bank and other agencies are playing in RCH program in the state?

4- Whether over the years there has been changes in the approach towards maternal and child health care in Orissa? If yes what are those changes?

5- Whether population control, HIV/AIDS and RCH is implemented in an integrated manner in the state?

6- What role do you visualize for the donor agencies for better performance of your department?

Interview Guide for the Director of Medical Education & Training (DMET)

1. As Administrator of three Government Medical Colleges and its attached hospitals what are the challenges you are facing? What are the constraints you are facing in updating the syllabus in medical colleges?

2. There are acute shortages of doctors in the state and the three medical colleges are not producing enough of them. What are your constraints to address this situation and how you are going to tackle them? Could you please tell us the level of unemployment among doctors in the state?

3. What was the idea behind Rural Health Centers and how the RHCs' of Jagatsinghpur/Digapahandi/Attabira are functioning? What are the strengths and weaknesses?

3. As Administrator of Sardar Vallav Bhai Patel Post Graduate Institute of Pediatric, Cuttack and selection of P.G.(Medical), in your opinion how the mandatory pre-PG rural posting has helped in addressing the problem of absence of doctors in remote areas?

4. As you are in charge of Nursing Selection & Training Programme could you tell us as to what are the constraints that you are facing to address the shortages of nurses in the state and how are you going to overcome these challenges?

5. Establishment of private Medical Colleges/Dental Colleges and of private Nursing Schools in the State comes under your office. Till now there is not a single private registered medical college/ nursing school in the state. What are the reasons for it?

6- As Orissa is facing acute shortages in Para-medics in the state, are you planning to establish newer Pharmacy Colleges in the state?

7. Have you received any application for establishment of private Physiotherapy/occupational therapy/speech therapy Colleges in the state?

8. As Registration of Clinical Establishments comes under your office (Nursing Homes, Patho Clinics etc), what are the initiatives you have taken for registration of private practitioners in the state? What are the constraints you have faced in this regard?

9. Medical Referral cases are the responsibility of yours. In tribal districts the traditional practitioners are being involved in referrals. What has been your experience so far in this regard?

10. As you select in-service candidates for training, inside the country and abroad, what are the areas you focus for training?

11- The whole society values success and the more one consume the better status one has. In this situation is it not an injustice to ask the aspirants for a PG degree for mandatory rural posting for one year, where they will face difficulties for providing quality education for their children and maintaining a status in the society?

Interview Guide for the Director of State Institute of Health & Family Welfare (SIHFW) Orissa

1- As the objectives of the institute are to develop the skills of health personnel for demand generation by public and promote voluntary action by people in Health & Family Welfare services, how far the multi-skilling of health personnel has helped in tackling the shortages of manpower?

2-Your Institute takes a comprehensive view of Reproductive and Child Health Programme, could you please elaborate on this?

3-You are also involved in other health programmes by which you want individual's families and community to accept and adopt desirable health behaviors and practices. Please elaborate on this aspect also.

4- What has been the change towards the approach to RCH over the years?

5- Do you have any research reports in this regard?

Interview Guide for the Director of Indian Medicine & Homeopathy in the State of Orissa

1- What role homeopathy and Ayurveda play in health care provisioning in Orissa?

2- What are the constraints you face in regularizing the traditional practitioners in the state?

3- In tribal districts these traditional practitioners are being used for referral services. What has been your experience so far in this regard?

4-What is the attitude of allopathic practitioners towards these traditional practitioners?

5-Your views on AYUSH (Aurveda, Unani and Siddha).

6- Whether the indigenous systems practitioners are being posted in primary health care centers? What are the advantages and disadvantages of this phenomenon?

Interview Guide for the Director of Drugs Control, Government of Orissa

1-How far the essential drugs list of World Health Organization and shifting towards generic drugs from the brand names and centralized procurement of drugs has helped in reducing cost and rational prescription of drugs?

2- What is the situation of availability of drugs after the implementation of these new measures?

3- How far have you been successful in making available to the public, effective and safe drugs in required quantities and in appropriate dosage forms with acceptable quality, at all public/Government Health Care Institutions in the state in time?

4- What are the constraints you have faced in ensuring that banned, misbranded, and adulterated drugs, irrational and sub-therapeutic formulation (both Allopathic and Homoeopathic) are not available in the state and that the labeling, storage and preservation of drugs at appropriate temperature are carried out properly and effectively to preserve the potency of the drugs in all places before consumption by the patient?

5- What was the nature and forms of corruption that existed before the introduction of new drugs policy? What kind of pressures you faced when you restructured the new drugs procurement and delivery system?

6- What are the constraints you have faced in ensuring the availability of quality drugs in the state?

7- Has the system of weir-housing for drugs are in place in the state? If yes, then has it improved the situation in terms of availability of drugs in the state?

8- As you are responsible to ensure availability of essential drugs at a fair price to all patients of the state, what are the constraints you face in this regard and what steps you have taken to address these issues?

9- Another of your role is: grant of manufacturing and sales licenses of narcotic drugs and formulations containing narcotic drugs, allotment and utilisation of narcotic raw materials etc. under the provision of Narcotic Drugs and Psychotropic substances Act, 1985. What are the constraints you have faced in this regard?

10-What is the situation at the government, private clinics and stores functioning under the CDMOs and missionaries hospitals in terms of procurement, storage and distribution of drugs in the state?

Interview Guide for Project Director OHSDP (Orissa Health Systems Development Project)

1- Whether the OHSDP is being implemented separately or within the structures of the health services in Orissa?

2- What were the compulsions and motivations for the state to approach the World Bank for implementing this project?

3- What was the basis for opting for this project?

4-How the components of this project were prioritized and decided? Was there consultation with the state government and whether the state government had consulted with the CDMOs, MOs; and Health Officers etc.? Describe the process of consultations and different actors who all were involved.

5- The World Bank is implementing the Orissa Economic Revival Package. Whether funds for OHSDP are subject to fulfilling the conditionalities in the Economic Revival Package?

6- What are the elements of OHSDP?

7- OHSDP aims to strengthen the planning, management and implementation capacity at the state, district and lower levels. How this is being implemented and in which parts of Orissa? What has been your experience so far in this regard?

8- It also aims to strengthen the Health Management Information System and the capacity for surveillance of major communicable diseases. Which part of Orissa it has been implemented and how it has been implemented and what is your experience so far in this regard?

9- This project intends to improve service quality, access and effectiveness by:
a. Upgrading area, sub-divisional, district hospitals.
b. By upgrading clinical, managerial and support services at the facility level (CHC/PHC level. How far this component has been implemented and in which part of Orissa and your experience in this regard.

10-Is there any valuations across districts in the state and specifically in the districts of Sundergarh and Khurda?

11- Another aim is to improve access to basic health services at the community level through:
a. selective upgrading of community health centers.
b. Promoting health services in tribal areas and for disadvantaged groups.
c. Improving referral mechanisms and strengthening linkages between the different tiers of the health care system.

Which components of the above mentioned has been implemented and your experience in this regard.

12- What about the sustainability of the reform measures initiated in this project in terms of financing, infrastructure, equipments and drugs?

APPENDIX II

INTERVIEW GUIDE FOR THE DONOR AGENCIES AT STATE AND CENTRAL LEVEL

The background and history of donor's operation in the state in general and health sector in particular. What prompted the agency to move into the health sector? What were the specific areas of intervention and the reasons for choosing those areas? Were these areas for intervention based on an assessment of the health sector? (Was there a report that was available? What was the experience of the donor agency with regard to the state government (Opportunities and Constraints)? What kind of changes these interventions have brought about, say in terms of infrastructure, drugs and governance? The experience with other donors and their role for the next ten years.

APPENDIX III

INTERVIEW GUIDE FOR THE OFFICIALS AT THE DISTRICT LEVELS AND BELOW

Interview Guide for CDMOs/ADMOs (Public Health, Medical and Family Welfare)

1- What are the *strengths and weaknesses* in the *health care delivery structure* in the district?

2- Are you aware of HSR? Did you participate in the consultative process of HSR?

2- In district hospitals *user charges* has been introduced. What are the services for which user charges have been introduced? What is the proportion of those below poverty line and other income groups in the district? How this scheme has performed so far? What are the mechanisms for identifying BPL population? What has been the perception of people who are paying user charges? Whether the income from user charges has been able to sustain the recurrent expenditures of these institutions?

3- For *petty maintenance of buildings and equipments* funds has been allocated to the MOs in the PHCs/CHCs. How this scheme has performed in your district?

4- *New Drugs Policy:* At present Orissa has an essential drugs list prescribed by WHO. Also generic drugs are being used rather than branded drugs and central purchasing of drugs is being done. What is the scenario in the district in terms of availability of essential drugs? What is the difference the new drugs policy has created compared to the earlier policy? Whether you views were taken before introduction of this drugs policy?

5- Whether the *district cadre for paramedics* has been introduced in this district? If yes, then how far the scheme has been successful in boosting the morale of the paramedics? And whether under the scheme you can recruit the required number of paramedics for your district?

6- There are *shortages of doctors and paramedics* in the district. What are your constraints to address this situation?

7- Whether the *mandatory pre PG rural scheme* is applicable to the district? If yes, how far it has performed in addressing the availability of doctors in remote areas?

8- Whether any *PHCs were handed over to NGOs* in this district? If yes, what has been your experience till now?

9- How is the *Zilla Swasthya Samiti* functioning in the district? Has the situation improved with creation of this body?

10- What is the *role of World Bank in the RCH* program of this district?

11- Whether *population control, HIV/AIDS and RCH* is implemented in an *integrated manner* in the district? If yes, do you see any difference in terms of results at the ground level?

12- Whether there has been *changes* over the years *in the approach* towards *maternal and child health care* in the district? If yes, what are those changes?

13- Whether *traditional practitioners at the primary level care* are being involved in the *referrals* in your district? If yes, what are the terms for involvement of traditional practitioners? What are the inputs from government in terms of training etc.? For what diseases/ conditions are they expected to do referrals? And where do they refer?

14- What is multiskilling and at what level is it happening? Does multiskilling result in downsizing staff? How does it address the shortage of human resourses?

15- Medical Internship training introduced in 2000. Under the Internship training, the interns are sent in groups of two and three to community health centers under the control of the CDMOs. They are exposed to real community health situations and get 'hands on' training. They are supervised both by the medical officers in charge of the institutions as well as the medical college teachers.

Whether these trainings produce better trained doctors than the earlier scheme? And has it led to better attendance of doctors in rural health institutions, as it was the intension of this training?

16-Pancha Byadhi Chikitsa (Five Diseases Treatment) Scheme introduced in 1999, reintroduced in 2001.Objective: To ensure that every patient who goes to a public hospital is guaranteed treatment at government cost for diseases such as malaria, leprosy, diarrhoea, acute respiratory infection, and scabies.

How this scheme has performed in the district?

17- Before introducing the above mentioned changes whether your views were taken into consideration?

Interview Guide for Medical Officers at the CHC/PHC level

1- For *petty maintenance of buildings and equipments* funds has been allocated to the MOs in the PHCs/CHCs. How this scheme has performed in your PHC/CHC?

2- Under the new drugs policy whether the essential drugs are available in your institution?

3- Whether this PHC/CHC has adequate staff in terms of MOs and paramedics? In case of shortage in the staff what are the challenges that you face in your day to day functioning?

4- What is your opinion on mandatory pre- PG rural scheme in Orissa?

5- There are talks about handing over PHCs to NGOs. What do you think about this?

6- There is an idea that the multiskilling of health personnel would help in overcoming the shortages of paramedics in the state. What is your opinion on this?

7- For increasing the referrals, the traditional practitioners are being involved in tribal districts? Do you think that this will increase the referrals? Will it not legitimize the quacks in the state?

8- The earlier existing different societies at the district level have been amalgamated to create one society. Has it improved the situation?

9- Do you think that over the years there has been change in the approach towards maternal and child health care in this district? If yes, what are those changes?

10- What are your strategies for Population control, HIV/AIDS and RCH?

11- For Internship Training, two to three medical interns are sent to CHCs under the supervision of CDMOs. Do you think that this has helped in better training of doctors and whether it motivates the interns to work in the rural areas after training?

12- The objective of the Pancha Byadhi Chikitsa scheme has been to ensure that every patient who goes to a public hospital is guaranteed treatment at government cost for diseases such as malaria, leprosy, diarrhoea, acute respiratory infection, and scabies. How do you evaluate this scheme?

13- What is your opinion about introduction of user charges in district hospitals and medical colleges in the state?

14- In your opinion what are the strengths and weaknesses in the health services structure in the state? What measures you would suggest for their amelioration?

15- There are problems of communication, infrastructure, and lack of better schools in remote areas of Orissa. And the government expects you to perform in those conditions. Don't you think that this is an injustice to those in service and the aspiring doctors in the state?

16- Don't you think that the syllabus in the medical colleges are not updated from time to time and hence is not equipping doctors to face the challenges in the field?

17- Any other matter you would like to mention.

ANNEX I

INTERVIEW GUIDE FOR THE HEALTH SECRETARY GOVERNMENT OF ORISSA

1- Brief overview of Orissa's health services during the last decade (in terms of provisioning, financing, training, manpower and drugs).

2- Motivations for reforms and the role of donor agencies. Among the donor agencies whom do you think as the major player in the health care sector in Orissa?

3- Why the House Committee on health sector reforms was formed?

4- Why did the Committee focused on the following areas of reform only? Or how did the committee prioritized the areas for reform?

   i-Introduction of *user charges in medical colleges and district hospitals*. What is the proportion of below poverty line families using these services? (How the below poverty line families are identified).

   ii-Granting greater autonomy to major hospitals. What are the components of grater autonomy? What has been its experience?

   iii-Abolition of private practice by government doctors. Has the government been successful in implementing this scheme and what are the hazards faced?

5- DFID suggested reforms in three areas after going through an evaluation of their earlier work. How did the government react to the DFID evaluation? Did they agree with the DFID on the following areas of reform namely:

   i- Maintenance of buildings and equipments.

   ii- ii- Medicine (a new drugs policy) and

iii- Mobility of Para-medics.

How far have the reform measures had an impact on these areas?

6- There are shortages of doctors and paramedics in the state. The three medical colleges are not producing enough number of doctors. How the state plans to address this situation? Could you please tell us the unemployment level among doctors in Orissa?

7- Health care budget has not increased in Orissa in the nineties and the state is also in a fiscal crisis. In this context how do you visualize about achieving the goal of universal health care in Orissa?

8- In the last decade where has the health sector budget stagnated and where it has increased? (Like in Curative, Preventive, and Family Welfare etc.)

9- The mandatory Pre-PG rural scheme was introduced in the state. How it has performed?

10- What has been the role of World Bank in the health care sector in Orissa?

11- Are there conditionalities attached to loans from the Bank?

12- In "Orissa Economic Revival Package", are there any components of health sector reforms?

13- Whether the Bank is able to put pressure on health sector reforms through this package?

14- There are allegations that the World Bank even though contributes a little in terms of money, it influences in the policymaking. In case of Orissa how far do you think it to be true?

15- Interviews with the donor agencies have suggested that the health services structure in the state is not a pyramidal one, which is hampering in implementation of policies in the long run. What are the constraints faced by the state government in making the structure a pyramidal one?

16- The vision document 2010 talks about introduction of public-private initiatives in the state. But the private sector in Orissa is very small and these are concentrated in urban areas. Further the experience of handing over PHCs to NGOs suggests that it has not worked due to lack of experience and resources on behalf of NGOs. Hence is not it a difficult task?

17- It seems that the reforms are heading towards an idea where the health care cost has to be borne by the people? (For example measures like introduction of user charges and contracting out cleaning etc. and plans for encouraging the private sector). In a state where 47percent of the people are living below the poverty line, how is it going to improve the health care situation?

Interview Guide for the Director of Health Services

1- What are the components of health sector reforms being addressed by your department?

2- As Technical Head and expert of General Health care delivery services of the government of Orissa, in your opinion what are the strengths and weaknesses in the health care services structure of Orissa?

3- As Cadre controlling authority of State Cadre non-Gazetted employees and also disciplinary authority, how do you plan to address the shortages of Para-medics in the state?

4- The introduction of district cadre for paramedics, whether it has helped in maintaining the morale of the cadre?

5. As head executive & Inspector of various health related projects operating in the state, which donor agency in your opinion is the major foreign player in the health sector reforms in Orissa?

6- Whether and how do the donor agencies play a role in influencing health policy in Orissa? (Pathways of influence).

7- As budget controlling authority of primary and secondary health care services of the state, is there any evaluation of the quality of services?

8- As you are responsible for portfolio management including financial restructuring and reformation, what are the financial constraints Orissa is facing for achieving universal healthcare?

9- As appellate authority of district cadre employees under health directorate administration, what are the problems of the district cadre employees and what are your constraints in addressing them? How are you going to overcome these constraints?

10- As you hold key position in Central Purchase of Drugs and Consumables, instruments and equipments, after the introduction of new drugs policy has it improved from the earlier situation? If so, how and what are the areas of improvement? What is the proportion of high tech equipment procured during the last five years? (X-ray, ECG, EEG etc.)

11- As you assist government of Orissa in formulation of Budget, what are the constraints you face in formulating the health budget in the state as the state is in a deep fiscal crisis?

12- As a member of various health related committees and societies under sanction of state government, can you elaborate the role of House Committee on health sector reforms? What are the changes those have occurred after the amalgamation of various societies at the district level?

13- Why the health care cadre structure in the state is not pyramidal in nature. What are the constraints you are facing to address these issues?

Interview Guide for the Director of Family Welfare

1-As the principal objective of the Directorate is to stabilize the population and to provide health services including (Immunization) to both pregnant mother and children, it seems that you have been successful in lowering the population growth rate in Orissa significantly and in Immunization also you have done very good job.

However there is an area that remains unexplained which is that the poor opt for more children for economic reasons and by this logic Orissa should have higher population growth rate than India as a whole. Hence in a poor state like Orissa how your population control strategies were different than other states?

2- In immunization Orissa has done really well whereas other states that started simultaneously with Orissa have not done so well. What are the reasons for this?

3- What role the World Bank and other agencies are playing in RCH program in the state?

4- Whether over the years there has been changes in the approach towards maternal and child health care in Orissa? If yes what are those changes?

5- Whether population control, HIV/AIDS and RCH is implemented in an integrated manner in the state?

6- What role do you visualize for the donor agencies for better performance of your department?

Interview Guide for the Director of Medical Education & Training (DMET)

1. As Administrator of three Government Medical Colleges and its attached hospitals what are the challenges you are facing? What are the constraints you are facing in updating the syllabus in medical colleges?

2. There are acute shortages of doctors in the state and the three medical colleges are not producing enough of them. What are your constraints to address this situation and how you are going to tackle them? Could you please tell us the level of unemployment among doctors in the state?

3. What was the idea behind Rural Health Centers and how the RHCs' of Jagatsinghpur/Digapahandi/Attabira are functioning? What are the strengths and weaknesses?

3. As Administrator of Sardar Vallav Bhai Patel Post Graduate Institute of Pediatric, Cuttack and selection of P.G.(Medical), in your opinion how the mandatory pre-PG rural posting has helped in addressing the problem of absence of doctors in remote areas?

4. As you are in charge of Nursing Selection & Training Programme could you tell us as to what are the constraints that you are facing to address the shortages of nurses in the state and how are you going to overcome these challenges?

5. Establishment of private Medical Colleges/Dental Colleges and of private Nursing Schools in the State comes under your office. Till now there is not a single private registered medical college/ nursing school in the state. What are the reasons for it?

6- As Orissa is facing acute shortages in Para-medics in the state, are you planning to establish newer Pharmacy Colleges in the state?

7. Have you received any application for establishment of private Physiotherapy/occupational therapy/speech therapy Colleges in the state?

8. As Registration of Clinical Establishments comes under your office (Nursing Homes, Patho Clinics etc), what are the initiatives you have taken for registration of private practitioners in the state? What are the constraints you have faced in this regard?

9. Medical Referral cases are the responsibility of yours. In tribal districts the traditional practitioners are being involved in referrals. What has been your experience so far in this regard?

10. As you select in-service candidates for training, inside the country and abroad, what are the areas you focus for training?

11- The whole society values success and the more one consume the better status one has. In this situation is it not an injustice to ask the aspirants for a PG degree for mandatory rural posting for one year, where they will face difficulties for providing quality education for their children and maintaining a status in the society?

Interview Guide for the Director of State Institute of Health & Family Welfare (SIHFW), Orissa

1- As the objectives of the institute are to develop the skills of health personnel for demand generation by public and promote voluntary action by people in Health & Family Welfare services, how far the multi-skilling of health personnel has helped in tackling the shortages of manpower?

2-Your Institute takes a comprehensive view of Reproductive and Child Health Programme, could you please elaborate on this?

3-You are also involved in other health programmes by which you want individual's families and community to accept and adopt desirable health behaviors and practices. Please elaborate on this aspect also.

4- What has been the change towards the approach to RCH over the years?

5- Do you have any research reports in this regard?

Interview Guide for the Director of Indian Medicine & Homeopathy in the State of Orissa

1- What role homeopathy and Ayurveda play in health care provisioning in Orissa?

2- What are the constraints you face in regularizing the traditional practitioners in the state?

3- In tribal districts these traditional practitioners are being used for referral services. What has been your experience so far in this regard?

4-What is the attitude of allopathic practitioners towards these traditional practitioners?

5-Your views on AYUSH (Aurveda, Unani and Siddha).

6- Whether the indigenous systems practitioners are being posted in primary health care centers? What are the advantages and disadvantages of this phenomenon?

Interview Guide for the Director of Drugs Control, Government of Orissa

1-How far the essential drugs list of World Health Organization and shifting towards generic drugs from the brand names and centralized procurement of drugs has helped in reducing cost and rational prescription of drugs?

2- What is the situation of availability of drugs after the implementation of these new measures?

3- How far have you been successful in making available to the public, effective and safe drugs in required quantities and in appropriate dosage forms with acceptable quality, at all public/Government Health Care Institutions in the state in time?

4- What are the constraints you have faced in ensuring that banned, misbranded, and adulterated drugs, irrational and sub-therapeutic formulation (both Allopathic and Homoeopathic) are not available in the state and that the labeling, storage and preservation of drugs at appropriate temperature are carried out properly and effectively to preserve the potency of the drugs in all places before consumption by the patient?

5- What was the nature and forms of corruption that existed before the introduction of new drugs policy? What kind of pressures you faced when you restructured the new drugs procurement and delivery system?

6- What are the constraints you have faced in ensuring the availability of quality drugs in the state?

7- Has the system of weir-housing for drugs are in place in the state? If yes, then has it improved the situation in terms of availability of drugs in the state?

8- As you are responsible to ensure availability of essential drugs at a fair price to all patients of the state, what are the constraints you face in this regard and what steps you have taken to address these issues?

9- Another of your role is: grant of manufacturing and sales licenses of narcotic drugs and formulations containing narcotic drugs, allotment and utilisation of narcotic raw materials etc. under the provision of Narcotic Drugs and Psychotropic substances Act, 1985. What are the constraints you have faced in this regard?

10-What is the situation at the government, private clinics and stores functioning under the CDMOs and missionaries hospitals in terms of procurement, storage and distribution of drugs in the state?

ANNEX II

INTERVIEW GUIDE FOR THE DONOR AGENCIES

The background and history of donor's operation in the state in general and health sector in particular. What prompted the agency to move into the health sector? What were the specific areas of intervention and the reasons for choosing those areas? Were these areas for intervention based on an assessment of the health sector? (Was there a report that was available? What was the experience of the donor agency with regard to the state government (Opportunities and Constraints)? What kind of changes these interventions have brought about, say in terms of infrastructure, drugs and governance? The experience with other donors and their role for the next ten years.

ANNEX III

Interview Guide for CDMOs/ADMO (Public Health, Medical and Family Welfare)

1- What are the *strengths and weaknesses* in the *health care delivery structure* in the district?

2- Are you aware of HSR? Did you participate in the consultative process of HSR?

2- In district hospitals *user charges* has been introduced. What are the services for which user charges have been introduced? What is the proportion of those below poverty line and other income groups in the district? How this scheme has performed so far? What are the mechanisms for identifying BPL population? What has been the perception of people who are paying user charges? Whether the income from user charges has been able to sustain the recurrent expenditures of these institutions?

3- For *petty maintenance of buildings and equipments* funds has been allocated to the MOs in the PHCs/CHCs. How this scheme has performed in your district?

4- *New Drugs Policy:* At present Orissa has an essential drugs list prescribed by WHO. Also generic drugs are being used rather than branded drugs and central purchasing of drugs is being done. What is the scenario in the district in terms of availability of essential drugs? What is the difference the new drugs policy has created compared to the earlier policy? Whether you views were taken before introduction of this drugs policy?

5- Whether the *district cadre for paramedics* has been introduced in this district? If yes, then how far the scheme has been successful in boosting the morale of the paramedics? And whether under the scheme you can recruit the required number of paramedics for your district?

6- There are *shortages of doctors and paramedics* in the district. What are your constraints to address this situation?

7- Whether the *mandatory pre PG rural scheme* is applicable to the district? If yes, how far it has performed in addressing the availability of doctors in remote areas?

8- Whether any *PHCs were handed over to NGOs* in this district? If yes, what has been your experience till now?

9- How is the *Zilla Swasthya Samiti* functioning in the district? Has the situation improved with creation of this body?

10- What is the *role of World Bank in the RCH* program of this district?

11- Whether *population control, HIV/AIDS and RCH* is implemented in an *integrated manner* in the district? If yes, do you see any difference in terms of results at the ground level?

12- Whether there has been *changes* over the years *in the approach* towards *maternal and child health care* in the district? If yes, what are those changes?

13- Whether *traditional practitioners at the primary level care* are being involved in the *referrals* in your district? If yes, what are the terms for involvement of traditional practitioners? What are the inputs from government in terms of training etc.? For what diseases/ conditions are they expected to do referrals? And where do they refer?

14- What is multiskilling and at what level is it happening? Does multiskilling result in downsizing staff? How does it address the shortage of human resourses?

15- Medical Internship training introduced in 2000. Under the Internship training, the interns are sent in groups of two and three to community health centers under the control of the CDMOs. They are exposed to real community health situations and get 'hands on' training. They are supervised both by the medical officers in charge of the institutions as well as the medical college teachers.

Whether these trainings produce better trained doctors than the earlier scheme? And has it led to better attendance of doctors in rural health institutions, as it was the intension of this training?

16-Pancha Byadhi Chikitsa (Five Diseases Treatment) Scheme introduced in 1999, reintroduced in 2001.Objective: To ensure that every patient who goes to a public hospital is guaranteed treatment at government cost for diseases such as malaria, leprosy, diarrhoea, acute respiratory infection, and scabies.

How this scheme has performed in the district?

17- Before introducing the above mentioned changes whether your views were taken into consideration?

Interview Guide for Medical Officers at the CHC/PHC level

1- For *petty maintenance of buildings and equipments* funds has been allocated to the MOs in the PHCs/CHCs. How this scheme has performed in your PHC/CHC?

2- Under the new drugs policy whether the essential drugs are available in your institution?

3- Whether this PHC/CHC has adequate staff in terms of MOs and paramedics? In case of shortage in the staff what are the challenges that you face in your day to day functioning?

4- What is your opinion on mandatory pre- PG rural scheme in Orissa?

5- There are talks about handing over PHCs to NGOs. What do you think about this?

6- There is an idea that the multiskilling of health personnel would help in overcoming the shortages of paramedics in the state. What is your opinion on this?

7- For increasing the referrals, the traditional practitioners are being involved in tribal districts? Do you think that this will increase the referrals? Will it not legitimize the quacks in the state?
8- The earlier existing different societies at the district level have been amalgamated to create one society. Has it improved the situation?

9- Do you think that over the years there has been change in the approach towards maternal and child health care in this district? If yes, what are those changes?

10- What are your strategies for Population control, HIV/AIDS and RCH?

11- For Internship Training, two to three medical interns are sent to CHCs under the supervision of CDMOs. Do you think that this has helped in better training of doctors and whether it motivates the interns to work in the rural areas after training?

12- The objective of the Pancha Byadhi Chikitsa scheme has been to ensure that every patient who goes to a public hospital is guaranteed treatment at government cost for diseases such as malaria, leprosy, diarrhoea, acute respiratory infection, and scabies. How do you evaluate this scheme?

13- What is your opinion about introduction of user charges in district hospitals and medical colleges in the state?

14- In your opinion what are the strengths and weaknesses in the health services structure in the state? What measures you would suggest for their amelioration?

15- There are problems of communication, infrastructure, and lack of better schools in remote areas of Orissa. And the government expects you to perform in those conditions. Don't you think that this is an injustice to those in service and the aspiring doctors in the state?

16- Don't you think that the syllabus in the medical colleges are not updated from time to time and hence is not equipping doctors to face the challenges in the field?

17- Any other matter you would like to mention.

ANNEX IV

INTERVIEW GUIDE FOR PROJECT DIRECTOR OHSDP (ORISSA HEALTH SYSTEMS DEVELOPMENT PROJECT)

1- Whether the OHSDP is being implemented separately or within the structures of the health services in Orissa?

2- What were the compulsions and motivations for the state to approach the World Bank for implementing this project?

3- What was the basis for opting for this project?

4-How the components of this project were prioritized and decided? Was there consultation with the state government and whether the state government had consulted with the CDMOs, MOs; and Health Officers etc.? Describe the process of consultations and different actors who all were involved.

5- The World Bank is implementing the Orissa Economic Revival Package. Whether funds for OHSDP are subject to fulfilling the conditionalities in the Economic Revival Package?

6- What are the elements of OHSDP?

7- OHSDP aims to strengthen the planning, management and implementation capacity at the state, district and lower levels. How this is being implemented and in which parts of Orissa? What has been your experience so far in this regard?

8- It also aims to strengthen the Health Management Information System and the capacity for surveillance of major communicable diseases. Which part of Orissa it has been implemented and how it has been implemented and what is your experience so far in this regard?

9- This project intends to improve service quality, access and effectiveness by:
a. Upgrading area, sub-divisional, district hospitals.
b. By upgrading clinical, managerial and support services at the facility level (CHC/PHC level. How far this component has been implemented and in which part of Orissa and your experience in this regard.

10-Is there any valuations across districts in the state and specifically in the districts of Sundergarh and Khurda?

11- Another aim is to improve access to basic health services at the community level through:
a. selective upgrading of community health centers.
b. Promoting health services in tribal areas and for disadvantaged groups.
c. Improving referral mechanisms and strengthening linkages between the different tiers of the health care system.

Which components of the above mentioned has been implemented and your experience in this regard.

12- What about the sustainability of the reform measures initiated in this project in terms of financing, infrastructure, equipments and drugs?

BIBLIOGRAPHY

Books

Aschengrau Ann and George R Seage III. 2003. *Essentials of Epidemiology in Public Health.* Jones and Bartlett Publishers.

Banerji D. 1985. *Health and Family Planning Services in India: An Epidemiological, Socio-cultural, and Political Analysis and a Perspective.* Lok Prakash: New Delhi.

—. 1982. *Poverty, Class and Health Culture in India.* Vol. 1. Prachi Prakashan: New Delhi.

Baru R. V. 1998. *Private Health Care in India: Social Characteristics and Trends.* Sage Publications: New Delhi.

Becker Howard and Harry Elmer Barnes. 1961. *Social Thought from Lore to Science.* Dover Publications Inc: New York.

Becker Saul and Alan Bryman ed. 2004. *Understanding Research for Social Policy and Practice.* SPA: Policy Press.

Bennett S. Mcpake. Bijaud Mills A. ed. 1997. *Private Health Providers in Developing Countries.* Zed Books: London.

Berman Peter ed. 1995. *Health Sector Reform in Developing Countries: Making Health Development Sustainable.* Harvard University Press: Cambridge MA.

Blau Peter and Marshall Meyer. 1987. *Bureaucracy in Modern Society.* 3rd edition. New York: Random House.

Bossert T. 1994. *Chilean Health Care Social Insurance Innovations.* Latin American and Caribbean Health and Nutrition Sustainability. Washington, D.C.

Bourdieu Pierre. 2004. *Science of Science and reflexivity.* Translated by Richard Nice. Polity Press: Cambridge.

Breman V J and Akitoshi Shimizu. ed. 2000. *Anthropology and Colonialism in Asia and Oceania.* Curzon Press.

Bryman Alan. 1988. *Quantity and Quality in Social Research.* Unwin Hyman: London.

Castro Arachu and Merrill Singer. 2004. *Unhealthy Health Policy: A Critical Anthropological Examination.* Alta Mira Press: A Division of Rowman and Littlefield Publishers Inc.

Chaturvedi Abha and Anil Chaturvedi ed. 1995. *The Sociology of Formal Organizations*. Oxford University Press.

Cleaves P S. 1987. *Professions and the State: The Mexican Case*. University of Arizona Press: Tucson.

Cohen Stephen F. 2000. *Failed Crusade: America and the Tragedy of Post-Communist Russia*. W. W. Norton: New York.

Cooper H M and A J Culyer ed. 1973. *Health Economics*. Penguin Books.

Coote A and Hunter D J. 1996. *New Agenda for Health*. Institute for Public Policy Research: London.

Curtis Sarah and Ann Taket. 1996. *Health and Societies: Changing perspectives*. Arnold and Halsted Press.

Dahl Roberts A, 1972. *Who Governs? Democracy and Power in an American City*. New Haven: Yale University Press.

Das Veena ed. 2004. *Handbook of Indian Sociology*. Oxford University Press.

Das Veena. 1999. *Critical Events: An Anthropological Perspective on Contemporary India*. Oxford University Press.

Dent Mike and Stephen Whitehead ed. 2002. *Managing Professional Identities: Knowledge, Performativity and the 'New' Professional*. Routledge. London and New York.

Donabedian A. 1980. *The Definition of Quality and Approaches to Its Assessment*. Ann Arbour, Health Administration Press.

Dreze J and Sen A. 1989. *Hunger and Public Action*. Oxford University Press. Oxford.

Duckett S J. 2000. *The Australian Health Care System*. Oxford University Press: Victoria. Australia.

Enthoven Alain. 1985b. *Theory and Practice of Managed Competition in Health care Finance*. North-Holland: Amstardam.

Esping-Andersen G. 1985. *Politics against Markets*. Princeton. NJ: Princeton University Press.

—. 1990. *The Three World's of Welfare Capitalism*. Princeton. NJ: Princeton University Press.

Ferlie E. Pettigrew A. Ashburner L and Fitzgerald L. 1996. *The New Public Management in Action*. Oxford University Press. Oxford.

Field Mark G ed. 1989. *Success and Crisis in National Health Systems: A Comparative approach*. Routledge. London.

Foucault Michael. 2003. *The Birth of the Clinic*. Routledge. London and New York.

—. 1991. *Discipline and Punish: The Birth of the Prison*. Translated from the French by Alan Sheridan. Penguin Books.

—. 1980. *Power/Knowledge: Selected Interviews and Other writings 1972-1977*. Harvester Wheat Sheaf.

—. 1985. *The History of Sexuality: The Use of Pleasure*. Volume 2. Translated from the French by Robert Hurley. Penguin Books.

Frenk J. Gomez-Dantes O. Cruz C. Freeman P. 1994. *The North American Free Trade Agreement and Medical Services*. 2nd ed. Mexico City: National Academy of Medicine.

From Eric. 1970. *The Crisis of Psychoanalysis*. Jonathan Cape. Thirty Bedford Square. London.

Gardner H. ed. 1997. *Health Policy in Australia*. Oxford University Press. Melbourne.

—. ed. 1995. *The Politics of Health: The Australian Experience*. 2nd edition. Longman Australia. Churchill Livingstone. Melbourne.

Garrett Laurie. 2000. *Betrayal of Trust: The Collapse of Global Public Health*. Hyperion. New York.

Good J Byron. 1994. *Medicine, Rationality and Experience: An Anthropological Perspective*. Cambridge University Press.

Goode William J and Paul K Hatt. 1981. *Methods in Social Research*. McGraw-Hill Book Company.

Gough I. 1979 *The Political Economy of the Welfare State*. Macmillan. London.

Graham Hilary. ed. 2001. *Understanding Health Inequalities*. Open University Press. Philadelphia.

Gray Bradford. 1991. *The Profit Motive and Patient Care: The Changing Accountability of Doctors and Hospitals*. Harvard University Press. Cambridge.

Grindle M.S. and Thomas J. W. 1991. *Public Choices and Policy Change: The Political Economy of Reform in Developing Countries*. Johns Hopkins University Press. Baltimore.

Habermas Jurgen. 1971. *Toward a Rational Society: Student Protests, Science and Politics*. Translated by Jeremy J Shapiro. Heinemann. London.

Hadenius Stig. 1998. *Swedish Politics during the 20th Century*. 2nd edition. Stockholm: Swedish Institute.

Hammersley Martyn and Paul Atkinson. 1983. *Ethnography: Principles in Practice*. Tavistock Publications. London.

Harris Marvin. 1999. *Theories of Culture in Postmodern Times*. Altamira Press. A Division of Sage Publications Inc.

Harrison Mark. 1994. *Public Health in British India: Anglo-Indian Preventive Medicine- 1859-1914*. Cambridge University Press.

Hurrelmann Klaus and Ulrich Laaser. ed. 1996. *International Handbook of Public Health*. Greenwood Press. London.

Jones Linda J. 1994. *Social Context of Health and Health Work.* The Macmillan Press Ltd.

Khilnani Sunil. 1999. *The Idea of India.* Penguin Books.

Kishore J. 2002. *A Dictionary of Public Health.* Century Publications. New Delhi.

Koop Everett C. Clarence E Pearson and M Roy Schwarz. ed. 2001. *Critical Issues in Global Health*. Jossy-Bass. A Wiley Company.

Korpi Walter. 1978. *The Working Class in Welfare Capitalism: Work, Unions and Politics in Sweden*. Routledge. London.

Kuhn Thomas. 1962. *The Structure of Scientific Revolution*. Chicago University Press.

Leys Colin. 1996. *The Rise and Fall of Development Theory.* Indiana University Press. James Currey. Oxford.

Mac Mahon Brian and Dimitrios Trichopoulos. ed. 1996. *Epidemiology: Principles and Methods*. Second Edition. Little Brown and Company.

Matcha Duane A. 2001. *Readings in Medical Sociology*. Allyn and Bacon.

McCarthy T. 1984. *Critical Theory of Jurgen Habermas.* Polity Press.

Merton R K. 1968. *Social Theory and Social Structure.* Amerind Publishing Company.

Miringoff Marc. Marque-Luisa Miringoff and Sandra Opdycke. 1999. *The Social Health of the Nation: How America is Really Doing*. Oxford University Press. New York.

Mishra B D. Ali Ashraf. Ruth S Simmons and Geroge B Simmons. 1982. *A Systems Analysis of Family Planning in Rural India*. Family Planning Foundation. Radiant Publishers.

Neale Arthur Frederic. 1997. *Narrative of a Residence in Siam.* White Lotus Press.

Neutens James J and Laurna Rubinson. 1997. *Research Techniques for the Health Sciences*. Second Edition. Allyn and Bacon.

Nichter Mark and Mimi Nichter. 1996. *Anthropology and International Health: Asian Case Studies*. Gordon and Breach Publishers.

Oxford Dictionary Thesaurus. 2003. Indian Edition. Oxford University Press Inc. New York.

Petersen Alan and Deborah Lupton. 1996. *The New Public Health: Health and Self in the age of Risk.* Sage Publications.

Phadke A. 1998. *Drug Supply and Use: Towards a Rational Policy in India*. Sage Publications.

Popper K R. 1992. *The Logic of Scientific Discovery.* Routledge. London.

Qadeer Imrana. Kasturi Sen and K R Nayar. ed. 2001. *Public Health and Poverty of Reforms: The South Asian Predicament*. Sage Publications.

Roberts Marc J. William Hsiao. Peter Berman and Reich M R. 2004. *Getting Health Reforms Right: A Guide to Improving Performance and Equity*. Oxford University Press. USA.

Rosen G. 1988. *History of Public Health*. MD Publications. New York.

Sainath P. 1996. *Everybody Loves a Good drought*. Penguin Books. New Delhi.

Sambler Graham. ed. 2001. *Habermas, Critical Theory and Health*. Routledge. London.

Samson Colin. ed. 1999. *Health Studies: A Critical and Cross Cultural Reader*. Blackwell Publishers.

Scamblem Graham and Paul Higgs. 1998. *Modernity, Medicine and Health*. Routledge. London.

Sen A. 1999. *Development as Freedom*. Oxford University Press. New York.

—. 1997. *On Economic Inequality*. 2nd ed. Clarendon Press. Oxford.

—. 1991. *The Political Economy of Hunger*. Oxford University Press. New York.

Shah G. 1997. *Public Health and Urban Development*. New Delhi: Sage Publications.

Silverman William A. 1998. *Where is the Evidence: Debates in Modern Medicine*. Oxford University Press.

Steuerman Emilia. 2000. *The Bounds of reason: Habermas, Lyotard and Melanie Klein on Rationality*. Routledge. London.

Strauss-Levi Claude. 1968. *Structural Anthropology*. Penguin Press. Allen Lane.

Stroup Donna F and Steven M Teutsch. ed. 1998. *Statistics in Public Health: Quantitative Approaches to Public Health Problems*. Oxford University Press.

Suchman Edward A. 1963. *Sociology and the Field of Public Health*. Russell Sage Foundation. New York.

Symonds Anthea and Anne Kelly. ed. 1998. *Social Construction of Community Care*. MacMillan.

Teutsch Steven M and R Elliott Churchill. 2000. *Principles and Practices of Public Health Surveillance*. 2nd edition. Oxford University Press.

Turnock Bernard J. 2001. *Public Health: What it is and How it Works*. Aspen Publishers Inc. Gaithersburg MD.

Twaddle Andrew C. 1999. *Health care reform in Sweden 1980-1994*. Westport CT. Auburn House.

Twaddle Andrew C. ed. 2002. *Health Care Reform Around The World.* Auburn House. London.

Van Jan Bremen and Akitoshi Shimizu. ed. 2000. *Anthropology and Colonialism in Asia and Oceania.* Curzon Press. London.

Weber Max. 1978. *Economy and Society.* Vol I. University of California Press.

—. 1947. *The Theory of Social and Economic Organization.* Free Press. Glencoe IL.

Weiss Gregory L and Lynne E Lonnquist. 1997. *The Sociology of Health Healing and Illness.* 2nd edition. Prentice-Hall. Inc.

Young Kue T. 1998. *Population Health: Concepts and Methods.*Oxford University Press.

Zurbrigg Sheila. 1984. *Rakku's Story: Structures of Ill-Health and the Source of Change.* Sidma Offset Press P. Ltd.

Articles

Abel-Smith B and Dua A. 1988. Community Financing in Developing Countries: The Potential for the Health sector. *Health Policy and Planning*, 3: 95-108.

Abel-Smith B and Rawal P. 1992. Can the Poor Afford "free" Health Care: A Case Study of Tanzania. *Health Policy and Planning*, 7: 329-41.

Ackerman D. 1994. Economic and Medical Directions in the Czech Republic and Hungary. *American Journal of Surgery*. 167: 246-49.

Acuna C. 1994. Politics and Economics in the Argentina of the Nineties. In W Smith. C Acuna. and E Gamarra eds. *Democracy, Markets, and Structural Reform in Contemporary Latin America.* NJ: Transaction. New Brunswick.

Albert A. Bennett C and Bojar M. 1992. Health Care in the Czech Republic. *Journal of the American Medical Association*. 267: 2461-66.

Allen I.1997. Committed but Critical: An Examination of Young Doctor's Views of Their Core Values. *British Medical Association.* London.

Anderson G F and J P Poullier. 1999. Health Care Spending, Access and Outcome: Trends in Industrialized Countries. *Health Affairs*, 18: 178-92.

Angus Douglas E. 1992. A Great Canadian Prescription: Take Two Commissioned Studies and Call Me in the Morning. In Raisa B. Deber and Gail G. Thomption ed. *Restructuring Canada's Health Services System: How Do We Get There From Here?* p-49-62. University of Toronto Press. Toronto.

Anson Ofra. 2002. Rural Health Care Reforms in The People's republic of China. In Twaddle C Andrew ed. *Health Care Reform Around The World*. Auburn House. London.

Antia, N. H. 1993. World Bank and India's Health. *Economic and Political Weekly*, 25th December.

Arenas Luis Duran. Cervantes Malaquias Lopez. Dantes Gomez Octavio and Rubi Sandra Sosa. 2002. The Unbearable Homogeneity of Reform: The Mexican Health Care System Reform. In Twaddle C Andrew ed. *Health Care Reform Around The World*. Auburn House. London.

Aston Toni. 1998. Contracting for Services in New Zealand: A Transaction Cost Analysis. *Social Science and Medicine*. 46: 357-67.

Avah I. 1995. Primary Health Care Reform in Slovenia: First Results. *Social Science and Medicine*. 41: 141-4.

Baer Nicole. 1997. Despite Some PR Fallout, Proponents Say MD Walkouts Increase Awareness and May Improve Healthcare. *Canadian Association Medical Journal*. 157 (9): 1268-71.

Banerji Debabar. 1993. Simplistic Approach to Health Policy Analysis: World Bank Team on Indian Health Sector. *Economic and Political Weekly*. 12 June.

—. 1992. Health Policies and Programmes in India in the Eighties. *Economic and Political Weekly*. 21st March. 1992.

Baru R. V. 2002. Health-Sector Reform: The Indian Experience. In Twaddle C Andrew ed. Health Care Reform Around The World. Auburn House. London.

Baru R. V. and Sadhana G. 2000. Resurgence of Communicable Diseases: Gastroenteritis Epidemics in Andhra Pradesh. *Economic and Political Weekly*. 35 (40) 3554-3556.

Baru R. V. Nayar K. R. and Gopal M. 1996. Patterns of Funding by Bilateral and Multilateral Agencies in Health. *Paper Submitted to the Voluntary Health Association of India*. New Delhi.

Baru R. V. 2001. Health Sector Reforms and Structural Adjustment: A State Level Analysis. In Qadeer Imrana, Kasturi Sen and K R Nayar ed. *Public Health and The Poverty of Reforms: The South Asian Predicament*. Sage Publications. New Delhi.

—. 1994. Structure and Utilisation of Health Services: An Interstate Analysis. *Social Scientist*. Vol. 22: 9-12.

—. May 2000. Privatisation and Corporatisation of Health Care. *Seminar*.

Belmartino Susana. 2002. Health Care Reform in Argentina. In Twaddle C Andrew ed. *Health Care Reform Around The World*. Auburn House. London.

Berman A. Peter. 1995. Health Sector Reform: Making Health Development Sustainable. In Berman Peter ed. *Health Sector Reform in Developing Countries*. Harvard University Press.

Berman P. Gwatkin D. Burger S. 1987. Community based Health Workers: Head Start or False Start Towards Health For All? *Social Science and Medicine.* 25 (5) 443-459.

Beteille Andre. 2004. Sociology: Concepts and Institutions. In Veena Das ed. *Handbook of Indian Sociology.* Oxford University Press.

Bhat R. The Private/Public Mix in Health Care in India. 1993. *Health Policy and Planning*. 8 (1) 43-56.

Blades C. A. Culyer A. J. and Walker A. 1987. Health Service Efficiency: Appraising the Appraisers- A Critical Review of Economic Appraisal in Practice. *Social Science and Medicine.* Vol. 44.

Blendon Robert J. 1975. The Changing Role of Private Philanthropy in Health Affairs. *New England Journal of Medicine.* 292: 946- 50.

Bloom Gerald and Xinngyuan gu. 1997. Health Sector Reform: Lessons From China. *Social Science and Medicine.* Vol. 45. No.3. p-351-60.

Bloom Gerald and Gu Xingyuan. 1997. Health Sector Reforms: Lessons From China. *Social Science and Medicine*. 45: 351-60.

Bodenheimer T and Grumbach K. 1994. A Clinical Approach: Paying for Health care. *Journal of the American Medical Association.* 272: 634-639.

Bogg Lennart. Hengjen Dong. et. al.1996. The Cost Of Coverage- Rural Health Insurance in China. *Health Policy and Planning.* 11(3). p-238-52.

Broomberg J. 1994. Managing the Health Care Market in Developing Countries: Prospects and Problems. *Health Policy and Planning.* 9: 237-251.

Burger Edward J. Mark G Field and Judyth L Twigg. 1998. From Assurance to Insurance in Russian Health care: The Problematic Transition. *American Journal of Public Health.* 88 (5): 755-58.

Canadian Medical Association. 1997a. Financial and Geographic Barriers to Fee-For-Service-Practice. *Canadian Medical Association Journal.* 156:616.

—. 1997b. Physicians Moving Abroad. *Canadian Medical Association Journal.* 156: 744.

—. 1998. Qubec Latest to Face Obstetricians' *Anger. Canadian Medical Association Journal*. 158-160.

Cassels A. 1996. Aid Instruments and Health Systems Development: An Analysis of Current Practice. *Health Policy and Planning.* 11:4: 354-68.

—. 1995. Health Sector reform: Key Issues in Less Developed Countries. *Journal of International Development*. 7:3: 329-347.

Chelimsky E. 1991. On the Social Science Contribution to Governmental Decision-Making. *Science*. 254: 226-231.

Chen X M. Hu T W and Lin Z. 1993. The Rise and Fall of the Cooperative Medical System in Rural China. *International Journal of Health Services*. 23: 4: 731-42.

Chernichovsky Dov and Chinitz David. 1995. The Political Economy of Health System reform in Israel. *Health Economics*. 4: 127-41.

Chinitz D. 1995. Israel's Health Policy Breakthrough: The Politics of Reform and the Reform of Politics. *Journal of Health Politics Policy and Law*. 20:909-32.

Chinitz David. 1996. Israel's Health Policy Breakthrough: The Politics of Reform and reform of Politics. *Journal of Health Politics Policy and Law*. 20: 909-32.

—. 1994. Reforming the Israeli Health care Market. *Social Science and Medicine*. 39:10: 1447-57.

Collins C and Green A. 1994. Decentralization and Primary Health Care: Some Negative Implications for Developing Countries. *International Journal of Health Services*. 24 459-475.

Collins C. Green A and Hunter D. Health Sector Reform and Interpretation of Policy Context. *Health Policy*. 47: 69-83.

Creese A. 1991. User Charges for Health Care: A Review of recent Experience. *Health Policy and Planning*. 6: 309-319.

Crogan M. Colleen. 1995. Urban Economic Reform and Access to Health Care Coverage in the People's Republic of China. *Social Science and Medicine*. Vol.41.

David J Hunter. 2002. Health Systems Reforms: The United Kingdom's Experience. In Twaddle C Andrew ed. *Health Care Reform Around The World*. Auburn House. London.

Deppe H and Oreskovic S. 1996. Back to Europe: Back to Bismarck? *International Journal of Health Services*. 6: 4: 777-803.

Dev S. Mahendra. 19th August 1995. Economic Reforms and Rural Poor. *Economic and Political Weekly*.

Diderichsen Finn. 1995. Market Reforms in Health Care and Sustainability of the Welfare State- Lessons from Sweden. In Berman Peter ed. *Health Sector Reform in Developing Countries*. Harvard University Press.

Dobson F. 1999. Modernizing Britain's National Health Service. *Health Affairs*. 18: 3: 40-41.

Dong H. Bogg L. Rehnberg C and Diwan V. 1999. Drug Policy in China: Pharmaceutical Distribution in Rural Areas. *Social Science and Medicine*. 48: 777-86.

Dorozynski A. 1996. Shock Treatment for French Health Insurance System. *British Medical Journal*. 313: 840.

Duckett S J. 1984. Structural Interests and Australian Health Policy. *Social Science and Medicine*. 18: 959-966.

Duggal Ravi. Sunil Nandraj and Asha Vadair. 12th June 1993. Health Expenditures Across States, Special Statistics. Part 1. *Economic and Political Weekly*. 15th April 1995. Part II. Regional Disparities in Expenditure. *Economic and Political Weekly*.

Ellis R P. 1987. The Revenue Generating Potential of User Fees in Kenyan Government Health facilities. *Social Science and Medicine*. 25: 995-1002.

Ellman Michael. 1994. The Increase in Death and Disease under 'Katastroika'. *Cambridge Journal of Economics*. 18: 329-55.

Enthoven A. C. 2000. In Pursuit of an Improving National Health service. *Health affairs*. 19: 102-17.

Farmer Paul. 1999a. Pathologies of Power: Rethinking Health and Human Rights. *American Journal of Public Health*. 89:10: 1486-96.

Fiedler J L. 1993. Increasing Reliance on User Fees as a Response to Public Health Financial Crises: A Case Study of El Salvador. *Social Science and Medicine*. 36: 6: 735-47.

—. 1996. The Privatisation of Health Care in Three Latin American Social Security Systems. *Health Policy and Planning*. 11: 4: 406-17.

Field Mark G. 2002. The Inelasticity of Institutional Patterns: An Impediment to Health Care Reform in Post-Communist Russia. In Twaddle C Andrew ed. *Health Care Reform Around The World*. Auburn House. London.

Field Mark. 1995. The Health Crisis in the Former Soviet Union: A Report from the 'Post-War' Zone. *Social Science and Medicine*. 41: 11: 1469-78.

Fooks Catherine. 1999. Will Power, Cost Control, and Health Reform in Canada 1897-92. p-151-72. In F D Powell and A F Wessen ed. *Health Care Systems in Transition: An International Perspective*. Thousand Oaks. CA. Sage.

Frenk J. 1992. Balancing Relevance and Excellence: Organizational Responses to Link Research with Decision-Making. *Social Science and Medicine*. 35:11:1397-1404.

Friedman Milton. 2001. How to Cure Health care. *Public Interest*. No. 142, Winter, p-3-30.

Ghosh Arun. 23rd July. Ideologues and Ideology: Privatisation of Public Enterprises. *Economic and Political Weekly*.

Gidadhubli R. G. and Kumar Sampat Rama. 12th June 1993. Privatisation in East Europe, *Economic and Political Weekly*.

Gill Sucha Singh. 6th January 1996. Punjab: Privatizing Health Care. *Economic and Political Weekly*.

Gilson Lucy and Mills Anne. 1995. Health Sector Reforms in sub-Saharan Africa: Lessons of the Last 10 Years. In Peter Berman ed. *Health Sector Reform Developing Countries*. Harvard University Press.

Ginzberg Eli. 1991. Philanthropy and Non Profit Organizations in U.S. Health Care: A Personal Retrospective. *Inquiry*. 28: 179-86.

Godbeng C and S Kishovsky. 16th December 2000. Russia's Doctors are Beggars at Work, Paupers at Home. *New York Times*.

Griffin C. 1992. Welfare Gains from User Charges for Government Health Services. *Health Policy and Planning*. 7:177-180.

Gross Revital and Ofra Anson. 2002. Health Care Reform in Israel. In Twaddle C Andrew ed. *Health Care Reform Around The World*. Auburn House. London.

Gross Revital and Harrison Michael. 2001. Implementing Managed Competition in Israel. *Social Science and Medicine*. 52 (8): 1219-31.

Gross Revital. Rosen Bruce and Chinitz David. 1998. Evaluating the Israeli Health Care Reform: Strategies, Challenges and Lessons. *Health Policy*. 45: 99-117.

Gu, X. Y. et al. 1993. Financing Health Care in Rural China: Preliminary Report of a Nation-Wide Survey. *Social Science and Medicine*. 36 (4), 385-391.

Gupta S. P. 3rd June 1995. Economic reform and its impact on poor. *Economic and Political Weekly*.

Haber Manfred. 1999. Health Expenditure Trends in OECD Countries 1970-1997. *Health Care Financing Review*. 21 (2): 99-118.

Ham C. Hunter D J and Robinson R. 1995. Evidence Based Policymaking. *British Medical Journal*. 310: 71-72.

Harris M G and Harris R D. 1998. The Australian Health System: Continuity and Change. *Journal of Health and Human Services Administration*. Spring. 442-67.

Hayo B. 1997. Eastern European Public Opinion on Economic Issues: Privatisation and Transformation. *American Journal of Economics and Sociology*. 56: 85-102.

Healy Judith and Martin McKee. 1997. Health Sector reform in Central and Eastern Europe: The Professional Dimension. *Health Policy and Planning*.12:4. p-286-295.

Hebrang A. 1994. Reorganization of the Croatian Health care System. *Croatian Medical Journal*. 35: 130-36.

Hellander I. D Himmelstein and S Woolhandler et.al. 1994. Health Care Paper Chase, 1993: The Cost to the Nation, The States, and the Districts of Columbia. *International Journal of Health Services*. 24 (1): 1-9.

Henderson G. Jin S. Akin J. Li X. Wong J. Ma H. He Y. Zhang X. Chang Y and Ge K. 1995. Distribution of Medical Insurance in China. *Social Science and Medicine*. 41:10: 1119-30.

Hesketh T and Zhu W X. 1997. Health in China: From Mao to Market Reform. *British Medical Journal*. 314: 1543-1545.

Himmelstein D U. Lewontin J and Woolhandler S. 1996. Who Administers? Who Cares? Medical Administrative and Clinical Employment in the United States and Canada, *American Journal of Public Health*. 86: 172-78.

Ho Lok Sang. 1995. Market Reforms and China's Health Care System. *Social Science and Medicine*. Vol.41. No-8. p-1065-72.

Hsiao W. 1994. Marketisation: The Illusory Magic Pill. *Health Economics*. Vol. 3: 351-357.

Hsiao William. 1995. The Chinese Health Care System: Lessons For Other Nations. *Social Science and Medicine*. Vol. 41. No 8.

Huang S M. 1988. Transforming China's Collective Health Care System: A Village Study. *Social Science and Medicine*. 27:9: 879-88.

Huber J. 1993. Ensuring Access to Health Care with Introduction of User Fees: A Kenyan Example. *Social Science and Medicine*. 36:485-94.

Hunter D J. 1992. Doctors as Managers: Gamekeepers Turned Poachers? *Social Science and Medicine*. 35: 557-66.

—. 2002. Health System Reforms: The United Kingdom's Experience, in Health Care Reform Around the World. In Twaddle C Andrew ed. *Health Care Reform Around The World*. Auburn House. London.

—. 1998. Medicine. In M. Laffin ed. *Beyond Bureaucracy? The Professions in the Contemporary Public Sector*. Ashgate. Aldershot.

—. 1996. The Changing Roles of Health Care Personnel in Health and Health Care Management. *Social Science and Medicine*. 43: 799-808.

Hurley. Jeremiah. Lomas. Jonathan and Bhatia. 1996. When Tinkering Is Not Enough: Provincial Reform to Manage Health Care Resources. *Canadian Public Administration*. 37: 490-514.

James O and Manning N. 1996. The Public Management Reform: A Global Perspective. *Politics*. 16: 3: 143-49.

Jara Jorge Jimenez de la and Bossert J. Thomas. 1995. Chile's Health Sector Reforms: Lessons from Four Reform Periods. In Peter Berman ed. *Health Sector Reform in Developing Countries*. Harvard University Press.

Jayal N. 1999. The Gentle Leviathan: Welfare and The Indian State. In M Rao ed. *Disinvesting in Health: The World Bank's Prescription for Health*. Sage Publications, New Delhi.

Kalman I. Massaro T and Nemec J. 1994. Health System Reform in the Czech Republic: Policy Lessons from the Initial Experience of the general Health Insurance Company Caring for the Uninsured and the Underinsured. *Journal of the American Medical Association*. 271: 1870-74.

Kan X. 1990. Village Health Worker in China: Reappraising the Current Situation. *Health Policy and Planning*. 5:1: 40-48.

Karcher H. 1996. German Health Insurance System faces New Deficits. *British Medical Journal*. 312: 74-75.

Kent Heather. 1998. Reduced Activity Days A Way of Life in BC. *Canadian Medical Association Journal*.159:913.

Klein R. 1998. Why Britain Is Reorganizing Its National Health Service-Yet Again. *Health Affairs*. 17: 4:111-25.

Kobayashi Y and M R Reich. 1993. Health Care Financing for the Elderly in Japan. *Social Science and Medicine*. 37: 3: 343-53.

Korte R. Richter H. Merkel F. Gorgen H. 1992. Financing Health Services in sub-Saharan Africa: Options for Decision Makers during Adjustment. *Social Science and Medicine*. 34: 1-9.

Krishnan T. N. 1999. Access to Health and Burden of Treatment in India: An Interstate Comparison. In M Rao ed. *Disinvesting in Health: The World Bank's Prescription for Health*. Sage Publications, New Delhi.

Lawson J S and Lin V. 1994. Health Status Differentials in the People's Republic of China. *American Journal of Public Health*. 84 (5): 737-41.

Le Grand J. 1999. Competition, Cooperation, or Control? Tales from the British National Health Service. *Health affairs*, 18: 3: 27-39.

Lennart B. Dong H. Wang K. Cai W and Vidon D. 1996. The Costs of Coverage: Rural Health Insurance in China. *Health Policy and Planning*. 11 (3):238-52.

Light Donald. 1995b. Equity and Efficiency in Medical Care. *Social Science and Medicine*. 35: 4: 465-70.

Litvack J and Bodart C. 1993. User fees Plus Quality Equals Improved access to Health Care: Results of a Field Experiment in Cameroon. *Social Science and Medicine*. 37: 369-383.

Liu Y. Hsiao W C and Eggleston K. 1999. Equity in Health and Health Care: The Chinese Experience. *Social Science and Medicine*. 49: 1349-56.

Liu Yuanli. et. al. 1996. Is Community Financing Necessary and Feasible for Rural China? *Health Policy*. 88.

Liu Yuanli. et. al. 1995. Transformation of China's Rural Health Care Financing. *Social Science and Medicine*. Vol. 41.

Lomas Jonathan. 1997. Devolving Authority for Health Care in Canada's Provinces: 4. Emerging Issues and Prospects. *Canadian Medical Association Journal*. 156: 817-23.

Lomas Jonathan. Woods John and Veenstra. 1997. Devolving Authority for Health Care in Canada's Provinces: 1. An Introduction to the Issues. *Canadian Medical Association Journal*. 156: 371-77.

Macintyre Sally. 1997. The Black Report and Beyond. What are the Issues? *Social Science and Medicine*. Vol. 44. 1997.

Macrae J. et al. 1996. A Triple Burden for Health Sector Reform: 'Post Conflict' Rehabilitation in Uganda. *Social Science and Medicine*. Vol. 42.

Mannen Van John. 1995. An End to Innocence: The Ethnography of Ethnography. In John Van Mannen ed. *Representations in Ethnography*. Thousand Oaks, Sage Publications. London.

Maynard A and Bloor K. 1996. Introducing a Market to the United Kingdom's National Health Service. *New England Journal of Medicine*. 334: 604-8.

Maynard A and Bloor K. 1996. Occasional Notes: Introducing a Market to the United Kingdom's National Health Service. *New England Journal of Medicine*. 334: 9: 604-8.

McKee M. Bobak M. Kalina K. Bojan B and Enachescu D. 1994. Heath Sector Reform in the Czech Republic, Hungary and Romania. *Croatian Medical Journal*. 35: 238-44.

McKinlay John B. S Mckinlay and R Beuglehole. 1989. A Review of the Evidence Concerning the Impact of Medical Measures on Recent Mortality and Morbidity in the United States. *International Journal of Health Services*. 19: 181-208.

McPake B. Hanson K and Mills A. 1993. Community Financing of Health Care in Africa: An Evaluation of the Bamako Initiative. *Social Science and Medicine*. 36: 1383-1395.

McPake B. 1993. User Charges for Health Services in Developing Countries: A Review of the Economic Literature. *Social Science and Medicine*. 36:1391-1405.

McPherson K. Wennberg J. Hovind O and Clifford P. 1982. Small Area Variations in the Use of Common Surgical Procedures: An International Comparison of New England, England and Norway. *New England Journal of Medicine*. 307: 1310-14.

Musgrove P. 1987. The Economic Crisis and its Impact on Health and Health Care in Latin America and the Caribbean. *International Journal of Health Services.* 17:3: 411-441.

Nambissan G and Batra P. 1989. Equity and Excellence in Indian Education: Issues in Indian Education. *Social Scientist.* 17: 9-10. 56-73.

Normile D. 2000. Chinese Awakens to Fight Projected AIDS Crisis. *Science.* 288:2312-13.

Omvedt G. 26th December 1981. Capitalist Agriculture and Rural Classes in India. *Economic and Political Weekly.* 16:52.

Oreskovic S. 1995. Health System Reorganization in Croatia in Light of Major Reform Tendencies in OECD. *Croatian Medical Journal.* 36: 47-54.

Oreskovic Stipe. 2002. Introducing Compulsory Health Insurance in Central Europe: Redirecting a Wheel? In Twaddle C Andrew ed. *Health Care Reform Around The World.* Auburn House. London.

Pannikar P. G. K. April 1994. High Cost of Medical Care in Kerala: A Tentative Hypothesis. *Economic and Political Weekly.*

Patnaik P. 1999. The Political Economy of Structural Adjustment: A Note. In M Rao. ed. *Disinvesting in Health: The World Bank's Prescription for Health*, Sage Publications, New Delhi.

Perry Seymour and Mac Thamer. 1997. Health technology Assessment: Decentralized and Fragmented in the U.S. Compared to Other Countries. *Health Policy.* 40: 177-98.

Pollock A. 1995. The NHS Goes Private. *Lancet.* 346: 683-84.

Popkin B M. Paeratakul S. Ge K and Zhai F. 1995. Body Weight Patterns Among the Chinese: Results From the 1989 and 1991 China Health and Nutrition Surveys. *American Journal of Public Health.* 85 (5): 690-94.

Prabhu K. Seetha. April 1994. The Budget and Structural Adjustment with a Human Face. *Economic and Political Weekly.*

Prabhu S. 1994. World Development Report1993: structural Adjustment and the Health Sector in India. *Social Scientist.* Vol. 22. No-9-12.

Price M. 1989. Explaining Trends in the Privatisation of Health Services in South Africa. *Health Policy and Planning.* 4:2: 50-62.

Purohit B. and Siddiqui T. 1994. Utilization of Health Services in India. *Economic and Political Weekly*, Vol. 29, No 18.

Qadeer I. 2000. Health Care Systems in Transition III, India, Part I: The Indian Experience. *Journal of Public Health Medicine.* 22:1: 25-32.

—. 1985. Health Services System in India: An Expression of Socio-Economic Inequalities. *Social Action.* 35: p- 35-60.

—. 1994. The Brave New World of Primary Health Care. *Social Scientist.* Vol. 22. No 9-12.

Rafkin S. Walt G. 1986. Why Health Improves: Defining the Issues Concerning Comprehensive Primary Health Care and Selective Primary Health Care. *Social Science and Medicine.* 23: 559-566.

Reich M. 1995. The Politics of Health Sector Reform in Developing Countries: Three Cases of Pharmaceutical Policy. In Peter Berman ed. *Health Sector Reform in Developing Countries.* Harvard University Press.

Rimashevskaia Natalia. 1993. The Individual's Health Is the Health of Society. *Sociological Research.* May-June, p- 28-34.

Ryten Eva. Thurber A D. and Buske L. 1998. The Class of 1989 and Physician Supply in Canada. *Canadian Medical Association Journal.* 158: 723-28.

Sawanpanyalert Panthom. 2002. The Health Care Reform Initiative in Thailand. In Andrew C Twaddle ed. *Health Care Reform Around The World.* Auburn House. London.

Schofield T. 1995. The Health of Australians of Non-English Speaking Background: Key Concerns. *Australian Journal of Public Health.* 19: 2: 117-19.

Sen A. 1992b. Missing Women: Social Inequality outweighs women's survival advantage in Asia and Africa. *British Medical Journal.* 304: 587-588.

Sengupta A. 30th November 1996. Economic reforms, Health and Pharmaceuticals: Conferring Legitimacy to the Market. *Economic and Political Weekly.*

Sheiman Igor. 1997. From Beveridge to Bismark: Health Financing in the Russian federation. In G. Scheiber ed. *Innovations in Health care Financing.* World Bank Discussion Paper No. 365, Washington DC: World Bank, p-65-76.

Sheiman I. 1994. Forming the System of Health Insurance in the Russian Federation. *Social Science and Medicine.* 39:10:1425-1432.

Shi L. 1993. Health Care in China: A Rural-Urban Comparison after the Socio-Economic Reforms. *Bulletin of World Health Organization.* 71:6: 723-36.

Shirom Arie. 1995. The Israeli Health Care Reform: A Study of an Evolutionary Major Change. *International Journal of Health Planning and Management.* 10: 5-22.

Shishkin Sergei. 1999. Problems of Transition from Tax Based System of Health care Financing to Mandatory Health Insurance Model in Russia. *Croatian Medical Journal.* 40: 195-201.

Smith David R. 1999. Porches, Politics and Public Health. *American Journal of Public Health.* 84: 5: 725-26.

Smolen M. 1992. The Past and the Present of the Polish National Health Services. *Polish Journal of Occupational Medicine and Environmental Health*. 5: 1-11.

Soboron G. J Frenk and J Sepulveda. 1986. The Health Care Reform in Mexico: Before and After the 1985 Earthquakes. *American Journal of Public Health*. 76: 673-80.

Stambolovic Vuk. 2002. The Reform That, Alas, Succeeded: The Case of Serbia. In Twaddle C Andrew ed. *Health Care Reform Around The World*. Auburn House. London.

Stewart Donald and England Ian. 2002. Reform of the Australian Health Care Landscape: The Contested terrain of Development and Innovation. In Twaddle C Andrew ed. *Health Care Reform Around The World*. Auburn House. London.

Taylor C. Jolly R. 1988. The Strawmen of Primary Health Care. *Social Science and Medicine*. 26:9.

Twaddle Andrew C. 1996. Health System Reforms- Towards a Framework for International Comparisons. *Social Science and Medicine*. 43:5: 637-54.

—. 1997. EU or Not EU? The Debate on Swedish Entry into the European Union 1993-1994. *Scandinavian Studies*. 69:2: 189-211.

—. 1994. Salvaging Medical Care: Views of Swedish Opinion Leaders and Decision Makers on Dealing with the Medical Care Crisis (If There Is One). *Linkoping*: *Tema H*, Universitet i Linkoping, 1994.

—. 2002. Ideology and Interests: Explaining Swedish Medical Care Reform, 1991-1994: An Overview. In Twaddle Andrew C. ed. *Health Care Reform Around The World*. Auburn House. London.

Viveros-Long A. 1986. Changes in Health Financing: The Chilean Experience. *Social Science and Medicine*. 22: 3: 379-85.

Walsh J A. 1988. Selectivity within Primary Health Care. *Social Science and Medicine*. 26 (9) 899-903.

Warren K S. 1988. The Evolution of Selective Primary Health Care. *Social Science and Medicine*. 26: 9.

Wennberg J E and A Gittlesohn. 1973. Small Area Variations in Health Care Delivery. *Science*. 182: 1102-8.

Wessen Albert F. 2002. The United States: Live Free and Die. In Twaddle Andrew C. ed. *Health Care Reform Around The World*. Auburn House. London.

Wloch T. 1993. The Potential for Changing the Health care System within the Current Polish Transformations. *Public Health*. 107: 437-39.

Woodward Christel A and Charles Catherine A. 2002. The Changing Faces of Health Care in Canada. In Twaddle Andrew C. ed. Health Care Reform Around The World. Auburn House. London.

Woolhandler S and D Himmelstein. 1991. The Deteriorating Administrative Efficiency of the U.S. Health Care System. *New England Journal of Medicine*. 324: 1253-58.

Woolhandler Stephanie and David Himmelstein. 1985. Militarism and Mortality: An International Analysis of Arms Spending and Infant Death Rates. *Lancet*. June 15th. P- 1375-78.

Yip W P. Wang H. and Liu Y. 1998. Determinants of Patient Choice of Medical Provider: A Case Study in Rural China. *Health Policy and Planning*.13:3:311-22.

Yishei Yael. 1982. Politics and Medicine: The Case of Israeli National Health Insurance. *Social Science and Medicine*. 16: 285-91.

Yoder R. 1989. Are People Willing and Able to Pay for Health Services. *Social Science and Medicine*. 29:35-42.

Yuan Xing Gu and Lan Sheng Tang. 1995. Reform of the Chinese Health Care Financing System. In Peter Berman ed. *Health Sector Reform in Developing Countries*. Harvard University Press.

Zaidi S. 1988. Poverty and Disease: Need For Structural Change. *Social Science and Medicine*. 27: 119-127.

Zhou X and Hou L. 1999. Children of the Cultural Revolution: The State and the Life Course in People's Republic of China. *American Sociological review*. 64:1: 12-36.

Reports/Working Papers

American Hospital Association (AHA). 2000. *Hospital Statistics 2000*. Chicago. (American Hospital Association) Healthcare Infosource.

—. April 2001. *Profile of Hospitals*. Hospitals and Health Networks, 75:4: 50.

Angus Reid Group. February 6th 1999. *Press Release*: *Restore Healthcare Funding Taken from Provinces Full Majority Say (80%)*. Angus Reid Group.

Australian Institute of Health and Welfare. 1998a. *Australia's Health 1998: The Sixth Biennial Health Report of the Australian Institute of Health and Welfare*. Canberra: AIHW.

—. 1995. *Health in Australia*. Canberra: Australian Government Publishing Service.

—. 1998b. *International Health: How Australia Compares*. Canberra: AIHW.

Baru Rama V. 1998. *Health Sector Reform in India: A Review of Literature*. Paper Submitted to the Indian Statistical Institute. Calcutta. As Part of the Project Sponsored by the European Commission. Unpublished Document.

Bergstrom Hans. 1992. *Pressures behind the Swedish Health reforms*. Viewpoint Sweden. Bulletin No. 12. New York: Swedish Information Service.

Berrios X. Koponen T. Huiguang T. et. al. *Distribution and Prevalence of Major Risk Factors of Non-Communicable Diseases in Selected Countries: The WHO Inter-Health Programme*. Bulletin of World Health Organisation, 75 (2): 99-108, 1997.

Cassels A. 1997. *A Guide to Sector-Wide Approaches for Health Development: Concepts, Issues, and Working Arrangements,* Geneva: World Health Organization.

Central Bureau of Health Intelligence. 2003. *Health Information of India: 2000 and 2001* DGHS. MOHFW. Government of India.

CEHAT. January 2005. Gangolli Leena V. Ravi Duggal. Abhay Shukla ed. *Review of Health Care in India*. Centre for Equity into Health and Allied Themes.

Creese A. 1994. *Global Trends in Health Care Reform.* World Health Forum. Vol. 15.

Department For International Development. 2001. *Orissa Health and Family Welfare Sector Reform Project: Output to Purpose Review and Evaluation- 7th- 22nd June, 2001*. Undertaken by Paul Thornton of Verulam Associates Ltd. & Nalini Abraham of Plan International India on Behalf of DFID.

Dezhi Y. 1992. *Changes in Health Care Financing and Health Status: The Case of China in the 1980s.* UNICEF Economic Policy Series 34.

Enthoven A. C. 1985. *Reflection on the Management of NHS*. Nuffield Provincial Hospitals Trust. London.

Enthoven Alain. 1985a. *Reflections on the Management of the National Health Service*. Nuffield Provincial Hospital Trust. London.

European Commission. March 2000. *The Sector Reform Cell.* ECTA Working Papers. 1999/22. European Commission.

European Health Management Association. 2000. *The Impact of Market Forces on Health Systems: A Review of the Evidence in 15 European Union Member States*. EHMA. Dublin.

Evans David B. A Tandon. C Murray and J Lauer. 2002. *The Comparative Efficiency of National Health Systems in Producing Health: An Analysis of 191 Countries.* GPE Discussion Paper Series. No 29. Geneva. World Health Organization.

Government of India. 1991. *Census of India.*

—. 1987. *Enterprise Survey 1983-84*. Central Statistical Organization. Government of India.

—. 2003. *Health Information of India, 2000 & 2001.* CBHI. DGHS. MOHFW. New Delhi.

—. 1998. *Morbidity and Treatment of Ailments.* NSS 52nd Round. NSSO. Government of India.

—. 1989. *Morbidity and Utilisation of Medical Services: 42nd Round of NSSO*. No. 364, CSO. Government of India.

—. 2002. *National Health Policy 2002*. Ministry of Health and Family Welfare, Government of India.

—. 2001. *National Commission on Population: District Wise Indicators.* Yojana Bhawan. Government of India.

—. 1989. *NSSO 42nd Round 1986-87*. Government of India.

—. 1998. *NSSO 52nd Round 1995-96.* Government of India.

—. 2003. *Proceedings of Workshop on India's Health System: Role of Health Sector Reforms.* September 4-5. India International Centre. Ministry of Health and family welfare in Collaboration with WHO.

—. 1946. *Report of the Health Survey and Development Committee.* Vol-1. Manager of Publications. Delhi.

—. 1946. *Report of the Health Survey and Development Committee* (Bhore Committee). Vol. IV. Manager of Publications: Delhi.

—. 2001. *Census of India.*

Government of Orissa. 1979. *Annual Plan: 1980-81* draft. Government of Orissa.

—. 1983. *Annual Plan: 1984-85.* Government of Orissa.

—. 1985. *Annual Plan: 1986-87.* Government of Orissa.

—. 1992. *Annual Plan: 1992-9.* Government of Orissa.

—. 1992. *Annual Plan: 1993-94.* Government of Orissa.

—. 1994. *Annual Plan: 1994-95.* Government of Orissa.

—. 1995. *Annual Plan 1995-96.* Government of Orissa.

—. 1996. *Annual Plan: 1996-97.* Government of Orissa.

—. 1999. *Annual Plan: 1999-2000.* Government of Orissa.

—. 1990. *Annual Plan: Volume II. 1990-91.* Government of Orissa.

—. 2001. *Annual Plan: Volume II. 2001-02.* Government of Orissa.

—. 2001. *District Statistical Handbook: Khurda.* Directorate of Economics and Statistics. Bhubaneswar. Orissa.

—. 1997. *Economic Survey: 1997-98* Ministry of Finance. Government of Orissa.

—. 2002. *Health Statistics of Orissa 2000-2001.* State Bureau of Health Intelligence. Directorate of Health Services.

—. 2005. *Health and Family Welfare Department: An Overview*. Unpublished report.
—. 2004. *Navajyoti: A Strategy to Improve Maternal and Child Care with Focus on Prevention of Neonatal mortality and Morbidity*. Department of Health and Family Welfare. Government of Orissa.
—. 1997. *Ninth Five Year Plan: 1997-2002*. Government of Orissa.
—. 2004. *Orissa Budget at a Glance- 2004-05*. Finance Department. Government of Orissa.
—. 1983. *Orissa Budget in Brief: 1983-84*. Government of Orissa.
—. 1991. *Orissa Budget in Brief: 1991-92*. Government of Orissa.
—. 1994. *Orissa Budget in Brief: 1994-95*. Government of Orissa.
—. 2002. *Orissa Budget in Brief: 2002-03*. Government of Orissa.
—. 1998. *Orissa Health Systems Development Project: Project Implementation Plan*. Health and Family Welfare Department. Government of Orissa.
—. 2003. *Orissa Vision 2010: A Health Strategy*. Ministry of Health and Family Welfare Department. Government of Orissa.
—. 1985. *Seventh Plan: 1985-90*. Government of Orissa.
—. 2005. *State Level Conference of Chief District Medical Officers: 10th and 11th January 2005*. Directorate of Health Services. Health and Family Welfare Department. Government of Orissa. Unpublished Report.
—. 2003. *Statistical Outline of Orissa*. Directorate of Economics and Statistics. Government of Orissa.
—. 2002. *Tenth Plan: Volume II. 2002-07*. Government of Orissa.
—. 2004. *Unserved and Underserved Areas in 17 Districts of Orissa for RCH Delivery Intervention*. Documented by NGO Cell. Ministry of Health and Family Welfare Department. Unpublished Report. Government of Orissa.
—. 2001. *District Statistical Handbook: Sundergarh*, Directorate of Economics and Statistics. Bhubaneswar. Orissa.
Gupta Meena. 2002. *State Health Systems: Orissa*. Working Paper No. 89. Indian Council for Research on International Economic Relations. New Delhi.
Hazell R and Jervis P. 1998. *Devolution and Health*. Nuffield Trust Series No. 3. The Nuffield Trust. London.
Health Canada. Policy and Consultation Branch. 1997b. *Canada Health Act Annual Report*. 1996-1997. Ottawa.
—. 1997b. *National Health Expenditures in Canada. 1975-1996*. Ottawa.
Hurley J. Goldsmith J. Lomas J. Khan H. Vincent V. 1997. *A Tale of Two Provinces: A Case Study of Physician Expenditure Cap as Financial*

Incentives. McMaster University Centre for Health Economics and Policy Analysis. Working paper. P- 96-112.

Indian Council of Social Science Research and Indian Council of Medical research. 1981. *Health For All: An Alternative Strategy*. Indian Institute of Education. Pune.

International Institute for Population Sciences ORC Macro. 2001. *National Family Health Survey: II. Orissa*. 1998-99. India.

—. 1995. *National Family Health Survey-I*. 1992-93.India.

—. 2000. *National Family Health Survey-II*. 1998-99. India.

Iyer Aditi and Sen Gita. 2000. *Health Sector Changes and Health Equity in the 1990s in India: Health and Equity Affecting Change*. Tech. Report Series 18. ed. Shobha Raghuraman. HIVOS Publications. Bangalore.

Jesani A and Anatharam S. 1993. *Private Sector and Privatisation in Health Care Services*. Foundation for Research in Community Health. Bombay.

Kumar Shiva N and Paul Thornton. 2002. *Review of the Policy and Strategic Planning Unit (PSPU).Government of Orissa*. For Health Department. Government of Orissa and DFID: India. Unpublished Report.

Landstingsforbundet. 1991. *Crossroads: Future Options for Swedish Health Care*. Stockholm: Landstingsforbundet.

—. 1990. *Some Innovative Projects of Swedish County Councils*, Stockholm: Landstingsforbundet.

Nanda P. 2000. *Health Sector reforms in Zambia: Implications for Reproductive Health and Rights*. Working Paper. Centre for Health and gender Equity. Washington DC.

National Council of Applied Economic Research. 1992. *Household Survey of Medical Care*. New Delhi.

Pillai Radhakrishna S and R Prakasam. 1999. *User Charges in Government Hospitals in Orissa*. Institute of Management in Government. Thiruvananthapuram. Kerala.

Preker Alexander S and Richard G. A. 1995. *Market Mechanisms and the Health sector in Central and Eastern Europe*. World Bank Technical Paper. No. 293. Washington DC: World Bank.

United Nations Development Program. 1990. Human Development Report 1990: *Concept and Measurement of human development*, UNDP.

—. 1991. Human Development Report 1991: *Financing Human Development*. UNDP.

—. 2003. Human Development Report 2003: *Millennium Development Goals: A compact among nations to end human poverty*. UNDP.

Waddington Catriona. 1999. *Orissa Health and Family Welfare Project: Design of Program of Work in Health Economics*. Report to DFID. Institute for Health Sector Development. London.

World Bank. 1987. *Financing Health Services in Developing Countries: An Agenda For Reform*. World Bank. Washington D.C.

—. 1992. *Indian Health Sector Financing: Coping with Adjustment.* Report No. 10859-IN. New Delhi.

—. 20th February 1996. *India Health Systems Project II*. Report No. 15106-IN. New Delhi.

—. 20th February 1996. *India Health Systems Project II*, Report No. 15106-IN. New Delhi.

—. 1998. *Project Appraisal Document: Orissa Health Systems Development Project*. Report No. 17653-IN. Health Nutrition and Population Sector Unit. World Bank.

—. 2000. *World Development Indicators*. Washington DC: World Bank.

—. 1993. *World Development Report 1993*: *Investing in Health*. New York: Oxford University Press.

—. 2000. *World Development Report 1999*. New York: Oxford University Press.

—. 1993. World Development Report 1994: *Infrastructure for Development*. World Bank.

—. 1994. World Development Report 1995: *Workers in an Integrating World*. World Bank.

—. 1995. World Development Report 1996: *From Plan to Market.* World Bank.

—. 1996. World Development Report 1997: *The State in a Changing World*. World Bank.

—. 1998. World Development Report 1998-99: *Knowledge for Development*. World Bank.

—. 1999. World Development Report 1999-2000: *Entering the 21st Century*. World Bank.

—. 2000. World Development Report 2000-2001: *Attacking Poverty.* World Bank.

—. 2001. World Development Report 2002: *Building Institutions for Markets*. World Bank.

—. 2002. World Development Report 2003: *Sustainable Development in a Dynamic World.* World Bank.

—. 2003. World Development Report 2004: *Making Services Work for Poor People.* World Bank.

—. 2004. World Development Report 2005: *A Better Investment Climate for Everyone*. World Bank.

—. 2005. World Development Report 2006: *Equity and Development.* World Bank.

World Health Organization. 1978. *Primary Health Care.* A Joint Report by the Director General of WHO and the Executive Director of UNICEF. Geneva.

—. 1995. *Decentralization and Health System Change: A Framework for Analysis.* WHO. Geneva.

—. 2000. *The World Health Report 2000: Health Systems: Improving Performance.* WHO. Geneva.

—. 2000. *World Health report: 1999.* WHO. Geneva.

—. 1997. *World health report: 1997.* WHO. Geneva.

Unpublished PhDs/Documents

Baru Rama V. 1992. *Some Aspects of the Private Sector in Medical care and Its Inter-relationship with the Public Sector: A Study of Hyderabad and Secunderabad.* Unpublished PhD Thesis. Centre of Social Medicine and Community Health. Jawaharlal Nehru University. New Delhi.

Dasgupta Rajib. 1992-93. *24-Parganas (South) West Bengal.* District Health Profile Series: 1. Unpublished Report. Centre of Social Medicine and Community Health. Jawaharlal Nehru University. New Delhi.

Kundu Subrata. 2001. *Socio-Economic Conditions of Agricultural Labourers and its Implication for Health: A Review.* Unpublished M. Phil Dissertation. Center of Social Medicine and Community Health. Jawaharlal Nehru University. New Delhi.